THE AZERBAIJANI TURKS

STUDIES OF NATIONALITIES

Wayne S. Vucinich, founding General Editor of series

The Crimean Tatars
Alan W. Fisher

The Volga Tatars: A Profile in National Resilience
Azade-Ayşe Rorlich

The Making of the Georgian Nation
Ronald Grigor Suny
(copublished with Indiana University Press)

*The Modern Uzbeks: From the Fourteenth Century to the Present;
A Cultural History*
Edward A. Allworth

Estonia and the Estonians, updated second edition
Toivo U. Raun

The Azerbaijani Turks: Power and Identity under Russian Rule
Audrey L. Altstadt

The Kazakhs, second edition
Martha Brill Olcott

The Latvians: A Short History
Andrejs Plakans

The Moldovans: Romania, Russia, and the Politics of Culture
Charles King

Slovakia: From Samo to Dzurinda
Peter A. Toma and Dušan Kováč

The Czechs and the Lands of the Bohemian Crown
Hugh LeCaine Agnew

Macedonia and the Macedonians: A History
Andrew Rossos

THE AZERBAIJANI TURKS

Power and Identity
under Russian Rule

Audrey L. Altstadt

HOOVER INSTITUTION PRESS
Stanford University
Stanford, California

www.hoover.org

Hoover Institution Press Publication No. 410

First printing, 1992
16   15   14   13   12   11   10   09   10   9   8   7   6

Manufactured in the United States of America
The paper used in this publication meets the minimum requirements
of the American National Standard for Information Sciences
Permanence of Paper for Printed Library Materials, ANSI Z39.48-1992.

Library of Congress Cataloging-in-Publication Data
Altstadt, Audrey L., 1953–
    The Azerbaijani Turks : power and identity under Russian rule / by Audrey L. Altstadt.
      p.   cm.—(Hoover Institution Press publication ; no. 410)
    (Studies of nationalities)
    Includes bibliographical references and index.
    ISBN-10: 0-8179-9181-6 (cloth: alk. paper)
    ISBN-13: 978-0-8179-9181-4 (cloth: alk. paper)
    ISBN-10: 0-8179-9182-4 (paperback: alk. paper)
    ISBN-13: 978-0-8179-9182-1 (paperback: alk. paper)
    1. Azerbaijan S.S.R.—Politics and government.   2. Azerbaijanis—
Social life and customs.
I. Title.   II. Series: Hoover Institution Press Publication ; 410.   III. Series.
DK696.6.A48   1992
947'.91—dc20   91-41684
                                                          CIP

Design by P. Kelley Baker

In memory of
Alexandre A. Bennigsen (1913–1988)
and Arcadius Kahan (1920–1982)

Contents

List of Maps

Foreword

With this timely and important book Professor Audrey Altstadt gives us a comprehensive history of Azerbaijan and its people—heirs to a long succession of cultures and civilizations. Systematically examining the major stages of the historical development of Azerbaijan and the Azerbaijanis, she emphasizes the modern and contemporary period. In this task she not only consulted a large quantity of primary and secondary sources but also painstakingly examined Soviet historiography, which was written in accordance with the teachings of Marxist philosophy of history and in compliance with the goals of the Soviet state. Altstadt objectively assesses the place in history of prominent Azerbaijanis, who were calumnied and at times expunged from Soviet historical writings, and evaluates the significance of events and artistic creations frequently slighted or distorted by Soviet historians.

Starting with Media and other ancient precursors of modern Azerbaijan, Altstadt takes us through the early period of Azerbaijan's history, focusing on the emergence of Caucasian Albania, an early Christian community, which, according to some historians, was the core of the Azerbaijani nation. Particularly important are Islamization in the seventh century and the subsequent Turkification, both of which played a decisive role in the Azerbaijanian ethnogenesis. Persian rule over Azerbaijan from the sixteenth century on and the acceptance of the Shi'a form of Islam gave the Azerbaijanis their present religion and influenced their culture. Thus today the Azerbaijanis share Shi'a Islam with the Iranians, although ethnically and linguistically they identify with the Ottoman Turks, who are Sunni Muslims.

Altstadt also explains how Russia, under Peter I in the early eighteenth century, initiated the move into the Caucasus and how, early in the next century, Alexander I established Russia in that region. Giving Russian rule over Azerbaijan critical scrutiny, Altstadt discusses the effects on Azerbaijan of the cultural conflict between the Azerbaijanis and the Russians, the changes in the colonial administrative system, and the effects of the revolution of 1905 and the First World War.

The Azerbaijanis viewed the Russians as foreign oppressors, people of another language and religion. In the eyes of the Azerbaijanis, Russia's Caucasian policy was anti-Muslim and an outright colonial conquest. Throughout the nineteenth century the Azerbaijanis, individually and collectively, voiced their national and religious grievances and yearned for independence. As time passed, especially after the turn of the century, the Azerbaijanis articulated their discontent vocally and effectively through nationalist organizations and the press.

Among the most insightful sections of Altstadt's work are those on traditional Azerbaijani society, communal relations, and social categories and classes. The author superbly analyzes demographic changes and the challenges posed by modernism to traditional Azerbaijani society. Education contributed significantly to the growth of Azerbaijani literacy and to the founding of modern Azerbaijani culture. A few Azerbaijanis were exposed to modern European political and philosophical thought, as well as to such movements as Pan-Islamism and Pan-Turkism. By the end of the nineteenth century, Azerbaijan had its own small but dynamic intelligentsia, which included literati, artists, and political thinkers. Baku became a flourishing center of secular culture and burgeoning Azerbaijani nationalism.

Despite the repressive policies of the tsars, Altstadt notes that Azerbaijan made important economic gains under Russian rule. She looks at how the oil industry developed, largely through foreign investors, particularly the Nobel Brothers Company and the Rothschild Caspian Black Sea Company, but also examines how the oil industry stimulated the growth of related industries and building construction in Baku. Only a small part of the oil industry was owned by Azerbaijanis, but they dominated in several related branches of the economy.

Altstadt closely analyzes the role of Azerbaijan in the First World War and in the February and October revolutions of 1917, a revolutionary period characterized by clashes between ethno-confessional groups (e.g., Azero-Armenian), by political activities of competing native and Russian parties, by the successes and failures of the nationalist Azerbaijani Musavat party, and by British, Turkish, and German military expeditions into the Caucasus.

Covered in detail are the fighting between the Bolsheviks and their adversaries, the ever changing Bolshevik organization along with its tactics and clandestine operations, political agitation, and the incitement of strife in the region.

This period of Azerbaijani history is complex, and Altstadt does a masterly job of clarifying it. The Azerbaijani struggle in the revolutionary period of 1917–1921 was political and military. The brief existence of Azerbaijan's independence and statehood, proclaimed in May 1918, had deep psychological implications even though it was cut short by the Communists' seizure of Baku. The Musavat survived, withdrew into the hinterland, and continued to exist. In September 1918 the advancing Turks entered Baku but were forced to relinquish it after the collapse of the Ottoman Empire in 1918. In early 1919 independent Azerbaijan sent a delegation to the Peace Conference in Paris. The realization of independence fell short, however, as the Bolshevik Red Army advanced on and occupied Baku on April 27, 1920. The actual power was wielded by the Kavbiuro (the Caucasian Bureau of the Bolshevik party). From the Azerbaijani perspective, the Red Army imposed communism on the country and acted as an army of occupation. Altstadt explains how the country was integrated into the Soviet system.

In 1922, at the instigation of the Bolsheviks, Azerbaijan, Armenia, and Georgia combined to form the Transcaucasian Socialist Federative Soviet Republic (TSFSR), which then, along with the Russian Socialist Federated Soviet Republic (RSFSR) signed the treaty forming the Union of Soviet Socialist Republics. The treaty was put in force in July 1923. Azerbaijan was quickly subjected to sovietization, antireligious campaigns, collectivization, and the sedentarization of the nomads; industrialization was accelerated. Altstadt records important developments in the history of the Transcaucasian republic until its dissolution in 1936 into three separate Soviet Socialist republics. After briefly examining the 1936 constitution, she provides a detailed examination of the barbarous "Great Terror" from 1920 to 1941.

In the chapters that follow, Altstadt turns to Azerbaijan during the Second World War (e.g., how its human, material, and cultural resources were used) and developments in the transitional period from war to peace. This is followed by comments on Stalin's death in March 1953 and the removal from office of Mir Jafar Abbasovich Baghirov, the first secretary of the Azerbaijan Communist party, and his trial and execution in 1956. Altstadt continues with some comments on de-Stalinization and brief assessments of the first secretaries that followed Baghirov's demise.

The postwar period, under the more lax conditions of de-Stalinization, saw Azerbaijani scholars and writers beginning to reassert their nation's historical identity and dignity. Altstadt, noting the controversies over the interpretation of major historical events, literary creations, and the contributions of prominent men in Azerbaijani history, finds that national forces gradually became more assertive. State control over literature and culture continued, as did the battle over the place of the Azerbaijani language in schools and government. Yet Azerbaijan made impressive advances at all levels of learning and education. The Academy of Sciences, the University of Baku, a polytechnic school, and a number of other centers of learning and culture were founded. Illiteracy was almost stamped out.

The rapidly growing population, however, has long faced the possibility of increasing economic deprivation. The level of social and cultural benefits in Azerbaijan has always been among the lowest in the Soviet Union, as has the average per capita income. Azerbaijan's failing economy—owing to the decline in oil production and the unrestricted siphoning of Azerbaijan's national production for the benefit of the larger Soviet community—resulted in popular demands for economic independence.

As a people the Azerbaijanis have shown remarkable vitality and impressive natural growth. Altstadt points out that in Azerbaijan the Soviet Union failed to achieve a unified and harmonious "international" Soviet community. Instead, the trend in Azerbaijan has been toward "nativization," not "internationalization."

The Azerbaijanis, who were under Russian and Soviet rule for a little less than two centuries, throughout the period in one way or another manifested opposition to that rule. In the past few years, when a modicum of freedom of thought was allowed, the Azerbaijanis seized the opportunity to demand their national and religious rights. What they needed however, was to rally popular opposition to the existing order into a broader and more vigorous national movement. This came with Mikhail Gorbachev's ascendancy to power in the Soviet Union in 1985. In the final section of her book, Altstadt discusses at length Azerbaijan's reaction to Gorbachev's call for "openness" (*glasnost*') and "restructuring" (*perestroika*).

The Azerbaijanis began vigorously voicing their demands in 1987, when the Armenians demanded the annexation of the Nagorno-Karabakh region. Because neither the Armenians nor the Azerbaijanis accepted the borders established for their republics by the Soviet government, the enmity between the two peoples has been aggravated by frequent clashes in modern times. The Armenian demand to annex Nagorno-Karabakh was followed by demonstrations, strikes, and armed attacks.

The unrest first started in Erevan on February 21, 1988, and from there spread to Sumgait, Baku, and smaller towns and villages. Altstadt details specific encounters and gives a full account of the conflict between the two republics and the subsequent Soviet political and military intervention.

The indecisiveness of the Azerbaijani and Moscow governments in introducing reforms and in handling the Nagorno-Karabakh question swelled popular opposition. The most vocal opposition force was the Azerbaijan Popular Front (APF) established in July 1989 to promote Gorbachev's reforms. The APF demanded an immediate solution to the Nagorno-Karabakh conflict, democratic elections for the republic's Supreme Council, political pluralism, and economic and cultural independence for Azerbaijan. The Azerbaijanis, however, never forgot that they once were independent, and in our own day this memory fires their imagination and national spirit. Despite the long period of foreign rule and the powerful influence of modernism, the Azerbaijanis have managed to preserve their ethno-confessional identity and their distinctive life-style. Their national pride has remained strong.

Under popular pressure the republican Communist party was forced to recognize the APF in September 1989. Moscow later dissolved the special commission in charge of Nagorno-Karabakh and nominally restored the Azerbaijani government.

In the meantime armed clashes between the Azerbaijanis and Armenians continued, and some Azerbaijani groups claimed the no-man's-land along the border with Iran. The flow of Azerbaijani refugees to Baku increased, and, during January 12–13, 1990, a bloody, communal conflict broke out. The Azerbaijani Supreme Soviet proved unable to cope with the situation, and there was danger that the government would fall. On January 20, Moscow troops arrived in Baku and opened fire on the civilian population ("Black January"). Nearly two hundred were killed and many more were wounded. A number of APF leaders were arrested and jailed.

According to Altstadt, the use of Soviet armed forces against the native population deepened anti-Soviet and anti-Russian sentiments among the Azerbaijanis. The opposition criticized the government for being ineffective and for its soft attitude toward the Soviet army and militia. The first secretary of the Communist party, Abdurahman Vizirov, resigned and was replaced by Ayaz Mutalibov. Almost from the start Mutalibov began using the rhetoric of the popular causes; in preparing for democratic elections of the Supreme Council, he offered a program much like that of the APF.

To better its own position in the forthcoming elections, the APF joined several other political groups to form an electoral block known as "Democratic Azerbaijan." Mutalibov's group won by a landslide. The opposition protested in vain against the irregularities that had accompanied the election. Once the election was over, the government felt secure in its position and, despite its democratic line, strove to isolate the opposition.

Moscow saw in the Azerbaijani-Armenian clash an infectious movement that, unless contained, could spread to other Soviet republics and communities. Thus, in November 1991 the president of Russia, Boris Yeltsin, and the president of Kazakhstan, Nursultan Nazarbaev, negotiated an agreement between Azerbaijan and Armenia. According to the agreement Nagorno-

Karabakh would remain part of Azerbaijan and a joint Russian-Kazakh committee would oversee the government of the Nagorno-Karabakh Autonomous Region (NKAO). But sporadic fighting along the Armenian and Azerbaijani borders continued, and the refugee problem was not resolved.

Azerbaijan—steadfast in its demand for political and economic independence—refused to sign the proposed Soviet treaty calling for the establishment of a "Union of Sovereign States," an association of Soviet sovereign republics that would reserve a great deal of power for a central authority. For similar reasons it also refused to sign an economic pact. As of this writing, Azerbaijan's relationship to the newly announced "commonwealth" of former Soviet republics has not been determined.

Altstadt suggests that, as it builds an independent state, Azerbaijan will face severe social and economic problems. The country will be obliged to regulate relations not only with Russia but also with other former republics of the USSR, especially those dominated by Muslims. The political factionalism and conflicts between nationalists and reborn nationalists will be an enduring source of irritation. Finally, the new Azerbaijan will certainly seek closer relations with countries abroad, although it is difficult to predict the direction it will follow. Altstadt leaves speculation on this topic to others. Her important contribution is her excellent coverage and sophisticated presentation of Azerbaijan's rich history and unrelenting struggle for independence.

Wayne S. Vucinich
Series Editor and Professor Emeritus
History Department, Stanford University

Acknowledgments

This work was begun at the University of Chicago as a doctoral dissertation from which chapters 1–4 are drawn. Sincere thanks go to the many individuals and institutions connected with that early endeavor. The University of Chicago, the university's Hilman Fund and Center for Middle Eastern Studies, NDEA Title VI, the International Research and Exchanges Board (IREX), and the American Association of University Women all provided generous funding at various stages in research and writing the dissertation. Postdoctoral support was provided by the Harvard Russian Research Center, the University of Illinois Summer Lab (for four summers), Central Connecticut State University and the American Association of University Professors– Connecticut State University Foundation, the George F. Kennan Institute for Advanced Russian Studies, and again by IREX.

Thanks go also to my many teachers and colleagues who guided, taught, and prodded me or otherwise assisted my efforts over the years: to H. B. Paksoy, to the late Alexandre A. Bennigsen and Arcadius Kahan, to Olga Andriewsky, Jeremy Azrael, Jeffrey Brooks, Steven L. Burg, Richard L. Chambers, James Critchlow, Robert Dankoff, Ralph T. Fisher, Jr., McGuire Gibson, Paul Goble, Peter B. Golden, Keith Hitchins, Akira Iriye, Roger E. Kanet, James R. Millar, John R. Perry, A. J. Plotke, Teresa Rakowska-Harmstone, Andras Riedelmeyer, Azade-Ayşe Rorlich, Alfred E. Senn, Ronald Grigor Suny, Tadeusz Swietochowski, S. Enders Wimbush, John Woods,

Richard S. Wortman, Richard E. Wright, and many Azerbaijani friends, colleagues, and acquaintances.

The faculty of Azerbaijan State University (Baku), the Central Historical Archive of the Republic, and the M. F. Akhundov Library provided assistance and challenges during my two periods of work there. Special thanks are extended to Dr. Suleiman Serdaroglu Aliyarov, Professor Mir Yusuf M. Mirhadiyev, other members of the history faculty, and the *Kafedra* of Azer-baijani history, and to Mrs. Shamsidikhan N. Sosiuksh of the History Archive. I would also like to thank the History Department and the Cartog-raphy Laboratory of the University of Massachusetts at Amherst for providing the maps.

Throughout the research that produced this book, numerous libraries and their directors and staffs lent assistance: the libraries of the Universities of Chicago, Illinois (Urbana), Harvard, the Library of Congress, and of Yale, and Bodley Library of Oxford University (England). Thanks to Dr. Marianna Tax Choldin and Helen Sullivan (University of Illinois), Harold M. Leich (Library of Congress), June Pachuta Farris and the late Vaclav Lashka (University of Chicago), and Dr. Christopher Murphey (Library of Congress).

Sincere thanks to Professor Wayne Vucinich, Patricia Baker, Ann Wood, Tom Lacey, and the staff at Hoover Institution Press.

Terms and Transliteration

The Turks of Azerbaijan were classified as Tatars or Muslims in the imperial period and as Turks until 1937. Thereafter, they and their language were called Azerbaijani by Soviet or "Azeri" by some Western sources. An apparently Iranian language called Azeri was spoken in Atropaten; thus, the term is inappropriate for today's Azerbaijani Turks and their language.* Some historians in Soviet Azerbaijan have suggested the most correct usage is "Azerbaijan Türkleri," for it reflects both ethnicity and location. I have used this term, translated as Azerbaijani Turk, occasionally using only Azerbaijani or Turk for brevity. In the language of the Turks, there is no distinction between Turkish (in Russian, *turetskii*) and Turkic (*tiurkskii*). The former has been used, following Russian imperial and Soviet precedent, to refer to Turks of the Ottoman Empire or the Turkish Republic; the latter, to Turks elsewhere. Because of the artificiality of this distinction in a cultural or ethnic sense, I have used Turkish throughout.

The ancient city of Ganje was renamed Elizavetpol by the Russians, 1806–1918, and Kirovobad by the Soviet government, 1934–1989. I have used Ganje throughout except for official usage, including the name of the imperial era, Elizavetpol *guberniia* (province).

Transliteration is always a problem when dealing with multiple languages

---

*From *Istoriia Azerbaidzhana/Azärbayjan Tarikhi* (Baku, 1958–1963), 1:49.

and alphabets. I have transliterated Russian according to the standard Library of Congress (LC) system. Azerbaijani Turkish has been transliterated directly rather than from Russian spellings. Spelling has been determined on the basis of a modified LC system for Cyrillic, with adjustments to account for letters that exist in Turkish and English but not in Russian: *j* as in *just* is used, not *dzh* as when transliterating from Russian, and *h* as in *house* rather than *g*. Thus it is Azerbaijan rather than Azerbaidzhan and Huseinov rather than Guseinov. Citations of works in Russian are transliterated from Russian.

Vowels present greater difficulty because there are more of them than in English and because the Cyrillic spellings were designed to distance Azerbaijan's Turkish dialect from others, like Modern Turkish to which it is closest. In the text, diacritics have been avoided and vowels chosen to approximate sound. The closed and open *e* (in Cyrillic, e and ə, respectively) are both transliterated as *e* and the Cyrillic ч and ы as *y*. Exceptions have been made for personal and place names that have a standard spelling in English or if the use of *e* would make the name unrecognizable: Ali (Äli) rather than Eli. Personal names are transliterated from Azerbaijani unless the individual is known with the Russian form.

In bibliographic citations and with the first use of proper nouns in the text (noted in parentheses), a precise system is used as noted below. For Latin script Azerbaijani Turkish (used circa 1926–1939), no changes have been made; for Arabic script, words have been transliterated according to the IJMES system for Ottoman Turkish. For Modern Turkish, no change has been made (unfamiliar letters: ç = *ch*; c = *j* [as in *just*]; ş = *sh*; ğ as an intervocalic glide; ı (undotted i) pronounced as *i* in *nation*; and ö and ü as in German).

Transliteration of Cyrillic Letters Not Found in Russian

Vowels	Consonants
Ə, ə = *ä* (like *bat*)	Ч, ч = *j* (like *just*)
Ы, ы = *ï* (*i* in *nation*)	J, j = *y* (like *year*)
Y, y = *ü* (same as German)	F, ғ = *gh* (guttural *g*)
Ө, ө = *ö* (same as German)	К, к = *g* (like *gate*, used with ä, e, ö, ü)

Note on pronunciation: *h* is always pronounced (like *hot*); all vowels are pronounced, including final *e* (like *bet*) or *ä*, without diphthong.

Because family names were not traditional among Turks, the titles Bey (initially, landowner; in the nineteenth and twentieth centuries, a generic form of respect), Hanim (female Bey), and Pasha (general in Ottoman army) follow first names (e.g., Enver Pasha).

Physical Profile

The Azerbaijan Republic (Soviet Socialist Republic, SSR, until 1991) is situated on the western shore of the Caspian Sea, on the Iranian border. The republic occupies 86,600 square kilometers, including the Nagorno-Karabagh Autonomous Oblast (NKAO) in the west (4,400 sq km) and noncontiguous Nakhjivan (Autonomous Soviet Socialist Republic, ASSR) in the southwest (5,500 sq km). Elevation varies greatly, from the coastal lowlands and basin of the Kura and Aras (Araxes) rivers in the east and southeast to the mountains in the north at the Daghestan border (4,243 meters in the Greater Caucasus range) and in the west near the Georgian and Armenian borders (Lesser Caucasus), with peaks rising to 3,581 meters in far western Karabagh. Within the republic are seven microclimates, suitable for cultivating wheat, grapes, tea, cotton, figs and pomegranates, mulberry trees (for silk), saffron, and forest products. Sheep, cattle, and goats are kept. Among natural resources are copper, salt, iron ore, and the most famous—oil.

The capital, Baku, is located on the south side of the Apsheron Peninsula that protrudes into the Caspian. Like much of the eastern part of the republic, the Apsheron Peninsula has a semiarid climate; grape, fig, and pomegranate cultivation are widespread. Baku has the best natural harbor on the Caspian and has been a commercial port for more than a millennium. The republic's "second city," historic Ganje (called Elizavetpol in tsarist times and Kirovobad from the mid-1930s until January 1990), is 320 kilometers west of Baku. A journey there from Baku would entail a rise in elevation from sea level to

500 meters above. A traveler continuing south by southeast to the old town of Shusha, the traditional capital of Karabagh, now in the NKAO, or farther to the Nakhjivan ASSR (via the Armenian SSR) would go around or through mountains of over 3,500 meters.

The eastern and central portions of the republic are relatively dry, receiving 200–400 millimeters (mm) of precipitation annually. Higher elevations receive more, to extremes in mountainous regions of over 1,000 mm in the far northern and western mountains and over 1,600 mm in the south near the Iranian border. The average annual temperature is 14–14.5 degrees Celsius in the eastern and central parts of the republic, dropping to an average of 2 degrees at the highest points in the Caucasus range. Extremes in Baku range from 40 (over 100 degrees Fahrenheit) to −13, though the climate is mostly Mediterranean with early springs and long, sunny summers; winters may pass without freezing temperatures or snow. In the mountains temperatures range from highs of 39 to 43 to lows of −19 (north) or −30 (Nakhjivan).

Introduction

Since the Russian conquest early in the nineteenth century, the central issue in the political life of Azerbaijan has been the relationship with the Russians. Relations with other peoples, though historically significant and sporadically crucial, have become secondary. Because of the nature of Russian imperial policy, the state intruded into Azerbaijani Turkish society and culture as well as into its economy, administration, and judiciary. In each of these arenas, the Azerbaijani Turks fought back. Although the Bolsheviks called tsarist policy "colonial," they borrowed from it and embellished it to implement their own policies—building socialism and communism, creating the "new Soviet person," and establishing "friendship of people," "drawing nearer" (*sblizhenie*) and even "merging" (*sliianie*).

This book is a study of central government policies and of Azerbaijani Turkish responses during nearly two centuries of Russian rule. Evidence suggests that the Azerbaijani Turkish leadership strove to maximize political autonomy, especially in times of transition. When the tsarist empire fell, Azerbaijan seceded. As the USSR crumbled, Azerbaijan declared independence. The political and cultural elite carried on the battle in other areas, too—economic, social, and cultural. Cultural endeavors became especially important when political action was restricted under both tsars and commissars. Whenever the political arena was closed, Azerbaijani Turks laid the intellectual groundwork for future political opportunities.

Part of this struggle entailed the articulation of an historical identity and national aims in the late imperial period and in the late 1970s to 1990s. Emphasizing ethno-national identity, the place of Islamic identity was and is debated. As a result, the writing of literature and history, particularly cultural history, occupies a central position in the political struggle. Because the imperial Russians claimed to have a "civilizing mission" and the Soviets have proclaimed themselves "elder brothers" in politics and culture, the Azerbaijani Turks use the antiquity of their history, language and literature as a weapon of self-defense, as proof they need no tutelage in self-government, economic management, education, or literature.

THE
AZERBAIJANI
TURKS

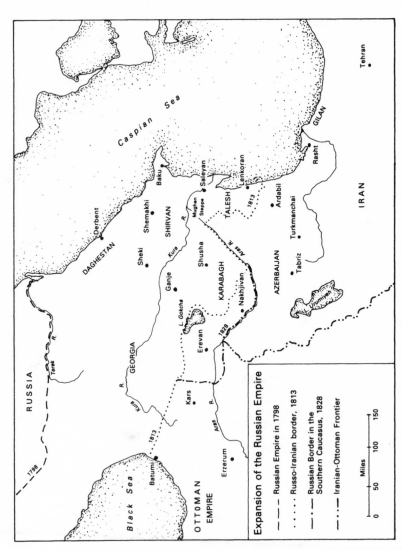

Azerbaijan Area/Location Map

Expansion of the Russian Empire

- - - Russian Empire in 1798
· · · · Russo-Iranian border, 1813
- · - Russian Border in the Southern Caucasus, 1828
- · · - Iranian-Ottoman Frontier

Miles

0   50   100   150

RUSSIA

1798

Terek R.

DAGHESTAN

Derbent

Caspian Sea

Sheki

Shemakhi

SHIRVAN

Baku

Kura R.

Ganje

Shusha

KARABAGH

Mughan Steppe

Seleyan

Aras R.

TALESH

Lenkoran

1813

GILAN

Rasht

GEORGIA

Kura R.

L. Gokcha

Erevan

1828

Nakhjivan

AZERBAIJAN

Urumiyeh

Ardabil

Turkmanchai

Tabriz

IRAN

Tehran

Kars

Aras R.

Erzerum

Batumi

1813

Black Sea

OTTOMAN EMPIRE

I Origins of the Azerbaijani Turks

When I saw ten thousand enemies, I attended to them,
When I saw twenty thousand enemies, I dented them . . .
When I saw a hundred thousand enemies I thundered at them,
I took up my unswerving sword . . .
Even then I did not boast: "I am a warrior, I am a prince":
Never have I looked kindly on warriors who boasted.

The Book of Dede Korkut*

Soviet historians seek to clarify the ethnic and cultural roots of Azerbaijani Turks in the distant past. The land that constitutes present-day Azerbaijan has been inhabited since earliest times. Over the centuries this territory has been invaded and ruled by different peoples and influenced by a number of great civilizations, each passing on some of its legacy to posterity. Ancient Media,[1] the land of today's Azerbaijan, was invaded by Persian king Cyrus the Great in the 6th century B.C.E., by Alexander of Macedonia two centuries later, and by Roman legions under Pompey three centuries after that. A boulder bearing what is believed to be the eastern-most Roman inscription survives just southwest of Baku.[2]

---

*The Book of Dede Korkut, trans. G. L. Lewis (London: Penguin Books, 1974). Recorded not later than the 16th century, though the contents are far older.

In late Roman (Byzantine) times, Caucasia was invaded by constantly warring Sasanian and Byzantine forces as well as by various Turkish tribal confederations who controlled the steppes north of the Caucasus chain and often acted as Byzantine allies against Iran. The Islamic caliphate extended its domain as far as the Caucasus Mountains by the middle of the 7th century, but Muslim control was consolidated during the 8th century after wars with the Khazars to the north.[3] Part of the population was gradually converted to Islam.

Eastern Caucasia was incorporated into a series of empires that included the Iranian plateau, portions of Central Asia, and often eastern Asia Minor: the Seljuk Turks' in the 11th century, the Chinghizid Ilkhanid, then the Timurid empires from the 13th to the 15th centuries, and the Karakoyunlu and Akkoyunlu states, with their base in southern Azerbaijan, in the 15th century. From the 16th to the mid-18th centuries, all Azerbaijan would be part of Safavid Iran, interrupted only by two occupations—first by Ottomans in the late 16th–early 17th centuries and then by Ottomans and Russians under Peter I during the early 18th century.

CAUCASIAN ALBANIA AND
THE SHIRVANSHAHS

By the 4th century B.C.E., two states had emerged to whose history Azerbaijani Turks attach special importance—Caucasian Albania, on the territory of present-day Soviet or northern Azerbaijan, and Aturpatkan or Atropaten in southern, now Iranian, Azerbaijan. The word Azerbaijan may have been formed from Atropaten,[4] named for Atropat, a satrap of Alexander of Macedonia in 328 B.C.E. His state lasted until circa 150 B.C.E. Azerbaijani scholars regard both states as predecessors of modern Azerbaijan and contend that the name Azerbaijan has been used since pre-Christian times for both areas, two issues of considerable controversy for historical and political reasons. (Because of its location Soviet scholars concentrated on Albania as a major predecessor state to the Azerbaijan SSR.)

Twentieth-century non-Azerbaijani scholars have argued that Azerbaijan is a recent, artificial creation (following to some extent Allied claims during World War I that it was created by the Ottomans) and that the Turks of Azerbaijan are such newcomers to the Caucasus that their claim to land—and indeed their living there—is not legitimate. Azerbaijani scholars have responded by writing histories of pre-Islamic and pre-Christian Caucasia in which they draw on works of Russian and European orientalists of the 19th century and on early works of Greek, Arab, Persian, Armenian, and other geographers and chroniclers and argue that modern Azerbaijan is an heir to the Albanian state and its territory. In a historical geography of Azerbaijan written in the mid 1980s, academician Ziya M. Buniatov, director of the Oriental Institute of the Azerbaijan Academy of Sciences and an internationally known scholar, maintained,

> The idea of Azerbaijan . . . is correctly used with respect to the territories of Northern and Southern Azerbaijan beginning with the 6th century [B.C.E.] . . . According to Arabic and Persian sources . . . from the 8th century, both Northern and Southern Azerbaijan were understood by the name Azerbaijan.[5]

In writing about the Albanian state, Soviet scholars have cited Greek and Roman sources of the late pre-Christian and early Christian eras, including the works of Strabo, Ptolemy, and Pliny, which indicated that Albania lay between the Caspian Sea and Iberia (Georgia), from the country of the nomad Sarmatians (the steppe north of the Greater Caucasus range) in the North to the Araz River in the South. A rich country with diverse economic activity, it had gardens, orchards, viticulture, arable land, pastures, large herds of cattle and horses, fishing, and hunting.[6] Around the 3d century, numerous cities famous for trading and crafts or as administrative and cultural centers were established: Ganje, Barda (Partva), Sheki, Nakhjivan, Baku, and others.[7] Armenian and Albanian historians of the 5th to the 8th centuries described Albania as a large state having essentially the same borders described by Ptolemy.[8] The *Syriac Chronicle . . . of Zachariah of Mitylene* (mid-6th century) described Albania as a separate state, having its own language, people, and a king who was a vassal of the Persian shah.[9]

Albania (sometimes called Aghvan; later, Aran)[10] appears to have retained considerable autonomy despite formal vassalage to larger states, notably Sasanian Iran. The Albanians recognized the Sasanian rulers as their suzerains and paid them tribute but maintained political autonomy.[11] Albanians reportedly joined Sasanian armies in fighting the Muslim Arabs in the 630s, but Albanian prince Javanshir finally negotiated his vassalage to the caliphate in 667.[12] Although Arab garrisons were placed in several strategic towns—Ardebil, Barda, Nakhjivan, Derbend, Maragha—the Khuramit movement, led by Babek from 820 to 837, resisted their control.[13]

Although Albania survived until the 9th century, the ruling dynasty lost power over the left bank of the Kura River in the Northeast early in the 6th century. According to Dr. Sara B. Ashurbeyli (Ashurbeili), in the region of Shirvan (Sharvan), "a small political entity called the state of the Shirvanshahs appeared." The state, initially created by the Sasanians to defend the frontier against the Khazars,[14] expanded in later centuries to include Derbend, Sheki in the Northeast, and the Mughan steppe south of the Araz River.[15]

The dynasty, however, was regarded by some medieval writers as being of great antiquity. Rashid al-Din (1247–1318), whose son married the daughter of the reigning Shirvanshah, placed the dynasty's origins in Achaemenid times: "It is already about two thousand years that rulership belongs to their lineage."[16] Ashurbeyli cited Ibn Khordadhbeh, writing in the 9th century, that the first Sasanian shah, Ardashir I (ruled 224–240) elevated local rulers in Caucasia to the title shah:

> In the name of Sasanian Khosrow I Anushirvan an organization of local vassal princes and significant settled colonies of their citizens was organized, especially from the Caspian regions, to fortify the northern borders against incursions of Turkish nomadic tribes. Among these kings who received the title shah, Arabic sources name . . . Sharvan-shah.[17]

Ashurbeyli and Russian orientalist Vladimir Minorsky agreed there were four dynasties that successively ruled as Shirvanshahs: the first, which the Sasanians used to defend the northern frontier, the Arab Mazyadids (9th–early 11th centuries), the Kesranids (so-called by Minorsky, 11th–14th centuries),[18] and the Derbend Shirvanshahs, a branch of the Kesranids (1382–circa 1539).[19]

The peak of Shirvan power appears to have been the 10th century when it expanded and reached its greatest size, incorporating major cities such as Ganje and Barda, the former capital of Albania.[20] Shirvan was as wealthy as Albania had been, and according to 10th-century chronicler Ibn Hauqal, Shirvan paid 1 million dirhams tribute in 955, compared with 300,000 for the second largest state of Caucasia.[21] During the 10th and 11th centuries, according to Arab sources, oil and salt were among Shirvan's most important economic assets.[22]

The strength of the Shirvanshahs is perhaps best measured by their resilience and adaptability. Ashurbeyli traces the fortunes of Shirvanshah Ibrahim I ibn Sultan Muhammad (ruled 1382–1417), who accepted Timur (13??–1405) as his suzerain, minting coins with Timur's image, saying the Friday prayer in his name, supporting him against Tokhtamysh of the Golden Horde and the Ottomans, and thus retained his title. After Timur's death and the rise of Kara Yusuf Karakoyunlu in southern Azerbaijan, Ibrahim agreed to recognize Kara Yusuf as his suzerain in 1410, in exchange for which Kara Yusuf granted Ibrahim lands from Sheki to Derbend, enlarging Shirvan once again.[23]

The end of the Shirvanshah state and dynasty is connected with the rise to the Iranian throne of the Safavids of southern Azerbaijan, who annexed

Shirvan and incorporated it directly into the imperial administrative system. Resistance to Safavid rule lasted for several decades.[24]

The first Safavid shah, Ismail I (ruled 1501–1524), emerged as a political leader within his prominent Ardebil family while still a young man. As shah, Ismail elevated Twelver Shi'ism to his state religion.[25] Caucasian Muslims, like the rest of the empire, came under heavy pressure to accept Shi'ism. The conversion was accomplished during Ismail's lifetime and that of his first successor, Tahmasp I (1524–1576), whose sister was the wife of the last effective Shirvanshah, Halilullah (1524–1535). Shi'ism was adopted by Ismail at least partly as a political tool in his ongoing warfare with two neighboring Sunni Muslim Turkish empires, the Ottomans to the West and the Central Asian Shibanids on the Northeast.[26] For the Turks of Azerbaijan, the result was twofold: (1) a strengthening of the bonds with the Iranian state and what was by the 16th century its Turco-Persian culture (the Safavid court language, according to various European scholars and travelers, was Turkish)[27] and (2) a sectarian division from other Turks. Realignment along ethnic lines would become a serious issue for Azerbaijani Turkish intellectuals in the 19th and 20th centuries.

THE ARRIVAL OF THE TURKS

The time of arrival of the Turks in Caucasia and of the complete Turkization of eastern Caucasia, like the history of Caucasian Albania, is a controversial topic. Azerbaijani scholars strive to illuminate their early ethnographic history and to quash their neighbors' claims (based on different interpretations of historical documents and/or other sources) to land that the Azerbaijanis have long inhabited and regard as their patrimony.

The History of Azerbaijan noted incursions by Turkic-speaking groups from "the beginning of our era," which increased in the 5th to the 7th and the 9th to the 11th centuries.[28] Ashurbeyli stated that "from antiquity" the Shirvan region had been a place where Caucasian-, Iranian-, and Turkish-speaking tribes mingled and argued that "in the 6th century intensive migrations of Turks into Aran, Shirvan, and Mughan occurred."[29] Soviet Azerbaijanis often cite historians and chroniclers who seem to regard Huns and Khazars as purely Turkish confederations (rather than partly Turkish, which is more accurate). They quote historian Tabari's (d. 932) description of invasions of Caucasia from the North during the 4th and 5th centuries by Huns and Khazars, whom he called Turks, and his statement that by the mid-6th century, there was a significant Khazar presence in Albania. Also cited are Byzantine sources of the mid-6th century that refer to the "settlement of Khazars" in "left bank Albania" (the left bank of the Kura)[30] and the 7th-century work of Ubeid ibn Shariyya al-Jurhumi, who told Muslim Caliph Mueviyyen I (661–680) that Azerbaijan "has long been a land of Turks. Having gathered over there, they have mixed with one another and become integrated."[31] Albanian historian Moisey Kaghankatli referred to a "Hun state" on the left bank of the Kura River in the 7th century. This state established "brotherhood and friendship" with Javanshir, the Albanian prince who ruled on the right bank of the Kura, that is, between the Kura and Araz rivers.[32]

Recently, some Azerbaijani scholars have argued for a direct ethnic link between the Albanians and Turks, both of whom have come to be regarded as ancestors of today's Azerbaijani Turks:

> In the 3rd century, the names of the Albanian Basileus, Zoberin, and of one of the Hun leaders (Zobergan) were the same; in the book "Aghvan tarihi," that is Albanians' own historical tradition, one of the religious leaders who signed church laws in the year 488 also had a name of Turkish origin— Manas; Gazan and Gor (Gor + gut) which appear in the same work written in the 7th century, conform to the names of the Oghuz leaders in the dastan ["ornate oral history"] "Kitabi-Dede Gorgut."[33]

Furthermore, on the basis of Moisey Kaghankatli's *The History of Albania*, it is argued that the Christian Albanians (Christian since the 4th century) had begun to take brides from the Turkish nomads to the north no later than the 7th century, for the *History* speaks of "condemning the Aghvan [Albanian] aristocracy for intermarrying with the Buddhists," and of members of eight aristocratic families who "married aliens and profaned themselves."[34]

According to Professor Peter B. Golden, early sources are not sufficiently clear to form detailed and definitive conclusions. Only some pieces of information are certain. He has written that "genuine interaction" between Turkic peoples and the Caucasian population can safely be dated from the middle of the 4th century. Contacts in the succeeding centuries were part of the complex interplay of Byzantine-Sasanian-nomadic forces who waged war in Caucasia:

> In the course of the seventh century, the two major tribal unions emerged in this region under the Türk banner: the Khazars and the Bulgars . . . [there is] confusion in our sources of *Khazar* and *Türk* (the two are virtually interchangeable at this time) . . . [and] it is not until the seventh century that we can trace the outline of Khazar involvement in Transcaucasian affairs with any degree of clarity. Prior to this they operated in close concert with their Türkic overlords. Thus the Khazars formed the bulk of the Türk forces used by the Byzantine Emperor Heraclius (610–641) in this counter-offensive against the Sasanids in Transcaucasia.[35]

These events do not refer to settlement by Turks. Complete Turkization of eastern Caucasia can be dated from the arrival of the Seljuks in the 11th century and more fully consolidated with Turkish migrations during the 13th-century Mongol eruption.[36]

The Arab Muslim invasions brought Arabs and Islam to Caucasia in the 7th century. The settlement of Arabs in Albania and the fact that non-Muslims paid higher taxes led eventually to the Islamization of most of the Albanian population, a matter that is not without disputation. Nineteenth-century Russian caucasologist I. P. Petrushevskii argued that a majority of the Albanians converted to Islam; those who remained Christian became Armenianized.[37] Some have argued further that Muslim Albanians merged more easily with recently Islamized Seljuk Turks in the 11th century,[38] an idea that is sometimes coupled with the popular, but erroneous, notion that the Seljuks were the first Turks to come to Caucasia.

A closely related and equally controversial matter concerns the status of the Albanian Christian church prior to Islamization. Put simply, the dispute concerns whether the Albanian church was separate and had its own liturgical language or whether it was part of the Armenian church. Without repeating arguments that have been stated elsewhere,[39] it can be noted that Azerbaijani and some Russian, Armenian, and Western scholars have confirmed the existence of an independent Albanian church and language. One scholar cited a 15th-century Armenian-language "textbook" that contained the Albanian alphabet.[40] Professor Keith Hitchins has concluded that "although much of the religious history of Albania is obscure, evidence indicates that at least by the latter part of the fifth century a regular [Albanian] church organization headed by a Metropolitan (or Catholicos) and numerous bishops did exist."[41] As Petrushevskii suggested, what was left of that church after Islamization apparently merged with the Armenian church. Diplomatic notes of 705 C.E. between the Armenian Catholicos and the caliph showed how the caliph sanctioned the absorption of the Albanian church by the Armenian:

> Caliph Abd al-Malik answered the Armenian Catholicos: "I have read your letter, Iliya God's Slave, Catholicos of the Armenian people. And to you as a sign of favor, I am sending you one of my own faithful servants with many troops. We have given him orders that the Aghvans who raised a rebellion against our suzerainty be subordinated to the laws of your religion."[42]

THE EVE OF THE RUSSIAN CONQUEST

Safavid rule had been consolidated in Caucasian Azerbaijan by the end of the 16th century. Ottoman-Iranian wars led to Ottoman occupation of Caucasia between 1578 and 1603, and, in the waning years of the Safavid dynasty, the area was fought over by both Russians and Ottomans. The Russians under Peter I during the 1710s and 1720s held the Caspian coast, but Empress Anna returned the lands in the 1730s.

In the middle of the 18th century, after the end of the Safavid line and the assassination of Nadir Shah (Afshar) in 1747, central control over former Safavid lands ended and local rulers asserted their independence. Among the Caucasian khanates were Baku, Kuba, Sheki, Shemakhi, Karabagh, Nakhjivan, and Erevan; the khans who ruled these small states were Muslim and apparently Turks. Struggles for power, often bloody, took place within khanates or among them, making for turbulent times. The population was mixed in terms of ethnicity, religion and sect, and nomadism-sedentarism. The largest component of the population of eastern Caucasia has been called "Turcoman tribes," some of whom were nomadic, some seminomadic, and others settled as farmers or town dwellers.[43] Among the settled were the Javanshirs of Karabagh. Kurds, Lezghi, and Avars were found throughout the region. Sunni-Shi'i antagonism was muted late in the century, though it had been bloody some decades earlier. There were also non-Muslim minority communities of Georgians, Armenians, and Jews in all regions except Talysh near the Caspian coast. According to Professor Muriel Atkin,

> Non-Muslims lived under certain disadvantages, notably a higher rate of taxation, but they do not seem to have been actively persecuted. . . . Christians and Jews lived in their own villages and enjoyed certain advantages, especially the local governance of their coreligionists. Some of the Armenian village chiefs were extremely powerful . . . as "people of The Book," [Christians and Jews] were able to maintain their houses of worship, obtain religious literature, and employ the clergy of their faith for their congregations.[44]

The Christian populations, both Armenian and Georgian, appealed to Russia to extend sovereignty over them, bring Caucasia under their control, unseat the khans, and even invade central Iran.[45] Catherine the Great (1762– 1796) signed a treaty with Georgia in 1783 bringing that kingdom under Russian protection but did not engage in military action there until 1796. Professor Atkin noted that "for all Catherine's professed concern over Christians living under Muslim rule, her actions in the Caucasus showed that she never allowed that issue to force her along a course that was not chosen first and foremost on the basis of Russia's best interests."[46] Expansion and the prestige of amassing colonies to pursue a "civilizing mission" were perhaps more important factors in the decision to expand in Caucasia, and Catherine was always careful to avoid provoking the Ottomans by action too close to their border.

Catherine's expansion clashed with the attempts of a new Iranian dynasty to reestablish control over former Safavid territories. Aga Muhammad Khan (effective rule circa 1785–1797) established the Qajar dynasty in southern Azerbaijan in 1791. Aga Muhammad gathered most of the former Safavid lands south of the Araz River under his control by 1794. Thereafter, he began to look northward. In 1796 his forces and Catherine's would clash. The protracted and bitter struggle for the Caucasus would bring the khanates under Russian domination during two Russo-Iranian wars, 1804–1813 and 1826–1828.

Law and Administration

From the Arab conquest to the consolidation of Soviet power in the 1920s, a dual system of justice existed in Azerbaijan, as it would throughout most of the Islamic world, in which holy and secular laws coexisted. Law, in Islamic thought, is regarded as "flowing from or being part of the concept of Shari'a (the divinely ordained pattern of human conduct)."[47] Furthermore, in theory, Islam knows no such dichotomy as "render to Caesar the things that are Caesar's and to God the things that are God's." In Islam, the state and the faith are conceived as one fabric and the goal of the Islamic state is to create and safeguard conditions for the individual believer to fulfill his duties as a Muslim. This, at least, is the theory.

In practice, alongside the religious laws were customary laws (*adet*) and temporal laws made by the ruler (*kanun*). The relationship of these bodies of law and their relative purviews varied in history with the power of secular rulers and religious scholars (*ulema*). Furthermore, elements of Chinghizid law may also have existed, for Timur (in the late 14th century) was reported to have given Ibrahim I of Shirvan the *yarlik* (khan's decree) to rule in Shirvan.[48] In former Chinghizid domains across the steppe, both the legitimacy of the Chinghizid lineage and its legal/administrative structure persisted into the 16th century.[49]

The Safavid conquest ended the independent existence of Caucasian states and, therefore, their administration. From the 16th century Caucasia was incorporated into the Safavid system, represented by its administrators, *beklerbeks*. The territory in turn was divided into four *beklerbekliks*: Tabriz (center at Tabriz city), Shukhur-Saada (Nakhjivan, with center at Nakhjivan city), Shirvan (center at Shemakhi), and Karabagh (center at Ganje). These four regions were called Azerbaijan by the Safavid administration, and their combined tax was between 300,000 and 500,000 *tumans*.[50]

The individual khanates that emerged in the mid-18th century were ruled by khans who were also tribal leaders; their first loyalty was to the tribes. *Beks* (*begs, beys*, or notables), who might be close relatives of the khan, served the khans and might have their own retainers. It was the job of the bek to serve his khan in any capacity required. In return the bek was exempt from taxes and might enjoy a great deal of local authority.[51]

Social Structure, Economy, and Culture to the 19th Century

From Strabo's time to the 20th century, the majority of the settled population in Caucasia was engaged in agriculture. Some, like nomads, kept herds. The Mughan steppe and other areas boasted fertile soil and pasture land, orchards and gardens. Fishing was profitable.

Trade was another major economic activity and involved commerce in agricultural goods (saffron, fish, salt) and handicrafts (silks, carpets and other textiles, and ceramics). The growth of Azerbaijan's many towns, some dating from pre-Christian times, is connected with trade. Towns grew rich and internationally renowned thanks to local artisans, traders, and crafts-people. Shemakhi became known for silks. Archaeologists in the 20th century have unearthed caravansaries that provided lodging for merchants of the 14th and 15th centuries in Baku and elsewhere in Azerbaijan. Merchants benefited from several prolonged periods of peace under the Seljuk, Chingh-izid, Timurid, and Safavid empires. The most famous trade, if not yet the most lucrative, was in oil. Early descriptions of the oil of the Apsheron Peninsula are found in writings of Arab geographers of the 10th century. Yaqub Hamawi mentioned yellow, black, and green oil and even some pits that produced "a white oil like mercury." A local geographer in the 15th century, Mawlana Abd al-Rashid al-Bakuwi, stated that 200 mule loads of oil were exported daily from the pits near Baku.[52]

Landowners were the mainstay of the ruling class and ruling dynasties themselves were landowners. Rulers depended on the landed nobility for taxes and soldiers. With the fall of the Shirvanshahs, the Safavid-appointed beklerbegs who came to administer Shirvan were reportedly absorbed into the local landowning nobility. The power of landownership reached a pinnacle with the emergence of the khanates; there all land was considered the personal property (*mülk*) of the khan.[53]

The ulema enjoyed prestige and privileges such as tax exemption. They do not appear to have played a particularly important political role, judging from local chronicles.[54] This may be explained by the distance between centers of the Shi'i hierarchy and Caucasia and by the fact that the khans were tribal chiefs not known for their submission to the religious establishment.

In the cultural realm as well as the political and economic, Azerbaijan's history cannot be separated from the developments of the larger Turco-Iranian world stretching, by the time of the Seljuks, from Turkistan into Asia Minor. Some periods and individuals are far better known than others, though ongoing research gradually is filling in the gaps. Perhaps the best-known aspects of cultural history are those connected with the autonomous kings and shahs of eastern Caucasian states who supported the arts in their courts. Traces remain of the work they fostered or commissioned, especially in architecture and written literature.

The surviving architectural monuments from the 12th century and earlier testify to this generous patronage as well as to defense and religious needs. Azerbaijan's oldest structure is a tower that stands in the middle of Baku on the bay. It is called the *Gyz galasy* (Maiden tower). Although it was once thought to be a 12th-century structure, archaeological work in the 1980s has confirmed that the tower is pre-Christian, probably dating from the 7th century B.C.E. or earlier, and apparently part of a defense system. When an enemy approached, a fire could be lit atop the tower. Sentinels at similar towers throughout the area would light fires, sending a message to prepare for battle. Despite the legend about a khan trying to seduce his daughter who then threw herself from the tower into the sea (which some members of the Soviet-period intelligentsia recognize as part of the state's "anti-khan" propaganda), the name of the tower refers to its strength, to the fact that it was impenetrable. Many other fortifications in Central Asia are also called by the same name.

The Shemkir minaret survives from the 9th or 10th century. More towers, mausoleums, fortifications, and bridges remain from the 12th and 13th centuries, and part of the Safavid-period wall still stands in Baku.[55] The *saray* (palace) of the Sheki khan (17th–18th centuries) displays decorative tiles, fountains, and several stained-glass windows. The Shirvanshah palace complex, built of fine local stone during the 15th and 16th centuries, has been preserved and stands as a museum in central Baku. There have been studies of these structures and of some architects.[56]

Modern studies of Azerbaijan's literary history discuss numerous poets, for poetry is perhaps the oldest genre in the written and oral literature of Azerbaijan. A 1982 textbook for institutions of higher education outlined the "ancient and medieval" literary history of Azerbaijan.[57] It included two works from the period before the 10th century (the Zoroastrian *Avesta* and the Turkish dastan *The Book of Dede Korkut*) and a selection of widely renowned poets from the 10th to the 18th centuries, including Hetran Tabrizi, poetess Mehseti Ganjevi, Khagani Shirvani, Nizami Ganjevi, Maraghali Evhedi, Arif Ardebili, Imameddin Nasimi, Shah Ismail, Muhammad Fuzuli, Mollah Veki Vidadi, and Mollah Penakh Vagif. Collected works of most of these poets and some others have been published in individual volumes.

Among the most prominent of these literati and those whose works have been most often and widely published in Soviet Azerbaijan are Khagani Shirvani (1126–1199), Nizami Ganjevi (1141–1209), Nasimi (1369–1417),

Shah Ismail Safavi ("Khatai") (1486–1524), and Fuzuli (1494–1556). Khagani Shirvani represented the impact of Shirvanshah patronage.[58] Nizami Ganjevi, because of his wide fame and enormous contributions to Persian-language literature, is seen as an example of the interconnections between Turkish and Persian cultural strands and of Azerbaijan's place in Turco-Persian culture. His collected works, in Turkish translation, have been printed along with individual volumes of particular types of poetry. His *Khamsa* of five epic poems, based on traditional tales and dastans, included "Leyla and Majnun," "Khosrow and Shirin," "The Seven Beauties," and other works.[59] Fuzuli, though he lived in Baghdad, wrote in Turkish, and his poetry and prose works are reprinted in transliterated but not translated editions.[60] He wrote versions of some of the same stories as Nizami, but his Turkish-language versions were the basis for early 20th-century dramatic and operatic productions.

Finally, Shah Ismail, who wrote much Turkish poetry under the name Khatai, is regarded not only as a political unifier of Azerbaijan but as an important contributor to its culture. He wrote as a member of his own court circle of poets, a common phenomenon for Turkish and Persian dynasties of the time.[61] The similarity of the language of Fuzuli and Shah Ismail to the modern Turkish dialect of Azerbaijan affirms the historical continuity and richness of the language. Such early works were models of subtle and sophisticated literature long before the advent of Russian power.

Cultural life was also manifested in libraries. Written works of the pre-Christian and early Christian eras suggest the existence of court and church libraries. The Shirvanshahs apparently maintained a library. Architects and literati had personal libraries, such as those of Khatib Tabrizi and Nizami Ganjevi.[62] A major library, reported to contain perhaps 400,000 volumes, was attached to the Maragha observatory (built 1258–1261) in southern Azerbaijan under the direction of a major scholar of that time, Nasreddin Tusi (1201–1274). Unfortunately, neither the library nor the observatory survived the Mongol invasions.[63] Shah Ismail established at least two libraries in Tabriz and Ardebil. Prince Behmen Mirza (17th–early 18th century) moved his personal library from Tabriz to Shusha using ninety-five camels (each could be expected to carry about 300–400 pounds).[64]

On the writing of history and philosophy in the 7th century, some aspects are well known, others are not known at all. Religious literature probably existed before that time in Albanian. Moisey Kaghankatli's history of Albania was written in the 7th century. The 12th and 13th centuries boasted a number of prominent and prolific philosophers and historians. Bakhmanyar al-Azerbaijani (d. 1169–1170) and Tusi have received special attention in contemporary Azerbaijan. Bakhmanyar's *Al-Tahsil*, "an encyclopedic work" on logic and metaphysics, was published in Russian in 1983.[65] Many of

Tusi's works have been published in Azerbaijani Turkish and Russian.⁶⁶ The 16th and 17th centuries, in connection with Safavid rule, were fruitful times for scholarship and the arts. A famous historian of that period was Hiyaseddin ibn-Muhamaddin al-Husein ("Khondemir" 1475–1536), who chronicled the consolidation of Safavid power in Azerbaijan. He and a contemporary, Mir-Yahya al-Husein al-Kazvini (1481–1555), wrote histories sympathetic to the Safavids; both works have been used by later historians.

Perhaps the oldest cultural and historical traditions are embodied in the dastans, which were composed in prose and poetry and often recited to music. They are "the principal repository of ethnic identity, history, customs, and the value systems of [their] owners and composers." Dastans combine the arts with the reporting of history and traditions using examples of heroism and morality. Being "an integral part of identity, historical memory and the historical record itself," the dastan "stands, as it always has, as the final line of defense against any attempts to dominate" its owners.⁶⁷

The dastans are part of the Central Asian tradition, and those which belong to the Turks in Caucasia reflect historic ties to the East and to other Turks. Dastans date from pre-Islamic and some from pre-Christian times. The two major dastans known among modern Azerbaijani Turks are *The Book of Dede Korkut* and *Köroglu*. Although these were written down in the 15th century, they were certainly carried orally by Turkish nomads in earlier centuries. *Dede Korkut* is "set in the heroic age of the Oghuz Turks" to whom the Azerbaijani Turks trace at least a part of their lineage. *Dede Korkut* is shared by the Turks of Asia Minor and by the Turkmen, as is the *Köroglu* dastan. Both, in their extant form, are set in Asia Minor and Caucasia—the twelve sections of *Dede Korkut* refer to "infidel" Georgians, to the Black Sea, to Trabzon, and other local places. Köroglu is known to have been a historical person. This is also true of at least some figures in *The Book of Dede Korkut*. Indeed, Dede Korkut himself, the reciter-compiler of the "book," may have existed. Professor G. L. Lewis wrote that "there is no need to go deeply into the question of whether Dede Korkut was a real person; certainly there is no evidence that he was not."

Although both dastans have Islamic elements, these are clearly overlays rather than integral parts of the action. Pre-Islamic customs and values are preserved. One obvious example is the required betrothal contest between a young man and woman that the man must win before they can marry. Thus, in the "Tale of Bamsi Beyrek of the Grey Horse," Beyrek and his betrothed, Lady Chichek, have three contests—shooting arrows, horse racing, and wrestling. Lady Chichek notes that Beyrek is the first to defeat her in these skills, and she willingly accepts him. ("Bamsi Beyrek" is a variant on the *Alpamysh* dastan) Elsewhere in the dastan, wives and mothers participate in hunting and battles. Loyalty to the family, clan, or tribe is fundamental, as are bravery and honesty. Both dastans describe struggles to protect the tribe or the homeland, or to free the people from a foreign invader-conqueror. Men and women are equal in these endeavors:

> [Kazan Khan] dismounted from his chestnut horse. . . . He blessed Muhammad, he foamed like camel, he roared like lion . . . and all alone he drove his horse at the infidel, his sword flashing . . . yet he could not overcome the infidel . . . Lady Burla [Kazan's wife] . . . with her forty slender maidens accompanying her, she sent for her black horse, she mounted, and grasped her black sword. . . . "To sword, Kazan, I am here!"
>
> Now the Oghuz nobles [arrived]. . . . Of counting the nobles of the Oghuz there could be no end . . . they charged at the infidels, they wielded their swords. On that day the manly warriors showed their mettle. On that day the unmanly spied out roads by which to slink away. . . . Lady Burla the Tall aimed a blow of her sword at the infidels' black banner and brought it down. The infidel king was taken and the unbelievers fled.[68]

2 Russian Colonial Rule

*Their sons worthy of becoming lords became slaves, their
daughters worthy of becoming ladies became servants.*

Kül Tegin inscription
Turkish, early eighth century*

Russian rule set the tone and established policies that shaped Caucasia for
at least two centuries. The cultural gulf between these Russian invaders and
the native population of Azerbaijan was great, perhaps the most pronounced
since the Muslim conquest. Russian imperial policies were very different
from the rule of other empires to control Caucasia in recent times; they strove
for a degree of economic, political, even cultural control that provoked nearly
continual resistance.

RUSSIAN CONQUEST AND FIRST YEARS
OF RUSSIAN ADMINISTRATION

The struggle between imperial Russia and a resurgent Iran for
possession of khanates north of the Araz River was long and difficult. Losses
in life and property were enormous. Intermittent military action had begun
in the 1790s, though an official state of war existed only from 1804 to 1813.

---

*Talut Tekin, *A Grammar of Orkhon Turkic*, Indiana University Uralic and Altaic
Series, vol. 69 (Bloomington, Ind., 1968), p. 264.

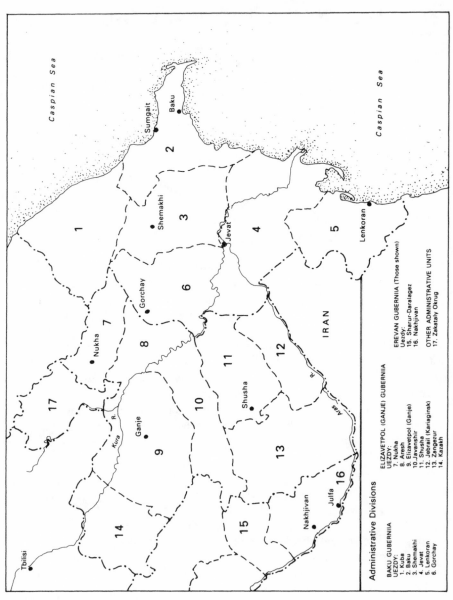

Administrative Divisions

BAKU GUBERNIIA
UEZDY:
1. Kuba
2. Baku
3. Shemakhi
4. Jevat
5. Lenkoran
6. Gorchay

ELIZAVETPOL (GANJE) GUBERNIIA
UEZDY:
7. Nukha
8. Aresh
9. Elizavetpol (Ganje)
10. Javanshir
11. Shusha
12. Jebrail (Kariaginsk)
13. Zangezur
14. Kazakh

EREVAN GUBERNIIA (Those shown)
Uezdy:
15. Sharur-Daralagez
16. Nakhjivan

OTHER ADMINISTRATIVE UNITS
17. Zakataly Okrug

Baku and Elizavetpol *Gubernii*, Late Nineteenth Century

Contrary to contemporary Russian and later Soviet accounts, the population and the khans strenuously resisted the Russian conquest, which was less a matter of Russo-Iranian armed conflict than of battles between khans and Russian forces. Initially, some khans thought to use the Russo-Iranian War to improve their own positions and supported the Russians because they seemed far away or because some traditional rival supported the Qajars. But contact with the Russians changed their minds. During the war Russians profaned mosques and forced their way into private homes. As the Russian forces neared a town or settlement, people would flee south. After the Russian victory, many khans and their families took refuge in Iran.[1] Russian gains were made only gradually, and the effort was interrupted by the wars against Napoleon. Indeed, European alliances and the larger European competition for land or influence or both in Asia—what Kipling called the "Great Game"—affected this Russo-Iranian War as well as the Russo-Ottoman wars about the same period.[2]

Among the casualties of the protracted campaigns in Caucasia was the infamous Pavel Tsitsianov. Commander-in-chief of the Russian war effort from 1803 until 1806, Tsitsianov was regarded as a great hero: "a man of indomitable courage . . . his soldierly qualities . . . secured him the love, the adoration almost of the army."[3] But in Caucasia his title was pronounced *ishpokhdor*, roughly meaning "his work is dirt." To an Iranian chronicler, he was "the shedder of blood."[4] The matter was more than the view of the defeated toward the conquering commander. Tsitsianov insulted his own men and the enemy; he was reported to have preferred the most brutal of methods. His writings referred to "Persian scum" and "Asiatic treachery." It has been suggested that he rarely planned attacks, expecting instead to intimidate the khans into surrender. Five of his six generals regarded his plan to capture Erevan as unsound.[5] He changed the name of Ganje to Elizavetpol and fined those who uttered the historic name. His destruction of that city was so thorough that it was "eliminated as a political entity." In 1806 he was lured into a trap outside Baku and shot dead.

Finally, the Russo-Iranian border was established roughly at the Araz River by the Treaty of Gulistan (1813) that ended the first Russo-Iranian War.[6] The second Russo-Iranian War was a brief recapitulation of the first. The populace was more pro-Iranian; the Russian victory, more decisive. During the fighting, Russian troops reached Tabriz. This war ended with the Treaty of Turkmanchai (1828), which handed over to Russia the Erevan and Nakhjivan khanates retained by Iran in 1813. Other provisions of the treaty concerned tariffs and legal concessions with broad implications for Russo-Iranian relations and the Great Game.[7] Resistance persisted.[8]

Administration

From the time of the Russian conquest until the 1840s, Azerbaijan was ruled directly by tsarist military forces. Even before the formal conclusion of the first war, Russian military rule was established. The former khanates were reorganized into *provintsii* (provinces), each governed by an army officer, a commandant. The military commanders had been charged with governing by a combination of local and Russian imperial law, the latter to be used only when the former was inappropriate or nonexistent. The Russian commandants, however, were entirely unfamiliar with local customary and religious law. As a result, Russian law was increasingly applied. The result was widespread popular discontent. Russian commander-in-chief Philip Paulucci (1811–1812) tried to remedy the situation by setting up judicial-administrative boards made up of the local commandant and representatives of the population, presumably including mullahs. Despite the efforts of these boards, the sphere of Russian law expanded.[9]

In the late 1830s plans were initiated to replace the commandant system with a civil imperial administration. The law was promulgated in April 1840, to take effect 1 January 1841. At that time, the entire region of "Transcaucasia" (so-called from Russia's perspective), was divided into a Georgian-Imeretian *guberniia* (province), with its center at Tiflis, and a Caspian *oblast'* (region), centered at Shemakhi. The line between the two was drawn so as to put Ganje (Elizavetpol) and Nakhjivan in the Georgian guberniia. Viceroy M. S. Vorontsov (1844–1854), made further administrative changes and consolidated the application of the empire's administrative and legal system.[10] He drew new administrative boundaries creating four gubernii in December 1846: Tiflis, Kutais, Shemakhi, and Derbent. The new borders, too, placed Ganje under Tiflis' jurisdiction. A new Erevan guberniia, created in 1849, included Nakhjivan. None of these divisions took account of the composition of the population or their wishes or of historic precedent. In 1859 when the town of Shemakhi was destroyed by an earthquake, Baku became the new capital and the guberniia was renamed.[11]

By the end of direct military rule in the 1840s, Russian law prevailed in all criminal and most civil matters. The jurisdiction of religious courts and their judges (sing.: *qadi*) was limited to family law such as marriage, inheritance and divorce, and continued to diminish. In an effort to control the application of Islamic law and the *ulema* (Islamic scholars), two Ecclesiastical Boards were created to oversee all religious activity. The head of each board, a mufti for the Sunni and a sheikh ul-Islam for Shi'i, were state appointees.

At the same time, the power of local imperial authorities grew. In November 1842 *uezd* (district) court officials received the right to decide legal matters involving up to 200 rubles, but lower officials could decide matters involving lesser sums. Tiflis and Shemakhi police chiefs on their own authority could decide matters involving up to 100 rubles. In 1844 local authorities received the right to send a convicted person to prison for up to five years, exile to interior provinces of Russia for up to eight years, or to Siberia for life. The Senate and individual ministries did not have the right to accept complaints about wrongful exile from Caucasia and were obliged not to act on such charges.[12] The matter of exile is significant in view of the practice of sending Russian criminals and dissenters to the Caucasus. This could result in potentially diluting the indigenous population by moving Russians in and natives out. Alone, it was not a large enough phenomenon to alter the population; with other types of resettlement carried out by the imperial government, it may have contributed to demographic shifts.[13]

Subjects of the empire were not equal before the law. Restrictions against non-Christians affected the Azerbaijani Turks. Tsarist censorship regulations of 1857, for example, granted Georgian and Armenian religious authorities oversight of censorship in their own ethno-religious communities. The local Muslim Ecclesiastical Boards did not receive such authority; Muslim religious works and books of any kind imported from the Ottoman Empire had to pass a censorship board in Odessa.[14] Treatment of the religious establishments was also prejudicial. Except for the viceroyalty of Prince Grigorii Golitsyn (1896–1904), state policy was firmly anti-Muslim and anti-Turkish. Golitsyn responded to Azerbaijani complaints about overrepresentation of Armenians in the civil service by removing many and replacing them with Azerbaijani Turks. In 1903 he confiscated Armenian church lands, provoking attacks by Armenian terrorists. Church lands were restored. Golitsyn soon left his post. The appointment of Count I. I. Vorontsov-Dashkov in May 1905 signaled a return to the traditional pro-Armenian posture. Except for the Golitsyn episode, Armenian church properties and priests were not threatened or their work obstructed.[15] In contrast, the Muslim mullahs were brought under direct state control and subjected to government regulations. Their religious properties were confiscated and they were subjected to intense Russian Orthodox proselytization.[16]

Economy

After being disrupted in the first Russo-Iranian War, agriculture and trade slowly began to recover. The process was set back by the second Russo-Iranian War, but the brevity of that war, which the Russian army carried into Iranian territory, meant relatively less damage to the North. To facilitate commerce, the separate currencies of the khanates were replaced by the ruble, tariffs between the former khanates abolished, and weights and measures standardized. Russians began to invest in joint-stock trading companies in Caucasia in the 1830s. The first steamship appeared on the Caspian in the 1840s, and the shipping company Caucasus and Mercury was founded in Baku in 1859. By the end of the century, the company would have offices in Paris, Copenhagen, Liverpool, Singapore, and New York. Telegraph lines linked major towns of the region during the 1860s.

Trade through the port of Baku increased steadily from an average of 400,000 rubles annually in the 1830s, to an average of 500,000 in the 1840s, and up to 700,000–900,000 after the Crimean War. The main exports through Baku's port in mid-century were iron ore, copper, and silk, reflecting the port's ties to the hinterland. In fourth place were petroleum products. Imports of cloth, fruits, and vegetables perpetually exceeded exports. Baku conducted more trade with Iran at that time than with Russia, but much of the trade through Baku was in transit between Russia and Iran.[17]

Azerbaijan's economy, like that of other colonies, grew because of trade with the empire even before the rapid industrialization of the 1870s. The city of Baku provides a prime example of such trade. Reestablishment of central control in Iran, the expansion of Russian trade (with advantageous concessions from Iran), and Baku's excellent natural harbor and tradition of commerce contributed to the city's vigorous commercial life. Yet the city remained physically small, almost entirely contained within the walls built by Shah Abbas the Great (1587–1629). By the time of the Crimean War, the Russians had built a "white Baku"[18] just north of the Inner City (Icheri Sheher). The Russians called it the Citadel (Krepost') because they had converted the remains of the Shirvanshah palace complex there into stables and an arsenal. According to Alexandre Dumas, the French novelist, who visited Baku in 1856, the narrow gates of the old walls made it impossible for more than three horses abreast to pass through. He likened entrance into the Inner City to "penetrating one of the strongest fortresses of the Middle Ages."[19]

THE ERA OF INDUSTRIALIZATION

The rapid industrial growth beginning in the 1870s sparked trade, banking, construction, and the creation of a communications and transportation network throughout the region. The result was a huge infrastructure similar to those in industrial Europe. It began with the oil boom.

The Oil Economy

Oil had been exported from the Apsheron Peninsula where Baku is located at least from the tenth century. The Russians took over the khans' monopolies in oil. By the end of the century, Baku would be the oil center of the empire and one of the top oil-producing areas of the world. From 1821 to 1872, the Russian state maintained some form of monopoly over oil extraction, refining, and trade. Except for an interval of state monopoly from 1834 to 1850, individual "tax farms" held state concessions. The last was a Baku Armenian, I. M. Mirzoev, who held the concession from 1863 until the system was abolished in 1872.[20] Mirzoev and others in the Armenian community in Baku were in a strong position when the auction of oil lands began.

Azerbaijan's first oil refinery was erected outside Baku in 1859, and the first kerosene plant was built in 1863. The "oil rush" began with the drilling of wells in the 1870s. Its impact on the economic and social character of the Baku area would be profound. Oil continued to bubble to the surface under the pressure of natural gas as the number of drilled wells increased. Traditional hand extraction of crude from shallow pits by means of buckets and pulleys continued to be widespread even into the twentieth century. Several factors at this time led to a jump in the output, refining, and export of oil.

Successful drilling by Mirzoev was the first element contributing to the oil rush. The year after his first well was sunk, the monopoly system was replaced by the auction of oil-bearing lands. The security of their holdings assured, oilmen now invested more money and care in their operations, which might yield long-term benefits.[21] Mirzoev became one of the major purchasers of oil lands. Most of the others were local Armenians and Russians, who constituted the financial elite of the oil industry. In contrast, few Azerbaijani Turks succeeded in buying oil lands, acquiring only 5 of the 51 plots sold at the first auction.[22] Azerbaijani Turks were more numerous in small-scale extraction and in refining. Of the 54 oil firms engaged in the extraction of oil in Baku in 1888, only 2 major companies were Azerbaijani-owned.[23] Of the 162 refineries, 73 were Azerbaijani-owned, but only 7 of them had fifteen or more workers.[24]

In 1873 another event contributed to the expansion of the oil industry. Robert Nobel, brother of the famous Alfred Nobel, arrived in Baku to purchase wood for the manufacture of rifle butts. He stayed and bought an oil refinery.[25] When Nobel arrived in Baku, there were twelve oil companies and a small industrial labor force.[26] Within ten years, the Nobel Company would be the largest in the Baku area; within thirty, it would be one of the major oil companies in the world. The Nobel Company came to symbolize the West for Baku. In contemporary socialist writings and subsequent Soviet historiography, it is the paradigm of European capitalist exploitation. More salient is the fact that the Nobels, their managers, advisers, technicians, and European fellow-investors like Rothschild brought new technology and business methods to Baku. They used their own capital to invest in innovation, marketing plans, and risky expansion on a scale totally foreign to Baku's pre-industrial oil industry. The Nobel Company was responsible for massive construction projects in and around Baku. It produced and exported more oil than all the other Baku firms combined—55 percent of the kerosene exports in 1883, the peak year. Even under the disadvantageous transportation conditions that existed before the completion of the Transcaucasian Railway in 1884, the Nobel Company was able to ship enough oil via the Volga-Baltic route to break the Standard Oil monopoly in Europe.[27]

To try to chip away at Nobel dominance, local oilmen copied Nobel's methods: improving the quality of their kerosene, turning waste into lubricants, and even forming storage and transportation networks to expand their marketing operations. They rejected Nobel's proposal for a marketing cartel in the early 1880s. After 1883 the Nobel Company's share of the market shrank. By 1893 the firm's kerosene constituted only 21 percent of all the Russian Empire's kerosene on domestic and foreign markets.[28] It remained the single most powerful and wealthy petroleum company in the Baku area. By the end of the 1880s oil extraction would be almost the exclusive preserve of big firms (Nobel, Rothschild's Caspian–Black Sea Society) and locally owned firms that had bought oil lands in the 1870s.

Despite the dominance of the "giants," the growth of the oil industry was such that many could turn a profit. From the 1870s to the turn of the century, the Baku oil industry grew in output (to its peak in 1901) and in the size of its labor force. Output rose from approximately 14,300 barrels (bbl) in 1872 to approximately 70,600,000 (almost 200,000 bbl/day) in the peak year 1901, more than the combined production of all U.S. fields for that year.[29] The number of oil workers increased from 1,254 in 1883 to 27,673 in 1901.[30]

Rapid expansion of the oil industry was primarily responsible for Baku's apparently well-deserved reputation as a wild boomtown replete with grand hotels, telephones, casinos, gaslit streets, prostitutes, and a "frontier" lawlessness. Musa Naghiyev, an oilman, was kidnapped from a carriage in front of his own house in the middle of the day.[31] Another community leader, Haji Baba Ashurov, was shot and killed one spring day in 1908.[32] Yet Baku held the same romantic excitement for its contemporaries as the American frontier did for the eastern tenderfoot. It conjured images of easily made fortunes and adventure. Young men came not only to work in the oil fields but to find oil and get rich themselves. Wildcat oil rigs proliferated so quickly and so close together that, as the saying went, one could not swing a cat by the tail between them. A novel set in Baku began:

There used to be a proverb among the Russian businessmen: "Whoever lives a year among the oil owners of Baku can never again be civilized." Thus spoke the honorable merchants from St. Petersburg. They always made their wills when they had to go to Baku.[33]

Other Industries, Commerce, and Rural Economy

Other industries grew up in the decades after the start of the oil rush. One of the first to respond to the financial and technical needs of the oil industry was the banking system of the empire. In 1880 a branch of the State Bank was opened in Baku. In its first year it discounted bills worth 438,000 rubles. Five years later that figure had risen more than ten times.[34] Other banking and financial institutions opened in Baku the following decade. By 1897 all Baku banking institutions issued a total of 5.6 million rubles in interest-bearing securities; in 1899, 11.4 million.[35] These financial institutions were supporting more than a burgeoning oil industry by the turn of the century.

Transportation served the oil industry and commerce. The number of ships on the Caspian Sea more than quadrupled between 1887 and 1899.[36] This crucial industry was the preserve of the Azerbaijani Turks.[37] By the beginning of the twentieth century, Azerbaijanis owned almost half the ships, constituting 42 percent of the carrying capacity of the Caspian merchant fleet, and 52 percent of the tankers.[38] That the Azerbaijani Turks maintained their dominance in this expanding commercial field attests to their vitality and ability to adapt to new conditions.

Railroad construction responded to the needs of the oil industry and had an impact beyond it. Baku's oldest rail line was built in 1880 to connect the city with the oil districts of Balakhano-Sabunchi and Surakhany. The Transcaucasian Railway was built to transport oil to the Black Sea to avoid the treacherous Volga-Baltic route. Because of the difficulty of the terrain and severity of the winters, the single-track line took four years to build, and was completed in 1884. It ran from Baku to Batum via Ganje (Elizavetpol) and Tiflis.[39] The years of its construction brought workers to formerly isolated areas of Caucasia and put villagers in contact with Russian, Iranian, or Daghestani workers. The railway drew the agricultural hinterland closer to industrial markets in Baku. A communication network enhanced their relationship. Telegraph lines connected Baku to Tiflis via Ganje in the 1860s. Within Baku a telephone system was created in the 1880s, laying the groundwork for a communications network as modern as those in contemporary Europe.

A construction industry also emerged during industrialization. Most of central Baku was built in the 1890s and 1900s. Much of the Inner City itself was rebuilt, often with new structures on top of the old, facilitating the archaeological excavations of the 1980s. Local stone was a major building material, rough or cut, the cut for government buildings and the estates of local officials and the wealthy. Streets, parks, and buildings were constructed according to a city plan designed to create a visual harmony. The buildings themselves were designed in popular European styles that included many Gothic elements. Most of the architects who designed these buildings were Russians, Azerbaijani Turks, and foreigners (especially Germans) resident in Baku; they were citizens of the Russian Empire who had been trained in the St. Petersburg Institute of Civil Engineering.[40]

Other industries contributed to the economic development and diversity of the region. The machine-building industry, though spawned directly by the demands of the oil companies, did not grow into a large industry until the twentieth century. From 1901 to 1903, there were 184 mechanical enterprises in Baku with a total of 9,349 workers. By the end of the decade, there would be 207 enterprises and 16,643 workers.[41] The textile industry, consisting exclusively of one huge factory complex in Baku owned by millionaire H. Z. A. Taghiyev, provided cloth and created 1,500 jobs.[42] Tobacco, silk, and carpet weaving outside Baku were dominated by Azerbaijani Turkish owners, growers, and merchants.[43] Regions would increasingly specialize production and feed via Baku into wider markets—silks in Shemakhi, Nukha, and Sheki; wheat on the Mughan steppe (in Lenkoran); orchards and madder (harvesting drew 9,000 workers from southern Azerbaijan by 1867) in Kuba and Zakataly.[44] Saffron, tobacco, and fruits were grown throughout the interior. Numerous towns produced handwoven carpets. Although merchants were sometimes Armenian, weavers were predominantly Azerbaijani.[45] Under tsarist orders cotton was planted at the expense of food crops. Loss of American cotton imports in the 1860s led to increases in the hated crop: Ganje guberniia cotton output rose from 1,500 puds in 1870 to 62,200 puds in 1894; in the Baku guberniia it rose from 4,000 puds in 1887 to 150,000 puds in 1900.[46]

The expansion of retail trade was reflected in the increase of Baku trading establishments—from 1,334 in 1881 to 1,620 in 1897.[47] Trade in food and other agricultural products, perhaps more than in any other area of economic activity, linked the hinterland to Baku and other cities and towns. One reason Azerbaijani Turks were numerous in agricultural trade throughout the area was that the merchants were often friends, partners, or members of the rural families who produced the food.[48]

Legal and Administrative Structure

The legal and administrative reforms of the industrial period were part of the Great Reforms of Alexander II. Though often regarded as progressive within the context of Russian history, many of these provisions, such as restrictions on non-Christians, reaffirmed imperial authority over the colonies. No *zemstvos* (committees for local self-government) were allowed in Caucasia and the rights of landowners over peasants were reinforced. For Baku the most important of the laws was the Urban Reform of 1870, which created the municipal Administration (*Uprava*) and the City Council (*Gorodskaia Duma*). The latter gave a voice in local government to an elite whose wealth would meet qualifications for suffrage.

The Urban Reform of 1870 was extended to the Caucasus in 1874 and was first applied in Baku.[49] Suffrage was based on property ownership and the value of trade turnover. As the majority of property owners in Baku, Azerbaijani Turks constituted more than 80 percent of the electorate. Restrictions on non-Christians, however, kept them from occupying more than half the seats in the council. From 1892 to 1900 the Urban Reform of 1890 allowed no more than one-third non-Christians. In 1908, despite the law and with only tepid opposition from the viceroy, a majority of Azerbaijanis were elected to the City Council. They ignored demands for new elections, remaining the majority until the end of the old regime.[50] Their victory in gaining a majority in the City Council was significant because it was a result of determined and organized political action within the established framework. It represented the exercise of power of the indigenous Turkish leadership who were flouting a prejudicial law. That their victory came in 1908 at a time of increasing intolerance at the center is surprising, but it reflects the degree to which Caucasia was "out of step" with the capitals. The Azerbaijani Turks' ability to gain control over the City Council, albeit decades after its creation, also reflected the degree to which they regarded Baku as their city, as it had been historically.

The city Administration, too, eventually came to include Azerbaijani Turks. It had three members (later, four)[51] who were elected by the City Council. The Administration controlled the disposal of the capital and property of the city, social services including public health and the care of the poor; guarded against fires and other catastrophes; and developed public education, trade, and industry. The Administration had the right to act as a legal person in litigation, borrowing, and disposing of and acquiring property.

The Urban Reform of 1870 provided for the independence of municipal institutions. It gave the care and oversight of the city's economy to the Administration. A governor (*gubernator*) was responsible for the legal execution of duties by the Administration and had the power to intervene in a conflict between the mayor (*gorodskoi golova*, head of both the City Council and the Administration) and the council or the other members of the Administration. The "counter reform" of 1892 said nothing about the independence of municipal institutions but put them under the jurisdiction of the *gradonachal'nik*. That officer then received power over both the legality and the "correctness" of the actions of the Administration. He could block decisions of the council if they were not in conformity with the law or with the "goals and needs" of the state. Appeal to the Senate was permitted, but its efficacy questionable.[52]

Owing to labor unrest, a "Temporary State (of Emergency)" was declared in Baku in January 1902. This allowed the extension of administrative and police power to permit restrictions of meetings or other "disturbances of the peace." In February 1905 martial law was extended to Baku and would remain in force until autumn 1906. The relaxation of martial law in October 1906 was accompanied by the establishment of the office of gradonachal'nik, a military officer, appointed by the viceroy to assume the duties of the gubernator in civil and administrative affairs, including the police apparatus. The gradonachal'nik was the senior authority of urban affairs in the guberniia, including the police of Baku, and the oil districts, and oil affairs.[53] Despite the overreaching power of the gradonachal'nik, the day-to-day affairs of the city were reportedly handled by the council and the Administration without special reference to him. Escalating violence in the years before World War I would occupy both administrators and security forces.

3 Industrialization, Conflict, and Social Change

All Russia is peaceful. The wolf and the lamb are grazing together.

The satirical journal *Molla Nasreddin*, April 1906

Russian colonial rule and an influx of Russian settlers evoked resentment among Azerbaijani Turks, and by the early twentieth century, rebellion was raised again. Industrialization also provoked violence, but it stimulated social change in the form of a native industrial working class and an industrial (as distinct from commercial) bourgeoisie. These classes emerged in Baku where the presence of Russians and industry was greatest. But until the late nineteenth and early twentieth centuries, much of the indigenous population of Baku, Ganje, and of other cities and the countryside remained relatively insulated from immigrants and industrialization—colonial rule had not changed social structure or behavior. Azerbaijani Turks continued to live in homogeneous *mahalle* (quarters) or villages, buying food at the bazaar, pursuing the careers of their fathers, speaking their native language, and arranging the marriages of their children within the usual circles. The presence of Russian administrators or new peasant villages did not immediately affect the inner workings of their society. The groups that changed most were those who genuinely interacted with some component of the changing environment— the merchants, the educated including those in the administration or newly developing industry, the oil and refinery workers, and perhaps those villagers through whose areas the railroad ran. Only gradually, and largely through the efforts of the financial and intellectual upper classes, did social change occur in Azerbaijani Turkish society.

The most intense interactions were in crowded Baku, where Russian administration and industrialization were unavoidable and hordes of immigrants outnumbered the indigenous Turks. Baku was not a melting pot and each community struggled for its own benefit. Leaders emerged from among the wealthy and educated, who were most familiar with Russian rule and its implications in a multinational environment, with the demands of industrializing society, and with European, Russian, and Ottoman attempts to resolve some of the same problems that Azerbaijan faced. The community leaders in Baku were influenced also by the labor movement and various political parties. Thus, Baku would be more influenced by socialism and would grow increasingly distinct from its hinterland. Social processes in cities like Ganje and in the countryside would have a more national character.

DEMOGRAPHIC CHANGE AND
EMPLOYMENT PATTERNS

In the first decade of Russian rule, immigration appears to have been confined to Russians—mainly military and later civil bureaucrats, political exiles, and a few traders—and Armenians from Iran, as provided in the Treaty of Turkmanchai. Armenian immigration affected mainly the Shemakhi, Ganje, and Karabagh regions and areas west including Erevan.[1] In the 1830s, with increased investment, the flow of Russians increased. Most went to Tiflis or Baku, the centers of administration and trade. Later in the century, peasants and exiles would be resettled in rural areas. Armenian immigration would grow as tens of thousands of families increased the size of Armenian communities in towns and created Armenian majorities in some rural areas. Russian imperial surveys of the 1860s called most of the rural population "Turkic tribes" (*tiurkskoe plemia*) and "Iranian tribes" (Tats and Talysh). Russians and Armenians in the Baku guberniia were less than 7 percent of the population.[2]

Classification of the Turks, a majority of the guberniia, was confused by official terminology. Turkic (*tiurk, tiurkskii*) was used by the Russians as a broad category for groups of tribes or for dialects in contrast to Turkish (*turok, turetskii*), which was then applied only to Turks in the Ottoman Empire. (In the Turks' language, there is no such distinction.) Furthermore, Tatar was the official designation used by the Russian state for settled urban Turkish speakers.

The first detailed data on the population of Caucasia came from the imperial census of 1897.[3] By 1897 the Baku guberniia had grown to 826,716 (from 486,000 in the 1860s), of which nearly 60 percent were Azerbaijani Turks (Tatars), 11 percent Tats, just under 10 percent Russians, and just over 6 percent Armenians; the latter two resided mainly in Baku. Azerbaijani Turks constituted a large majority in four of the six uezdy in the guberniia, and a plurality in the other two. They were also the most numerous (62 percent) in the Elizavetpol guberniia (the western half of today's Azerbaijan), where they were called Azerbaijani. In the eight uezdy of the Elizavetpol guberniia, the Azerbaijani Turks constituted a majority (52–74 percent) in all but one. They inhabited portions of other gubernii: in the Erevan guberniia they were 37 percent of the population (53 percent was Armenian). (See table 3.1.)

Russian peasants settled in the countryside in fertile regions like the Mughan steppe in the Lenkoran uezd. (Soviet sources have claimed that the "benefits" of Russian peasant settlement were that locals learned about potato cultivation and "modern technology," perhaps meaning the *sokha*, a primitive wooden plow, used in Russia for over a millennium.)[4] Thousands more went to Baku for industrial jobs. Baku had grown rapidly since the 1870s to a city of nearly 112,000. It became a city of immigrants: less than half the population had been born in the city, men greatly outnumbered women, and 62 percent were under age 30.[5] Baku had become the second largest city in the viceroyalty (after Tiflis), more than three times the size of the next Azerbaijani city, Ganje, with 33,600 inhabitants.[6] Baku had the region's largest Russian population outside Tiflis and a large and prosperous Armenian minority.

Immigrants from Iran were only partly reported because thousands were believed to have crossed the border without visas. The census listed "Iranian citizens" and "Tatar" speakers. Of the more than 9,000 Iranian citizens, only 3,369 were Persian speakers. Mahalle usually exhibited a distinct ethnic and/ or religious character; Daghestanis and Iranians clustered with local Turks while Russians lived among Armenians.

Radical demographic shifts coupled with the colonial administrative apparatus affected social structure. Russians controlled the top of the administrative and legal structure at the viceroyalty level, in the Baku guberniia, and in the city itself. They accounted for 700 of 1,100 in "administration" and, with other Slavs, constituted 70 percent of the "armed forces" category.[7] Russians were numerous in the judiciary, in credit and commercial institutions, and various professions, but were rarely merchants.[8] Numerous peasant immigrants were found in unskilled jobs in the city and oil districts. Outside Baku, Russians were overwhelmingly engaged in agriculture, railroad construction, mining, and soldiering.

TABLE 3.1
IMPERIAL CENSUS OF 1897, NATIONAL COMPOSITION
BY GUBERNII AND UEZDY IN AREAS OF
LARGE TURKISH POPULATION

	Azerbaijani Turks	Russians	Armenians	Total Population[b]
Baku guberniia	485,146	77,681	52,233	826,716
Baku	63,415	45,510	22,583	182,897[a]
Gökchay	92,962	2,475	12,994	117,705
Jevad	84,054	4,635	699	90,043
Kuba	70,150	3,971	1,191	183,242[a]
Lenkoran	84,725	9,728	483	130,987
Shemakhi	89,840	11,362	14,283	121,842
Elizavetpol guberniia	534,086	17,875	292,188	878,415
Ganje	103,970	10,428	43,040	162,788
Aresh	47,133	162	13,822	67,277
Jebrail	49,189	893	15,746	66,360
Jevanshir	52,041	208	19,551	72,719
Zangezur	71,206	1,006	63,622	137,871
Kazakh	64,101	3,444	43,555	112,074
Nukha	83,578	230	18,899	120,555
Shusha	62,868	1,504	73,953	138,771
Erevan guberniia	313,176	15,937	441,000	829,556
Erevan	77,491	3,713	58,148	150,879
Aleksander	7,832	6,836	141,522	165,503
Nakhjiran	64,151	1,014	34,672	100,771
Novobayazit	34,726	2,716	81,285	122,573
Surmalinsk	41,417	1,361	27,075	89,055
Sharur-Daralagez	51,560	122	20,726	76,538
Echmiadzin	35,999	175	77,572	124,237

[a]Tats represented 11 percent in the Baku guberniia of which 20 percent were in the Baku uezd and just under 20 percent were in the Kuba uezd.
[b]Totals include groups other than those listed.

Armenians in Baku were among the wealthiest merchants and oilmen. They were the second most numerous group in the judiciary and were prominent in the professions. Urban Armenians were primarily merchants, trading especially in clothing, food, metal equipment, and weapons; many were tailors and craftspeople. Most rural Armenians were peasants.

Few Azerbaijani Turks in Baku were in administration, the judiciary, or education, though after 1905 their numbers there increased. They owned most of the land and predominated in industries other than oil. Most small-scale traders were Azerbaijani Turks, especially trading in cattle, grain, and other agricultural products. They provided "employment networks" to absorb members of their own community. Baku Azerbaijanis who did engage in unskilled and physical labor worked in town as messengers, dockworkers, and servants, more often than in the oil districts where Russians, rural Azerbaijanis, and immigrants from the Daghestan and Iran worked. More than half those engaged in physical hygiene were Azerbaijani, probably because of the Islamic tradition of the *hamam* (bath) and associated religious prescriptions of cleanliness. Most of the women in this category, however, were Russian, as were most of the prostitutes.[9]

Outside Baku, Azerbaijani Turks participated in local administration. In other uezdy of the guberniia, Azerbaijanis held most administrative posts, though Russians were in second place. In the Elizavetpol guberniia administration nearly 50 percent of the posts were held by Azerbaijanis. In the city of Ganje itself, though Azerbaijanis were over 60 percent of the population, they held less than one-third of the posts. In only two uezdy of the guberniia were Azerbaijanis not the largest group in administration. In Zangezur, where they were 52 percent of the population and the Armenians 46 percent, Armenians held most administrative posts; and in Shusha, where they were 45 percent and Armenians 53 percent of the population, Azerbaijanis and Armenians were about equally represented in administration. In the Erevan guberniia, in two uezdy where Azerbaijani Turks were a majority—Nakhjivan and Sharur-Daralagez—they also dominated in the administration. As a result, many Azerbaijani Turks gained administrative experience in the years before independence.

Most Azerbaijani Turks were peasants and a large number were engaged in cattle-breeding and forestry, providing goods for their counterparts in trade or crafts (many were tanners and leather craftsmen). In the countryside many Azerbaijani were hereditary nobles, but few were personal nobles. Russians and Armenians in the region had the opposite pattern, suggesting that Azerbaijanis had less opportunity for advancement by service.

Data available only for Baku reveal a fundamental continuity to several social patterns.[10] The city censuses of Baku (taken 22 October 1903 and 1913) documented continued demographic, industrial, and commercial

TABLE 3.2

NATIONAL COMPOSITION OF BAKU, 1897, 1903, 1913

Nationality	1897	1903	1913
Azerbaijani Turks	40,148	44,257	45,962
Iranian citizens[a]	9,426	11,132	25,096
Russians	37,399	56,955	76,288
Armenians	19,060	26,151	41,680
Jews	2,341	n.a.	9,690
Germans	2,460	n.a.	3,274
Georgians	971	n.a.	4,073
Totals[b]	111,904	155,876	214,672

[a]Iranian citizens included a large but undetermined number of Iranian Azerbaijanis.
[b]Totals include groups other than those listed.
SOURCES: *Perepisi*, 1897, 1903, 1913

growth.[11] Data on the distribution of the city's nationalities show the persistence of traditional patterns[12] (Azerbaijanis, Persians, Daghestanis in the West, Russians in the industrial districts to the East, Armenians in a band between them, and a multiethnic business district in the center) and the relative homogeneity of the quarters, especially after the unrest of 1905.[13]

The three major ethno-religious communities continued to dominate the city, but their relative weights changed. (See table 3.2.) The Azerbaijani Turks, the Russians, and the Armenians were reduced from 92 or 93 percent of the city population at the turn of the century to 76 percent in 1913; the indigenous Azerbaijani Turks were reduced to 21 percent, nearly as small as the Armenian minority (19 percent in 1913). Immigration from Iranian Azerbaijan, however, kept the total Azerbaijani Turkish community up to 35 percent, nearly equal to the Russians (36 percent in 1913).[14] Despite the native's demographic disadvantage, Baku remained the "natural capital" and drew the educated, talented, and hard-working Azerbaijani Turks from Shusha, Ganje, Tiflis, and elsewhere in the region. At the same time, immigrants of other nationalities came to regard the city as their own and strove to give it their character.

Employment patterns had changed little since the 1897 census.[15] Russians had tighter control over security, surveillance, administration, and the judiciary. Approximately 4,100 of the 5,100 employed in "security" were Russians, as were 260 of 580 in the judiciary (Armenians were 150), and 106 of 120 were in "surveillance," most of whom were women.[16] There was a striking increase in the number of Azerbaijani Turks in the professions—

managerial and white-collar positions—and in education and the arts, a shift that is perhaps related to greatly increased literacy.[17] The trend reflected the social and cultural renaissance of this period.

MERCHANTS AND ENTREPRENEURS: THEIR ROLE IN SOCIETY

The prosperous upper layers of the commercial and industrial bourgeoisie of Azerbaijani Turkish society numbered more than five hundred in Baku (more than two hundred were guild merchants) and hundreds more throughout Azerbaijan. Some were from wealthy merchant or landed noble families from which the industrial-era generations inherited wealth as well as a network of relatives and friends.[18] This inheritance enabled them to grow with the upsurge in commerce and industrial productivity. Among the wealthiest businessmen were several from less prosperous families who began with modest funds and became millionaires through hard work and the good fortune of the oil rush.

The most famous among Azerbaijan's industrial and commercial elite were Haji Zeinal Adibin Taghiyev,[19] Musa Naghiyev,[20] and Shamsi Asadullayev, all of whom represented rags-to-riches stories. Starting in manufacturing and oil, they became millionaire philanthropists, patrons of the arts, and developers of other branches of the city's and the region's economy.[21] In 1914 Taghiyev and Naghiyev founded the Baku Merchant's Bank. Taghiyev's house in Baku later became the Azerbaijan History Museum.

The many wealthy industrialists and merchants formed the core of the Azerbaijani Turkish business community and an important part of the political stratum. Besides their economic and political clout, often exerted behind the scenes, this elite was instrumental in creating a cultural enlightenment movement.[22] Wealthy Azerbaijani Turks financed schools for children and adults and cultural-enlightenment and charitable organizations with branches in towns and villages. In Baku, Neshr Maarif, the Azerbaijani social democrats' Nijat, Saadet, Shahname, Sefa, and the Muslim Charitable Society were founded at the turn of the century.[23] Most established reading courses, libraries, and lecture series. The Muslim Charitable Society had the broadest scope, providing food and clothing throughout the region and building hospitals.

Significant branches of the major organizations were run by the women of industrialist and merchant families for causes like famine relief[24] and for improving the conditions and status of Muslim women. Taghiyev himself established the first Muslim Girls' School in Baku and provided stipends to young men and women to pursue their educations. The arts were not neglected. Taghiyev built Baku's first theater in the 1880s and, with other community businessmen, financed the plays, operas, and concerts performed there; they sustained the artists as well.

Azerbaijani entrepreneurs financed Baku's vociferous Azerbaijani press—the Russian-language *Kaspii* (Caspian) and, when the ban against Turkish-language periodicals was lifted after 1905, *Hayat* (Life), *Teze Hayat* (New Life), *Fuyuzat* (Abundance), and others. These were created and run by the same writers and editors who worked for *Kaspii*.[25] The press was primarily a forum for elite debate and carried reports from the City Duma for the regional and international press; it reported political controversies, strikes, and intercommunal violence when they rocked Caucasia. Debates on issues of the day, including the central questions of power and identity, were explored on the pages of Baku's many newspapers. As political actors and financiers of Baku's cultural developments, the merchants and industrialists were acting as partners of the intellectual elite, which concerned itself with political ideology and the substance of the era's broad Turkish cultural renaissance as manifested in Azerbaijan, the Crimea and Volga, and other parts of the Russian (and Ottoman) Empire.

SOCIAL CLASSES: *BAZARI*, PEASANTS, PROLETARIAT

Bazari

Traders and craftsmen of the bazaar (*bazari*), constituted a distinct class. The bazari were officially classified as *meshchane*, "townsmen" or "petty bourgeoisie." They worked for themselves in traditional occupations and in a traditional setting, the bazaar, and they were probably the most insulated group in urban Azerbaijani Turkish society. Together with their families, Baku's bazari numbered nearly 23,000 in 1897, or nearly 60 percent of the local Azerbaijani Turkish community. (The meshchane in Ganje were 75 percent of the Azerbaijani population.) They appear to have lived clustered together inside and adjacent to the Inner City. The wealthy of this group were probably the hundreds of merchants of the lowest *razriady* of the guilds, but most bazari were probably outside the guild structure altogether.[26] They owned 52 percent of all trade establishments and nearly half the inns and hotels.[27] They served mainly their own community.

Nothing is known about the political sympathies or actions of the bazari of Baku or other cities in northern Azerbaijan. In neighboring Iran the bazaar mobilized during times of rebellion. There were no reports from foreign consulates on the "closing of the bazaar" in Baku as there were from Tabriz or Tehran. Foreign diplomats were more likely to notice strikes. Nor has there been research on the bazari in northern Azerbaijan's towns. Some parallels may cautiously be drawn within the context of the religious establishment and intercommunal unrest.

Peasants and Nomads

Peasants formed the majority of the population (including most urban workers) in the Baku and Elizavetpol gubernii at the time of the 1897 census— 68 percent in Baku and 80 percent in Elizavetpol.[28] Most peasants were Azerbaijanis. The Russian state had large land holdings, retained since the conquest when khan monopolies in orchards, vineyards, and forests were taken over. About 85 percent of the peasants in Baku guberniia and nearly 60 percent in Elizavetpol guberniia were state peasants.[29] State land used by them measured about five million acres.[30] The Administration of State Lands, Forests, Agriculture and Industry of Transcaucasia and uezd officials administered these lands and collected taxes.

Peasants paid fees to landowners for use of land, animals, and water and taxes, including a military tax in place of service. No analyses of the actual burden of these taxes and fees are available. A law of 1 May 1900 permitted "continuous use" but not possession of land with payment of *obrok* (quitrent) to the state treasury. Lenin called it "state feudalism."[31]

Nomads and seminomads had been forced to abandon their traditional pastures as cash crops increased and the settled population grew due to the immigration of Armenians, then of Turks and Persians from Iran, and the settlement by Russians. By the late nineteenth century, nomads remained in a few regions, but there they were 30–40 percent of the population: in the Javad uezd (Baku guberniia near the Mughan steppe), Shusha and Jebrail uezdy in the western, mountainous part of Karabagh.[32]

Settlement by Russian and some Ukrainian peasants started in the 1860s and jumped in the 1890s. In 1893 *Kaspii* reported from the fertile Mughan steppe that every week Russian settlers arrived. They were given larger land allotments than native peasants were, sometimes ten times more per capita. Some Russian settlers were town dwellers who did not know what to do on their new land, reported *Kaspii*, so the goal of resettlement was at least partly to tip the demographic balance, not simply to give land to Russian peasants.[33] The local peasantry resented the "tsarist resettlement policies" and, presumably, the Russians themselves.[34]

Formation of the Azerbaijani Working Class

The Azerbaijani Turkish proletariat formed from peasants who came to work in factories and railroad construction throughout Azerbaijan and in the oil fields and refineries of Baku. This transformation was the single most dramatic social change of the era. Outside Baku, the Azerbaijani peasants formed a relatively homogeneous work force, but in the oil industry, Azerbaijani Turkish peasants became part of the "multinational proletariat."

The notion of an undifferentiated mass of "Muslim workers" is erroneous. Throughout Caucasia local Azerbaijani Turks, Iranian Azerbaijanis, Persians, Tats, Daghestanis, and Volga Tatars were employed in industry, construction, and as day laborers,[35] porters, dockworkers, and servants. There were significant differences among them depending on whether they were natives or immigrants and, among the latter, whether they planned to remain. The largest concentration of workers and of immigrant workers was in the oil industry.

Despite confusing and conflicting data on oil workers, it is plain that the oil-field hierarchy was structured along ethnic lines though perhaps less rigidly so by the eve of World War I than earlier (table 3.3).[36] Foreigners, Russians, and Armenians predominated as administrators and "enforcers" in law and surveillance, as managers of the larger companies, technicians, and skilled workers. In the numerous small companies, Azerbaijani Turks were managers, skilled and unskilled workers. "Muslim workers" were a majority of unskilled workers, but most of them, especially in the oil districts, were from Iran. The number of local Azerbaijani Turks was small, fewer than Russian and Armenian workers by 1913, as a progressively smaller proportion of Azerbaijani Turks ("Tatars" in the 1897 census and "Azerbaijani Tatars" by 1913) were found in working-class jobs. The growing number of "Persians" (many Iranian Azerbaijanis) constituted the bulk of the "Muslim workers" active in the labor movement.

The most detailed source on standard of living and ties to the village—issues that affected restiveness—is a study of oil workers' income and expenditures conducted in 1909 by A. M. Stopani.[37] His report was based on 2,244 (5.7 percent of the oil workers) income-expenditure schedules.[38] Stopani noted the coincidence of skilled jobs, nationality and "marital status."[39] About half the oil workers, but 85 to 90 percent of the unskilled in his sample, were "Muslim." The largest group was "Persian," with "Caucasian Tatar" (Azerbaijani Turks) a distant second. A large majority of these workers were classified as "single," meaning they were living without wives, not that they had none. Oil workers were the best paid in the empire,[40] with an annual average salary of 500 rubles, in a mix of cash and goods.[41] But over 70 percent of all workers, and over 90 percent of the "single" (*mutatis*

TABLE 3.3
NATIONAL COMPOSITION OF EMPLOYED PERSONS
IN BAKU OIL DISTRICTS, 1913

Occupation	Russian	Armenian	Azerbaijani	"Persian"	Total[a]
Owners					
Nonoil	125	255	510	254	1,275
Oil	3	6	347	25	397
Managers					
Nonoil	126	61	41	10	324
Oil extraction	585	666	305	54	2,083
Oil refining	73	36	1	1	149
Trade and credit	74	104	100	88	450
Workers					
Nonoil	2,542	1,697	472	1,484	7,015
Oil extraction	5,415	6,082	4,340	11,508	34,479
Oil refining	908	206	29	225	1,487
Professional					
Administration	74	68	34	46	258
Security	605	59	34	3	882
Judiciary	3	0	0	0	3
Medical	155	98	1	0	358

[a]Totals include national groups other than those listed.
SOURCE: Partial listing of jobs, from 1913 Baku City Census; *Perepis' naseleniia gor. Baku, 1913* (Baku, 1916), vol. 3, part 2, pp. 40–46.

mutandis Muslim) workers, earned less (probably the reason they were without their families and were, therefore, "single"). "Single" workers maintained a minimum standard of living for themselves, and roughly 73 percent sent over one-quarter of their earnings to support a family in the countryside. As a result, their diet consisted largely of grains (married workers' diets included more dairy and meat products), and they had to spend more on clothing,[42] but almost nothing on "cultural needs," including entertainment and education.[43] The use of alcohol was much lower among single men, reflecting either the Muslims' religious proscriptions on alcohol, the Christians' indulgence in it, or both. About half the "singles" used alcohol, spending about 9 rubles a year on it, while about 83 percent of the married workers drank, spending nearly 30 rubles.[44]

Stopani's data revealed three significant trends. First was the presence of undisbursed income, or savings, which may help explain the attraction of Baku's oil fields despite the onerous working conditions.[45] Second, his data emphasize the sharp wage differentials between skilled and unskilled workers. Keeping in mind the ethnic stratification of the working class, it becomes clear that there were economic reasons for friction between the unskilled ("Persian" or local Azerbaijani Turkish) and skilled (Russian or Armenian) workers. It suggests also why the "Muslims," being easily replaced unskilled workers, were reluctant to strike. Finally, many workers were separated from their families. Literary and anecdotal evidence suggest this group was heterogeneous. Some formed a large number of temporary workers interested in making money and going home to existing families or to marry. For them work in Baku was an opportunity for earning money and becoming "men of the world." Another subgroup was a core of immigrant but permanent workers intending to marry locally and stay. Professor S. S. Aliyarov, using Stopani's and other data, stated that approximately 80 percent of the workers from the villages in northern Azerbaijan (about 3,845 workers) maintained "agricultural households," but only 49.5 percent (4,038 workers) of the Azerbaijani Turks from Iran did so.[46] It may therefore be inferred that more than 4,000 Iranian Azerbaijanis and about 600 rural northern Azerbaijanis belong in the last subgroup of permanent immigrants.

These data must be interpreted with care, for they say nothing about extended family networks and the emotional and financial support they provided. Those whose ties to the village were cut might become "proletarianized" but transient, or they might constitute a stable urbanizing group of workers trying to obtain a skill and start a family. Such workers, with a stake in local conditions, would be receptive to attempts to organize labor and to the economic demands put forth by labor organizations. There are no data to show how many workers fit into each category, and in trying to analyze the working classes of Baku, both trends must be considered. If the Iranian Azerbaijanis were in fact becoming an urban proletariat, then they could be expected to participate increasingly in labor organizations and the labor movement.

There is no doubt that the conditions were appalling. Menshevik agitator Eva Broido described the oil district of Balakhany:

> Along both sides of the road, and completely dwarfed by the derricks, stood
> rows of squat, one-storied dwelling houses with windows darkened by soot

and sometimes covered with wire netting. . . . It was a picture of unremitting and hopeless gloom.

The "Persians" did not, she wrote, realize how bad their condition was.[47] A fictionalized account written by a Baku native, Essad Bey,[48] confirmed that "the Muslim workers" were seemingly satisfied with conditions in the oil fields, but that the Russian workers did less work for more pay and were always threatening to strike.[49]

Both writers reported on the *gochus* of the oil districts,[50] a small army of extortionists selling "protection" to local and foreign industrialists alike. According to Essad Bey, these men were impoverished beks of Azerbaijan who became "bodyguards" for companies or individuals and adhered to a strict code of honor. Broido was less reverent, noting that these "local Tatars" were "bitterly opposed to all workers' organizations."[51] Not only did the cossacks fail to disarm them, but they sometimes gave the gochus the confiscated weapons of others. The two views may reflect the difference between the writers—one an "insider,"[52] the other a European labor organizer.

Urban workers lived under conditions far better than those in the oil districts. The city was relatively clean with paved streets, garbage collectors, and, by early in the twentieth century, a tramway, telephones, and running water. There were schools, libraries, hospitals, restaurants, a theater, shops, a few department stores, and daily bazaars.[53] *Chaykhanas* were scattered throughout the city where, for a few kopecks, even the poorest workers could linger over a pot or two of hot tea with sugar.[54] The availability of cheap goods was important in the city, for wages were certainly lower there than in the oil fields. Although no study such as Stopani's was done on urban workers, those in cities were able to rely on families and available services and could live more comfortably with less money.

COMMUNAL RELATIONS IN CAUCASIA

The Russians had the greatest power to affect the Azerbaijani Turks. Russian control, with its Christianization and Russification policies and discriminatory laws, was pervasive and obvious. The Russian state strove to intrude even into spheres it could not directly control, such as religion and culture. Yet this pressure rarely led to Russification. The Azerbaijani Turks' cultural inheritance, both Turkish and Islamic, was of greater antiquity, with older written languages (Turkish, Arabic, and Persian) and cultural and historical ties to numerous empires across Asia (including the Chinghizid, which had ruled over the Rus). Adoption of Russian culture was regarded by many as a retrograde step.

The Azerbaijani Turks were the largest community in Azerbaijan and, until the turn of the century, in Baku. When they ceased to be the most numerous, they remained the largest indigenous group in Baku with their network of extended families throughout northern and southern Azerbaijan. They commanded wealth and influence. Discrimination was merely de jure—they felt themselves to be in de facto control of Baku. Their treatment as colonized people reinforced ethnic and cultural bonds with the rest of the empire's Turkish and Muslim peoples. Locally, political discrimination, the colonial attitudes of the Russians, and the influx of settlers inspired ethno-religious unity across class lines within the Azerbaijani Turkish community in Caucasia. The intellectual and business elites viewed themselves as leaders of the entire Azerbaijani Turkish community, despite the occasional strike, with a corresponding power and responsibility. This was eloquently expressed in their creation and direction of a cultural enlightenment movement that shaped the prewar decades. It was also demonstrated in their efforts to end the Armenian-Azerbaijani violence of 1905.

The Armenians also had significant interactions with the Azerbaijani Turks. Although far fewer than either the Russians or the Azerbaijanis, the Armenians were a wealthy minority who enjoyed a special relationship with the Russians. Numerous in conspicuous and sensitive administrative areas such as the judiciary, they were often regarded as surrogates for the Russians. Imperial law benefited them more than it did the Azerbaijani Turks. Economic growth, especially in and around Baku, led to sharpened competition for a larger share of the market while simultaneously creating a concern among members of all communities for overall economic prosperity and a favorable business climate. Thus, there was basis for conflict and cooperation.

Conflict manifested itself most vigorously among villagers and the urban lower classes. Some contemporary press accounts suggested that clashes often began and were sharper in the countryside. Violence erupted in and around Erevan in February 1905, in Nakhjivan in May, in Shusha in June, and in Ganje and Tiflis in November.[55] The Baku press echoed fears of rural violence in the summer of 1905, and community leaders worked in vain to shield the city from its effects.[56] After bloody fighting, inhabitants in Baku and Ganje moved to homes in mahalle where their own national group formed a majority, making the mahalle more homogeneous and the cities more polarized. In Nakhjivan and Sharur-Daralagez in the Ereven guberniia, and in Javanshir, Zangezur, and Shusha uezdy of the Elizavetpol guberniia (bordering the Erevan guberniia),[57] clashes occurred in spring and summer. Citing Armenian sources, one U. S. scholar stated that 128 Armenian and 158 Azerbaijani villages were "pillaged or destroyed."[58] These uezdy would later be claimed by independent Armenia and Azerbaijan, though only two of the five did not have an overwhelming Azerbaijani majority, suggesting that the armed conflicts of 1905 may have been linked to larger political issues.[59]

Press coverage of the intercommunal conflicts raised many possible causes of the violence but displayed the same anti-Turkish and anti-Muslim tenor embodied in state policy. Writers nearly always blamed "Muslims" for the unrest. A September issue of *Baku* reviewed various explanations of the disorders advanced by prominent newspapers in the empire.[60] The "right-liberal" *Slovo (Word)* blamed nationalism and national animosities; the "left-liberal" *Russkaia Vedomost' (Russian Bulletin)* and the more left-leaning *Syn Otechestva (Son of the Fatherland)* blamed "Pan-Islamism" and intrigues against the state by the Muslim bourgeoisie. But *Baku* claimed that the "Muslim people [*narod*]" were not guilty, but were merely victims of exploitation by "stupid pastors." This, *Baku* stated, does not reflect nationalism but democracy, and those who could not see this had been reading the "narrow chauvinism" of *Kaspii* (owned by Taghiyev and edited by Ali Mardan Topchibashi). *Baku* (edited by an Armenian) accused *Kaspii* of provoking national-religious animosities.

Baku's commentator, the pseudonymous Enen, discussed an article in *Peterburgskaia Vedomost' (Petersburg Bulletin)* by a Hungarian, Magda Neiman, who often wrote on the Caucasus. Her arguments were fully in line with official Russian policy. She blamed the "wildness" of the Muslims for disorders throughout Caucasia. She urged settling Russians among the Muslim villages on land that she claimed had been seized from Armenians in the eighteenth century. Enen explained that these lands were not Armenian but had belonged to the local Muslims for centuries. Enen went on to say that Muslims had no idea of law or legality because they had never seen any among the government officials with whom they had contact. The "wildness" of the Muslims was the result of unjust treatment meted out by the state, and it could be rooted out only with widespread humanitarianism and "culture." *Baku*'s commentator "defended" the Azerbaijani Turks by affirming that they had "no idea of law or legality" and needed to be "civilized."[61]

A few writers argued that the national loyalties of both communities were to blame and that the cultivation of class consciousness was the only solution.[62] Social Democrats expressed this view. Leaflets issued during the outbreaks called for an end to the "fratricide" (as reportedly urged by Azerbaijani peasant leader Gachag Zaid),[63] which distracted workers from antigovernment, anticapitalist strikes by setting traditional antagonists against each other.[64]

Only *Hayat* blamed the Armenians. As a Taghiyev-owned, Turkish-language newspaper edited by Ahmet Aghayev (Agaoglu), *Hayat* was regarded as too biased to be taken seriously. It wrote of Armenian plans to carve an independent state out of Caucasia, saying the Armenians felt they would have to fight to rule and had therefore decided on war against the Azerbaijanis to test Armenian strength and weapons. The Azerbaijani Turks were the chosen target because, first, they were the largest group in Caucasia. If they could be defeated, no other group would stand in the Armenians' way. Second, war with the Muslims could easily be disguised as a manifestation of the two groups' long-standing antagonism. Finally, the Armenians would be able to play on existing biases to claim that they had been attacked and to use an alleged threat from the Azerbaijanis as an excuse to stockpile weapons.[65] *Baku* dismissed *Hayat*'s accusations. The program of the Armenian party, the Dashnaktsutun, however, stated as its goal the creation of an Armenian state in eastern Asia Minor and/or western Caucasia, including the regions where most of the 1905 fighting took place. The Dashnaks regarded an "armed struggle" as necessary and terror as a political tool.[66]

In Baku, Peace Committees[67] were established in July 1905 with religious and lay members from each community. These committees strove to discover the causes of the outbreaks and discussed the means to prevent further disturbances. Religious spokesmen from each side urged calm. As part of one plan for maintaining peace after the August 1905 fires, twelve leaders of the Azerbaijani and Armenian communities assumed full financial responsibility for damage, injury, or loss of life resulting from trouble created by any member of their respective communities. The Azerbaijani Turks who accepted the role of guarantor were among the leading financial and political figures of Baku: Ali Mardan Topchibashi, Ahmet Aghayev, Mirza Asadullayev, Haji Aslan Ashurov, Haji Baba Ashurov, Isa and Memed Hasan Hajinskii, Hasan Agha Hasanov, Asadulla Ahmedov, Kerbelai Abdulla Zarbaliyev, Agha Baba Guliyev, and Kamil Safaraliyev, Baku's mayor.[68]

An investigation by these Peace Committees in conjunction with municipal authorities laid considerable blame on the militia and other forces for laxity and possibly for incitement.[69] In his testimony before the Baku Advocate's special committee on the February clashes, Meshadi Azizbeyov (Azizbekov, 1870–1918), a local engineer and member of the Socialist Hümmet, stated that local Muslims had told him they had been warned by the police that the Armenians were arming for a massacre of Azerbaijanis.[70] Azizbeyov added that not only were the gochus known to be linked to police chief Mamedbekov, but that such clashes could not have taken place without the acquiescence of the police.[71] At higher levels government representatives manipulated Azerbaijani-Armenian antagonism by favoring one side, then the other. After a short period of moderation toward Azerbaijanis, the anti-Turkish Vorontsov-Dashkov became viceroy in May 1905. Russian troops received orders to shoot "Tatars."[72]

The communal clashes revealed the fragility of class solidarity across national lines. The February and August 1905 events came at a time of prolonged unrest on the labor front. After the arson that destroyed vast areas of the oil fields in the August fighting, no other such riots took place during the remaining years of tsarist power. Perhaps the authorities saw that their own strategy to divert labor unrest—if one accepts this view—was a double-edged sword that, in August 1905, turned against the hand that wielded it, cut the flow of oil to Russian industry, and provoked the anger of industrialists who demanded financial aid and protection.

Some Soviet and Western scholars have perpetuated the view that the Azerbaijani community as a whole supported intercommunal violence because of its "weakness" in competition with the vigorous Armenian merchants and Russian rulers.[73] These interpretations do not recognize the areas of Azerbaijani strength. In fact, public disorder conflicted with the substantial commercial and civic interests of the Azerbaijani Turkish upper classes, as their personal financial commitment to peace demonstrated. The root of conflict must be sought in historical differences manipulated over decades by tsarist colonial policies meant to incite jealousy, perhaps violence, as a means of control. Azerbaijanis resented the Armenians as the Russians' surrogates, especially within the state structure. Azerbaijani Turkish and Armenian communities were experiencing a cultural renaissance with political implications. Both had established political groups pursuing national goals, though the Armenians operated in a larger arena. Both communities wished to alter the status quo but in different ways. The Azerbaijanis wanted to alter it at the Russians' expense; the Armenians, at the Azerbaijanis'.

REBELLION AND REVOLUTION IN COUNTRYSIDE AND CITY

Rebellions were a sporadic but regular feature of life in the countryside. Early recorded uprisings were protests of taxation or demands by peasants who worked on estates for greater use of land and water.[74] Like most peasant uprisings, these were usually uncoordinated and easily crushed. Most difficult for the authorities to subdue were the *gachags*. A gachag[75] was a young rebel who left his own village and family and, from mountain hideouts, carried out the fight against landowners or the government, sometimes rallying whole villages against a local administration or a particularly noxious landowner. There were quite a few famous gachags from the end of the nineteenth century to the early twentieth. One of those most renowned was Gachag Nabi, about whom a dastan was created.[76] Under Soviet rule he was lionized as an "anticolonial national liberation" leader.

According to Soviet historians,[77] a concerted and relatively coordinated resistance movement began around 1904 and grew into a mass movement during 1905 and 1906. The resistance began with the illegal cutting of timber in state forests as a protest against the state's gaining large revenues while depriving local peasants of the use of the forests. Illegal cutting was reported in many regions of both Baku and Elizavetpol gubernii. Guards posted were few in number and were often frightened off and completely ineffective.

By mid-1905, the illegal cutting was widespread. Elizavetpol guberniia peasants reportedly seized 12,000 rubles' worth of railroad property and fell on a village of settlers (probably Russians), stealing their cattle, then attacking a police station. Peasants sacked and burned estates of landowners. A few landowners were reportedly murdered.[78] More organized movements were reported elsewhere.[79]

In contrast to the labor movement (which petered out in the winter of 1905–1906), the peasants' illegal cutting, theft of state property, and refusal to pay taxes accompanied a marked upsurge in gachag activity throughout Azerbaijan.[80] By early 1906 peasants suspected of aiding gachags were being court-martialed. The army was mobilized in the summer of 1906, shooting villagers suspected of harboring or refusing to surrender gachags or setting fire to or using artillery to shell peasant villages. In one case a whole village was destroyed in retaliation for the alleged killing of four cossacks, and in another the official explanation for deploying troops (who opened fire on the population) was to "restore peace" between Azerbaijani and Armenian peasants.[81] The combination of arrest or summary execution and indiscriminate destruction of Azerbaijani villages finally crushed the peasant movement in the fall of 1906. It would reemerge in 1918.

The well-known labor movement of Azerbaijan was concentrated in cities and along the Transcaucasian Railway. Its center was Baku, whose volatile multinational labor force became the object of Bolshevik, Menshevik, and later historians' attention. Despite the standard notion that Muslim workers were too backward to participate in the labor movement, the evidence indicates otherwise.

The earliest period of sustained (sometimes organized) labor unrest can be dated from the general strike of the summer of 1903.[82] The significant general strike of December 1904 led to what is reportedly the first industry-wide labor contract in the Russian Empire.[83] The year 1905 was marked by strikes, bloodshed, and arson. From 6 to 9 February, several areas were engulfed in bloody battles between Azerbaijani and Armenian populations. Martial law was declared. Beginning in May, individual strikes broke out in the oil fields and in the city among dockworkers, typographers, porters, and textile workers. By summer Baku was declared to be in a state of siege. A general strike in August degenerated within a week into another round of the Azerbaijani-Armenian feud that ended with the burning of vast sections of the oil districts. Many social democratic activists were arrested or fled the town in the resulting police crackdown. The August events marked the end of serious labor unrest for some years, though individual strikes continued into spring of 1906. Martial law was lifted in October 1906, after being in effect for nineteen months.

The oil industrialists maintained a surprisingly moderate posture until the August fires, when they demanded the removal of the entire population of the districts, stationing a police force there, and the permission to organize their own protective forces.[84] The police were blamed for failing to contain clashes.[85] Even after August the oilmen continued to express their belief that workers' demands could be satisfied by concessions.[86] They recommended that the government grant freedom of speech and assembly, the right to form labor unions, and the right to strike.[87] The owners continued to advance such arguments until the eve of the war but especially while reserves were large and prices high, as they were in the spring of 1905 and again in 1913 and 1914. Because most strikers supported the constitution, not the overthrow of tsarism and capitalism, fear of radicalism was probably slight.

The local administration remained tolerant. As late as 1907 General Dzhunkovskii, the viceroy's representative, suggested a meeting between oil-company owners and labor representatives to discuss a general labor contract. The authorities waited for almost a full year while the unions (the Bolshevik-led Union of Oil Workers and the Menshevik Union of Mechanical Workers) and the labor press debated the merits of such a meeting.[88] Only an angry letter from Prime Minister Stolypin to Vorontsov-Dashkov ended the plan. The union movement petered out, and virtually all unions soon disappeared.[89] Bolsheviks from Caucasia maintained an underground and gained useful experience by participating in the Iranian Constitutional Movement (1905–1911) in southern Azerbaijan. They ran guns and distributed political leaflets by ship and across the border at Julfa (in Nakhjivan) and elsewhere.[90]

Baku remained peaceful until the summer of 1913. A report by the senior factory inspector of the Baku guberniia dated 21 August 1913[91] stated that between 1911 and 1913, workers' material position had deteriorated, including a 10 percent decline in earnings. Many workers had no days off, even those working twelve-hour shifts. With oil prices back up, workers saw a chance to make gains. Scattered strikes in July 1913 blossomed into a general strike in which about 40,000 workers took part. The strike was settled in August by a series of individual company agreements. In addition to economic demands, strikers wanted free education in their native languages for workers' children, with free textbooks and breakfast at school, libraries and reading rooms with materials in the languages of the workers, and days off during Muslim holidays (demands made earlier but apparently not observed). Political questions were raised about the recognition of unions and factory committees as representatives of the workers.[92] The Regulations for Oil Workers of 1913 included many such provisions.[93]

Whether the regulations were not observed, or whether discontent surfaced for other reasons, in 1914 strikes in Baku reached the 1905 level. By June 1914, 30,000 were on strike. Troops forced workers back to their jobs. Some returned to work without concessions, others attacked nonstriking workers. Police drove workers from their company-owned homes. The material hardship began to take a serious toll. By the end of July, only about 9,500 workers still refused to return to work. The beginning of the war and mobilization put an end to the strike but not to the underlying problems.

During the years from the revolution of 1905 to the eve of the war, the population had received a protracted political education.[94] Literacy programs, which were sometimes organized and led by Social Democrats, dealt with political themes in their reading classes. Civil liberties, the right to form unions, and the right to strike had become well-known issues.

The resurgence of a powerful strike movement in 1913, with its tacit threat of violence coupled with the rise in oil prices, made the owners willing to offer economic concessions while avoiding political issues.[95] Industrialists thought workers' demands had escalated, that workers themselves had become "less amenable" in that they now refused to settled without industry-wide capitulation.[96] Local officials kept up the pressure on industrialists to refuse discussion of "political" issues and to end the strike as soon as possible.[97] A telegram from the minister of trade and industry showed that the central government's main concern was that the flow of oil to Russian industry not be interrupted.[98]

Despite Soviet claims that the strikes of the early twentieth century had grown increasingly political, the majority of the 1913 demands seem to have been economic—wage increases, overtime pay, guaranteed days off, eight- or nine-hour work days, sick pay, and so forth.[99] Strike demands on the eve of the war were less political than in 1905 when the Russian Social Democratic Workers party (RSDWP) had called for an end to the Russo-Japanese War, the convening of a constituent assembly, equal, direct, and secret balloting, and equal representation for all nationalities. Demands advanced on the eve of the war seem tepid by comparison.

Concerning the response to the strikes, there was no difference in the behavior of European, Russian, and Armenian owners on the one hand and Azerbaijani Turks on the other. Azerbaijani owners were occasionally saved from the strike movement by some kind of religious or national loyalty on the part of "Muslim" workers[100] (especially before 1905 when labor organizers had yet to recruit any substantial number of Turks, Persians, or Daghestanis). When the Azerbaijani industrialists were struck, however, their response was no more paternal than that of other owners. When Taghiyev's

Muslim workers struck his textile mill in 1905, he closed the plant and threatened to fire all 1,600 strikers if they were not back at work in three days.[101] The senior factory inspector of the Baku guberniia in 1913 noted that small and medium-sized firms (among which were most Azerbaijani-owned firms) agreed quickly to settle conflicts by accepting virtually all the workers' demands. The management of those firms then replaced most of their small work force within the next few weeks and were thus able to revert to the previous conditions. For the larger firms a change in policy was likely to be permanent. Owners of large firms were, for that reason, more cautious in making concessions.[102]

This is not to say there was no difference in the behavior of Azerbaijani owners toward Muslim workers who struck. Azerbaijani owners seem to have regarded strikes by their "own" workers as particularly ungracious after many had been beneficiaries of night schools, charities, and student stipends that the rich had financed.[103]

The role of the RSDWP in making strike demands, organizing workers, and spreading revolutionary literature was sporadic over the years. Its efforts in the strategic oil center were successful mainly among Russian, Armenian, Georgian, and Jewish workers. "Muslim workers" were reticent but too numerous to ignore. Lenin paid close attention to the movement in Baku and maintained regular correspondence with local Bolshevik leaders.[104] Stalin spent his "apprenticeship" in the oil districts.[105] Despite the expanding propaganda and agitation efforts, Social Democrats' efforts to reach "Muslim workers" were handicapped by the association of socialist Russians and Armenians with tsarism and Christian missionaries.

The difficulty of conducting propaganda among the Turks and Persians led the Baku Committee of the RSDWP to accept into its ranks in 1904 and 1905 the Hümmet, a Muslim social democratic party exclusively for "Muslims." Such exclusivity of membership had been denied the Jewish Bund by Lenin,[106] and the Baku Committee accepted the Hümmet at a time when the Mensheviks, not the Bolsheviks, were a majority. Baku Bolsheviks, however, retained a cooperative relationship with the Hümmet until they took it over in 1920. The Hümmet conducted propaganda in Turkish, most vigorously opposing oppression, especially by the tsarist government, and promoting social justice and economic equality—in short, using rhetoric which could be construed by its audience as national as well as socialist. Because the leaders of this group were among the most respected men of the local Azerbaijani Turkish community, the Hümmet gained wide popularity and a large membership.[107]

Recognizing the differing needs of local and immigrant Azerbaijani Turks and the potential for Iranian Azerbaijanis to transmit socialist ideas to Iran, the Hümmet leadership formed a separate group for workers from Iran, the

Adalet (Justice). The two groups were closely tied and, for a number of years, seem to have shared the same Central Committee. Adalet was reportedly the first Iranian group to call itself social democratic. It would later become the basis for the Iranian Communist party.[108]

Participation by "Muslim workers" in the strike movement of 1905 suggests that agitation by socialists who held out the hope that a better life was within the workers' reach had produced a reaction. Records of the Nobel and Krasil'nikov companies showed that "Muslim workers" were among strikers who brought work to a standstill. They struck against oilman Bartdorf for equal pay with the Russian unskilled workers who, they charged, were paid more for doing the same work.[109] At Taghiyev's textile plant, 1,500 "Persians" struck for pay increases, the building of a *hamam* (bath), and the introduction of an eight-hour workday.[110] Some petitions reflected cooperation when they joined "Christian" strikers, demanding wage increases, pay for strike days, and prayer time for Muslims without loss of pay.[111] The degeneration of the strike actions into intercommunal violence twice in 1905 revealed the fragility of this class solidarity.

In comparison to the strikes of 1905–1907, Muslim, especially Persian, participation in the labor movement on the eve of World War I was more visible and widespread. Oil workers, dockworkers, porters, and carriage drivers struck.[112] Of the three hundred who attacked the office of the Russian Oil Association, most who appeared in the police report had Turkish or Persian names.[113] Police reports from Balakhany mentioned "Muslim strikers" at various oil fields persuading others to join strikes.[114] Some reportedly continued to work despite beatings by striking workers, usually Christians.[115] The typographers of the Orujev brothers' firm struck over an order for overtime work that was necessitated because so many other typographers (at Turkish-language newspapers) were already striking.[116]

Trudovaia Pravda of 15 June 1914 noted that the most active among the strikers were "Persian."[117] Various strikes of May 1914 were instigated by "Persian citizens"—two thousand dock porters struck over low wages;[118] at the Mukhtarov plant, a strike of 437 workers was generated by the firm's firing 4 "Persian citizens" for absenteeism.[119] Twenty-four workers at the Atlas brick factory, mostly "Persian citizens," demanded higher pay. In June 1914 some of the strikers were deported. A few days after the first deportations, eighty-four more immigrant workers were "evacuated" to Iran.[120]

Until recently, Western and Soviet scholars explained a perceived pattern of inactivity by "backward Muslim workers" by their being unskilled, easily replaced, and therefore afraid to strike. Because labor organizations were dominated by Christians, the Muslims, or so the argument went, were reluctant to join. Although these factors played a role, the potential for opposition and violence was not recognized. Restive and numerous Iranian

Azerbaijanis had been exposed to a profound and successful revolutionary experience at home in the Tobacco Rebellion of 1891–1892.[121] Later immigrants were veterans of the Constitutional Movement (1905–1911), the blockade of Tabriz (1910–1911), and organized guerrilla fighting. Iranians were responsive to the antitsarist aspect of social democratic propaganda since the Russian Empire had been the enemy even at home.

Russians and Armenians sometimes expressed their perception that Baku was their island in an "alien" ocean, forgetting that the ocean was the native population. Azerbaijani Turks in Baku, however, were conscious of links to the hinterland from which both intellectuals and workers had come. The political and cultural Azerbaijani elite saw themselves as leaders of a community beyond Baku, encompassing Shemakhi, Kuba, Shusha, Nakhjivan, Ganje (even as they called it Elizavetpol), and countless villages. Their efforts to clarify the identity of that community, to forge it into a conscious and active body, and to lead it to greater political and economic power were a central focus of their lives.

4 The Turkish Cultural Renaissance in Azerbaijan

*The following Turkish proverb has come down [to us] . . .
read it and take it to heart: To the man of intellect, intelligence is a sufficient companion; to the man of ignorance, a
curse is a sufficient name.*

Yusuf Khass Hajib, *Kutadgu Bilig,*
written circa 1069 B.C.E.*

The leaders of Azerbaijan's cultural and intellectual life were an educated
and active group of writers, composers, dramatists, journalists, teachers,
engineers, and medical doctors. Most resided in Baku, though few had been
born there. Many had been to Russian universities, others had been educated
in Europe (especially Paris) or Istanbul. They were the perpetuators in
Caucasia of a cultural renaissance that embraced the entire Turkish world—
Turkey, Crimea, the Volga-Ural region, Azerbaijan, and Turkestan—from the
second half of the nineteenth to the early twentieth century. The period was
characterized by a rediscovery of history, literature, and philosophy and by
a debate about politics, social change, religion and morality, and historical

---

Kutadgu Bilig, a seminal work of Turkish statecraft of the eleventh century, by
Balasagunlu Yusuf (made Chamberlain or "Khass Hajib" as reward), translated from
Turkish original by Robert Dankoff as *Wisdom of Royal Glory* (Chicago: University
of Chicago Press, 1983), p. 317.

identity. Interconnections among regions were many. Azerbaijani Turks were prominent in these contacts and often made their careers in Europe or Turkey as well as at home.

CULTURAL-INTELLECTUAL ELITES

The cultural-intellectual elite of Azerbaijan engaged in a diversity of activities apart from their chosen professions. Composer Uzeir Hajibeyli (Hajibekov or Gadjibekov, 1885–1948) wrote satirical verses and political commentaries. With his brother Jeyhun (1891–1962), Uzeir Hajibeyli taught in the Saadet school where local publicist Ali Huseinzade (1864–1941) was director. Nariman Narimanov (1870–1925) wrote plays, taught school, cochaired an education reform committee, then became a medical doctor. Memed Hasan Hajinskii, an engineer, had a seat in the City Council, wrote political tracts, and designed the boulevard along Baku's waterfront. Such a range of activities and breadth of knowledge was typical of the intellectual, social, and political elites, who were one group, formed by secular education and community consciousness. They were united in their efforts to improve the position of their community within the empire, to preserve their culture, and eventually to forge a national identity.

This elite came to its political maturity in the years before the Bolshevik revolution, led the independent republic, and played some role in Soviet Azerbaijan into the 1930s. The issues with which they struggled in the 1900s—language and educational reform, the development of the press, the arts and their social, political functions—became questions of policy after 1917. Their debate over identity, cut short by the purges, was revived after the death of Stalin.

LANGUAGE, THE ARTS, AND EDUCATION

The movement in the late nineteenth and early twentieth centuries toward the development and spread of a simplified Azerbaijani Turkish language was built partly on the foundations of the grammar texts of Mirza Muhammad Ali Kazembek (1802–1870). His work on the Azerbaijani dialect of Turkish began in the 1830s while he was a lecturer at Kazan University. His grammars, published in 1839 and 1846, provided a basis for school texts published in the 1850s.[1] Subsequent grammars calling the language Türki were published in Baku and Tiflis later in the century and early in the next.[2]

A significant contribution to language modification was made by dramatist Mirza Fath Ali Akhundzade (Akhundov) (1812–1878).[3] Akhundzade began his literary career in the 1830s while he worked as a translator in a Tiflis chancellery. His plays were often biting satires of traditional morals and mullahs. He wrote in colloquial Azerbaijani Turkish, so his plays had wide popular appeal and could reach the illiterate. For the educated they served as a model of form and language. Akhunzade's plays were translated in Europe—one translator called him the Molière of the Orient. His first translated play was *The Tale of Monsieur Jordan, Learned Botanist, and the Dervish Mastali-shah, Known Wizard.*

The Azerbaijani Turkish-language press became an important vehicle for the spread of the local language. The first Azerbaijani-language newspaper bore the name *Ekinji* (*Sower*, one who sows seeds). It was published between 1875 and 1877 and edited by Hasan Melikov-Zarbadi (1837–1907), a naturalist and educator who formed an intellectual bridge between early nineteenth-century intellectual leaders (like Akhundzade and the historian Abbas Kulu Agha Bakikhanli, 1794–1848) and figures of the twentieth-century cultural renaissance. The language used in *Ekinji* was widely emulated by subsequent periodicals published in the Azerbaijani dialect of Turkish, and it became the medium for the discussion and dissemination of a broad spectrum of ideas.[4]

After *Ekinji* was closed in 1877 (for alleged pro-Ottoman sentiments during the Russo-Ottoman War of 1877–1878), three other Turkish-language periodicals appeared between 1879 and 1891.[5] Periodicals in Turkish were then banned until 1904, so the Azerbaijani press consisted solely of the Russian-language daily *Kaspii*, edited by Ali Mardan Topchibashi (1862–1934). After 1904 there began a proliferation of Turkish-language newspapers using either the vernacular, as *Ekinji* had done, or a modified Ottoman Turkish.[6] The choice of literary form often reflected political inclinations. *Sharg-i Rus* (*The Russian East*), *Hayat*, *Taza Hayat*, and *Füyuzat* represented the nascent national movement based on ethnic, secular identity. *Füyuzat* used modified Ottoman because of the close ties its editor, Ali Huseinzade, maintained with Turkey. *Tekamül* (*Evolution*), *Tereggi* (*Progress*), *Davet-Koch* (*The Call*, in Armenian and Azerbaijani Turkish), and *Hümmet* (*Endeavor*) constituted the "socialist" press with some occasional overlap in views with the first group. The satirical *Ari* (*Bee*), *Zenbur* (*Wasp*), and the Tiflis journal *Molla Nasreddin* were extremely popular.

Language, however, was of less concern than substance. The press, whether right or left, represented exclusively the reformist, Westernized, socialist-tinted intellectual elite. Newspapers supported secularism, religious and social reform, a constitution and anticolonialism. Political commentators like Ahmet Aghayev (Agaoglu, 1865–1939), Mehti Hajinskii, Memmed Hadi, and others wrote for several newspapers. Baku boasted more than sixty prerevolutionary newspapers and journals, many of which were Azerbaijani-owned, if not printed in the local language.

The press was a medium for language development and was a "school" of literature, politics, and social reform. One of the most popular journals of the late imperial era was the Turkish-language *Molla Nasreddin*. Like its namesake, the legendary Molla Nasreddin (also called Nasrettin Hoja, a figure who appears in clever but didactic stories throughout the Middle East and Central Asia) whose feigned foolishness masked wisdom, the newspaper used elliptical language, ambiguity, satire, and cartoons against officialdom, religious conservatives, the unthinking person, the corrupt bureaucrat. The editor, Jalil Memedguluzade, and its most prominent contributors, like Alekper Sabir, were Azerbaijani Turks whose writings have been republished many times. More than one hundred countries around the world received the journal and translated its articles.[7] The first issue of *Molla Nasreddin* appeared in April 1906 and contained the following "latest news": "All Russia is peaceful. The wolf and the lamb are grazing together." To the contemporary reader, familiar with both the revolutionary upheavals of recent months and the censors who strove to keep all unrest from public view, the irony in this remark was plain. Concerning a heated debate about the election of the heads of the Muslim Ecclesiastical Boards of the empire (the state favored the current practice of appointment) *Molla Nasreddin* reported:

PETERSBURG, 30 March: It is said here that Senator Cherivanski will be appointed as the Orenburg mufti. The Orenburg mufti, his Excellency Sultanov, will become the servant of the Orenburg police.

To ridicule laziness and ignorance, the issue included several "proverbs":

Leave the chores of the morning to the evening and those of the evening to the morning.
A man becomes a scholar by remaining idle.
There is no remedy for what it is going to happen. Let it happen.

The press was a major vehicle for examining the role of women in traditionally Muslim Azerbaijani society. With the Westernization of Baku and the influx of Western styles, ideas, and Westerners themselves, the matter took on genuine urgency. Cartoons in *Molla Nasreddin* contrasted the veiled and secluded women of urban Muslim society with Edwardian London's bustle-clad gentlewomen. The stark differences in style were only the superficial aspects of a problem that aroused protests by Muslim women against polygamy and veiling. For the modernizers the veil became a symbol of men's control of women, of their forced seclusion, and of their illiteracy. Commentaries and editorials expressed the fear that educated men would hardly want such women as wives. The emancipation of women was therefore cast in broad social terms as a reform necessary for the preservation and growth of the nation.[8]

The performing arts also played a social and educational role. Azerbaijani Turks composed operas, ballets, and other works based on the classics of Turkish-language literature and folk traditions or of Islamic (especially Turco-Islamic or Perso-Islamic) culture. Dominating the performing arts in the early twentieth century were the brothers Uzeir and Jeyhun Hajibeyli, born in Shusha in Karabagh. At the end of 1907 the brothers wrote the libretto for Uzeir's opera, *Leyla and Majnun*, the "first opera of [the] Islamic East."[9] The brothers worked together on other compositions, but Jeyhun went to study in Paris and Uzeir continued with his circle of talented friends—Husein Kuli Sarabskii, Husein Bala Arablinskii, Muslim Magomayev—to write and produce a series of operas on traditional themes as well as satirical comic operettas. They were and still are often performed on traditional instruments. The serious works commemorate historical figures; the operettas poke fun at practices that the secular reformist intelligentsia were trying to change. Arranged marriages are the object of ridicule in two of the most famous comic operettas, *Arshin Mal Alan* and *Meshtibad*.[10]

In the comedic as in the dramatic performances, it was not yet acceptable for women to play the female roles. Uzeir Hajibeyli first put a woman performer, an Azerbaijani Turk who had been trained in Italy, on stage, though doing so was regarded as an insult to womanhood and to the community. Uzeir Bey and the other producers of the concert had to leave with her, hastily, in a carriage waiting at the rear door of the theater.[11]

Performing arts enjoyed the interest and support of the public. The repertoire at the "Taghiyev theater" included the plays of the venerated Ahkundzade and those of young local playwrights who also were teachers or community leaders: Narimanov, Hashin Vezirov, and Mehti Hajinskii.[12] From 1907 on the theater was also used for the operas and operettas of Uzeir Hajibeyli.

Formal Education

The struggle to introduce reformed primary schools was begun in the 1830s by Abbas Kulu Agha Bakikhanli.[13] He argued that education was the key to improved social conditions and the contentment of the populace. His proposal comprised eleven detailed items on all aspects of the school including courses of study and teachers, both Azerbaijani and Russian. Graduates would become scholars, teachers, and bureaucrats. An important part of Bakikhanli's plan, the essential components of which reappeared over the ensuing decades without crediting him, was its multilingual approach. Students were to be taught in Turkish, Russian, and Persian. There was no official response to the plan, but more than a decade later a modified form of it appeared in Tiflis attributed to "field-trained Orientalist" Khanykov. He proposed limiting language training to Russian and Turkish because the chief purposes of education were to train loyal bureaucrats for imperial service. Young men would be kept from going abroad (apparently to Iran or the Ottoman Empire) for advanced (religious) education. From the late 1840s to the turn of the century, attempts to bring native children into the schools with Russians failed.

The language of instruction was a continual point of contention. Muslim parents did not want to send their children to Christian, Russian-language schools, so teachers called for the use of Azerbaijani Turkish ("Tatar") as the language of instruction. They demanded Azerbaijani Turkish-language textbooks, the introduction of the "new method" of the *jadid* schools for teaching reading, and a revised training seminar for teachers. They complained of the Russification of their language and of the poor preparation of students for pedagogical work in their own language. Of forty-one primary schools in Baku in 1910, ten were "Russian-Tatar" schools and one was "Persian."[14]

Secondary schools might offer some courses in Turkish but only in the first years, giving way to Russian-language instruction at higher levels. Children could not be taught more than basic subjects in their native language. Preparatory schooling for work in the state bureaucracy or in higher educational institutions was entirely in Russian. Native-language instruction was widely offered only in religious schools, leaving students without preparation for higher secular education or for secular occupations that predominated in the new environment. Parents faced a dilemma at the root of which lay a mismatch between the values and skills needed to succeed under Russia rule and industrialization, including proficiency in Russian, and the traditional education and values of Azerbaijani Turkish society.

The Azerbaijani Turks saw that their own cultural traditions were being undermined. They shared their fear with other Turks and Muslims of the Russian Empire who had reformed the traditional *mekteps* (Koranic schools) in their own areas under a program formulated by Crimean Tatar Ismail Gasprali (Gasprinskii). His program, the "new method" (*usul-i jadid*), was aimed at reforming mektep education with secular subjects and a phonetic method for teaching reading. These jadid schools spread widely throughout the empire and to Egypt and India.

A Baku-area committee attempted in 1906 and 1907 to address these concerns. It included the most respected members of the community—

Melikov-Zardabi and Narimanov were cochairmen. The committee recommended a program of study conducted in the Turkish dialect of Azerbaijan, including language, literature, religious studies, and a variety of secular subjects.[15] Russian would be taught and courses such as accounting would be conducted in Russian. It is noteworthy that a plan for the "nationalization" of education that included provisions for religious instruction was produced by a committee with a large number of members (perhaps a majority) who were members of the RSDWP or in some way affiliated with the socialist movement.

Reformers in Baku planned to ensure bilingual and bicultural education to allow children to keep open their options of participating in both their traditional Turkish or Islamic milieu and the industrial West. Instead of having to choose between Europe and Asia, education would allow the Azerbaijani Turks of future generations to draw from, contribute to, and participate in both civilizations. The idea resembled the Bakikhanli plan of the 1830s and the goals were similar. The reform program of 1907 was aimed at preparing Azerbaijani children for life in the twentieth century without forcing them to sacrifice their intimacy with their own cultural heritage or their identity.

Bilingual education began at the Mikhailov *uchilishche*;[16] Baku's *real'noe uchilishche* opened a reading course for Azerbaijani children aged 7–8. The local school inspector prepared a project for a pedagogy course for those Azerbaijanis who had completed primary school.[17]

The problem of educating young women outside their homes was particularly difficult. Even so, parents wanted their daughters to be educated. The City Council received petitions for money to begin a pedagogical course for Muslim girls at the Aleksander Girls' School.[18] The following year residents in two western quarters of town petitioned the City Council to provide a school for their daughters in one of these mahalle because the only existing girls' school, the Taghiyev school, was overcrowded, expensive, and far away. Council representatives vigorously supported their request. Hajiyev made a rousing "down with the veil" speech on the need for education to make women good citizens and good mothers (the two roles were regarded as inseparable).[19] A commentary in *Kaspii* by Mehti Hajinskii pointed to examples of women's education among the Volga Tatars.[20] A new school was opened in a western quarter in 1910.

Adult Education

Adult education came within the purview of Baku's many charitable organizations and literacy societies.[21] Nijat, Neshr Maarif, and Saadet offered adult education in classes in Baku. Attendance increased and so did the need for greater funding, books, and instructors.[22] The 1913 Baku city census showed a large number of Azerbaijani Turks were educated in "irregular" educational institutions, the night classes of charitable and enlightenment societies. Much of the funding came from the wealthy. The cultural intelligentsia donated its money and, perhaps more significant, its time. Engineers, lawyers, doctors, and writers taught the workers and street sweepers to read.[23]

The evening courses were not nonpolitical. Nijat was an arm of the Hümmet and Nijat board members and officers were almost all Hümmetists (Mehmet Emin Rasulzade [1884–1954], Meshadi Azizbekov, and A. Haji-bababekov).[24] Neshr Maarif was more closely associated with industrialists and merchants (Taghiyev, Asadullayev, Naghiyev, the Ashurbekovs) and political "moderates" who would later form the core of the national movement (Topchibashi, Aga Mamed Dadashev). Hümmetists were not excluded. Aziz-beyov also was a contributor to Neshr Maarif.[25] Political lines were not sharp, but materials for reading courses were selected, at least in part, for their political content; literacy went hand in hand with the growing politicization of the lower classes. Reading rooms were opened in the oil districts.[26]

ISLAMIC ESTABLISHMENT

A religious establishment is conventionally regarded as the main antagonist of a secular elite such as that in turn-of-the-century Azerbaijan. Although this tension existed to some extent, there were reasons why the relationship between the groups was not merely antagonistic: (1) the Islamic establishment had been greatly weakened after a century of Russian rule; (2) a sectarian peace prevailed among the Shi'i and Sunni of the Russian Empire, and a reform movement within Islam divided the religious classes; and (3) secular elites never rejected Islam though they ridiculed some mullahs.

Traditionally, the religious classes played an important role in Muslim society as prayer leaders, administrators, judges (*qadis*), and scholars. They are not a clergy in the Christian sense, for Islam is not a sacramental religion. In northern Azerbaijan, as a result of Russian state policy, there were apparently no true scholars left by the end of the nineteenth century. The highest level in the local Shi'i hierarchy (the majority were Shi'a)[27] was the *akhund*, who stood rather low within Shi'i organizational structure. The urban mullahs (prayer leaders) seem to have come predominantly from the ranks of the bazari, and the mullahs of the villages were often peasants. Thus, mullahs came from insulated social groups and were sensitive to the interests of the class that traditionally sustained them. This bond was reinforced by education and appointment processes that kept young men near home throughout their careers.

The key tsarist policy that destroyed the ulema was the creation of Sunni and Shi'i Ecclesiastical Boards. These were reminiscent of the Holy Synod created by Peter I as a means of bringing the Russian Orthodox church under state control. Each board consisted of a president (called mufti for the Sunni, sheikh ul-Islam for the Shi'i), three board members, a secretary with two assistants, a registrar, an interpreter, and an archivist. Each presided over a judicial administration (*glavnyi kazii*) and four assemblies (*mejlis*), one for each guberniia: Tiflis, Erevan, Ganje, and Baku. The Sunni board had sixteen *qadis* (judges); the Shi'i, twenty.[28] This entire apparatus was under the control of the Ministry of Internal Affairs and the personal authority of the viceroy. The guberniia-level mullahs were under the legal jurisdiction of the guberniia and uezd civil authorities with regard to imperial law.[29]

The main function of this structure was to control and co-opt the ulema, who at the time of the Russian conquest were seen as the most likely leaders of opposition to Russian rule. The Russians had begun to curtail the power of the qadis with military rule. The qadis had effectively been removed from the realm of civil and criminal law long before industrialization. By the twentieth century they were confined to recording births, deaths, and marriages. The Shi'i Ecclesiastical Board processed 3,095 documents (mostly birth registrations) in 1904. The Baku uezd judicial administration heard only sixty-nine cases in 1904, and eighty in 1908—fewer than two per week.[30]

Regulations established parameters within which mullahs and qadis could act and designated their official rank (*chin*), qualifications, responsibilities, and privileges.[31] By granting rank and privilege, imperial authorities sought to co-opt these community leaders just as guarantees of land and titles (also granted in the 1840s) had been aimed at securing support from local landowners. To become a licensed Muslim "cleric" in the Viceroyalty of Transcaucasia, one could not be a known criminal or of ill repute and had to be a Russian citizen at least twenty-two years of age for instructing at lower levels and at least thirty for any "higher rank" (not defined). For a "title in the sciences" a special test and a license were required. The individual had to be willing to sign an affidavit that he was not and would not become a member of any proscribed society or sect, such as a Sufi order. (The Russians were particularly wary of contacts with Sufi brotherhoods after the Shamil's successful use of such groups during its long resistance to Russian rule in the Caucasus Mountains.)

The clerics were exempt from state property and most municipal taxes and from corporal punishment. Children had privileges commensurate with the rank of their fathers. The children of the mufti and the sheikh ul-Islam had the same privileges as the children of hereditary nobles; the children of board members of guberniia-level assemblies or qadis enjoyed the rights of a personal noble. Statutes even specified the numbers of horses allowed individuals of each rank when traveling.

Regulations defining the obligations of mullahs were concerned entirely with their duties toward the state and tsar. Before a "cleric" could occupy any post he had to pledge "loyalty to His imperial Majesty and conscientious fulfillment of his obligations." While fulfilling his duty to serve God according to his faith, he was also obliged to "fulfill unswervingly the laws and instructions of the government." A mullah must to the best of his ability inspire his coreligionists "with steadfast loyalty and devotion to the sovereign Emperor and obedience to the designated authorities." Other statutes prescribed loyalty and obedience and the necessity of informing the police in the event of "social disasters . . . or the celebration of Muslim holidays with solemn processions and popular assemblies." For mullahs serving under the boards and governed by these regulations, opposition to the central authority became a violation of duty, even a crime.

Provisions on education were absent from these regulations, perhaps because all state education was meant to make servants for the state. Those intending a religious career went to existing mekteps, some of which followed the jadid method or developed strong programs around leading scholars.[32] The few good mekteps reportedly provided a strong training in oriental languages and literature and, to a lesser extent, in history.[33] Then in the *medrese* students studied Arabic, logic, and Islamic law. Education here could take up to fifteen years, for a student remained in the medrese until a place opened for him in his home region.[34] Graduates moved directly into the state-regulated system. Those who received advanced education abroad were viewed with suspicion by tsarist authorities.[35] The strictures of the Ecclesiastical Boards and regulations must have discouraged them from returning home. Locally trained mullahs were few, and many mosque and religious-court posts remained unfilled. In 1904, 110 of 297 "parishes" in the Baku guberniia were without mullahs.[36]

The state had economic control over the religious as well. The economic strength of the ulema traditionally has been bound up with the *waqf* (plural: *awqaf*), a special religious endowment created by the contribution of some income-producing property for the perpetual support of a mosque, orphanage, or other charitable institution. Once created, a waqf cannot legally be alienated, divided, sold, or otherwise revert to its previous condition. (Throughout history many rulers, in disputes with the ulema, have seized awqaf.) Data concerning these properties in Caucasia are sparse. They were seized in Tiflis, Ganje, Baku, and other areas of Caucasia at the time of the

Russian conquest. Regulations concerning religious properties were formulated later.[37]

The regulations fundamentally altered the legal (Islamic) character of a waqf. Under Statute 107 it included "moveable and immoveable property, money capital, donations or loans for the use of mosques, mekteps, and medreses, the clergy of a given region or mosque, for the care of orphans, the poor, the aged, insane, or incurably ill, and in general for charitable purposes." The true waqf (as defined by Islamic law) thus was included with any other properties or capital used by religious institutions or the religious classes for the financial support of personnel, organizations, or programs. Other statutes also could be applied to both ordinary properties or to true awqaf: sale of waqf properties was permitted (Statute 112) by public auction; the punishment for maladministration of religious properties was the same as for state properties (Statute 115); and legal action concerning the properties of the Ecclesiastical Boards with other departments (of the state) was to be decided according to civil law established for state administration (Statute 116).

Insufficient data prevent definitive conclusions as to the effect of these legal provisions on the fate of religious properties and the ulema. Reports on mosque income suggest,[38] however, that for the four Baku mosques on which data were available, income from the renting of selling-stalls (*lavki*) at city bazaars covered all or most expenses, including wages for the mullahs, guards, an accountant and repairman, insurance on the lavki and hefty municipal taxes (though mullahs were exempt, mosques apparently were not).[39]

These figures demonstrate the mosques' dependence on rents from merchants but also suggest, in view of the low wages, that mullahs may have relied on good relations with merchants for supplements to their income. Contributions for services were a vestige of the preconquest economy in which mullahs might be paid sheep, oil, and other goods rather than cash.[40] Financial as well as family ties bound bazaris to mullahs.

The Russian authorities apparently believed that control over the Muslim hierarchy would lead to control over the Muslim population. Indirectly, state control did undermine clerical authority. Ulema were co-opted by "job security," tax exemption, privileges of rank, and high wages paid to those at the top—the president of each board received 6,000 rubles per year.[41] Over time, therefore, the legitimacy of religious officials in the eyes of the faithful was undermined. Distrust would develop under Soviet control (which copied tsarist methods), but the seed was planted early.

Russian state measures were not as successful in controlling, for example, the Russian Orthodox church. The role of the ulema in Islam is different from that of the Christian clergy. The ulema do not act as spiritual intermediaries, as in the sacraments, for the central relationship in Islam is between the individual and God. Authority is said to rest in the whole community, which is the great sustainer of the Islamic ethical and social milieu. Lines of authority in Islam are not so simple that the co-optation of a few ulema can alter the practices of the Muslim community. Shi'ism permits competing religious authorities so no single *alim* can speak with binding authority for all Muslims. The most learned Shi'i scholars resided in Iran or Iraq, beyond Russian control, and the Shi'a may practice *taqiyya* or "prudent dissimulation," the denial of belief with impunity when in danger.

The religious establishment itself was not homogeneous. The secular intelligentsia and the press it controlled criticized mullahs for "obscurantism" or "ignorance," for supporting the veiling and segregation of women, and rejecting secular skills and knowledge. Nonetheless, the press acknowledged those mullahs who supported school reforms and jadidism. The mullahs served as members of the Peace Committees, which strove to end the communal clashes in 1905; they made numerous appeals for calm and conciliation.

Sectarian differences were controlled. Although elsewhere in the Islamic world Sunni-Shi'i antagonism had led to division, even armed conflict, potential friction in Azerbaijan was progressively alleviated by pressure from Christian communities. At the All-Russian Muslim Congresses, the Sunni ulema in the Russian Empire in an unprecedented move accepted Shi'ism as a fifth *maddhab* or legal school, called the Jafari.[42]

The secular intelligentsia never attacked religion, despite a long tradition of anticlericalism represented by Akhundzade in the nineteenth century and *Molla Nasreddin* in the twentieth. Writing after the revolution, Narimanov remarked on the sensitivity of religion and the socialists' policy adjustments.[43] Even the Hümmet dated its leaflets by the Islamic calendar, [44] illustrating the diversity of both secular and religious leadership.

At a special conference of Caucasian Muslims in Tiflis in the fall of 1905, nine mullahs and twelve *intelligenty* (as the press called them) met to decide contemporary social questions. Two of the issues on the agenda concerned raising the minimum marriage ages from fifteen to eighteen for boys and from thirteen to sixteen for girls and condemning polygamy. Marriage age was settled in favor of the status quo; the conference did not condemn polygamy, though it was criticized by the press. For these positions to have dominated at least some of the secular leaders must have sided with the mullahs.[45]

Religious and lay leaders strove to gain community control over the appointment of the sheikh ul-Islam. In late 1907 the sheikh ul-Islam of Transcaucasia died. Shi'i Muslims from all over Caucasia convened in Tiflis to petition the viceroy for permission to elect the sheikh's successor (rather than accept a state appointee) and to determine the mechanism for that process.[46] The post remained empty through most of 1908 as debate and behind-the-scenes maneuvering went on. *Kaspii* stated that the "sheikh ul-Islam must enjoy the confidence of all Muslims," implying that a state appointee would not.[47] The community lost the fight when a new sheikh ul-Islam was appointed.[48]

POLITICAL ACTION

Baku City Council

With the Urban Reform of 1870, upper-class Azerbaijanis were able to expand the sphere of their activity and influence by engaging in local politics within an official framework. Despite early restrictions on non-Christian participation in the City Council, Azerbaijani Turks were active, even dominant there in the twentieth century. Their common concern and efforts on behalf of citywide issues like tax reform, water supply and sanitation, law enforcement, and budgeting demonstrate a genuine civic consciousness apart from religious or national particularism. The majority of those who regularly attended council meetings were Azerbaijani Turks. They took the initiative in raising problems and proposing solutions as though it was their prerogative to take the lead in Baku's only elective political body. The Azerbaijanis used a petition for a new Muslim girls' school to debate women's place in society and to support an end to veiling and segregation. They conducted the debates on and supported the distribution of municipal funds for the repair and construction of mosques and churches.[49] At the same time, they used their political power and their personal wealth and knowledge to bolster local education in their own community by allocating funds for schools and adult education. *Baku*'s commentator Enen complained that, despite the fact that they were not a majority, the Azerbaijanis dominated the City Council.[50]

In the city council the Azerbaijanis challenged the Nobel Company, a symbol for them of European imperialism, foreign capital, and exploitation of oil, their most valuable commodity. Although it had the right to a representative in the City Council, the Nobel Company seldom had anyone present. The company remained aloof generally from municipal affairs. When it wanted to build a tunnel connecting two of its buildings under a public street, however, it was obliged to petition the city Administration. The Administration agreed to permit construction but placed a tax on the unprecedented tunnel, perhaps to supplement the always-troubled city budget. The company manager, Lesner, was angered by the proposed tax and wrote a sharp retort. Lesner charged that there was no legal basis for the tax, that it set an unreasonable value on worthless land, and that it was proposed only to line the pockets of the city's officers. He demanded that the issue be brought before the City Council for a decision.

Although the question before the City Council was whether to permit construction of the tunnel, Lesner's letter dominated the debate. The mayor, head of the Administration and City Council, explained to the council the Administration's position that the letter was an insult and should have been returned as "unacceptable." Instead, the matter was placed before the council. Mehti Hajinskii rose first to argue that because of the tone of the letter, the council should deny the request to build the tunnel and should "inform St. Petersburg" (the Nobel office? the Senate?) that the refusal was due to the "unseemly excesses" of the company's local management. Other Azerbaijani Turks spoke in support of Hajinskii's position. A few others rose to advise caution, saying it would be better not to risk spoiling "good relations."

"I don't understand you," Hajinskii told one representative. "What kind of good relations are these? They slap your face. If later they give you sweets will you forgive everything?"

The debate continued in this lively vein. In the end the majority rejected the request for the tunnel because of the "incorrect tone" of Lesner's letter.[51]

In stark contrast to their strong role in the City Council was the weak position of Azerbaijani Turks in municipal administration. Of the seven members of the 1910 Administration, three were Azerbaijani Turks. Among the forty-nine officers of the various administrative departments, which included sanitation, financial, construction, land, water, schools, defense, and medical-sanitary, only five were Azerbaijanis.[52] This underrepresentation is especially significant because of the power and discretion of a bureaucracy in implementing plans and orders. An earlier shortage of Azerbaijani engineers, bookkeepers, veterinarians, and medical doctors had been alleviated to a large extent by 1910, and Azerbaijanis dominated elsewhere in this and neighboring gubernii. The continued underrepresentation of Azerbaijanis in the Baku municipal bureaucracy may be explained by the same sort of religious and national discrimination seen in other arenas.

Azerbaijani influence therefore depended on the power of the City Council and on the extent to which Azerbaijani Turks exerted power outside the municipal administration. The work load, not to say the power, of the City Council grew rapidly in the prewar years.[53]

Intellectual Currents and Political Parties

In their concern with the present and future of their community, the Azerbaijani Turkish elite agreed on several fundamental goals: ensuring political equality within the empire complemented by raising the status of women, workers, and peasants within their own nation; gaining state support for reforming education as a bilingual program of professional and traditional studies; participating in government through elected representatives; and safeguarding their native culture and way of life with legal guarantees. Those differences that did exist among intellectuals in the prewar period were more a matter of methods than goals.

Bound up with goals and methods was the question of identity. The secular intelligentsia rejected a fundamentally religious identity; the place of Islam in the national identity was problematic. Both Islamic and non-Islamic Turkish traditions were to be reconciled with selective borrowings from foreign ideologies such as socialism, liberalism, and European-style nationalism. One thing was clear—the Azerbaijani Turks were colonial subjects in an empire whose dominant nationality regarded itself as superior in every way, who supported policies of discrimination and assimilation, and whose government had no wish to share power or grant political or civil rights to any nationality.

With the political education of 1905, Azerbaijani Turks added political issues to their long-standing cultural agenda. To the earlier focus on language, literature, and education were added demands for civil rights, social justice, legal equality, and representative government. Political groups began to coalesce around such demands. They conducted a political and intellectual discourse through the periodical press, in pamphlets, at public meetings, in the City Council, even in music and theater.[54] Revolutionary doctrines that emphasized exploitation had great appeal and were understood to refer to tsarist colonialism (replete with Russian bureaucrats and settlers), Russification and Christianization, and nonnative capitalists enjoying the fruits of Azerbaijan's wealth. Rarely was exploitation seen in class terms within the Azerbaijani Turkish community. The anticolonial movement, which had begun as a cultural phenomenon, moved now to a political, but reformist, stage. Separatism was not a prewar goal.

A confluence of these and other elements is apparent in Hümmet.[55] Among its founders were members of the Azerbaijani intelligentsia: Rasulzade, Sultan Mejid Efendiyev, and Memed Hajinskii.[56] The Hümmet, despite its full title of Muslim Social Democratic Group, used Muslim as did tsarist officialdom, as a political designation. It did not regard itself as a Muslim organization in any religious sense, nor did it advance demands on behalf of the Azerbaijani Turks qua Muslims. Its views were articulated in its leaflets and party program. One leaflet answered "What does the worker need?" by listing political rights, education, and economic improvement.[57] To secure these, workers were urged to unite with the peasantry and intelligentsia. Education would enable workers to read newspapers and to participate in political life. Economic improvement would free them for greater spiritual development. In addition, the Hümmet demanded maternity leave for women, time on the job for nursing unweaned children, and medical care for all workers and rejected plans to build barracks near factories. The tone and substance of the demands were moderate compared to demands of the RSDWP for land expropriation and the creation of a republic. Despite some social democratic phraseology, the rhetoric was reformist but not revolutionary or Marxist.

A 1909 version of the Hümmet party program demanded civil rights and reform: freedom of speech, freedom to assemble, to form unions and strike; freedom of the press and from arbitrary arrest; an eight-hour work day; general, direct, secret elections to the State Duma; equal justice for rich and poor; free, public, compulsory education; a progressive income tax; and, at the end, two more radical demands: the abolition of a standing army and its replacement with a popular militia and the redistribution of all lands of the Treasury and nobility.[58]

If the Hümmet program displayed only a tepid socialism, individual Hümmetists clearly articulated diverse ideas. Hümmetist Nariman Narimanov, a member of the RSDWP, cochaired the conference for "nationalization" of education; Azizbeyov served in the Baku City Council and supported native-language education. He spoke once with indignation at the suggestion that a foreign company be granted a concession for building Baku's tramway. He asked "Why do they think *we* can't build the tramway?"[59] Hümmet's *Tekamül* declared itself a defender of the interests of the toiling masses,[60] as did RSDWP leaflets and other socialist publications, but did not specify the enemy against whom the oppressed should unite.[61] Memmed Hadi, a regular contributor to *Tekamül* and *Yoldash* (*Comrade*), wrote in "What Is Happiness?" that the greatest joy was to give one's life for one's *vatan*, homeland.[62]

In 1905 at the time of the Hümmet's greatest activity, community leaders outside that body placed hope in tsarist promises and worked for constitutional guarantees. The officially sanctioned petition drive of the spring and summer led to a substantial broadening of political participation. Ali Mardan Topchibashi was one of many who greeted the February promise of elections for a Constituent Assembly with great optimism. His *Kaspii* editorial predicted that the "new order" would spell the end of "bureaucratic tutelage" and of limitations on the development of "economic, political and cultural life of society." He anticipated greater independence for municipal and provincial self-government. The task of explaining to the government the needs of this region so far from the capitals should not be left in the hands of central government bureaucrats, Topchibashi argued. This task fell to the local elites who could now render a "great service to the government" by participating in the responsible legislative work.[63] Topchibashi articulated demands that emerged from the petitions collected from villages and towns: equalization of the rights of residents of the Caucasus with those of the internal provinces of Russia and the "inviolability of person and property, freedoms of conscience, press, speech and assembly." He called for the creation of zemstvos and jury trials in Caucasia, the lack of which had long been a major grievance.[64]

Although it has often been suggested that constitutional ideas came from Europe via Russia, many of the most prominent reformers had had European education, obviating the need for a Russian conduit. Furthermore, the ideas of humanitarian rule, social justice, and rational thought, though associated with Europe, can be found in earlier Islamic and pre-Islamic Turkish works.[65] Many Azerbaijani Turkish reformers knew of these antecedents and used them to popularize contemporary political programs. Yet their efforts to mobilize all those able to vote were sometimes frustrated.

Uzeir Hajibeyli wrote an "Open Letter to Caucasian Muslims" that ridiculed reluctance to participate in the State Duma and other excuses used to remain aloof from politics.

> Ay, Caucasian Muslims! The State Duma is approaching in a month's time. Russians, Armenians, Georgians, Poles strive so that the best of their men should be elected and sent to it. But you, Muslims, ought not to be taken in by such thoughts. It is not a matter worthy of you, that you should send a man to the Duma to sit down with Russians and Armenians. What is the Duma and what are you?
>
> [Russians and Armenians] are such ill-mannered and shameless nations that they wash in the *hamam* without a *fiteh* [loincloth]. . . . and now they want, when the Duma opens, to sit and rule with the Ruler, to minister with the Minister, command with the General. But that isn't your business. . . . And one day, some evil will probably come of it, and then that will be on their heads. . . . I am telling you this for your own good . . . on the day of the elections, don't leave your home. On that day, from morning to evening lie in bed as if you were fasting.[66]

At this time, the first All-Russian Muslim Congress took place. Topchibashi played a major role. Though the Congress was dominated by Tatars, the Azerbaijani Turks shared the demands and concerns—the political unity of all "Russian Muslims," equal representation of Muslims with Russians, the rule of law, freely elected popular representatives, the creation of schools, the publication of books and periodicals, and so forth. Topchibashi was cofounder of the Ittifaq al-Muslimin (Muslim Union) formed at the congress and subsequently allied with the Russian Constitutional Democrats (Kadets).[67] Although the headquarters of the Ittifaq was to be in Baku, Azerbaijan came to focus on local troubles—strikes, peasant unrest, communal violence throughout the region—and advanced its own causes.

In Ganje the political spectrum was narrower than in Baku, lacking a serious socialist component. Perhaps for that reason or because they felt more pressure from the militant Armenian Dashnaktsutun party's territorial ambitions, the Azerbaijani Turks of that region seem to have had a clearer national identity. They called themselves Azerbaijani, when the population around Baku still permitted the use of Tatar.[68] Ganje political rhetoric and organizations were more pointedly directed against Russian rule than those in Baku. Reportedly a small Ganje group first advanced the slogan of "Muslim, Georgian, Armenian unity" against Russian rule early in 1905.[69] Ganje would become the center of the national movement.

Difai (Defense) was a secret Ganje organization formed in 1905 in the wake of communal violence. According to one Difai leader, Naki Keykurun,[70] Difai was created by local intellectuals as a counterterror organization in response to the well-organized Dashnaktsutun and the Russian support for the Armenians. Among the founders were prominent Ganje intellectuals Aliakper and Khalil Khasmemetli, Nasib Yusufbeyli, and Dr. Hasan Agaoglu.[71] These men were among the community leaders who had taken the lead in ending the conflicts between their own community and the Armenians. The Ganje Azerbaijanis argued that the Dashnaks could not operate so freely without Russian backing and that the Administration, in fact, provoked intercommunal clashes. Ismail Ziyatkhan(ov), elected to the first State Duma and possible cofounder of Difai, described Russian policy:

> We, the Muslims were told by the administration . . . [Armenians] are arming themselves and plan to create their state; one day they will do away with you. The Armenians were told that the idea of Pan-Islamism had put down deep roots in all strata of the Muslim community, and one day the Muslims would massacre them. Such was the pattern of provocation. . . . In the past there had not been any armed clashes and if cases of murder happened, they were single exceptions and had never assumed any large proportions.[72]

Difai efforts were therefore directed against the Russian Administration. The Ganje governor's counsel, Kirijinskii, was assassinated first, then in Tiflis General Kalasjapov, who had been division commander in Karabagh. He was believed to have dressed Armenian soldiers from his division in civilian clothes to shoot Azerbaijani Turks. Difai took responsibility for the assassinations by displaying posters with the Difai seal. These deaths, Keykurun wrote, shook the Russian Administration and "caused them to be more reasonable." Despite home searches and a reward of 50 gold rubles, the authorities were unable to discover the identity of the Difai leadership. Reportedly, Difai had members in the Russian Administration and a sympathizer in the Russian secret service office. The latter revealed to Difai a plan to use a phony mullah to penetrate the community and gain information about Difai. When the "mullah" was assassinated, no local mullahs would say prayers over him. Difai carried out attacks against the Russian Administration from 1906 to 1909.[73]

After 1905 a National Committee (*Milli komite*) was established in Ganje, reportedly to "administer all-out efforts," overt and covert, against the Russian Administration. The chairman of the Executive Committee was Nasib Yusufbeyli,[74] prominent writer-publisher and cofounder of Difai in charge of covert affairs.[75] The secular character of the National Committee was demonstrated in a confrontation with the local religious establishment. Keykurun described the formation by Ganje mullahs of a political organization, called the Muhammediyye party, which claimed that Nasib Bey and other national leaders did not believe in the Koran. In a public meeting the National Committee refuted the charges and, reportedly with popular support, forced the mullahs to stay in mosques and deal exclusively with religious matters.[76]

The diversity of Azerbaijan's political action was reflected in the deputies elected to the first and second State Dumas.[77] At the former, Topchibashi,[78] Ziyatkhanov, and Aliakper Khasmemetli were among six Muslim deputies; at the latter, Ismail Taghiyev (Haji Zeinal Abedin's son), Kalil Khasmemetli (Aliakper's brother), Khan Khoiskii (then in the Ittifaq), and Hümmetist Zeynal Zeynalov (who joined the Muslim Labor Group) were the only four "Muslim deputies" from Transcaucasia. Their speeches reflected discontent with colonial status and the settlement of Russian peasants; and they demanded zemstvos, land reform, and various legal guarantees.

Despite the disappointments of the State Dumas and the fruitlessness of the Ittifaq-Kadet alliance, many Azerbaijani Turks retained their faith in a constitutional order. They were encouraged by the constitutions of neighboring Iran (1906) and the Ottoman Empire (1908).[79] They also saw a precedent in Islamic exhortations for "consultation"[80] and perhaps in the actual practice of early Turkish states.[81]

One prominent spokesman for the compatibility between Islam and democratic government was publicist Ahmet Aghayev. During an extended trip to the Ottoman Empire beginning in 1909, Aghayev wrote a series of "Letters from Turkey" published in *Kaspii*. One set was called "Islam and Despotism." He noted that some Russians and Europeans saw Islam as the enemy of culture and progress and that this created an environment that led to "unfair mistakes" in relations with Muslims. Aghayev discussed the common bases of the three major monotheistic religions, their belief in one God and in the triumph of good over evil. He argued that religion, like art or science, is a force that can be used for good or evil and noted that Catholicism in the Middle Ages opposed science and independent thought. In the same way, he wrote, Islam began as an enlightened religion but fell into the hands of those who used it as an evil force. The Koran was no more responsible for the errors of Muslims than the Bible was for the Inquisition.[82]

Aghayev's respect for Islamic ideals led him to argue for the education of Muslims in their own religion and for its development and *Weltanschauung*. But he clearly had in mind a "reformed" Islam, which would put aside sectarian differences and use secular learning to provide a viable basis for cultural revival and some degree of unity against Russian colonial pressure. Aghayev seems to have been thinking only of Turkish Muslims. In 1905 he wrote in *Hayat* that Arabs were responsible for "destroying the luster of Islam, filling the pages of its history with blood." He attributed the salvation of Islam to the non-Arabs who embraced it—thereby refuting occasional references[83] to him as a "Pan-Islamist[84]"—and to the inherent strength of Islam itself.[85]

Although Aghayev's support of Islam was perhaps greater than that of his colleagues, his cooperation with socialists was not unusual. He lauded *Tekamül's* "sacred ideas," saying that if there were a few more such newspapers, "our workers, our village toilers," would not be suffering.[86] He spoke at workers' rallies on the same platform with local Social Democrats, calling for resistance to the "Russian knout" and unity "under the banner of nationalism."[87] The softening of Aghayev's Shi'i identity, the pro-Iranian proclivities he expressed in his youth while studying in Paris, and the embracing of his ethnic Turkish identity[88] were symbolic of the evolving identity of many Azerbaijani Turks under Russian rule. The matter is one of degree, rather than of forsaking one identity for another.

Islam had powerful political implications for the entire community. For more than three hundred years, the Shi'i-Sunni split had strengthened the ties of Caucasian Turkish Muslims to Iran while separating them from fellow Turks in Crimea, the Volga, the Ottoman Empire, and Central Asia. It had even divided Azerbaijani Turks internally. Leaders of the embryonic national movement sought to raise national over religious consciousness. Yet they, and even the Social Democrats, had to employ the rhetoric of Islamic unity (with the anticolonial appeals of socialism and of guarantees of rights) to attract the bulk of the Azerbaijani population who had, as yet, little ethnic consciousness.

Ethnic identity was linked in part to the Ottoman Turks. Publicist and editor Ali Huseinzade, like Aghayev, advocated closer ties to the Ottoman Empire and the use of modified Ottoman Turkish in the Azerbaijani press.[89] Huseinzade had been a student at Istanbul's Military Medical School in the 1890s. He stressed the fundamental cultural and linguistic bonds among Turks rather than contemporary issues, which, like borders and administrative classifications, divided them. His poem "Turan," written during his student days, was the first poetic call to an ethnic-based unity of Turks.[90]

Huseinzade formulated the slogan "Türkleshmek, Islamlashmak, Avrupali-lashmak," an exhortation to the Muslim Turks to "be inspired by the Turkish way of life, to worship God in accordance with the Muslim religion, and to adopt present-day European civilization." Huseinzade's appeal symbolized the efforts of many intellectuals in Azerbaijan as well as throughout the Russian and Ottoman empires not only to reconcile but to amalgamate aspects of diverse cultures.

The Turkist cultural movement is not to be confused with a chimerical Pan-Turkism or Pan-Turanianism. The notion of the political unity of all Turks "from the Bosphorus to the Chinese wall" was formulated in the 1860s by Arminius Vambery, a Hungarian orientalist.[91] Articulated at the height of the "Great Game in Asia" when the English and Russians were vying for control over vast territories between the Russian-controlled steppe and British-dominated Afghanistan, the idea was attributed to the Turks them-selves and called "their" blueprint for world conquest. As a "menace" to the West, the Turks had to be stopped, Britain argued. Vambery was then working for British intelligence.[92] British officers worked to perpetuate this fear of a united Turkish state during World War I.[93] It was perpetuated by the Russian side in the Great Game, and even by "liberals" like A. N. Mandel'shtam and Alexander Kerensky in emigration after 1917.[94] Political Pan-Turkism had been advocated by Enver Pasha of the Young Turk triumvirate but had few followers in Azerbaijan.[95]

Most Azerbaijani intelligentsia recognized their identity as Turks but worked consciously to build a Turkish identity that was particularly Azer-baijani. An early example of this effort came in 1891 in the newspaper *Kashkül*.[96] In a fictitious dialogue, one speaker said he was "a Muslim and also a Turk" but not an Ottoman. Without the "Azeris" on the Iranian side of the border, he was "*bijanli*," or "soulless" (a play on Azer-baijanli). In one stroke, the writer conveys a distinction between religious and national identity while marrying the idea of Turkishness to the Azerbaijan land. He reflects the yearning for reunion with conationals in Iran, without whom the speaker's identity is incomplete. It suggests he call himself "Azerbaijani Turk," implying political, spiritual "reunion."

Turkish ethnic identity was expressed subtly in the arts and intellectual life. Akhundzade used Turkish in his mid-century plays rather than Persian, then the language of "high culture." Uzeir Hajibeyli used Fuzuli's Turkish-language *Leyle and Majnun* as the basis for his opera, rather than Persian-language versions. Poet and dramatist Husein Javid, living in Istanbul, wrote about Timur and the dastan *Köroglu*. As in education reform, in book publishing Azerbaijani Turkish became increasingly common. In 1912 the Petersburg newspaper *Mir Islama* carried a debate on the merits of Turk or Tatar as labels.

From 1905 on Azerbaijani Turks focused and acted on Azerbaijan's own political and economic needs within the Russian Empire, separating themselves from numerous natural allies against Russian colonialism and creating the same culturally artificial barriers as Shi'ism had. Azerbaijanis maintained some links and a short-lived political coordination with other Turks in the Russian Empire (in the Muslim congresses, the Ittifaq, and the "Muslim fraction" of the State Dumas). The primacy of local demands kept them from going beyond statements of general aims and loose coalitions. Only briefly after the fall of the Romanov dynasty would sentiments for unity with the Ottoman Empire surface and then only among a few. Rejecting political unity with other Turks would later be a major element delimiting the national program of the Azerbaijan republic. Molding a self-conscious community was a more complex process. Southern Azerbaijani Turks, a "natural constituency" for the northern elite, shared none of the economic or political pressures of industrialization and Russian rule and apparently saw their future in Tehran's orbit.[97] Focusing on the North, the Azerbaijani intelligentsia addressed a society being changed by colonialism and industrialization.

Class conflict did exist within the Azerbaijani community but did not lead to class solidarity across national lines. Azerbaijani workers might strike Azerbaijani owners, but solidarity with Russian or Armenian workers was infrequent and short-lived. In the countryside the presence of Russian settlers muted clashes between local peasants and landowners. For the industrialists, despite their inflexibility during strikes, competition with the Armenian bourgeoisie drove a wedge between the Azerbaijani and Armenian middle classes that was greater than that between the upper and lower classes within the Azerbaijani community. Commercial competition reinforced the gulf created by discrimination at the political level. As for intra-elite conflict within the Azerbaijani community, one finds little. At times, Social Democrats criticized the industrialists and supported the economic needs of the workers or peasants. Such clashes were confined mainly to Baku, but no estrangement appeared. The two groups continued to cooperate throughout the prewar period. For all classes, separateness from other communities and a colonial status in their own homeland provided a basis for national unity.

The Azerbaijani Turkish intellectual and commercial elites were forging that unity by defining a national community in their published and performed works and by trying to incorporate all classes into it. This concern lay at the root of their support for education and cultural-literacy societies. Like many workers, members of the upper classes came from the village. They tried to educate the working people and their children for white-collar, managerial, and, ultimately, professional and intellectual careers. The lower classes would be consumers, employees, and conscious supporters against external pressures. Ultimately, national unity consisted of more than filling jobs. The bookkeeper must be able not only to keep the books, but he ought to read national poetry and attend the national opera. Thus, Baku millionaires financed schools and theaters.

The establishment of a secular, ethnic identity was therefore a process of reaction to discrimination and pressure on one hand and, on the other, of bolstering awareness of the salient elements of history and culture. The elites worked to mobilize this conscious people to political action, drawing on the anticolonial impetus of socialism and the appeal to civil and political rights of liberalism, while rooted firmly in Turkish values and cultural norms and reformed Islam. No community could be formed that strove only to imitate others.

Jeyhun Hajibeyli, writing under the name Dzhey Daghestani or simply Daghestani, was a frequent contributor to *Kaspii*, even while studying in Paris. Jeyhun Bey, a native of Shusha in Karabagh, was multilingual in Turkish, Persian, French, and Russian and received his advanced education in St. Petersburg and Paris. But he understood that his intimacy with Russian and French language and culture was an asset but that he did not have to assimilate into those cultures. He criticized his countrymen who surrendered themselves to European fashion, abandoning their native and ancient Turkish culture, in this description of an "intellectual":

> In his native language he is illiterate. . . . In all that is native, national, he sees only signs of "excessive human stupidity." He looks down at his nation, deeply scorning it for its ignorance. He does not like the native literature because he does not know it. He does not like the native speech because it may "compromise" him in the eyes of the Europeans. He does not like native music because he cannot understand it, but condemns it as defective and savage before the European [music] of which he understands nothing; [he] tries to show himself an expert in all that seems European.[98]

Jeyhun Bey here made an explicit connection between knowing one's own culture and having a secure identity. Not to know one's own culture is to be disconnected from the people and from the historical past; not to know is to make one's self ridiculous. He defined the intellectual in terms of history and culture.

The national forces in Baku eventually coalesced into a political party, the Musavat (Equality); called the Muslim Democratic party, it was founded in 1911 or 1912. Because it was inactive before the October Revolution, some postrevolutionary historians claim it did not exist until 1917.[99] Nonetheless, the group had a program and statutes as early as 1912.[100] Soviet historians, writing in the 1920s, attributed a militant Islamic program to the Musavat. From 1913 its leader was former Hümmetist Mehmet Emin Rasulzade. Having fled Baku in 1908, he had published a proconstitution newspaper in Tehran but was forced to leave Iran owing to Russian pressure on the shah's government. He went to Istanbul and became committed to Turkism. With the 1913 amnesty, granted to commemorate the 300th anniversary of Romanov rule, he returned to Baku. Except for Rasulzade's participation, almost nothing is known about the early Musavat. Although the party was vocally pro-Ottoman before World War I began, it maintained public neutrality after 1914 and supported the tsarist empire. The Musavat became an important political group only after 1917.

5 War, Revolution, and Independence

*Then the Turkish common people apparently said as fol-
lows: "We used to be a people who had an independent
state. Where is our own state now? . . . We used to be a
people who had its own kagan [ruler]. Where is our kagan
now? To which kagan are we giving our services?"*

Kül Tegin inscription

The beginning of the war in Europe in 1914 appeared to have little impact
on the Azerbaijani Turks. The entrance of the Ottoman Empire and, later,
two revolutions within the Russian Empire, however, paved the way for
Azerbaijan's independence.

WARTIME HARDSHIPS

Despite general mobilization, Azerbaijani Turks, as Muslims, were
exempt from conscription. Anecdotal evidence suggests that they were not
particularly interested in a war so far from home, although public figures,
the press, and the Musavat party expressed support for the empire.[1] A few
prominent army officers were Azerbaijani, including General Khan-Nak-
hichevanskii, but their careers antedated this war. Because of deferments for
many skilled oil workers, conscription also touched the Christian workers in

Baku very little. Only about 20 percent of oil-related workers were drafted between 1914 and 1917, and the industry as a whole was not seriously hurt by mobilization. Turnover of the labor force appears to have been much more rapid during the war years, however, especially among the mostly Muslim field workers. The newest workers left their jobs most often.[2] As before, rural populations were still being exposed for short periods to industrial life, and workers functioned as conduits to the countryside.

Mobilization curtailed the labor movement and the social democratic organization in Baku. By 1915 little of it was left, though Armenian Bolshevik Stepan Shaumian wrote to Lenin that "respectable work goes on in legal organizations." The Bolsheviks had a lackluster conference in October 1915; Shaumian noted the "absence of interest on the part of the broad masses." By the end of the year, most labor leaders and Bolsheviks had been arrested or had gone elsewhere. Workers subject to conscription were less involved in strikes.[3]

As always, Baku oil was of critical importance to the empire. Shortages of coal led many companies to convert heating systems to oil.[4] By an imperial order of 4 March 1915, Nicholas II charged Minister of Communications S. V. Rukhlov with ensuring delivery of fuel to the military and industry. On 31 March the Council of Ministers instituted several measures. Where martial law or a state of emergency was in force (as in Caucasia), mineral fuel extractors were required to fill orders from the Ministry of Communications first; they were "freed from obligations" to other customers. A Committee for the Distribution of Fuel was formed with representatives of various ministries, the military, and industries.[5]

The price of oil went up: crude oil had been just 28⅜ kopeks/pud in January 1915 but was up to 43⅜ by mid-March. Shipping firms along the Volga demanded price controls. A delegation from Kazan asked Minister of Trade and Industry Prince V. N. Shakhovskii to fix oil prices at 25–27 kopeks/pud at the place of extraction, a rollback to the January 1915 price. Shakhovskii set the price at 40 kopeks. Price controls would be a last resort, and oil prices would be decided only in consultation with producers.[6] Shakhovskii had such consultations. He requested that the oilmen guarantee him a price ceiling at 40½. The owners said they would do so if he would guarantee them that oil enterprises would work without interruption, without strikes, and that there would be no depletion of oil lands or other interference with extraction, refining, and delivery.[7] No deal was ever struck. Oilmen disregarded government decrees while they argued with state agencies. In February 1917 the legal price was more than 95 kopeks/pud.[8] The Nobel Company, however, made an agreement with Volga customers in 1915 to sell oil in Baku at 38 kopeks/pud (excluding transportation costs).[9] Apparently, the industrialists objected to regulation rather than a special price for good customers.

Prices of consumer goods rose as well. In Baku "between September 1914 and January 1917, the price of bread rose 100 percent, sugar 51 percent, milk 205 percent, and eggs 292 percent." Increases in wages did not keep up.[10] The rural population was at least able to produce for its own consumption, but military requisitions from the countryside had a serious impact on the rural population and on the towns and cities they were to supply. Food riots broke out in the towns in each year of the war and strikes resumed during 1916.[11]

The Ottoman Empire entered the war in November 1914. If private attitudes changed, public statements remained loyal to the Russian state as long as the empire fought.[12] Azerbaijan was, however, the object of Ottoman aims, especially of the minority in the government who had supported entering the war on the German side.[13] Most prominent among these was Ottoman minister of war Enver Pasha, whose German training greatly influenced his strategy and tactics. Even his aim, to create a great "Turanian" state by uniting the Ottoman Turks with Turks in Caucasia and Central Asia, reflected German aims. He made contact with political groups in Azerbaijan. Those who spoke with him, including members of Difai and the National Committee at Ganje, placed independence at the top of their own political agenda and were disturbed by Enver's refusal to acquiesce.[14]

The Ottoman forces' Caucasus campaign began under the command of Enver's young uncle, Halil Bey, whose task was to reach the Caspian by a sweep through northern Iran, isolating the Russian forces.[15] Despite initial Ottoman victories in November 1914, a defeat at Sarikamish in eastern Asia Minor during December and January was costly both in lives and in demoralizing the Ottoman forces. Until 1917 Russian troops, supported by Armenian irregulars, maintained the upper hand, even establishing the core of an Armenian state in the city of Van during 1915 in the wake of the April deportations.[16] In January 1915 Ottoman forces took, then lost, Tabriz to Russian forces. They attempted to move against Tabriz later that spring but were stopped at Khoi, just south of Nakhjivan. In the spring of 1916 the towns of Erzerum and Trabzon were captured by the Russians, who held eastern Asia Minor until 1917. Casualties on the Caucasian front increased each year: 2,621 killed and over 15,000 wounded in 1914 on the Russian side; 3,086 killed and over 18,000 wounded in 1915; 9,913 killed and over 91,000 wounded in 1916. Total losses, killed and wounded, reached 146,998 soldiers and officers in the Russian imperial army.[17]

In all the military operations, the loss of civilian life, which sometimes was taken deliberately, was enormous among all communities. The tiny Laz and Ajar populations in and near Georgia were massacred by Russian forces for their support of the Ottomans; of 52,000, only 7,000 remained alive.[18] The anti-Turkish and anti-Muslim tenor of Russian rule, especially under the long tenure of Viceroy Vorontsov-Dashkov, was manifested in attacks on Azerbaijani villages in western Caucasia. State Duma representative Muhammed Jafar castigated Russian brutality in a speech to the Fourth Duma:

> In Transcaucasia this policy [of repression] has found its expression in open incitement against non-Russian nationalities in provinces either immediately affected by military operations or situated in the rear of the Caucasus Front. There, behind the roar of battle, horrible things have been perpetrated on the utterly helpless, peaceful Muslim population. Its lives and property are in jeopardy. The extortion, robbery, and murder of Muslims have become a matter of everyday occurrence. Wholesale expulsions of the male population, violation of the unprotected women left behind, ruined and devastated villages, an impoverished, hungry, terror-stricken and unprovided-for population—this is the situation of the Muslims in the region. We are in possession of facts and official data confirming every word that I have said . . . local and central authorities have been placed in possession of these facts but nevertheless, nothing has changed.[19]

In September 1915, shortly after Jafar's Duma speech, Vorontsov-Dashkov retired and was replaced by Grand Duke Nicholai Nikolaevich, who tried to improve relations with the Azerbaijanis. He permitted Musavat leader Mehmet Emin Rasulzade to publish the newspaper *Achik Söz* (*The Candid Word*). The newspaper continued to express support for the Russian effort, suggesting "Muslim citizens" work for the good of the empire. It was a position that Rasulzade's Bolshevik successors would ridicule, comparing Musavat's moderation to the aggressive national parties of Azerbaijan's neighbors.[20] *Achik Söz* reiterated the cultural demands that had been the hallmark of the prewar renaissance, highlighting the need for more schools.[21]

Achik Söz reflected the lingering political and philosophical dilemma of the Azerbaijani Turkish intelligentsia of Baku:

> Until the present time, there was no social idea among the Muslims, no clear final thought (idea) or final goal (ideal) worked out for the battle for national and social life . . . a huge majority of the intelligentsia also and the rest of the mass of the nation numbering in the millions, . . . know nothing about the idea or the ideal of the nation. . . . If there existed a defined idea and supported program, then undoubtedly the battle would be carried out differently for that idea and ideal would be nothing other than a compass for the action of every individual. For [lack of such an idea and program] we . . . remain without a compass; we do not know where to go and from where to seek aid, and our society, like a group of lunatics, fights among itself.[22]

The political climate in Ganje, however, was markedly different from that in Baku. In 1916 the Ganje leaders of the National Committee negotiated with the viceroy on the terms of military service. The Azerbaijani Turks desired active military service—in combat, not labor battalions—so that they, like their neighbors, would have military training. Proposals for significant military service were made in the second Duma by representatives Halil Khasmemetli and Ismail Khan (grandson of the last Ganje khan) but were rejected by the regime. In 1916 the state decided to conscript Muslims in Caucasia, as in Central Asia, into labor battalions. Three community leaders from Ganje went to Tiflis to meet with the viceroy to argue in favor of combat service.[23]

The group included Khasmemetli and Ismail Khan and one of the elder statesman of the community, Ali Ekper Rafibeyli. Rafibeyli, then seventy, had served in the Russian civil service all his life and had been awarded the Order of Stanislav. Rafibeyli told the viceroy: "The government has treated us with contempt. . . . For every hundred schools you built for our neighbors, the Georgians and Armenians, you built one for us. You have created an unlettered population and sown hatred among us, which you now reap." The viceroy admitted that the official treatment of the Caucasus Turks had been discriminatory and asked Ali Ekper Bey's recommendation. Rafibeyli suggested that the Azerbaijani Turks be allowed to volunteer into cavalry regiments, the only type of service that would be "honorable." The viceroy agreed and six regiments were formed. The Russians called these the Wild Division because they were not professional soldiers though the division had some Azerbaijani officers.[24]

The behavior of Rasulzade and other Baku-based national leaders on one hand and that of Rafibeyli and the Ganje group on the other reflected a deep cleavage between Baku and the rest of Azerbaijan, whose interests were more truly reflected by the Ganje leadership. In Baku non-Turks outnumbered the indigenous Azerbaijanis by the turn of the century. But many intellectuals counted as friends their Russian and Armenian counterparts with whom they shared a belief in the anticolonial and internationalist elements of socialist rhetoric, if not in socialism itself. The Azerbaijani national movement in Baku reflected this, and Azerbaijani Turkish intellectuals seemed to regard tsarism and the militant Armenian party Dashnaksutun as the enemy, not Russians and Armenians. In this spirit, they were willing to cooperate with all who articulated anticolonial and reformist policies. Azerbaijani national leaders would be taken by surprise when socialists of other nationalities, despite their rhetoric, displayed the same anti-Turkish and anti-Muslim prejudices as their "conservative" conationals. Committed to cooperation, even with hostile Bolsheviks, the Azerbaijanis in Baku diluted the force of the national movement in that city. Ganje, which became the center of the national movement, faced no socialist influence. The local population had already begun to call itself "Azerbaijani Turk" by 1897. Ganje leaders exhibited clarity of ideals and program that Rasulzade longed to see in Baku.

FEBRUARY 1917 REVOLUTION[25]

The fall of the monarchy brought about the resignation of the viceroy[26] and the emergence of multiple power centers. The Special Transcaucasian Committee (Osobyi Zakavkazskii Komitet, *Ozakom*) represented the Provisional Government. It included Russians and members of the three major nationalities in Caucasia and did little more than introduce the long-demanded zemstvos and approve legislation promulgated by competing political bodies. Among these competitors were soviets and national political parties. The two major soviets in Caucasia were in Tiflis and Baku; the main parties were the Azerbaijani Musavat and the Turk Federalist People's party (Türk Ademi-merkeziyet Halk Firkasi), which would later merge, and the Armenian Dashnaksutun. Smaller parties and cultural organizations were the branches of the Kadets and Socialist Revolutionaries (SRs) and the Bolsheviks and Mensheviks, who, with some SRs, were represented on soviets. Mensheviks dominated the Tiflis soviet; Bolsheviks, powerful in Baku, came to control the Baku soviet in 1918.

The city of Baku, because of its multinational population, reflected the Caucasian spectrum of political life and struggle. It was to some extent unrepresentative of the rest of Azerbaijan, for the Azerbaijani Turks of Baku were increasingly excluded from political life. An Executive Committee of Social Organizations, ECSO (Ispolnitel'nyi Komitet Obshchestvennykh Organizatsii, *IKOO*), for example, was formed by order of the Provisional Government. Its members, appointed by Baku's Russian mayor, L. L. Bych, included few Azerbaijanis. It had three representatives each from the Dashnak, Social Democratic (SD), and SR parties but none from the Musavat; five each from the Russian-dominated trade unions, cooperatives, and the Soviet of Soldiers' Deputies; and twelve from the Soviet of Workers' Deputies. Each ethno-religious community had one representative, so Poles and Molokans were represented equally with Muslims. There was one priest, but no mullah.[27] The Baku Soviet of Workers' Deputies also reflected nonnative power. Its fifty-two delegates—SRs, SDs, and Dashnaks—organized themselves in the Armenian Humanitarian Society building. Shaumian, an Armenian Bolshevik, was elected its head in absentia. The Musavat was excluded from its sessions for at least four months. The Hümmet, despite its long association with the Baku Committee of the RSDWP, was also apparently unwelcome: "Until October, the soviet represented primarily the Russian workers and soldiers and part of the Armenian community." The soviet and the Executive Committee began cooperative coexistence.[28]

The picture in Ganje was different.[29] The Ganje ECSO was organized by the mayor, Halil Bey Khasmemedli, beginning with twenty-five Azerbaijani Turkish[30] and twenty-five Armenian representatives, although as in Baku the latter were a minority in the city. During a debate decisions were made to add other members to the ECSO. At the suggestion of Halil Bey, they agreed to accept from among artisans and trade organizations one Turk (Keykurun's usage) and one Armenian from each group. When the representation of political parties was discussed, an Armenian socialist requested that two members from each of the two major socialist parties be added. Of the four men he proposed, two were Russian, one Armenian, one Georgian, all "veteran socialists." One of the Turks argued that such representation was appropriate for a socialist area, not a "nationalist" one. This guberniia, he said, should have national leadership. Turks and Armenians elected from those socialist parties should concern themselves only with matters of the guberniia and the local people. They should sever all relations with the headquarters of the respective socialist parties. This view prevailed at the meeting, and the men were not accepted.

Petitions from Russians living in Ganje and from soldiers' deputies asking to be admitted into the ECSO (to represent 15,000 soldiers in the city) were rejected. The Azerbaijani Turks declared that Russian soldiers "have no business" in Ganje and that one of the first duties of the Ganje ECSO would be sending them back to Russia. If the troops refused to go, they would be disarmed and turned over to the railroad administration for expulsion.

As representatives of the Azerbaijani Turks' and Armenians' national parties, members from the Turk Federalist Party and the Armenian Dashnaksutun were accepted. When an Armenian argued that the other important Armenian party, Hunchak,[31] should be represented, Keykurun quietly told a friend to agree on condition that Difai, which had been disbanded, also be admitted. Keykurun himself was proposed as representative. The quid pro quo was accepted.[32]

The Turks of Ganje, unlike their counterparts in Baku, showed firm resolve and a clear grasp of their own political goals and the realities of power. They succeeded in excluding the Russians, both settlers and soldiers, from political participation, thereby proclaiming the illegitimacy of the Russian presence. By insisting on de facto revival and representation of the Difai party in return for Hunchak representation on the Ganje ECSO, Azerbaijani Turks showed they were unwilling to place themselves at a disadvantage. After the meeting Keykurun and others began organizing local branches of the Difai. Anticipating a struggle with armed neighbors, the local branches provided military training. Within two months, wrote Keykurun, Ganje had a fighting force.[33]

Between 15 and 20 April 1917, the first Congress of Caucasian Muslims took place in Baku.[34] The Musavat, whose strength was mainly in Baku, and the Federalist party, centered in Ganje but popular elsewhere in Azerbaijan, agreed that a "new Russia" ought to be "democratic, representative Russia, organized on the territorial-federal principal." This position won the support of the congress and was brought before the All-Russian Muslim Congress by Rasulzade the next month.[35] The two parties agreed upon a new cultural program, calling for the creation of a university in Baku with native language instruction. Baku University would open in September 1919 but would lose its native character after sovietization.

This April congress laid the groundwork for the subsequent merger of the Musavat and the Federalist parties on the basis of shared principles. Ganje's Nasib Yusufbeyli articulated them as "nationalism, Türkchülük ["Turk-ness"], *halkchilik* [populism] and modernization." Differences did exist between the parties, especially concerning land reform, but they soon merged officially as Türk Ademi-merkeziyet Partisi—Musavat," or simply Musavat.[36] The original Musavatists would, during 1917, abandon their insistence on the socialist-inspired demand that expropriated land be distributed to the peasantry and would accept the Federalists' position requiring compensation to landowners, many of whom were active in that party.[37] Yusubeyli himself would later become minister of education and twice prime minister of the Azerbaijan Democratic Republic.

At the same time that major Azerbaijan parties were merging,[38] the Social Democrats in Caucasia were splitting into Menshevik and Bolshevik organizations. The Hümmet also was affected. Narimanov and other Azerbaijani Bolsheviks in Baku, both those who had been members of the RSDWP and those who had only been in the Hümmet, went with the Russian Bolshevik organization, while the Azerbaijanis in Tiflis and elsewhere in the region sided with the Mensheviks. The split, however, was not firm and the two groups continued to cooperate, maintaining joint representation as late as December 1917 at the Muslim Socialist Congress of the Caucasus. The Bolsheviks in Baku, mainly Russians and Armenians, were not entirely receptive to their Azerbaijani colleagues. Hümmet did not participate in elections to the soviet. Although some individuals were accepted into the Baku soviet on the basis of their RSDWP membership (Meshadi Azizbeyov, for example), the Hümmet as an organization was not represented in the soviet.[39]

The Baku soviet, intent on seizing power and isolating the native Azerbaijani Turks, also excluded the Musavat, despite that party's endorsement of the program of Russian socialist parties. The Council of Muslim Public

Associations, an umbrella organization for more than a half dozen Azerbaijani associations, complained that the soviet did not represent the largest group of workers, the Muslims. When the Musavat received the largest number of votes, more than twice that of the Bolsheviks, in October elections to the soviet, the Bolsheviks alleged election-law violations. They succeeded in nullifying the election results de facto and continued to operate in a "broadened soviet," which the Bolsheviks had padded with their supporters from district soviets, factory committees, and the military.[40] December elections under different conditions put the Musavat second to last and the Bolsheviks in the lead.[41]

Complicating conditions were food shortages and the accelerating collapse of the front, with deserting Russian soldiers traveling through Caucasia to Russia. Bolsheviks tried to recruit them into Red detachments with some success and Azerbaijanis tried to disarm them.[42] The problems related to these soldiers would sharpen after October 1917.

Elections to the Constituent Assembly in October 1917 revealed the differences between the city of Baku (with its adjacent oil districts) and the rest of the Baku uezd, guberniia, and Azerbaijan as a whole. In the city the most votes were won by the Bolsheviks, the Musavat, and the Dashnaks in that order, with first and third places separated by only 2,000 votes (of 111,050 cast). As in the October elections to the soviet, the garrison voted Bolshevik; its 7,699 votes put the Bolsheviks in first place, thereby vindicating the Ganje leadership's decision to exclude the Russian garrison from political participation. Elsewhere in the uezd, Ittihad, with its anti-imperial platform, won a huge victory; in the Baku guberniia, the big winners were the Musavat and Ittihad parties, with only a fraction of votes going to the SRs or Bolsheviks. In Transcaucasia as a whole, the Mensheviks, Musavat, and Dashnaks took the top three places, with the Azerbaijani parties getting about 30 percent or double the votes of the Bolsheviks.[43] The city of Baku was indeed a Russian and Armenian island but not a purely socialist one. Azerbaijanis regarded it as a colonial outpost in their country where foreigners stationed troops, controlled natural wealth, and wielded political power.

EFFECTS OF THE BOLSHEVIK COUP OF OCTOBER 1917

On 30 October/11 November,* the Transcaucasian Commissariat (Zakavkaz'skii Komisariat) was created to replace the Ozakom and administer Caucasia until the Constituent Assembly convened. In Baku the City

---

*Until March 1918, when the Bolsheviks brought their calendar into line with the

Council continued to operate. New elections produced an influential if small Bolshevik bloc.[44] The Baku soviet was divided by the Bolshevik coup in Petrograd. Mensheviks, Dashnaks, and right-wing SRs created a Committee of Public Safety to avert a Bolshevik takeover in the city, although they continued simultaneously to participate in the Bolshevik-dominated soviet. In the "broadened" soviet, Shaumian attempted to win passage of a resolution to transfer all power to itself. The Left SRs joined the Bolsheviks calling for support of Lenin; the Right SRs subsequently walked out of the soviet. The Musavat, despite exclusion from the soviet, refrained from joining the Committee of Public Safety. It stated its support for "revolutionary democracy" and argued against attempts to "crush the Bolsheviks." The Baku branch of the Musavat thus accepted the continuation of an uneasy modus vivendi with the Bolsheviks.[45]

The Bolsheviks, because of their control of the Baku soviet, their disproportionate influence in the City Council, and, most important of all, their command of the loyalty of the Baku garrison, became the most effective power in Baku. As an SR newspaper pointed out, "power no longer meant legal authority but rather real force."[46] Attempts by the City Council to claim power for itself and to organize countervailing bodies were not successful while the soldiers supported the Bolsheviks and the Bolsheviks were willing to use force. By year's end, the Bolsheviks had secured full support of the Left SRs and the Dashnaks. Although the garrison was disintegrating, the soldiers' section of the Baku soviet had decided in November to form a Red Guard unit. In January 1918 the Military-Revolutionary Committee of the Caucasian Army arrived from Tiflis and contributed men and weapons to the Red Guards; it also trained them.[47] The Red Guards represented Soviet, that is, Russian-Armenian, power, despite their "international" designation.

Because the Georgians, Armenians, and Azerbaijanis had armed national units, all Caucasia was set for armed conflict. In December the Armenians selected Andranik to command their forces in the West; Armenians in Baku organized under the local Dashnaks. The Azerbaijanis were least prepared because of their long exclusion from military service and a lack of equipment, training, and arms. Alexander Kerenskii, prime minister of the last Provisional Government, had earlier approved the formation of national units but had reportedly denied equipment and arms to the Azerbaijanis. With the collapse of the front in late 1917 and early 1918, the French and British, to bolster the frontier against Ottoman forces, encouraged formation of one corps each from Georgian, Armenian, and Azerbaijani communities. It appears that they financed and armed only the Georgians and the Armenians,

---

West (Gregorian), they used the Julian calendar. Thus, for this period, both dates are given, the first Julian, the second Gregorian.

however, telling the Azerbaijanis "to take weapons of Russians going through Azerbaijan."[48] With their neighbors armed (the Azerbaijanis were particularly fearful of the well-armed Armenian units in Baku and throughout the countryside)[49] and as Bolsheviks in Baku built up "international" Red Guard units, the Azerbaijani Turks increasingly relied on disarming Russian soldiers to gain weapons.

Two incidents in which Azerbaijanis disarmed Russian troops have been reported quite differently in Russian and Azerbaijani sources. The first concerned the disarming of the 218th and 219th regiments in Ganje in December 1917. The Soviet historian Sef, whose work is cited by Western historians,[50] described the disarming as follows: "The local organizations in Elizavetpol, including the Executive Committee of the Elizavetpol soviet, . . . were completely capable of protecting the city." He stated that the General Staff of the Caucasian front ordered the regiment to surrender its weapons for a "Tatar regiment being formed" and that the "Moslem National Council carried out the disarmament by force. . . . Everything down to their underwear was taken from the soldiers, who were then sent to the railroad station."

Keykurun's account agrees on two points only: the soldiers were disarmed and they were sent to the railroad station.[51] Keykurun mentions no soviet. He called the national organization the Ganje National Committee (Ganje Milli Komite), not the Muslim National Council, and called the city by its traditional name.

As for the incident itself, Keykurun provided minute detail. In Ganje there were two Russian reserve regiments, the 218th and 219th, whose soldiers had formed a joint military representation with local Armenians. They hoped to gain political control of Ganje, he said. The arrival in December 1917 of a cossack cavalry regiment from the front had emboldened the group: "Russian soldiers shot several civilians and in retaliation, several Russian soldiers were killed. That night . . . the mayor called an extraordinary meeting." The chief of the Russian military delegation told the meeting that "starting tomorrow, any civilian seen on the street with weapons will be disarmed and punished." Ganje National Committee spokesman Nasib Yusufbeyli "rose and in booming tones . . . stated . . . 'starting tomorrow, the weapons of any Russian soldiers appearing on the streets will be taken.' These words were loudly applauded." As the soldiers' representatives were leaving the room, the cossack colonel rose to say that he would not support the Russian troops against the local population. The cossacks left town by dawn.

The next day armed Russian soldiers seen on the streets were disarmed and held in a basement of the Umid cotton factory. Sixty Russian soldiers were imprisoned, and the National Committee decided to disarm the rest before sunrise:

By 4 A.M. the barracks were surrounded. . . . I told [the sergeant who opened the gate] the orders of the Committee and told him to surrender. . . . The sergeant asked how we would guarantee their lives. Loudly, so both sides could hear, I said, "The population that have surrounded you and are taking your weapons are Turks. . . . They possess every power and ability, but they are not barbarians. After disarming you we will send you to the railroad station and you will go back to Russia to your home." Those disarmed were sent to the station that day. As a result, no Russian soldiers remained in the city of Ganje. The national Committee had full control.

Azerbaijani Turks also disarmed Russian troops in January 1918 at Shemkir (Shamkhor) station less than 40 kilometers west of Ganje.[52] According to Keykurun, the Russian soldiers attacked as one contingent, coming forward ostensibly to surrender their weapons.

Our people's forces seeing Russian treachery counterattacked; fighting continued until nightfall . . . the Russians started throwing their weapons down and surrendering. The next day, those Russians were put on trains and sent back to Russia. The weapons were distributed to those who had none. We were not jubilant because of the casualties.[53]

Sources agree on the outcome. Numerous Russian casualties and mutual distrust between the two communities contributed to the final rupture of already strained relations between Musavatists and Bolsheviks. It would be the Baku Azerbaijanis who would pay the price in the "March Days."

Throughout January 1918 the Baku City Council continued to lose power while the soviet gained it.[54] By February the soviet established tribunals to replace law courts. Commissars began to oversee banks and other institutions in Baku in a clear usurpation of legitimacy. Rasulzade, like most Azerbaijanis, suspected that the soviet was biased and was arming only Russians and Armenians, whose forces continued to grow. Armenian forces in Baku alone numbered in the thousands. The Dashnaks remained pro-Russian, cooperated with the Bolsheviks, opposed separation from Russia, and "identified counterrevolution, as did the Bolsheviks, with . . . Muslim federalists."[55] So when Shaumian—an Armenian, a Bolshevik, and Lenin's "Extraordinary Commissar" for seizing power in Caucasia—declared in favor of "civil war," the Azerbaijanis understood the desperation of their position. By February there was a complete break between the Musavat and the Baku soviet.[56] In March Shaumian proclaimed that the soviet must "move against counterrevolutionaries."[57] Azerbaijani families fled an increasingly tense Baku.

On 17/30 March the Azerbaijani "Wild Division" arrived at the Baku harbor.[58] The division had already demonstrated its immunity to revolutionary appeals, for it had not broken discipline or turned against its officers;

the men returned home with their mounts, a sign of normalcy.[59] The division had disarmed a pro-Bolshevik garrison in Lenkoran earlier that month. Its presence would tip the power balance in the city, so the Baku soviet sent "inspectors" to their ship. The division was somehow persuaded to disarm. The Azerbaijani community regarded this as an attempt to deprive it of its own force while other communities had large, well-armed units. During the night barricades went up in Muslim quarters in the western half of the city, and on the morning of 18/31 March, Azerbaijani spokesmen demanded that their community be armed like the others.

Events moved quickly. According to the Azerbaijani Bolshevik Nariman Narimanov, Shaumian held talks with Musavatists and agreed to turn the division's arms over to the Hümmet. Other Azerbaijani representatives approached Prokofii Japaridze (Dzhaparidze) with the request for the arms. Shots were fired. Japaridze ended the talks and reportedly called Narimanov to say the "Muslims" had started a "political war." Shaumian later admitted, "We exploited the opportunity of the first armed assault on our cavalry unit and began an attack on the whole front."[60] The 6,000 men of the Baku soviet faced an estimated 10,000 Azerbaijani troops. The Dashnaks, with 4,000 well-armed and experienced troops, joined the soviet force.

The next day, on 19 March/1 April, Bolsheviks decided to use artillery against Azerbaijani residential quarters. Shelling forced immediate capitulation and the acceptance of the soviet's ultimatum: unconditional recognition of the soviet's power and withdrawal of all "Muslim" forces from the city, in return for which Armenian forces were also to be withdrawn.[61] Armenians expressed dissatisfaction at these "mild terms."

After the Azerbaijani representatives accepted the terms, the Dashnaks "took to looting, burning and killing in the Muslim sections of the city."[62] By Shaumian's estimate, more than 3,000 were killed during two days. "The Armenian soldiers became more brutal as resistance subsided, and for a day and a half they looted, killed, and burned."[63] Thousands of Azerbaijani Turks fled the city. The British vice consul in Baku, Major A. E. R. McDonnell, wrote, "not a single Musulman of any importance remain[ed]."[64] The exodus shifted the demographic picture even further in favor of the nonnative elements. The Baku branch of the National Council was disbanded. The Azerbaijanis, from those "March Days" until the following August, would play no political role in Baku.

Now there was no obstacle to soviet control over Baku. On 9 April, all "bourgeois" newspapers were closed down. The soviet's Committee of Revolutionary Defense began to act as the government and assigned administrative duties. Armenians had charge of trade, finance, and food supplies; Narimanov, the sole Azerbaijani, was in charge of "welfare."[65] The soviet demanded 50 million rubles in "tax" for its military campaigns and abolished the "elitist" Naval Aviation School and the City Council.[66] A Bolshevik Sovnarkom (Soviet of Peoples' Commissars) was established. Here, too, Narimanov was the sole Azerbaijani. Shaumian was chairman and commissar of foreign affairs, the Georgian Japaridze was in charge of internal affairs, the Armenian A. B. Karinian (Gabnelian) was in charge of justice, and the Russians were responsible for military-naval affairs, economy, and public education. It is hardly surprising that Azerbaijani Turks regarded soviet power as Russian-Armenian rule.

The image was reinforced by other actions of the Baku soviet. In February the soviet aided Russian settlers on the Mughan steppe in their clashes with Azerbaijani peasants. Even a full year later, Baku Bolsheviks would establish an armed force on Mughan to fight "counterrevolutionaries."[67] Shaumian had insisted on the need for more active establishment of Soviet power but was in fact defending the results of tsarist colonization policy, which the Bolsheviks criticized in the abstract. At the same time to the West, Armenian units "often engaged in massacres of local Muslims."[69] Rasulzade stated publicly that the Bolsheviks favored the Armenian cause while threatening the Musavat. Although Shaumian denied the charge, the Azerbaijani Turks remained unconvinced.[69]

By early March advancing Ottoman forces had already crossed the 1914 Russo-Ottoman border. A delegation from the newly established Transcaucasian Diet met with Ottoman representatives in Trabzon. There they heard the Brest-Litovsk Treaty provisions calling for the return to the Ottoman state of Kars, Ardahan, and Batum, lands taken by Russia in the 1877–1878 war.[70] The Ottoman commander insisted that the Diet representatives, if they were to continue to negotiate, would have to do so as representatives of an independent state.[71] After much hesitation, the representatives declared independence. The Transcaucasian Federation was reluctantly born on 9/22 April 1918.[72] The Baku soviet, with Dashnak support, denounced separation from Bolshevik Russia.[73]

Ottoman forces occupied the rail line from Aleksandropol through Julfa at the Iranian border in order to pursue the war against the British in Iran. The Azerbaijanis admitted that they could not take up arms against their fellow Turks and maintained a separate delegation, hoping to get Ottoman recognition of their independence. The Germans, meanwhile, encouraged Georgian independence in hopes of making further gains in the region and getting a step closer to Baku oil. On 26 May (all dates Gregorian hereafter) the Georgians withdrew from the federation and proclaimed their independence. Armenia and Azerbaijan, in unprecedented agreement, accused the Georgians of collusion with the Germans, then declared independence two days later.[74]

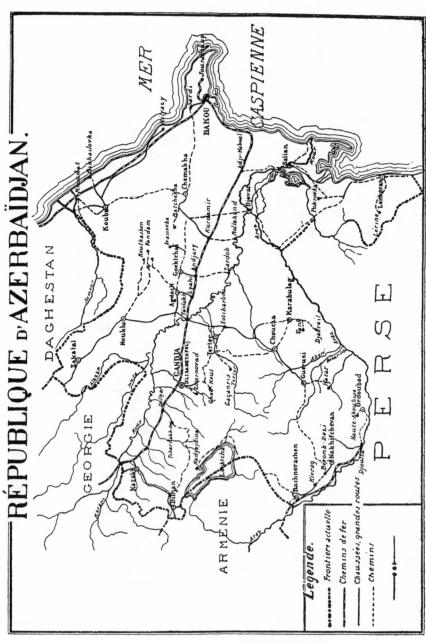

Official Map Issued by the Azerbaijan Democratic Republic, 1919

6 The Azerbaijan Democratic Republic (1918–1920)

From this day, sovereign rights belong to the Azerbaijan people . . .

Declaration of Independence, 1918

In its creation of a republic, the Azerbaijani leadership built on prewar intellectual, social, and political foundations. The Azerbaijan Democratic Republic (ADR) exercised only limited independence during occupations, continual border disputes with neighbors, and internal strife.

The ADR was formed on 28 May 1918. Its name, Azerbaijan Khalg Jumhuriyeti, meaning "People's (Popular or Democratic) Republic," emphasized the populist and sovereign character of the new state in contrast to its former colonial status. The republic's declaration of independence bore a similar message: "Sovereign rights belong to the Azerbaijan people. . . . Independent Azerbaijan is a democratic republic. . . . All citizens . . . are guaranteed full civil and political rights regardless of their nationality, religion [the only mention of religion in this declaration], social position, or sex." Another provision established universal suffrage.[1]

The republic's history can roughly be divided into three periods: (1) when Baku was politically separated from the rest of Azerbaijan (until August 1918), the national government was located in Ganje, and the Bolshevik Baku Commune, then the Centro-Caspian dictatorship, controlled Baku; (2)

when Baku was reincorporated until the departure of British troops in August 1919, a period of unified but "occupied" independence; (3) when the ADR was unoccupied and independent, a period that lasted until the Bolshevik conquest of Baku in April 1920 and the defeat of the republican forces outside Ganje that summer.

CONSOLIDATING POWER

On Azerbaijan Independence Day, Khan Khoiskii became prime minister and formed his first cabinet in Ganje. One week later Azerbaijan signed a friendship treaty with the Ottoman government. The treaty promised Ottoman armed assistance "to ensure law and order and the security of the country," that is, to defeat Armenian bands and retake Baku. By one account, Enver Pasha told Mehmet Emin Rasulzade that the cost of keeping an Ottoman force in Azerbaijan was so high that Azerbaijan should form its own army.[2] Shortly thereafter, an Army of Islam was assembled as an irregular force around one Ottoman unit, filled out by Azerbaijani and Daghestani volunteers. The force grew to between 16,000 and 18,000 under the command of Nuri Pasha, Enver's half-brother.[3] The relationship of this Army of Islam to the Azerbaijan republican army and the nature of Nuri's own role before and after the taking of Baku are murky. Most secondary accounts argue that Nuri (accompanied by Ahmet Aghayev) blatantly interfered in the ADR government, treating its National Committee as a product of the Bolshevik revolution, encouraging religious opposition to the new secular government, and finally forcing a cabinet reshuffle.[4] Enver still nursed his dream of building an empire on former Russian-held lands and Nuri surely supported him. Nuri's force and his later intelligence activities were completely separate from Gen. Kazim Karabekir's forces to the South and his intelligence network (first in the Ottoman army, then in the Turkish national movement).

The Ottoman-Azerbaijan treaty did not recognize Azerbaijan's independent statehood, thereby offending ADR leadership. Relations had initially been friendly. Azerbaijani Turkish intellectuals had kept close contacts with Istanbul and admired their self-governing kin. But Azerbaijan did not want to be part of the Ottoman Empire.[5] Nuri Pasha aggravated tensions by opposing reforms that had been so painstakingly negotiated by the Ganje and Baku branches of the Musavat.

Two things saved the relationship. The Azerbaijani Turks gladly received teachers that had been sent to help "Turkicize" the school system, and the Ottoman and Azerbaijani Turks closed ranks in the face of an offensive by the Baku soviet in June. The Army of Islam held the soviet's forces at Gökchay, near the former Baku-Elizavetpol provincial boundary. The battle (27 June–1 July) turned the tide against soviet forces and the advance on Baku began.[6]

Like the Bolsheviks in Moscow and Baku, the Germans feared Azerbaijani control over Baku oil. The former enemies made a deal: the Germans would try to use their influence in the Sublime Porte (seat of Ottoman government) to stop the move on Baku, claiming that the involvement of Ottoman forces constituted a violation of the treaty of Brest-Litovsk and might provoke the Bolsheviks to renew hostilities (of course, they were in no position to do so). In return Germany would get a share of Baku oil. Rasulzade, then in Istanbul, lodged an official protest against German pressure and the recognition of Russian sovereignty over Baku. He stated that Baku "is the natural capital of Azerbaijan, its political, cultural, and economic center."[7]

The British, too, were eager to penetrate Caucasia, though access to the oil reserves was only one consideration. In January 1918 Whitehall authorized the creation of the Dunsterforce under Gen. Lionel C. Dunsterville of the Indian Army.[8] The mission of the Dunsterforce was primarily political—to gather and act on intelligence and to train local forces to prevent the spread of German propaganda, regarded as a potential threat to Afghanistan and India. Its secondary goals were to take and protect or to destroy the Baku oil fields. Later, Dunsterville was told to gather information on Bolsheviks and to lead at least two known tsarist units (mostly Armenian), without officers, against the Ottomans. Because of its mission, the Dunsterforce was made up only of officers and noncommissioned officers. They were to start from Baghdad and go to Tiflis via Rasht and Baku. Those close to the scene of action doubted the likelihood of the Dunsterforce's success (General Marshall, commander of the Mesopotamian theater, suggested the population of Baku certainly would not stand by while the British blew up their oil wells) and in various ways subverted it.[9] Not until summer did Dunsterville's force, now enlarged with technical support, reach the Caspian coast.

Meanwhile, British political agents in Baku and Tiflis had been trying to arrange for Dunsterville's transport there. According to a report by Maj. G. M. Goldsmith,[10] Shaumian had agreed to allow Dunsterville's passage as early as February 1918. Dunsterville, however, was not prepared to move, nor would he be until summer. With the approach of the Army of Islam in July (regarded by the British as an Ottoman force and therefore the front in the war effort) and because of the inadequacy of the Bolshevik force to hold them off,[11] the Baku fleet and the non-Bolsheviks of the soviet decided to invite Dunsterville to Baku. Shaumian then opposed the invitation, and the Bolsheviks resigned from the soviet. The others in the soviet joined the Fleet (Centro-Caspian) Committee in calling Dunsterville to Baku.[12] After the twenty-six Bolshevik commissars departed by boat for Astrakhan on 12

August, it was discovered that most of the city's military stores were missing. The boat was intercepted and forced to return to Baku. The missing supplies were retrieved from the Bolsheviks, who were arrested. With the fall of the city a few days later, they fled again by sea and wound up in Krasnovodsk, where they were arrested and shot by anti-Bolshevik (White) forces.[13]

The British under Dunsterville arrived in Baku in mid-August with three battalions, field artillery, and armored cars. The local inhabitants were disappointed with so small a force, and Dunsterville was sorry to discover there were no effective local forces for him to lead.[14] He discovered war matériel "unguarded and unused" throughout the city and had it gathered and repaired. Meantime, the Army of Islam, stopped in its August assault, was now reinforced. It attacked on 15 and 16 September. A colleague of Dunsterville reported:

> There was no lack of equipment and ammunition for the defence of the city; what was lacking was the willingness to fight. . . . The Armenians, who formed the major part of the Baku troops, despite their fear of the Turks, showed no disposition to fight, abandoning their position on the slightest sign of enemy movement.[15]

Dunsterville evacuated his force.[16] On 16 September the Army of Islam took Baku, and the Azerbaijani population took the opportunity to avenge themselves for the March Days. Many Armenians perished or fled.[17] The government of the Azerbaijan Democratic Republic moved to Baku.[18]

Baku was reunited with the rest of Azerbaijan, marking the second period of the republic's independence. The cabinet now resided in Baku and claimed jurisdiction over the prewar Baku and Elizavetpol gubernii. On the basis of population composition, Azerbaijan also claimed the Nakhjivan region that had been in the Erevan guberniia. That claim and Azerbaijani claims to Zangezur and Karabagh (in the former Elizavetpol guberniia) would be continually disputed with Armenia.

Ottoman troops remained. The Mondros (Mudros) Armistice signed by a new Ottoman cabinet[19] and the Entente on 9 October 1918 included provisions for their evacuation from Caucasia, for Entente control of the Transcaucasian railroad, and for British occupation of Baku. The Azerbaijan government wrote a note of protest to the Ottoman government for agreeing to terms concerning Azerbaijan, a declared sovereign state, but to no avail. Ottoman soldiers were permitted to join Azerbaijan's military as individuals, but not as units.

Maj.-Gen. W. M. Thomson came to administer Baku and arrived with 2,000 troops on 17 November.[20] The previous day he had met with a delegation from the Musavat government made up of Nasib Yusufbeyli, Ali Ekper Rafibeyli, and Ahmet Aghayev, who went to Enzeli to discover his intentions. Thomson outlined his tasks: to ensure that Azerbaijani national units as well as Ottoman forces left Baku (he did not restrict the movements of Azerbaijani forces elsewhere in the republic), to prevent armed Armenian forces from entering Baku, and to establish British control over the local militia. He was to supply the British with Baku oil and hold the eastern terminus of the Transcaucasian Railway. One underlying principle of his occupation was that he would not make political decisions. "The principle of self-determination of peoples will be decided at the [Peace] Conference from which Azerbaijan will not be excluded," he said.[21]

Thomson did not then recognize the legitimacy of the ADR, and he ordered that its flag be removed from the pier where he landed. He spoke of Caucasia as a part of Russia that would eventually be handed over to a reestablished Russian state. The presence of cossack Commander Bicherakov, who openly worked for Russian control in Baku, amplified Azerbaijani fears; nonetheless, Thomson met no resistance. His own statements did not appear bellicose and in any case the republic's armed force was scattered throughout its territory.[22]

Thomson's initial actions coincided with the views of many in London and Europe and with the Russians, both Bolshevik[23] and White, who regarded the separation of Azerbaijan from Russia as temporary.[24] According to a report by a British officer:

> As regards the Caucasus, there appears to be only one point of view, namely, that they were an integral part of Russia; . . . as soon as the time came, they had got to come back to Russia, peaceably if possible, but if not, force would be used.[25]

Not everyone in Britain agreed. According to various specialists in Anglo-Russian relations, men like Thomson who had India experience regarded Russia as England's main rival throughout Asia, and they were favorably disposed toward border states that seemed to "contain" Russia.[26] According to a later Foreign Office memorandum: "The Mesopotamian division were said to adore Muslims, despise Eastern Christians, and to have the traditional Anglo-Indian suspicion of everything pertaining to Russian imperialism."[27]

As the Ottomans had regarded the Azerbaijan National Committee as a child of the Russian Revolution, so Thomson thought of the Azerbaijan Democratic Republic as an Ottoman product. Nonetheless, he came to accept the republican government as the "only legitimate authority" in Azerbaijan and Prime Minister Khan Khoiskii as "one of the ablest men in Baku."[28] The government established a modus vivendi with Thomson. The general assumed control of all state affairs, including the Baku militia and the ADR's Ministry of Internal Affairs.[29] The British used their occupation to secure ports and Baku oil and to gather intelligence, driving through the countryside mapping physical features, roads, and railways and taking photographs. Public figures, including government ministers, complained that the ADR's sovereignty was being violated.[30] The Musavat and the coalition government it led were accused by internal opponents and the Turkish military of being pro-British. Because Britain embodied the imperialism that was now so despised and had aided Armenian forces, the accusation was meant to damage popular support for the Musavat and the republic.

Thomson's tenure as governor general was not so grim for Azerbaijan as it initially appeared. He did adhere to the policies outlined in his statements of 16 November 1918 and, from the outset, maintained civil order, overseeing the railroad, oil exports, and a new currency issue by the Azerbaijan State Bank. Industries nationalized by Shaumian were privatized. Predictably, it became impossible to maintain order in such a setting without making political decisions, and Thomson came to accept the de facto authority of the Musavat government. After the December multiparty elections for Parliament, he regarded the Azerbaijan government as a legitimate representative of the popular will. His actions provided the young republic with security and an opportunity to enact reforms.[31]

In March 1919 Thomson disarmed the Russian Caspian fleet and ejected White recruiters from Baku. He reined in the Kadets when they attempted to assert Russian authority over the city, saying that "at the moment Russia simply did not exist and that the future status of Transcaucasia was to be resolved by the peace conference." Thomson's force arrested and deported a few Bolsheviks, though others remained. In the dispute with Armenian forces over Karabagh and Zangezur, Thomson recognized Azerbaijani claims in keeping with Entente policy to recognize former guberniia boundaries.[32] He asked Armenian general Andranik to cease his efforts to seize the areas and appointed an Azerbaijani governor, Dr. Khosrow Sultanov, over both. To sharp Armenian criticism he responded, "The fact is that in Azerbaijan some Armenians are much disappointed that the British occupation is not an opportunity for revenge. They are reluctant to accept it that [the] peace conference is going to decide and not military forces."[33] A few months later, however, Thomson placed the Nakhjivan region, with its Azerbaijani population, under Armenian administration to prevent it from being used as a corridor between the ADR and Turkish national forces in eastern Asia Minor.[34]

Under Thomson's occupation the ADR was able to operate its multiparty Parliament, which had been elected by universal suffrage.[35] Dozens of political groups and parties flourished: Azerbaijani, Armenian, Russian, Georgian, Jewish, and Estonian national councils (the Russian council proclaiming

Baku a "Russian city"); the Ukrainian Rada of Baku; a Council of Polish Organizations; a Jewish Zionist National Fraction; a Society of Muslim Citizens of Karabagh; the Dashnaksutun; the SRs; the Russian nationalist Edinaia Rossiia; and an array of student, charitable, and cultural societies.[36] After parliamentary elections, the ADR sent a delegation led by Ali Mardan Topchibashi to the Paris Peace Conference.[37] The anti-Bolshevik Russians were already well established and had the ear of Allied leaders, however, so it was difficult for the non-Russians to get a hearing.

Thomson's support for multiparty politics provided an opportunity for the revitalization of the Hümmet. The party produced a new program shortly after Parliament was elected in December 1918 and repaired its internal division by accepting Bolshevik Hümmetists. The door was open to renewed Bolshevik activity. Anastas Mikoyan returned in March 1919 to manage the work, most of it semilegal, of the Baku Committee of the Russian Communist party (Bolshevik), RCP(b). Bolsheviks, Mensheviks, and SRs resumed their struggle for primacy.[38]

During the struggle for independence, the Azerbaijani Turks embarked on a cultural program that was high on the agenda of the national movement. The Azerbaijani Turkish language and the study of history and literature now dominated education and, as far as possible, the business of the republic. Baku University (established 1919) made Azerbaijani Turkish the language of instruction and could have prepared a new generation for state service. (Latinization of the alphabet was already being considered.) At the time, the shortage of trained indigenous cadres forced concessions. In the midlevel state bureaucracy, for example, so few individuals could use Turkish that Russian continued to be the language of government. A two-year deadline was set for all to learn the language of the ADR.

Azerbaijan's army expanded to a fighting force of about 30,000 in which new conscripts and guerrillas joined men who had served in the Russian or Ottoman armies. For training, the new army employed Ottoman officers and Generals Shikhlinskii and Suleyman Sulkevich (a Lithuanian Tatar). The minister of war was former tsarist general Samed Mekhmandyarov. A military academy in Ganje staffed with Ottoman officers produced "young officers 'educated in the national spirit.'"[39] Establishing a regular military force ate up 13 percent of the republic's 1919 budget.[40]

General Denikin, a White, posed a constant threat of attack. The general needed Baku oil and considered the republics a "power vacuum" into which Bolsheviks might go. The British War Office warned that "the states of the Caucasus . . . must not attack Denikin and that, unless they cooperated with him at least to the extent of supplying him with petroleum and denying it to the Bolsheviks, the British government could not insist that he stay north of the [defense] line."[41] Denikin crossed the first and subsequent lines the British drew in their "defense" of Caucasia. By June 1919 his forces were so near the Azerbaijan and Georgian borders that the two republics signed a defense pact against him. Although invited to join the pact, the Armenians refused.[42]

In February of 1919 British prime minister David Lloyd-George decided not to commit further resources to the Russian civil war and informed Thomson he would be removed.[43] By August 1919, when Thomson's forces left Baku, the republic had its third coalition government in sixteen months and no party had a majority in Parliament. Denikin had crossed British defense lines and was rapidly approaching the northern border. Communist party organizations in Astrakhan were funding pro-Bolshevik publications in Baku. The Baku Committee of the RCP(b) was well on its way to absorbing the Hümmet.[44]

UNOCCUPIED INDEPENDENCE

After the withdrawal of Thomson and his troops, the Azerbaijan republic entered its final stage of independence. The ADR leadership faced the departure of the English with some trepidation, especially in view of the strength of Denikin to the North and the lukewarm reception their delegation had received at the Paris Peace Conference. The European Powers had not yet granted even de facto recognition to the ADR. Ties with both the Turkish national forces and Iran were strengthened in what proved to be the final months of the republic's existence.

The ADR was plagued by political trouble. The government was a series of coalitions. Although the Musavat was the senior partner, it could not enforce its will on members of other parties or those unaffiliated with any party. Cabinet crises would sharpen as Communist party strength increased.

During the second half of 1919, the RCP(b) Baku organization gobbled up the Hümmet cells, beginning with the smallest part and going on to absorb the entire party, circumventing objections by the Azerbaijani leadership. The quasi-independent Azerbaijani socialists were eliminated as a political force, making Azerbaijani Turks a minority within the Azerbaijan Communist party, the AzCP(b), which had been officially founded in February 1920.[45] Some Azerbaijani Bolsheviks received places on the Central Committee: Mirza Davud Huseinov and A. H. Karayev, who had returned after their earlier association with the Menshevik Hümmet, and Ali Bayramov, M. B. Kasimov, and Dadash Buniatzade.[46] The new AzCP(b) would undermine the divided coalition government from inside the country while Bolshevik Russia, employing its Tiflis organizations and the Red Army, would pressure the ADR from outside.

Denikin's losses in battle before Moscow during October and November

1919 enabled the Red Army to counterattack, advancing like a steamroller toward the Caucasus intent on Baku's oil, not on its "toiling masses." As Lenin informed the head of the North Caucasus Revolutionary Committee (revkom), Grigorii K. ("Sergo") Ordzhonikidze, on 17 March 1920: "The taking of Baku is absolutely, absolutely essential. Devote all your efforts to it."[47]

Recognizing the untenability of a two-front war against Russians in the North and Armenians in the West, the ADR attempted to secure its northern border by getting diplomatic recognition from the Bolsheviks. It was repeatedly rebuffed.[48] The process culminated in a series of diplomatic notes written between January and April 1920 by Grigorii Chicherin, foreign affairs commissar of the Russian Soviet Federative Socialist Republic (RSFSR), and Fath Ali Khan Khoiskii, alternately prime minister and foreign minister of Azerbaijan. In January 1920, the Red Army was driving Denikin's forces from Daghestan and positioning itself on Azerbaijan's northern border. Chicherin's notes were more propaganda than diplomacy, declaring Bolshevik respect for "the territory of others" while invoking the superior right of the "working stratum" of every society to shape its people's destiny. To a republic with a largely Russian proletariat, the slogan was ominous. The notes, which were published by the Azerbaijan Communist party as they were handed to ADR representatives, were part of the combined military and diplomatic offensive the Bolsheviks used to subdue many parts of the former Russian Empire.[49]

Relations with Russia led to a dispute within the Musavat along the lines of the premerger Baku-Ganje division and to a debate within the ADR government. In the ADR cabinet a faction led by the internal affairs minister, Baku resident Memed Hasan Hajinskii, favored making "broad concessions" to the RSFSR (including an oil deal) in the hope of gaining diplomatic recognition. Khan Khoiskii's supporters rejected any concessions and agreed to Hajinskii's removal and the appointment of anti-Communists to several cabinet posts. Hajinskii lost his post but became minister of commerce and industry. He and his followers were able to continue lobbying, an option that would not be open under the Bolshevik government that was to follow. The political pressure brought to bear by Chicerin's notes, by Hajinskii's group at a Musavat party congress in mid-March, and by the presence of the 11th Red Army on Azerbaijan's border led the ADR government to grant favorable trade terms to Russia, mainly for the sale of oil. Negotiations on price continued until 27 April 1920, the day the Red Army occupied Baku.[50]

On 8 April the RCP(b) created a Caucasian Bureau (Kavbiuro) to coordinate the conquest of Caucasia, starting with Azerbaijan. Ordzhonikidze was chairman, and vice-chairman was Sergei M. Kirov, a political commissar in the 11th Red Army. They gave the orders that would lead to the seizure of power in Baku and the overthrow of the ADR government. The creation of the Kavbiuro seems to have reflected Lenin's belief that the local party (now grown to 4,000 members) was unable to manage the task unaided.[51] Yet the AzCP(b) had to play a visible role in order to "give the appearance of an internal revolution."[52] It was to hand an ultimatum to the ADR Parliament, then call for "fraternal assistance" from the Soviet Russia. But the Red Army crossed the undefended northern border ahead of schedule, perhaps indicating the degree of trust the AzCP(b) enjoyed in the Kavbiuro and Moscow. The border was unguarded because ADR forces had been moved west to defend against an Armenian attack on Karabagh.[53] The possibility that the two moves were coordinated has been suggested but not demonstrated.

Early on 27 April, with the Red Army already inside Azerbaijan, the AzCP(b) proclaimed the overthrow of the "'treacherous, criminal, counter-revolutionary' government of the Musavat Party, and declared that the only lawful authority was now the Provisional Azerbaijani Military-Revolutionary Committee (Azrevkom)."[55] Representatives of the Azrevkom handed their ultimatum to the Parliament. A cabinet headed by Yusufbeyli (assassinated by Bolsheviks in Tiflis, 1921) had fallen early in April, having lost the support of the socialists.[56] Hajinskii had failed to form a cabinet despite talks with potential allies. The Azerbaijan republic had only a caretaker government when it fell.

With the Caspian fleet's guns trained on the Parliament building, the Bolshevik ultimatum was debated in Parliament by those who urged accommodation and those determined to fight. Their positions were influenced by the strife within the coalitions governing the republic. The Musavat had, to some degree, been tainted by its association with British forces under Thomson. In contrast, the anti-imperialist, prosocialist buzzwords recalled prewar native socialists who had been full partners in national reforms like Nariman Narimanov. He and other former Hümmetists who had shared leadership in prewar cultural and political movements were proposed as the Soviet government for Azerbaijan. Current leaders were also offered posts.[57]

Former Hümmetist Rasulzade supported "revolutionary Russia" though his position seems to have been ambiguous. Only his Musavat party, he said, was willing to defend the republic's independence. Because it could not do so alone, he abnegated responsibility for the outcome of the coming struggle. Menshevik-Hümmetist Aghamalioghlu took an openly defeatist position, saying: "Let no one risk bringing destruction upon the city and shedding innocent blood!"[58] His words evoked memories of March 1918, when despite its acceptance of Bolshevik terms, the community fell victim to random slaughter by the Bolsheviks' Armenian allies. Aghamalioghlu seemed to accept the notion that "unification" with Bolshevik Russia would mean rule by Azerbaijani Bolsheviks.

Perhaps the parliamentary deputies, confronted by their own political division, by the defeatist elements in their midst, by the absence of their armed forces, and by the military strength of their enemies, thought resistance useless. Perhaps hoping that the Bolshevik terms were genuine, Parliament voted—at 11 P.M., 27 April 1920, just one hour before its time ran out—to accept them.

Contrary to the fiction about voluntary unification with Russia, the Bolshevik ultimatum demanded immediate surrender. It also offered specific guarantees—Azerbaijan's "independence and territorial integrity . . . would be protected," the national army would remain intact, individual political parties would remain free—a whole list of provisions that were ignored once the Bolsheviks had control.[59] The guarantees, which were recorded by Rasulzade, differ significantly from those published in the official newspaper *Kommunist* in May 1920 and subsequently republished in Soviet volumes. Apparently, the Bolsheviks changed their terms as soon as they had power.[60]

Azerbaijan could not get more than diplomatic support from the Turkish national movement that was now engaged in a life-or-death struggle to establish a republic in Asia Minor. The commitment to the preservation of Azerbaijan, at least on the part of Gen. Kazim Karabekir,[61] is evident from his statement that it was necessary to come to a speedy agreement with the Bolsheviks "if Azerbaijan is not to be swept away."[62] Just a few days later, with the Red Army poised on the Daghestan-Azerbaijan frontier, Karabekir instructed a military mission going to Baku for talks with Bolshevik Russian representatives to walk a tightrope:[63]

> If Bolshevik forces take up operations against Georgia, and if they can persuade Georgia to become Bolshevik and include them in a Bolshevik union, expelling the British, the [nationalist] Turkish government will mount military operations against the imperialist Armenian government and have the Azerbaijan government completely agree to Bolshevik principles and have them incorporated into a Bolshevik union. Therefore, we do not see any reason for Russian Bolshevik operations against Azerbaijan.

It was a subtle policy meant to spare Azerbaijan from military confrontation by persuading Azerbaijan to accept "Bolshevik principles." The speed of Bolshevik action and internal conditions in Baku rendered Karabekir's arguments moot.[64]

TERRITORIAL DISPUTES

All the independent republics had territorial disputes with their neighbors. Some were more heated than others. The Azerbaijan-Georgian border was settled, after months of dispute, as part of a military pact against

Denikin in June 1919.[65] The Armenian-Georgian conflict over the region of Borchalo continued as did disputes between Azerbaijan and Armenia over three contiguous regions. The borders of the two republics coincided only roughly with those of prerevolutionary provincial boundaries—Armenia was formed from the Erevan guberniia and Azerbaijan, from the Baku and Elizavetpol gubernii. With independence, control of territory and, therefore, placement of borders became serious matters. The western part of Karabagh (in the Elizavetpol guberniia) and Zangezur to the southwest were claimed by both sides, as was Nakhjivan west of Zangezur, bordering Turkey and Iran.[66] Both republics issued official maps reflecting their claims.

The land of the former khanate of Karabagh that was absorbed in the first Russo-Iranian War lay entirely within the Elizavetpol province.[67] Its historic center was Shusha. The former Erevan and Nakhjivan khanates (the latter included much of Zangezur) had been added to the Russian Empire during the second Russo-Iranian War. The main towns were Nakhjivan, Julfa, and Ordubad. The two khanates were dissolved, and in March 1828 the Russian administration established an Armenian *oblast'* in their place even though 80 percent of the population of these two khanates, including Turks and Kurds, were classified "Muslim." The name of the oblast' signaled Russian intentions to establish an Armenian enclave there.[68] During the wars with Iran and during a Russo-Ottoman war in the second half of the century, many Turks emigrated. This emigration coupled with Armenian immigration (provided for in the Turkmanchai Treaty, 1828) led to an Armenian majority in some regions. In 1840 Erevan and Nakhjivan uezdy replaced the Armenian oblast' inside the Georgian-Imeretian guberniia, then in 1846 in the Tiflis guberniia. In 1850 an Erevan guberniia was formed from (northwest to southeast) Aleksandropol, Novobayazit, Sharur-Daralagez, and Nakhjivan uezdy and the Ordubad *okrug*.[69]

KARABAGH AND ZANGEZUR

Armenian-Azerbaijani relations in this period were marred by the dispute for control over the "mountainous" portion of Karabagh. Both sides published maps and articles and deployed military forces to enforce their claims to the region. Each accused the other of aggression and infringing on the rights of the other. In October 1918 the ADR's semiofficial newspaper, *Azerbaijan*, reported on clashes there:

> The news from Karabagh is that the adventure of a group of Dashnaks has been completely liquidated: it is finally known that the Armenian masses were not involved in the Karabagh events. Armenian population in town

and in the villages met our forces with bread and salt [a sign of welcome], accepted Azerbaijani citizenship.[70]

A later report stated that "life has returned to normal . . . relations between Muslims and Armenians have become friendly."[71]

The optimism was premature. General Andranik's operations in the region continued. Early in 1919 General Thomson sent Dr. Khosrow Sultanov to be governor general of Karabagh and Zangezur. When he returned to Baku in March, newspapers reported his "journey in Karabagh had produced no results." Representatives of the Armenian National Council in Karabagh went to Baku for talks on the region's status.[72] In early April 1919 the Baku newspaper *Bor'ba* summarized the dispute:[73]

> The Armenian government advances its claims to Karabagh and protests the appointment there of an Azerbaijani Governor General. . . . The Azerbaijani government, for its part, protests Armenian claims to Karabagh, which it considers its own undisputable territory and protests excesses[74] carried out by Armenian forces on Muslims in the Erevan and Sharur-Daralagez uezdy.

Bor'ba quoted the Dashnak newspaper *Ashkhatavor*:

> After centuries of living together, these three republics are divided from one another by artificial borders; their mutual relations cannot be based on force or provocation.
>   Underground work of Azerbaijan in Sharur, Nakhjivan, the claims of Georgia on Zakatala *okrug*— these are all phenomena demonstrating the abnormal relations, and therefore it is necessary to put an end to them. . . . The future of Transcaucasian democracy compels us to raise the question on the necessity for solidarity of action.

Bor'ba picked up the phrase "solidarity of action" and stated that such united action in the interests of democracy "can only hearten us." Noticing the *Ashkatavor* mentioned only Azerbaijani and Georgian "incitement," *Bor'ba's* writer predicted that "the 'Dashnaktsutun' Party tomorrow will insinuate and spread all kinds of meanness against the neighboring republics, then run to *Ashkhatavor* with the charge of 'provocation,' the sole goal of which is to summon the interference of the Great Powers in our internal affairs." Later in April a conference on border issues met in Tiflis[75] but did not lead to a resolution of disputes.

Despite many discussions about the dangers of European interference, the Allied Powers were courted by all the Caucasian republics to recognize their independence and territorial claims. The English historian Col. H. W. V. Temperly, who headed an English mission to Erevan in 1919, asked the

Armenians which portions of the former tsarist empire they considered their own. They responded with a list encompassing the entire Erevan guberniia, including Nakhjivan; half the Elizavetpol guberniia, to a point east of mountainous Karabagh; the entire Kars oblast'; and parts of the Tiflis guberniia.[76] Mikoyan characterized it as "a grandiose plan for the expansion of Armenia."[77]

In summer 1919 Col. W. N. Haskell, former chief of the American Relief Mission to Romania, was appointed both as an Allied high commissioner, with full charge of all relief measures in Armenia, and as an agent of the Department of State.[78] In September he visited Baku and spoke with Yusuf-beyli. *Azerbaijan* reported Haskell's saying that he was not a representative of the Armenians and was entirely nonpartisan concerning the republics. Following Entente policy he declared that Karabagh and Zangezur should be confirmed as part of Azerbaijan but that Nakhjivan, Sharur, and Daralagez should be made a "neutral zone" between the Caucasian republics and Turkey.[79]

Shortly after Haskell's visit to Baku, the Armenians of mountainous Karabagh resolved to include Karabagh in Azerbaijan pending a final decision by the Paris Peace Conference. The resolution was based on the granting of "territorial autonomy for all Karabagh and national-cultural autonomy for its Armenian population." *Bor'ba* noted that "the agreement between Armenians and Muslims in Karabagh is already a fact. . . . In the present case, we see the first serious attempt at resolution of the Armenian-Muslim conflict not by means of violence but by means of negotiation." The newspaper added that other populations in Caucasia—the Armenian minority in Zangezur and the Azerbaijani Turks "under Erevan"[80]—were in a position analogous to the Armenian minority in Karabagh. Haskell reported to the Peace Conference in December that the two republics agreed to settle all their differences by negotiation or, failing that, to accept the high commissioner's (Haskell's) arbitration.[81]

Early in 1920, the Peace Conference recognized Azerbaijan's claim to Karabagh. The decision upheld earlier Entente policy. It may have been bolstered by reports of Allied observers in the field, like Haskell, and by a recognition of the veracity of what Mikoyan told Lenin: "The unification of Karabagh to Armenia would mean, for the population of Karabagh, deprivation of their source of life in Baku and being tied to Erevan, with which they have never had any kind of connection."[82] The decision also may have reflected a shift in Allied tactics in the wake of Denikin's defeat by the Bolsheviks and the likelihood of a Bolshevik advance on Caucasia. England, in response to this new threat, in January 1920 urged de facto recognition of Georgia and Azerbaijan, the two states that had already resolved their differences and committed themselves to defend their independence against a Russian threat from the North. Perhaps Karabagh was "awarded" to Azerbaijan as a way of bolstering it against the new Russian, now Bolshevik, threat. Such Allied recognition did not obstruct plans to make a "neutral zone" out of other disputed territories or the much-touted possibility of expanding Armenia at the expense of the nascent Turkish republic in the West.

The "Armenophile movement" was not without effect. In recognition of the Armenian minority in Karabagh, the Allied Powers' representatives stipulated that the police of Karabagh be made up of equal numbers of Armenians and Azerbaijani Turks. Relations were not improved, however. In late March 1920, just after this decision, the Armenian half of the police force was reported by a British journalist to have murdered the Azerbaijani half during the latter's traditional Novruz Bayram holiday celebrations.[83]

Attacks by local Armenian forces reportedly resumed at this time, coordinated with an offensive on the Azerbaijan border by forces of the Erevan government. Fighting was reported in Zangezur, Nakhjivan, and Karabagh.[84] *Azerbaijan* expressed outrage at "intrigues" that led to this attack:

> The rights of the Armenians, the inviolability of their property and lives, [are] fully guaranteed. . . . Concerning the cultural needs of the Armenian population of Karabagh, the government of Azerbaijan has devoted much attention to the matter of education and not only has removed obstacles, but has taken all sorts of steps to facilitate the success and flourishing of their social life.

The ADR sent its forces to the western frontier, leaving the northern border unguarded as the Bolsheviks began their invasion. The problems in Karabagh would be inherited by the next government.

Nakhjivan

Nakhjivan's political situation was shaped by its having been in the Erevan guberniia and its close proximity to the front. The Azerbaijani Turks were harassed, even murdered, during the war years under the ancien régime. They fared no better under the Provisional Government,[85] whose representatives exacerbated tensions by "secur[ing] warehouses and property for Russian forces at the front." They "requisitioned produce and cattle without payment and accused local Azerbaijani Turks of being agents of the [Ottoman] Turks and punishing them."[86] Peasants seized irrigation systems, harvests, and animals from local landowners and clashed with the militia. The governor of the Erevan guberniia reported a "loss of faith" by the local populace in the Provisional Government's local representative body, the

Ozakom.[87] Bolshevik land decrees, giving "land to the toilers," would sharpen the conflicts.[88]

The Ozakom was not without competitors for power in Nakhjivan. Least influential of these were the few soviets of soldiers' deputies which had formed along the railroad in the towns of Nakhjivan, Julfa, and Shakhtakht.[89] The socialists were not a significant force in Nakhjivan and the Bolsheviks even less so. The Azerbaijanis had a national committee in Nakhjivan as did the Armenians. Jafar Kuli Khan, briefly a leader of the Azerbaijani Turks' National Committee, rejected the Ozakom and turned for protection to Ottoman forces and to his relative, the khan of Maku (Iran).[91]

As in Baku the October Revolution did not shift power in Nakhjivan.[92] Jafar Kuli Khan continued to fight Russian forces, both the remnants of the imperial army and the Reds. His forces reportedly blew up Russian army warehouses at Shakhtakht station. He also may have fought the Shakhtakht garrison, reportedly Bolshevik-dominated, which strove to spread its influence along rail lines.[93] The Nakhjivanis were not interested in being part of an Armenian state whose forces cut off Nakhjivan from the ADR and carried out frequent attacks on border villages. The Armenian threat cemented National Committee ties to the Ottoman army and the Maku khan and later led them to seek Allied aid against Armenian forces trying to incorporate Nakhjivan into Armenia.[94]

In spring 1918 during an Ottoman-Azerbaijan attempt to retake Baku along a northern approach, General Karabekir was headquartered in Nakhjivan. He helped the Azerbaijanis establish their own military units to face Armenian General Andranik, who was then besieging Nakhjivan.[95] When the Ottoman forces evacuated Nakhjivan in December 1918, they left behind the "Araz Republic," apparently founded by the local National Council with Ottoman backing (though Soviet sources insist it was created by Ottoman commanders with Musavat assistance). The Araz Republic, according to one report, was united with a "South West Caucasian Democratic Republic" formed from a strip of territory that would have linked Nakhjivan with the Black Sea coast.[96] The paper creation of the republic (for it was never a reality) was clearly designed to offset Entente plans to make the same strip a buffer between Turkish forces and Caucasian states.

When the British occupied Nakhjivan in January 1919, they regarded the Araz Republic, like the regime in Baku, as merely an Ottoman creation and accorded it no recognition.[97] In the summer of 1919, according to Soviet accounts, an American colonel, James Ray, arrived in Nakhjivan. After discussion with various parties, he suggested to Jafar Kuli Khan that an American governor general oversee the territory.[98] Colonel Haskell suggested the same in a letter of 1 September 1919 to the ADR government. He reportedly traveled through Nakhjivan and Sharur-Daralagez and, in his report to the Peace Conference, supported "neutral zone" status for these areas under an American governor general. In October, *Azerbaijan* published notices signed by Ray and Haskell that U.S. Army colonel Edmund D. Daily would be the U.S. governor general of Nakhjivan.[99] Daily apparently never assumed the post.

Karabekir returned to the East (Erzerum) in 1919 to fight in the resistance against the sultan's capitulationist government. He activated his intelligence network and resumed his assistance to Nakhjivan. As before, he responded to requests for aid by sending officers (they had been withdrawn after the armistice) to revive the defense units.[100] Karabekir's forces occupied Nakhjivan in March 1920. Their support would subsequently assist Azerbaijan in reclaiming Nakhjivan after the establishment of soviet power.

EUROPEAN POWERS
AND THE REPUBLIC

All belligerents had interests in Caucasia during World War I because of that region's location and Baku's oil fields. The Bolshevik withdrawal from the war led the Entente to try to reestablish the eastern front by intervention. When the war ended and fighting Germans gave way to fighting Bolsheviks, all former belligerents adjusted their policies. Some wanted Russia reestablished as a Great Power, whether tsarist or not. Many desired to control Baku oil and the Baku-Batum railroad that brought that oil to the Black Sea. Britain, which had been playing the "Great Game in Asia" with Russia for over a century, had the most to gain.

Thus, Britain remained intent on controlling the eastern Mediterranean and on protecting India with a "forward" posture between the Mediterranean and Afghanistan. Some strategists regarded the Caspian Sea and Caucasia as an approach to India that must be under British control. The port of Baku would service a proposed British Caspian fleet, for it was the eastern terminus of the Baku-Batum railroad linking the Caspian and Black seas. Baku oil was significant though secondary; to use the oil, control of the Caspian and the rail link to Batum was needed. London debated whether India's defense perimeter ran through Caucasia;[101] whether England had enough men and money to sustain a force throughout Caucasia (Lloyd-George stated flatly that extensive aid would bankrupt England) or only in selected locations and to what end; and how to treat the new republics.[102]

Because the British wanted to prevent bolshevism from infecting the eastern Mediterranean, they backed Denikin and, after his defeat in early

1920, hoped to use the Caucasian states as buffers.[103] Their support for Denikin, however, angered Georgia and Azerbaijan. Accusations about British imperialism appeared fully justified when British officers appeared throughout Caucasia fretting about supply lines to the Whites. When the Armenians refused to join the anti-Denikin pact and the Dashnak government maintained a permanent liaison officer with Denikin,[104] the seemingly close ties Erevan and émigré Armenians maintained with the Entente seemed to bond Russian Whites, Armenia, and Britain into a grand alliance.

Some in the West thought the Caucasian states, especially Armenia because of its anti-Turkish posture, would serve as buffers between the Bolsheviks and the eastern Mediterranean. (Churchill thought otherwise, likening the use of small republics against the Red Army to "using a piece of putty to stop an earthquake."[105]) Nevertheless, England armed and funded Armenian forces, though not out of a sense of commitment to the Armenians. In discussing possible mandatory Powers for Caucasia, Lord Curzon, former English viceroy to India, stated that France, whose merely "sentimental or chauvinistic" interest in Caucasia threatened British interests, "must be given Armenia, because nobody else wants to have anything to do with that singularly unattractive people!"[106]

The United States, too, took some interest in the Christian Armenians and the possibility of establishing an Armenian state, perhaps because of Armenian lobbying in the United States. Many Americans' belief in self-determination was another factor, though it was usually not applied to Turks or other Muslim populations. Moreover, the United States was extremely fearful in those years of the spread of bolshevism. Some may have thought about Armenia as a buffer, but it was unlikely that U.S. politicians would have used such "imperialist" language publicly.[107]

Thomson's actions in Caucasia reflected disagreements in London. Lord Hardinge, permanent under secretary of state at the Foreign Office, wrote in June 1917 that "we have two diplomacies—one of the Foreign Office and the other 'amateur' running side by side." The "amateur" policy was associated with so-called ideological notions like self-determination.[108] Initially, Thomson supported self-determination and the decision of the Peace Conference on Azerbaijan's independence; arriving in Baku, he stated that the Caucasian states were "Russian." Later, however, he ejected White Army recruiters from Baku and supported the elected ADR parliamentary government.

Churchill, reflecting the imperial school of thought, argued that it was all right to support self-determination in the abstract but that no vital interests were at stake in the Caucasus; owing to their weakness, these states would be reabsorbed into Russia eventually.[109] In early 1919 Foreign Secretary Arthur James Balfour said,

I feel much disposed to say with [Secretary of State for India] Mr. [Edwin] Montagu . . . If they want to cut their own throats why do we not let them do it. . . . I should say we are not going to spend all our money and men in civilizing a few people who do not want to be civilized. We will protect Batum, Baku, the railway between them, and the pipe-line.[110]

In January 1920, when Denikin had been defeated and the Bolsheviks were moving toward the Caucasus, Sir Henry Wilson, chief of the imperial general staff, argued against committing British troops to these "buffers." He said that just keeping communications open would take seven divisions. That evening Sir Henry wrote in his diary that Georgia and Azerbaijan would certainly "go Bolshevik."[111] A few days later, he told Sir Louis Mallet, British consul in Baku, that he did not see why Lenin would not (and thought Lenin would and ought) declare these states part of Russia and retake them. Lloyd George "is totally unable to offer a solution and simply drifts from one crisis to another," Sir Henry noted in his diary.[112]

At the urging of Oliver Wardrop, British high commissioner for Transcaucasia in Tiflis, Lloyd-George asked representatives of the Powers on 10 January 1920 for quick decisions on recognizing the republics; Georgia and Azerbaijan received de facto recognition right away.[113] Lloyd-George then gave his flabby support to protecting Transcaucasia as a barrier against bolshevism. He claimed that the Soviet danger was mostly political, not military, in its use of "gold and propaganda." The Soviets attack by propaganda and military action was of little use against such tactics, he said. He was "not averse," however, to sending arms to Caucasia to make coming to terms more attractive to the Bolsheviks, nor did he oppose sending British sailors to reclaim the Caspian flotilla—they could always escape through Enzeli; he saw no need to send troops.[114]

7 The Sovietization
of Azerbaijan

*Entry of the 11th Red Army into Azerbaijan in April 1920
was a shining example of that fraternal assistance which the
Russian people gave to the toilers of Azerbaijan.*

Notes on the History of Soviet Azerbaijan*

THE BATTLE FOR AZERBAIJAN

The acceptance of the ultimatum of the Azerbaijan Communist party (Bolshevik) (AzCP[b] by the interim government in Baku just before midnight on 27 April 1920 formally ended the existence of independent Azerbaijan. The Azerbaijan Revolutionary Committee, Azrevkom, had only been named the previous day by the Baku Bureau of the Kavkraikom (Caucasian regional committee) of the Russian Communist party (Bolshevik) (RCP[b]) and the Central Committee of the AzCP(b), predominantly non-Azerbaijani bodies. Azrevkom ostensibly directed the takeover.[1] Now officially the "supreme organ of state power," Azrevkom cabled Russia for "fraternal assistance." Already on its way, the 11th Red Army arrived in Baku on 28 April. Ordzhonikidze and Kirov came with it to set up head-

---

*E. A. Tokarzhevskii, *Ocherki istorii sovetskogo Azerbaidzhana v period perekhoda na mirnuiu rabotu po vosstanovleniiu narodnogo khoziaistva (1921–1925 gg)* (Baku, 1956), p. 24.

quarters for directing the sovietization of Azerbaijan and the neighboring republics. An "independent Soviet Republic" of Azerbaijan was proclaimed.

The official version of the "voluntary" unification of Azerbaijan with Soviet Russia rests on the claim of Azerbaijani support. The Kavbuiro's selection of the Azrevkom, like the role assigned to the AzCP in the fall of the ADR government, reflected the need to associate Soviet power with native Communists. The highly respected Dr. Nariman Narimanov was appointed chairman of Azrevkom, and the other members—Mirza Davud Huseinov, Ali Heydar Karayev, Ghazanfar Musabekov, Hamid Sultanov, and Dadash Buniatzade—were Azerbaijani Turks, prominent Communists, and former Hümmetists. Narimanov and most other Azrevkom members were not in Baku, however, when Azrevkom was created or when the ADR Parliament accepted the communist ultimatum.

Like Musabekov, Sultanov, and Buniatzade, Narimanov had worked in an Azerbaijani party cell in Astrakhan. Narimanov had also served as a deputy commissar to Stalin at Narkomnats.[2] He had gone to Petrovsk (now Makhachkala) from Moscow on 21 April, then returned to Moscow to "confer" with Lenin and Stalin. Subsequent events suggest he may have argued against invasion. He arrived in Baku on 16 May to assume the presidency of the Azrevkom.[3] Therefore, it was not the men named to the Azrevkom who called for the Red Army on 27 April. In fact, both the Red Army and the AzCP(b) were playing parts assigned to them in a drama directed by the Kavbiuro under Ordzhonikidze and Kirov.

The Azrevkom was replaced as an organ of the state by Sovnarkom (Soviet People's Commissars)[4] but included many of the same people: among others, Sovnarkom president and foreign commissar posts were held by Narimanov; Huseinov became commissar of finance; Chinghiz Yildirim, head of the navy; Sultanov, head of internal affairs; Karayev, head of labor and justice, Gh. Musabekov, head of land, trade, industry, and food; and Buniatzade, head of education and state control.[5] This overlap was less significant than the fact that most of the power was in the hands of the Red Army's Revvoensovet (Revolutionary Military Soviet), in which Musabekov was the only Azerbaijani Turk,[6] and the army's "Special Department," which was concerned with opponents of communist power. The Special Department, which reportedly sent hundreds to the firing squad or Arctic exile,[7] was complemented by the Soviet Caspian fleet's Cheka (MorCheka) and an Azerbaijan Cheka (AzCheka), created on 28 April.[8] Also exercising power in Baku was the Baku *revkom* (revolutionary committee), with half non-Azerbaijani membership,[9] and the AzCP(b), an *oblast'*-level organization of RCP(b) with a native minority. Most powerful of all was the RCP(b) Kavbiuro led by Ordzhonikidze, through whom Lenin's and Stalin's orders were carried out. Khan Khoiskii, Sulkevich, and others were executed.

By means of party and revolutionary committees, the Bolshevik center undermined the much-touted, but purely pro forma, independence of Azerbaijan. "Whatever form Soviet power assumes in the Caucasus . . . we cannot tolerate here the creation of any isolated or independent communist parties," proclaimed the Kavbiuro in April 1920.[10] Like the viceroyalty and the Baku Commune, this was nonnative rule, for the party-state division coincided with national differences. The state apparatus was made up mainly of Azerbaijani Turks; in the party, they were a minority.[11] As late as 1925, after a long drive to "indigenize" local organs of power, less than half the AzCP's members would be Azerbaijanis.[12] Its leadership was primarily Russian and Armenian.

Consolidation of Bolshevik power throughout Azerbaijan was a difficult task, for, as shown by 1918–1919 voting data, there was no support for the Bolsheviks outside Baku. Communist power would be imposed by military force and other forms of coercion.

The Battle of Ganje: Resistance in the Countryside

After securing Baku, the Red Army moved out to occupy the rest of the republic during May 1920.[13] Soviet sources refer to "counterrevolutionary uprisings" against the Red Army throughout Azerbaijan in the months, even years, after the seizure of Baku.[14] Although resistance has been attributed to "propaganda by beks and khans" and to "Musavat counterrevolutionaries," the strength of that resistance has never been denied. One source recorded that "in May to June 1920 in Azerbaijan arose several powerful uprisings, connected with counterrevolution. The situation originated in Ganje on 26 May. On 5 June an uprising began in Karabagh, on 9 June, in Zakatala."[15] Armed resistance was reported in the Jevad uezd (involving 3,000–5,000 people), in the Lenkoran region (with 1,500 people under command of General Selimov), and at various points along the Azerbaijan-Armenian border. Azerbaijani national forces were fighting both Armenian units and the Red Army in these areas.[16] The Red Army employed maximum security in all units. The Red Air Force commander was under the jurisdiction of the army general staff.[17]

The defense of Ganje in May and June 1920 marked the beginning of the real "Battle of Azerbaijan."[18] The defense of the city was led by loyalists to the fallen ADR government. Col. Jihangir Kazimbekov (1887–1955) commanded the 3d Ganje Infantry Regiment; other forces were under the command of Gen. Jevad Shikhlinskii. Kazimbekov had fought Bolsheviks in the Crimea; he escaped Azerbaijan after the Battle of Ganje and lived more than three decades abroad.[19] Shikhlinskii died in 1920; sources do not indicate where or how.

The Red Army laid siege to the city. Reinforcements arrived almost daily as the Bolsheviks pulled troops from the Georgian frontier. By the end of the battle, despite defections to ADR loyalists,[20] Reds greatly outnumbered the national force. During the last days of the siege, one Red Army unit that had been arrested and jailed as the battle began succeeded in escaping and attacked the defending force from inside the city.[21] This "error of leniency"—merely jailing Red Army or revkom members—would be repeated in other Azerbaijani towns. The Bolsheviks would not make such mistakes in the treatment of their political adversaries. Soviet sources acknowledge that at least one thousand Ganje defenders were killed. Of those who survived, some went to other towns and villages to face the Red Army again. Many took refuge in the mountains where they carried on the fight as guerrillas. Their memories are preserved in oral accounts of their fighting, in new dastans. A few novelists and painters refer obliquely to these heroic figures.

The Ganje battle was the beginning, not the end, of armed resistance to the Bolshevik takeover of Azerbaijan. After the crushing of Ganje, uprisings occurred in Karabagh and Zakatala. In the northern region of Zakatala, a local revkom's order to surrender weapons sparked resistance by as many as a thousand people. With the aid of the local militia, they seized the telegraph and arrested the revkom. Their force, which grew to three thousand within a week, fought Red cavalry and rifle units brought again from the nearby Georgian border. Although the locals held out for ten days, they were finally defeated. Many fled to remote mountain bases to continue their fight.[22] Similar battles were fought in every major town of Azerbaijan—Shusha and other towns in Karabagh, in Nukha, Barda, and in the Zangezur and Nakhjivan regions.[23] The battle the Red Army did not fight at Baku it fought over and over throughout Azerbaijan.

To secure Soviet power in the Ganje region after the bloody success of the Bolshevik forces, Sultan Mejid Efendiyev,[24] an Azerbaijani Turk and longtime Bolshevik, was sent as extraordinary commissar to enforce the Ganje party committee's authority. To accomplish this, he established (or reorganized) a local revkom, which, in turn, created a *kombed* (Committee of Poor, a "temporary organ of state power") "to deepen the revolution in the village and to destroy parasites and kulaks who were enemies of Soviet rule." Efendiyev carried out land seizures and nationalization, formed *sov-khozy* (state farms), and "protected" grain in the near-famine conditions. These measures were advertised as counterweights to alleged attempts by local landowners and Musavatists to attack Soviet power by destroying the economy. "Terrorists" were "quickly seized and destroyed."[25]

Armed resistance to communist rule was widespread and would continue at least into 1924. To expand party and state control beyond Baku, the Bolsheviks sent experienced party workers (Azerbaijani Turks like Efendiyev as often as possible) to establish revkoms, kombedy, and other organs of surveillance and coercion. By August 1920 there were revkoms in 16 uezdy, 46 districts, and 435 villages of the republic.[26] Revkoms with numerous kombedy carried out the ruthless grain-requisitioning policy, which, like the kombedy, was part of War Communism that Moscow still followed in 1920. (Kombedy were not established in Armenia and Georgia, where Bolshevik control was not consolidated until 1921.)[27] The revkoms and kombedy with AzCheka branches supplemented the efforts of the Red Army. On 28 May Azrevkom organized a Soviet of Worker-Peasant Defense of Azerbaijan "to which was given wide power for the quick and decisive liquidation of counterrevolutionary uprisings, with the aid of units of the 11th Red Army."[28] Early in August a "small Sovnarkom" was established with only four members—the president of the republic's Sovnarkom and the heads of the Cheka, the Military-Revolutionary Tribunal, and the Military Field Tribunal.[29] The purpose of such a group could only be speedy trial and punishment. In the fall of 1921 summary execution of "bandits" in the Karabagh region was ordered by the Orgbiuro (Organization Bureau) CC AzCP(b); villages sheltering them were to be fined "not less than 10 million rubles."[30]

CONSOLIDATION OF SOVIET POWER

Republican Industry and Agriculture

As the army and other instruments of coercion worked to subdue the population, party and Azrevkom decrees brought economic resources, industry, trade, communications, and transportation under their control. War Communism began to be implemented once the Red Army occupied Baku. Among the many steps taken were the nationalization of industry,[31] mining, banking, and joint stock-companies (including power plants). The state began monopolizing some trade and goods, including cotton,[32] and took control of transport and communications.

The earliest nationalization decree, however, was aimed at the fundamental area of printing and publishing. An Azrevkom decree of 8 May made all polygraph and typographic machinery and equipment the property of the state.[33] Not until 24 May did Azrevkom nationalize the oil industry.[34] "The oil fields, constituting an extremely important branch of our economy, must . . . be marked by the sign: soviet communist!" Kirov proclaimed.[35] Thereafter, oil was requisitioned for use in Russia and, as the conquest in the South proceeded, for Armenia and Georgia. This "free oil" policy continued, despite New Economic Policy (NEP) provisions, into 1922.

Smaller enterprises were prepared for nationalization by state-imposed directives and quotas.[36] The Ganje revkom expropriated warehouses of raw materials, mechanical equipment, factories, and workshops. Revkoms elsewhere followed suit.[37] Despite Azrevkom warnings that such actions "disturb the economic plan of the state [and] deepen the difficulty of industrial recovery,"[38] seizures continued. Personal valuables were lost by legalized robbery. The decree of 31 July "On the requisitioning of precious metals, money and various valuable objects" led to the requisitioning, by the end of 1920, of "10 puds [360 pounds] of gold, 200 puds [7,200 pounds] of silver, 800 gold rings, several thousand carpets and so forth."[39]

There is no indication that control and confiscation facilitated economic recovery. Regional industries had been seriously damaged in the continuing fighting; mines and factories were not functioning, and production levels of cotton, cloth, cement, oil, and coal were at a fraction of their prewar levels.[40] Even by official estimates, however, 1913 levels were not achieved until the second half of the decade or into the 1930s.[41] Many Soviet secondary sources do not begin describing industrial and infrastructural construction until 1926. Fighting in the early 1920s must have set back recovery begun by the ADR.

Control over communications networks was vital for Soviet power. Telegraph, printed publications, and radio came under official control early in the process of sovietization.[42] Newspapers, a key element in Leninist propaganda, proliferated. Museums, film studios, and theaters were brought under state power.[43] Radio broadcasting appealed to Lenin, for it could send to all republics "speeches, reports, and lectures given in Moscow."[44] Mercifully, these programs were only on the air for short intervals. Because broadcasts from Moscow were in Russian, they had a small audience. Local broadcasts fulfilled educational and propaganda needs with programs called "Workers' Radio University" and "Peasants' Radio Journal."

In the countryside, too, recovery was subordinated to control. Agriculture had suffered extensive destruction from prolonged fighting. Although tens of thousands of village homes had been destroyed and the population displaced,[45] no figures are available on the total number of those who died, were injured, or fled during the prolonged struggle for independence. Land under cultivation was reduced 33 percent from the 1913 level.[46] "Land reform" and "pacification" meant dispossessing and arresting or shooting landowners ("class enemies") who resisted Bolshevik power and the nationalization of land. As in Russia, land belonged to the state and was provided for peasants' use. Even those whose land was not nationalized were required to meet production quotas.[47] The old court system was replaced with a Soviet system.[48]

In May 1921, almost a year after his arrival in Ganje, Efendiyev, a member of the Central Executive Committee (CEC) of the AzCP, was named commissar of lands. Although Efendiev was charged with ensuring food production and delivery, the expanded irrigation that he oversaw in the Mughan steppe led to more cotton acreage. Officially encouraged, as it had been in tsarist times, cotton production began to expand at the expense of food crops; according to official statistics, it doubled from 3,000 *desiatina* in 1920 to 6,000 desiatina in 1922.⁴⁹ Recovery in agriculture thus did not necessarily benefit the republic or its population but certainly did benefit the central government, which acquired cotton, like grain, at low fixed prices. In May 1922 Efendiyev would be moved from the Commissariat of Lands to the Worker-Peasant Inspectorate (WPI), a state power enforcement arm.⁵⁰

Refugees and nomads complicated matters. Armenians from Julfa demanded space in Zangezur; Azerbaijanis fled Zangezur to Shusha in Karabagh.⁵¹ They numbered in the thousands and made regional food shortages worse. Nomads, whose summer pastures (*yaylak*) were in Daghestan, the mountains of western Karabagh, or the new Armenian SSR, had been prevented for several years from moving their herds to higher elevations in summer. The resulting losses of animals impoverished thousands, and many of the nomads died.⁵²

This human, political, and economic catastrophe was almost unknown to the outside world; U.S. government observers monitoring events from Istanbul reported in the summer of 1921 that

> it has been a matter of common knowledge that the extreme policies of Lenin and Trotsky were gradually being replaced by more liberal ones. One of the first instances . . . was [Moscow's] attitude toward the republics of Azerbaijan, Georgia, and Armenia. These three republics were all recognized autonomous states which accepted a form of Soviet Communist Administration, and while amenable to the jurisdiction of Moscow, there was little confiscation of private property and practically no reign of terror such as prevailed in other parts of the old Russian Empire.⁵³

Regional Integration

After the loss of national independence, remaining a separate and distinct Soviet republic became Azerbaijan's major challenge. The Bolshevik conquest of the neighboring republics of Armenia and Georgia allowed de facto reconstitution of the former viceroyalty of Transcaucasia. "Vitally necessary for the existence of the Georgian and the Armenian soviet republics was the unhindered receipt of bread and other food products from Soviet Russia, and oil from Azerbaijan."⁵⁴

On 9 April 1921 Lenin telegraphed Ordzhonikidze: "I demand urgently the creation of a regional [oblast'] economic organ for all Transcaucasia."⁵⁵ Because the Communist party of each republic was already an oblast'-level branch of the RCP(b), economic unity would reinforce existing political control. Indigenous leaders opposed economic integration as diminishing their sovereignty.

Ordzhonikidze's first steps toward regional economic integration were in the fundamental and related areas of the railroad and trade. Narimanov's reluctance to accept the proposed integration (despite Georgian and Armenian agreement) forced Ordzhonikidze to go to Baku to address a plenum of the CC AzCP(b). Ordzhonikidze told party members that each republic's own railroad system was too small to be effective. "It's funny," he said, "to see Voskanov in the role of commissar of transport [of Armenia] when he has only one broken-down train car, in which he himself rides, with one broken-down engine."[56] Furthermore, trade had to be unified to eliminate damaging competition. Each republic, he said, used oil it received free from Azerbaijan as foreign currency. This had to stop, said Ordzhonikidze. "The Azerbaijan and Georgian republics must assume the task of supplying Armenia."[57]

These words confirmed Azerbaijani fears that their republic was to support its neighbors while more than half a million people, perhaps 20 percent of the Azerbaijan population, starved at home.[58] Azerbaijan Sovnarkom member Hamid Sultanov articulated their concern by delicately asking if the proposed unification would benefit some republics and hurt others. Ordzhonikidze answered boldly, turning the question inside out:

> If we pose the question in a soviet, communist fashion, then no republic will be offended. If we pose the question egotistically, it is necessary to answer directly—Azerbaijan will be hurt, Georgia to a lesser degree, and Armenia not at all. . . . Who among you would get up and say that anything we get from the exchange of Baku oil should be refused to our Armenian comrades?[59]

Narimanov continued to oppose the plan and those who backed it. Ordzhonikidze neatly removed himself from the dispute, saying: "Comrade Narimanov has no disagreement with me, he has a disagreement with comrade Huseinov and comrade Kaderli."[60] A resolution approving rail and trade unification was passed by the AzCP plenum. Agreement among republics followed.

Seizing the precedent, Lenin immediately ordered recognition of the Georgian State Bank as "a Bank for all Transcaucasia."[61] In June a Kavbiuro plenum established a "commission on the unification."[62]

Steps toward economic integration continued. Soviet sources admit opposition existed but only among "those with nationalist tendencies."[63] In August 1921 creation of an Economic Bureau of Transcaucasian Republics was proposed in the Kavbiuro plenum. The sole no vote was cast by

Narimanov.[64] Subsequent opposition forced Moscow to vote on the matter; Stalin, Molotov, and Kamenev favored creation of the bureau, Lenin voiced "no objection," and Trostkii abstained. Ordzhonikidze was prepared to move immediately, but continued opposition led by Narimanov forced him to delay. Ordzhonikidze said, "We will go by quiet steps and will not fight."[65] Narimanov later wrote to Stalin:

> The Muslim toiling masses have suffered enough from the policies of the Russian tsar, and they know well what are tsarism, democracy, and Soviet power . . . when the Azerbaijani citizen sees that kerosene is cheaper in Tiflis than in Ganje, he [begins to see] the guilt of colonizers.[66]

For all the attention given to economic matters, the question of republican borders was also complex. After the republics were reconquered by the Russians, the border issue had to be considered by the Communist party. Concomitantly with the conquest of Azerbaijan in April 1920, the new Soviet republic's possession of all disputed lands was upheld by the communist hierarchy against the claims of "bourgeois" governments.[67] In July the Red Army occupied Nakhjivan and declared it to be the Nakhjivan Soviet Socialist Republic (SSR), with "close ties" to the Azerbaijan SSR.[68] The sovietization of neighboring Armenia during the winter changed the equation. A November 1920 declaration by the Azrevkom celebrating the "victory of Soviet power in Armenia" declared that both Zangezur and Nakhjivan should be awarded to Armenia to signify Azerbaijan's support for the Armenian people in their battle against the Dashnaks (whose bands under General Dro were still operating in Zangezur) and to prevent any territorial matter from coming between these centuries-old friends.[69] But the December 1920 treaty between the Russian Soviet Federative Socialist Republic (RSFSR) and Armenia recognized Armenian claims to Zangezur, not to Karabagh or Nakhjivan.[70]

Nakhjivan's strategic position made it, with Zangezur, either a corridor between Turkey and Azerbaijan or, if controlled by Armenia, a barrier between them. With Zangezur under Armenian control, Nakhjivan could not be a bridge. Although Lenin welcomed Azrevkom's offer to cede Nakhjivan to Armenia as a "fraternal act," he did not agree to it: "Soviet power in Armenia, as the power of the people itself, sees that its own strength lies only in the clear expression of the will of the population itself, among them, the toiling population of Nakhjivan."[71] A referendum taken early in 1921 demonstrated that "nine-tenths" of the Nakhjivan population wanted to be included in Azerbaijan, "with the rights of an autonomous republic."[72] Perhaps not coincidentally, the Turkish national movement, then engaged in their Independence War, insisted that Nakhjivan be confirmed as part of Azerbaijan because of demographic composition, strategic significance, and the local population's fear of Armenian annexation.[73] Lenin, who intended to sign a treaty with the Kemalist forces, was willing to accept this demand. The provision was embodied in the 1921 treaties of Moscow (signed in March between the Bolsheviks and the Kemalist forces) and of Kars (in October between the Kemalists and the Caucasian republics). The treaties were nearly identical.[74] According to both, Nakhjivan's separate status and "close ties" with Azerbaijan were confirmed.[75] Nakhjivan temporarily remained a separate SSR.

Between the signing of the Moscow and Kars treaties, a protracted territorial dispute took place among the three republics. In the spring of 1921 Kavbiuro established a commission for the demarcation of borders under Kirov's chairmanship.[76]

During the border commission meetings in June, the newspaper *Soviet Armenia* published a notice that the Azerbaijan SSR had agreed to hand over to Armenia the mountainous Karabagh region. Records of a discussion among CC AzCP members show they knew nothing of such an "agreement." Erevan, asserting its claim, appointed a representative and sent him to Karabagh. Narimanov demanded his recall in telegrams to the Kavbiuro in Tiflis and the Soviet government in Erevan.[77] The CC AzCP and Sovnarkom rejected the surrender of mountainous Karabagh to Armenia on the basis of its economic ties with Azerbaijan but said that Azerbaijani Turkish and Armenian citizens should be "widely involved" in "soviet construction." Privately, Narimanov told Mirza Davud Huseinov that Ordzhonikidze had said that the issue of mountainous Karabagh "is a matter of honor to all Soviet Russia and that *he [Ordzhonikidze] must decide the question* in that spirit."[78] As Shaumian had done in padding the Baku soviet with Bolshevik supporters, Ordzhonikidze here sought to "broaden the constituency" to win his point.

In early July a further step was taken in a "broadened plenum" of the Kavbiuro with representatives of each republic, the soviets, the unions, the army, and the railroad administration. Stalin was present. After a lengthy discussion a resolution to transfer mountainous Karabagh was carried against Narimanov's opposition. Voting for the resolution were Ordzhonikidze, Miasnikov (Miasnikian), Kirov, and Figatner.[79] Narimanov argued that the importance of this issue for Azerbaijan was so great that it should be referred to the CC RCP(b) for a final decision. The Kavbiuro adopted a resolution to that effect.[80]

Stalin apparently did not speak in this debate but seems to have made his opinion known after the session, as the ensuing backdoor tactics bear his mark. The next day (5 July),[81] Ordzhonikidze and Nazaretian, an Armenian Communist, called for a reconsideration of the previous day's resolutions for which they had voted. Those were rescinded and the following resolution was passed:

Proceeding from the necessity for national peace among Muslims and Armenians and of the economic ties between upper (mountainous) and lower Karabagh, of its permanent ties with Azerbaijan, mountainous Karabagh is to remain within the borders of the AzSSR, receiving wide regional [oblast'] autonomy with the administrative center at Shusha, becoming an autonomous region [oblast'].[82]

   b) The CC AzCP is entrusted with the delineation of the border of the autonomous oblast.

Within two weeks, Kirov became first secretary of the CC AzCP.[83] He had been Ordzhonikidze's right-hand man in the Kavbiuro since its creation and had voted with him in the Karabagh dispute. Kirov, then, was to be the instrument of Ordzhonikidze's and Stalin's influence in Azerbaijan in the wake of conflicts with Narimanov over territorial and economic issues.[84]

Narimanov apparently took the position that existing constitutional provisions were adequate to protect Armenian autonomy in mountainous Karabagh, so that a separate administrative unit, which would further diminish Baku's control there, was not needed.[85] Borders for an autonomous oblast' were not drawn.

In August AzCP member Levon Mirzoyan began a campaign to force the issue. He told a party meeting in Shusha that mountainous Karabagh's autonomy would be safeguarded against "the possibility of a national knout" by the creation of a separate administrative unit. Mirzoyan telegraphed the CC AzCP (sending a copy to the Kavbiuro), saying that the "normalization" of conditions required the creation of an independent administration.[86] On 6 October Kirov sent a soviet (made up of three Armenians, one Jew, two Azerbaijani) to mountainous Karabagh to carry out the Kavbiuro decision. He ordered the commissar of finance to allot 1 billion rubles for work in mountainous Karabagh.[87] A meeting of the Orgbiuro CC AzCP(b) under Kirov's chairmanship decided to appoint a special commission "for the delineation of borders for an autonomous part of Karabagh."[88] Coming just eleven days after the Kars Treaty, the action on mountainous Karabagh may have been intended, if only in part, as compensation to Armenian sensibilities, though not to the Armenian SSR.

The Karabagh issue was only partly a competition between the state apparatus (primarily Azerbaijani Turkish) and the party apparatus (largely non-Azerbaijani with a Russian first secretary). Some Azerbaijani Turks who held party and state posts supported Kavbiuro (Ordzhonikidze-Kirov) efforts in Karabagh as they had on economic integration. Others in the AzCP echoed Narimanov's argument in an unsigned statement of December 1921 that "there is no so-called Karabagh question; [there is] general weakness of party and soviet work in Karabagh."[89] Rather, the dispute entailed a conflict of interests. Some young, indigenous Communists may have been persuaded, by a lifetime of Bolshevik rhetoric, of the cultural "backwardness" of their own nation, which they sought to suppress and from which they sought to distance themselves by association with "European" communism and its "Progressive" Russian and Georgian representatives. Forsaking their national identity, they forsook the cause of their nation.

The party exercised direct control over the organs of the state, despite official claims that the two institutions were separate and that the state was independent and sovereign. The conflict would not be resolved for more than a year, as higher levels of the party apparatus were busy establishing the Transcaucasian Soviet Federated Socialist Republic (TSFSR).[90]

TRANSCAUCASIAN FEDERATION (1922–1936)

The Formation Process

Early in November 1921 the Kavbiuro "declared the necessity for the organization of a federative union of the republics of Transcaucasia." With Kirov at the helm, the AzCP became an enthusiastic supporter of Kavbiuro policies. All Baku party organizations and the AzCEC supported the call for federation.[91]

Some dissent, however, was voiced. M. D. Huseinov and Ruhulla Akhundov said that the pace of integration was being forced by the Kavbiuro. Although their objections were officially rejected by the Politburo CC RCP(b),[92] Lenin began criticizing the Kavbiuro's clumsy handling of the matter. He wrote to Stalin that immediate creation of the TSFSR would be "premature, i.e., it required a certain period of time for discussion, propaganda, and soviets' action from below."[93] The campaign to drum up support for federation began in December 1921 and was to last four months. The target date for establishing the federation was March 1922. Narimanov remained unsatisfied and in January 1922, midway through the propaganda campaign, protested the plan's rapid imposition.[94]

One campaign theme was antinationalism. Kirov made this the cornerstone of his own propaganda, warning the Fourth AzCP Congress in February 1922 that "ultranationalism" existed in Azerbaijan among high party and state officials. He made acceptance of the federation plan a test of communism in Azerbaijan.[95]

As the campaign for federation reached a climax, meetings of party organizations proliferated. Despite Kirov's control of the AzCP, Narimanov's continual opposition and influence could not be ignored. In view of the stiff opposition from Georgia, the Kavbiuro faced potential dissent at the final stages. Ordzhonikidze continued to accord Narimanov the recognition due him as senior Azerbaijani Communist but managed to dilute his power. Narimanov was included on major regional committees such as the RCP Transcaucasian Regional Committee (Zakkraikom), where he was the only Azerbaijani of nine full members. He would be elected to the TSFSR soviet after unanimous acceptance of the federation on 12 March 1922. But Narimanov was not there to accept posts or influence policy.

Narimanov's criticism of party policies was an irritation not only to Ordzhonikidze who, after all, was merely charged with their implementation, but to Lenin, with whom the policies had originated.[96] Thus, when the Western powers proposed an economic conference in Genoa for early March 1922, Lenin's selection of Narimanov to represent Azerbaijan in the Soviet delegation may not have been merely a recognition of Narimanov's prestige. Whatever the intent, it effectively removed Narimanov from Caucasia at the critical moment. While he was being elected the sole Azerbaijani on the Zakkraikom in late February, he was in Moscow preparing for the Genoa Conference. The delegation finally left Moscow in late March, in the wake of Narimanov's election to the TSFSR soviet. He was gone until late May, during the formative months when early policies and precedents were being established.[97] His election to both bodies followed the announcement of his participation in the Genoa Conference, so his absence was assured. The Georgian representative to the Genoa Conference, Budu Mdvani, was elected as the Georgian representative on the TSFSR soviet.[98] Thus, the representatives of the two troublesome republics were absent and "honored" at the same time. The Armenian representative to the TSFSR was A. F. Miasnikov, who had voted with Ordzhonikidze and Kirov on Karabagh issues.[99]

The agreement for federation was accepted by the plenipotentiaries in the Central Executive Committees (CEC) of each republic on schedule in Tiflis, 12 March 1922.[100] The TSFSR soviet would have jurisdiction over military affairs, finances, foreign affairs and trade, communication and transportation, the battle against counterrevolution, and the economic policies of each constituent republic.[101] The process of establishing the TSFSR lasted from the March agreement until December 1922 when, despite several disputes, the federation was established. The nominally independent republics lost their sovereignty.[102]

Having rejected Stalin's "autonomization plan,"[103] Lenin proposed creating a Union of Soviet Socialist Republics (USSR) with rights guaranteed on paper.[104] The republics of Caucasia would join as components of the TSFSR. The final months of the formation of the TSFSR coincided with the drafting of the USSR constitution.

On 30 November a document entitled "Basic Points of the Constitution of the USSR" was accepted by the Politbiuro of the CC RCP(b). All republican party CCs, not organs of the states, accepted the draft in two weeks as did the first Congress of Soviets of Transcaucasia and the representatives of the individual republics.[105] Narimanov was elected to the Presidium of the CEC USSR by Ordzhonikidze's nomination.[106]

Creating the TSFSR relied on (1) a growing degree of central control over Caucasian administration, economy, and trade; (2) the supremacy of the party over the state apparatus; and (3) the use of propaganda and "public discussion" to make central decisions palatable. Azerbaijan thus found itself back in the "prison house of peoples," with new and zealous jailers. The proselytization rhetoric of the new "religion" was different, but little of the substance had changed. Now, however, the Azerbaijanis were compelled to call it freedom.

TSFSR Control through Federation

The Transcaucasian Federation was a control mechanism that used means similar to those by which the Bolsheviks had consolidated power in Azerbaijan—administrative hierarchies, economic control, organs of surveillance and security, and the Communist party. The TSFSR Congress of Soviets met only seven times between 1922 and 1935; thus power rested with the small CEC and the Presidium. Most republican commissariats were subordinated to corresponding TSFSR bodies.[107] In the late 1920s industrialization and collectivization would be administered by the TSFSR Higher Economic Soviet.[108] With the inauguration of full central planning, all economic and budget decisions would shift to Moscow.[109] Few Azerbaijani Turks held posts in TSFSR organizations. Narimanov was on the Presidium, though he moved in 1923 to Moscow; Sultan Mejid Efendiyev was elected to the CEC in 1922; and M. D. Huseinov was on the TSFSR CEC and Commissariats of Finance and Foreign Affairs until 1929, when he was transferred to Tajikistan, then Moscow.[110] Georgians seemed to dominate, usually holding the presidency.

A small group of young Azerbaijani Communists built their careers in Azerbaijan under TSFSR oversight. Ghazanfar Musabekov succeeded Narimanov as president of AzSovnarkom in 1923 or 1924 and was succeeded by Ali Heydar Karayev in 1927.[111] Efendiyev held a series of posts. Mustafa Kuliyev was deputy chairman of the Sovnarkom and commissar of education in the mid-1920s.[112] Mir Jafar Baghirov was commissar of internal affairs (1921–1933) and would be AzCP first secretary (1933–1953).

TSFSR's "operational direction" over economies of the republics was vital for regional control and to funnel resources—especially oil—to bolster the USSR. Perhaps as important as oil were the railroads that carried it. In 1926, TSFSR Gosplan (State Planning Committee) established a plan for railway repair and construction.[113] Despite its high priority, railroad construction seems to have come to a standstill after 1929. Rail in use increased from 2,162 kilometers in 1929 to just 2,188 kilometers in 1932.[114] Such a small increase is especially surprising in an era of *udarniki* (shock workers). By 1 February 1930 Azerbaijan railroad construction was said to have had an "udarnik brigade" of 1,279.[115] By the end of the Second Five-Year Plan period, 6,331 of 11,132 workers in Azerbaijan were udarniki, which "speaks of their high degree of socialist consciousness,"[116] but not, apparently, of their productivity.

The shortage of new rail lines may have been deliberate. Existing lines took oil where Moscow wanted it and allowed movement of troops from Russia into and within Caucasia. Other lines, the promise of which made good propaganda, did not necessarily serve the regime's interest. Such a case was the planned railroad from Baku to Julfa in Nakhjivan over relatively flat terrain. An economically logical link, it crossed Armenian-held Zangezur, undermining that territory's role as a barrier between Nakhjivan (and therefore the Turkish border) and the rest of Azerbaijan. Work had reportedly started on the 408-kilometer line in 1920 during Azerbaijan's independence but was not completed until 1930 or later.[117] The completion of that line with a trunk into Iran coincided with expanded Soviet-Iranian trade.[118] But trains carry soldiers, too, and would in the following decade.

Organs of surveillance and coercion—AzCheka, the Commissariat of Internal Affairs, GPU (state political directory, a surveillance organ), and others—were permanent features. The WPI-CSC (Worker-Peasant Inspectorate–Central Surveillance Committee) "inspected" the Sovnarkom, individual commissariats, and even the State Planning Committee and "economized" on their personnel and structure. Among other cuts, WPI-CSC eliminated thirty-two missions for interrepublic relations "without harm." In the court system one level of appeals courts was eliminated.[119]

The best control mechanism was the party, which acted as an effective check on government and the soviets through its members in those bodies. The AzCP continued to represent Russian power. Most Russian Communists in Caucasia in 1925 were in Azerbaijan: of 10,245 Russians, 7,795 were in Azerbaijan (2,255 in Georgia and 195 in Armenia).[120] Less than one-half of one percent of the Azerbaijani Turks were party members, and they were a minority in their own republic's party. In January 1925 AzCP membership was almost 25,000, four times larger than in February 1923.[121] The swelling of the AzCP under Kirov was not due to the recruitment of Azerbaijanis, despite the regime's *korenizatsiia* (indigenization) policy.[122] In contrast to the Armenian and Georgian parties (93 percent and 71 percent indigenous cadres), the Azerbaijan party apparatus in 1925 included about 43 percent Azerbaijani Turks (called Tiurk in official documents), 38 percent Russians, and 18 percent Armenians.[123] That represented a growth in the proportion of Russians and Armenians from 35 percent and 12 percent in February 1923 and a decline in Azerbaijani Turks from 47 percent.[124] If the size of the party and the number of nonnative members in it indicate the measure of force needed to impose Soviet rule, then Azerbaijan must have been a troublesome republic for the Bolsheviks. The party in Azerbaijan was larger and included more nonnatives than the other two Caucasian republics five years after the Red Army reconquest.

More important, the AzCP had many nonnatives in its leadership—Kirov, Mirzoyan, Sarkis, Kaminskii (president of the Baksovet [Baku soviet]), Serebrovskii (Baksovet), Armenak Karakozov (Karakozian),[125] and others.[126] Not all Azerbaijani Turks, however, could be presumed to represent Azerbaijani interests; thus korenizatsiia in Azerbaijan was used to enforce central, not local, power despite the use of native cadres. Efendiyev supported centralization and TSFSR power,[127] as did Huseinov and Karayev. Those who worked for local interests, like Nariman Narimanov, were discredited or removed from the scene. Narimanov was a significant threat to advocates of central control, for he was a respected Communist who had believed that Marxism would liberate his native land from Russian colonialism. He argued as a Marxist for Azerbaijan's "own" way to communism under native rule.[128] Removing him from Caucasia when the TSFSR was created and again the year after (by election to the CEC USSR) did not silence him.

Narimanov wrote "Toward a History of Our Revolution in the Borderlands," which he directed as a memorandum to Stalin, Trotskii, and Karl Radek in late 1923.[129] In it he informed Stalin that "Ordhonikidze put forward my candidacy for . . . CEC USSR so that in Azerbaijan there would be no more discussion about [the republic's] interests [and he] places his trust in those petty individuals who kowtow before him in order to secure their own positions and cry about nationalist tendencies in Azerbaijan." Narimanov warned that the "national tendency will last as long as an opposite tendency exists against it."

Narimanov argued that when AzCP policies were carried out by non-Azerbaijanis, it provoked national hostility. The Musavat, he stated, had handed over power to "Muslim-Communists." In fact, power was held by Armenian Communists and Azerbaijanis with no concern for Azerbaijan's well-being. Narimanov numbered Huseinov and Karayev as uncaring about Azerbaijan and castigated Mikoyan and his protégés, Mirzoyan and Sarkis, for remaining in Azerbaijan to carry out "Dashnak work under the flag of communism." Mirzoyan recruited into the party nationalistic Russian workers who evoked a nationalistic response from the local population. Answering Mikoyan's suggestion that Narimanov was a nationalist, Narimanov recalled his 1890s novel, *Sona and Bahadur*, about the love between an Armenian girl and an Azerbaijani boy, written "when Mikoyan was still a Dashnak."

Several months later, Narimanov added that "the CC AzCP in the persons of Sergo [Ordzhonikidze] and Stalin do not believe us, the Turks. . . . The honorable worker-Turks will never forget such disregard for Azerbaijan on the part of the CC RCP." Within a year, Narimanov died in Moscow at age fifty-four under unknown circumstances. The official cause of death was heart failure. His body was cremated.

Cultural Control

More subtle than organizational control were regime policies toward language, literature, and education. Cultural policy was crucial in shaping the future communist person: "In a socialist state, there is and can be no neutral art," proclaimed a CC CPSU resolution of 1925.

One fundamental element of culture policy was alphabet "reform." Adoption of the Latin alphabet had been suggested in the nineteenth century by Mirza Fath Ali Akhunzade and was anticipated by the ADR. When the Bolsheviks supported Latinization, taking sides in an existing debate, they saw in the alphabet change a rare chance to cut off the Azerbaijani Turks from the new, emphatically anti-Bolshevik, Turkish republic. Over time, Latinization would also block new generations from reading pre-Soviet publications that might perpetuate religion or "bourgeois" ideas of liberty or cultural autonomy. Latinization was adopted by the AzCEC in 1924 but phased in gradually.[130]

Other Turks in the USSR and the Iranian Tajiks followed suit, as did the Turkish republic, where numerous Turkestani and Azerbaijani émigrés wrote anti-Bolshevik tracts. Thus in 1937, in conjunction with other cultural purges, the Latin alphabet was denounced and the Cyrillic alphabet proposed. Touted as "progressive," it was admitted that using the Cyrillic alphabet would facilitate learning Russian.[131] The script was changed officially in January 1940, when Cyrillic replaced all the republics' Latin alphabets but the script was slightly different in each, with the letters in a different order.

With the change in the script came artificial differentiations in the language. New official vocabulary was introduced, often substituting Russian words for Turkish, Persian, or Arabic ones: *partiia* instead of *firka*, *respublika* for *jumhuriyet*, *sovet* for *shura*. Language histories proclaimed the languages "separate and distinct"—Türki became Azerbaijani, Uzbek, and Turkmen. The names of the nations were changed to conform. To speak of being Turks was now considered dangerous "nationalism."

Literature, too, came under attack, especially after 1927, for "national-ist" and "sentimental" themes.[132] Criticism of pre-1920 works and their authors escalated as "proletarian" literature, based on Russian models, was put forward as the only appropriate literature for the new society.[133]

Schools were to convey the values of the "new society," which, with its rhetoric of "nationalization" or "Turkization," seemed to favor the arguments of pre-Soviet Azerbaijani community leaders. These terms referred to the form, not the content, of education. Officially, communist ideology, class struggle, and proletarian leadership, the cornerstones of all cultural policy, were stressed. An all-union conference of teachers in January 1925 adopted a resolution that highlighted these points.[134] Teachers proclaimed their acceptance of party leadership in "cultural construction."

After this declaration was adopted in Azerbaijan, other goals were proclaimed:[135] (1) to strengthen the class basis of education and spread communist values, (2) to create stronger ties to the village, (3) to establish social organizations for workers, and (4) to establish the school system on the basis of the polytechnicum: every boy and girl by age seventeen should have a basic general and polytechnical education. The main themes appear to have been "communization" (spreading communist ideology and combating national or other loyalties); "proletarianization" (establishing ties to, among, and for the "proletariat," using the Russian worker as a model, to bring children of workers and peasants into schools and to enforce "proletarian" values, again according to the Russian model); and "technicumization" (enhancing technical training at the expenses of "liberal" education, the study of the humanities, or "esoteric" scholarship). The national form, that is, use of the native language, would be supported and much touted, but central directives would soon make the content of curriculum and texts conform to the CPSU, essentially Russian, norms.

TERRITORIAL "APPLES OF DISCORD": KARABAGH AND NAKHJIVAN

Creation of the Autonomous Oblast' of Nagorno-Karabagh

In December 1922, after more than a year of "party work" in Karabagh by primarily Armenian Communists,[136] armed clashes in mountainous Karabagh were still being reported, but whether against Soviet power or on a national basis was not stated. The Presidium of the CC AzCP established a three-man Central Commission on Karabagh Affairs[137] made up of Kirov (Russian), Mirzabekian (Armenian), and A. N. Karakozov (apparently Armenian) to administer the area.[138] The Presidium also appointed a seven-man committee headed by Karakozov to pursue the creation of an autonomous oblast' in mountainous Karabagh. On the committee were two Azerbaijanis and four Armenians (besides Karakozov) including a party secretary of Zangezur and a member of the Armenian Sovnarkom.[139] The commission that would administer the hotly disputed territory included no representatives from one of the claimants. Its working committee on the equally controversial matter of separate administration would be made up of twice as many members from one contending nation as from the other. Karakozov, while working in Karabagh in 1922, served simultaneously as the representative of the Azrevkom, the CC AzCP, and the Armenian revkom. Many party workers brought into mountainous Karabagh during his tenure appear to have been Armenians, reinforcing the Armenian character of the Communist party there.[140]

In June 1923, Karakozov's committee recommended to the Presidium of the CC AzCP that mountainous Karabagh become an autonomous administrative unit.[141] The Zakkraikom ordered the AzCP to comply within one month. A protocol of 1 July 1923 from the Presidium of the CC AzCP over Kirov's signature "suggested" to the Azerbaijan CEC the creation of an "Autonomous Karabagh oblast'" with its center at Khankend (later Stepanakert), not the historical capital, Shusha. Land and water would henceforth belong to the current residents, a provision that undercut the nomads' claims to their traditional pastures. A revkom was to be established under Karakozov and an oblast' committee (*obkom*) under comrade Manutsiyan. A special commission was appointed to draw borders, and an agitation department would carry out a campaign to "explain . . . to Turkish and Armenian populations the significance of this reform."[142] Decrees conforming to these "suggestions" were soon issued. The Azerbaijan Sovnarkom provided the new revkom with 15,000 gold rubles immediately, 20,000 in August, and 2 million in September.[143]

Disputes over land and water rights, nomads' access, and boundaries continued for more than a year. In November 1924 the Autonomous Oblast' of Nagorno-Karabagh (AONK) was officially proclaimed and confirmed as a constituent part of the Azerbaijan SSR. It was mandated, however, that "all business, legislation and instruction in schools in the AONK will be conducted in the native [Armenian] language." [144] AONK's own CEC, Sovnarkom, and Congress of Soviets were established, Karakozov chairing the Sovnarkom until 1928. The party and state organs were staffed primarily by Armenians who not only ensured Armenian cultural autonomy with Armenian-language newspapers, schools, and arts but strengthened it. Armenian type from Shusha was moved to the new capital, Khankend, and Turkish type (then Arabic script) was moved to Aghdam in a neighboring uezd designed as the administrative center for "lower" Karabagh.[145] The AONK allotment in the republican budget was generous relative to that of the larger and more populous Nakhjivan: in 1924–1925 AONK received more money than Nakhjivan and in 1925–1926 slightly less but still more per capita.[146] These figures do not include extra subsidies, such as a 125,000-ruble grant to Azerbaijan by the Zakkraikom, which was turned over to the AONK in May 1925.[147]

The AONK was carved out of the mountainous portions of the districts in Azerbaijan that constituted historic Karabagh. North to south they were Javanshir, Shusha, Kariaginsk (formerly Jebrail), and a small portion of Kubatlinsk (formerly part of the Zangezur uezd). These four districts bordered the Armenian republic; the AONK initially touched the Armenian border at one point, as shown in the first volume of the *Bol'shaia Sovetskaia Entsiklopediia* published in 1926. By the time the volume on Nagorno-Karabagh was published in the early 1930s, the borders had been changed and no part of the oblast' touched Armenia.[148] The AONK borders were drawn to include Armenian villages and to exclude as much as possible the Azerbaijani Turks' villages. The resulting amoeba-shaped district ensured an Armenian majority as well as numerous disputes among villages (which led to border changes) and with nomads.[149] The Russian term *Nagorno* (mountain) was affixed to the Turkish name *Karabagh*. The rest of Karabagh remained separate, though Karakozov tried to speak for it as well.[150] The name was changed to the Nagorno-Karabagh Autonomous Oblast' (NKAO) in 1937.[151]

Creation of the Nakhjivan ASSR

In the final stages of the Nagorno-Karabagh debate, the status of Nakhjivan as an autonomous but indivisible part of the Azerbaijan SSR was confirmed by organs of the TSFSR and the RCP(b), by the third All-Nakhjivan Congress of Soviets (February 1923), and by the AzCEC in June 1923, just before the final decision on AONK. The AzCEC and the Sovnarkom under Musabekov, perhaps seeking compensation for the loss of mountainous Karabagh, demanded not only administrative but also political autonomy for Nakhjivan within the Azerbaijan SSR. Moscow accepted the demand, and political autonomy was secured in March 1924 with the formation of the Nakhjivan ASSR.[152]

In its handling of Karabagh, Nakhjivan, and Zangezur, Moscow achieved a subtle balancing act: Zangezur was given outright to Armenia as a barrier between Nakhjivan (which was confirmed as part of Azerbaijan) and Karabagh, a portion of which was removed from direct control of Baku and placed under a nominally Azerbaijani republican but de facto Armenian party administration. For Azerbaijan the loss of Zangezur was bitter medicine, but it was quickly accepted as the price of peace. The manipulation of

Karabagh and Nakhjivan was carried out simultaneously, with steps in each process offsetting the other. Azerbaijan gained nominal sovereignty over Karabagh and Nakhjivan but lost actual control of western Karabagh. The cultural and administrative character of that enclave encouraged Azerbaijani emigration and renewed Armenian claims. Armenia lost nominal control over both but won special cultural rights and great political power for its conationals inside Azerbaijan without surrendering comparable rights for Azerbaijanis inside the Armenian SSR. This embittered the Azerbaijani Turks in Armenia and in Azerbaijan. The AONK was proclaimed as a "shining example of Leninist nationality policy," and it was. The territorial settlement demonstrated the primacy of Moscow, particularly of the Communist party. Neither republic could feel safe from border adjustments or interference in its internal affairs, despite written guarantees of republican sovereignty. Tension was perpetuated; "apples of discord" remained.

THE "STALIN CONSTITUTION" AND THE END OF THE TSFSR

By 1936 "historical conditions" allowed the dissolution of TSFSR. The old problem of national animosities having been officially solved, proletarian internationalism reigned.[153] Each republic became part of the USSR under the 1936 "Stalin constitution," the model for new constitutions in all union and autonomous republics. The republican constitutions echoed a commitment to Marxism-Leninism, the construction of socialism, and the equality of citizens and nationalities.[154] Azerbaijan's draft constitution was published in local newspapers in February 1937 and debated and officially ratified, with characteristic Soviet rapidity in constitutional matters, in three weeks.[155] The constitution proclaimed republican power over its own territory but also affirmed Moscow's control over the republic. Included were guarantees of freedoms and autonomy.

The 1937 Azerbaijan SSR constitution, which contained 154 articles, grouped into fourteen chapters,[156] declared the republic to be a "socialist state of workers and peasants" (Article 1). Among the achievements of the "dictatorship of the proletariat" was the liberation of the populace from "the national knout of tsarism and the Russian imperialist bourgeoisie and from clashes of nationalist counterrevolutionaries" (Article 2). The economy was declared to be "a socialist system of economy and socialist property," though socialist property was equated primarily with state property including land, water, forests, raw materials, mines, railroads and other means of transportation, the means of communication, banks, and factories. Socialist property was cooperative-*kolkhoz* property that included the inventories and products of the *kolkhozy*, including "small" parcels of land and livestock "for personal use" (Articles 4–7).

For Azerbaijan the greatest change was the removal of the TSFSR layer of state bureaucracy. Azerbaijan was now a "voluntary" member of the USSR on an equal footing with all other union republics. Its right to secede was confirmed (Articles 13, 15). No changes to its territory could be made without the republic's approval (Article 16). At the same time, the ties to Moscow were clear: sections of this constitution were copied directly from the USSR constitution;[157] all USSR laws were in force on the territory of the republic and all citizens of the republics were citizens of the USSR (Articles 17, 18). Most telling was the division of "union-republic" and "republic" commissariats (Article 52). The union-republic commissariats included those of lands, finance, internal trade, internal affairs, justice, and health (Articles 53, 55), and their power was limited by their all-union counterparts.

The rights of the republic over both the Nakhjivan ASSR and the NKAO were affirmed through the subordination of local organs of the state and judiciary to those at the republic level. Article 47 stated that the republic Sovnarkom had the right to nullify decisions of the Nakhjivan Sovnarkom or the NKAO Soviet of Deputies.

Although the constitution defined the limits of power, it could not indicate the true power relationships. Despite the guaranteed right of secession, attempts to exercise that right have been regarded as "counterrevolutionary" actions carried out by "bourgeois nationalists." Only an examination of actual policies can clarify the meaning of this constitution. The policy of the era was dominated by purges.

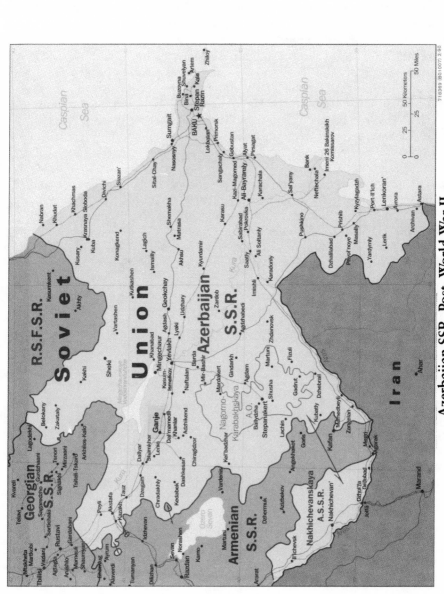

Azerbaijan SSR, Post–World War II

8 Azerbaijan's "Great Terror" (1920–1941)

> We the undersigned Musavat party members, [admit] we
> were deceived and mistaken . . . the present [Soviet] govern-
> ment has brought the best and highest system of labor, and
> peace and brotherhood in the Caucasus. . . , which no
> capitalist government could ever achieve.
>
> Newspaper *Kommunist*, 14 September 1928

> Under the spreading chestnut tree, I sold you and you sold
> me.
>
> George Orwell, *1984*

The "terror" in the second half of the 1930s, described in Robert Conquest's *The Great Terror*, was characterized by exile, imprisonment, or execution on trumped-up charges. In Azerbaijan it lasted almost continuously from the sovietization of the country until World War II in roughly three stages. The early 1920s witnessed the attempt to crush initial opposition to Soviet rule and the Communist party. Thousands of individuals with no special prominence in politics or society as well as members of the former government and those in the resistance movement at Ganje and elsewhere were killed or exiled. Other victims were rebellious peasants, "kulaks," and religious leaders. Mosques were closed and an antireligious campaign was launched.

A second, more focused purge took place in the second half of the 1920s and the early 1930s that affected all Turks in the USSR, with former political leaders, Communists, and others being charged with "Sultangalievism" or "national communism."[1] During those years, in Azerbaijan "nationalists," especially former Musavat party members (an alternative political leadership), and sympathizers were "unmasked" and arrested or killed.

The third period was broadest in scope and in many ways the most perilous era in Azerbaijan's history under Russian rule. This purge, which liquidated the Azerbaijani Old Bolsheviks and the prerevolutionary writers and artists and their works, also threatened to obliterate historical memory. These purges went beyond the elites to encompass all levels of society, rooting out "wreckers," "saboteurs," and "spies," as depicted by the contemporary press. These campaigns took place during the second half of the 1930s, coinciding with Russia's "Great Terror" and incorporating some of Azerbaijan's Old Bolsheviks into the show trials in Moscow. These second and third stages are covered in the present chapter.

A major villain in this drama was Mir Jafar Abasovich Baghirov (1896?– 1956), whose career was tied up with the prolonged reign of terror in Azerbaijan. Baghirov, who had been a party member since 1917, was commissar for internal affairs in the early 1920s and continued to head republican security forces until 1933, when he became first secretary of the Central Committee of the Azerbaijan Communist Party (CC AzCP). He was also president of the Soviet of People's Commissars (Sovnarkom), holding both posts until his removal in June 1953, a few months after Stalin's death.[2]

NATIONAL DEVIATION AND COLLECTIVIZATION: MID 1920s–MID 1930s

Purges of the Political Leadership

The hunt for *nationalists* (the word *always* carries negative connotation in Soviet parlance) is a preoccupation of communist power. One of the earliest victims of an AzCP purge not linked with the creation of Soviet power was Ayub Khanbudaghov who had been a secretary of the AzCP since 1922. At the sixth Congress of the AzCP in May 1924, Khanbudaghov was accused of heading a "splinter faction" with "nationalist tendencies." S. M. Efendiyev, supported by Ghazanfar Musabekov, A. H. Karayev, and Hamid Sultanov, rejected Khanbudaghov's criticism of AzCP national policy (which Soviet sources do not discuss). At the same congress the merger of the Worker-Peasant Inspection (WPI) and the Central Surveillance Committee (CSC) was confirmed. Purges of the regime's opponents came within the purview of

Efendiyev's WPI-CSC, overlapping with the Cheka (of which Khanbudaghov was former chairman) and perhaps other departments of the state. In December 1926 Baghirov spoke of the arrests of members of the Central Committee, but gave no names.[3] Khanbudaghov was removed from the CC AzCP but apparently not from the party; he later held posts in the Azerbaijan Agriculture Bank and commissariats of the TSFSR.[4]

At the eighth AzCP Congress in November 1927, Efendiyev (who was assistant chairman of the Azerbaijan Central Executive Committee [AzCEC] until December 1931 when he became chairman) took on an "antiparty group" in his report on the work of the CSC. The group, "comrade Sarkis and other Trostkiites," was criticized for factionalism and failing to put an end to that factionalism, thereby attempting to break the unanimity of the members of the Baku party organization, harming the construction of socialism, and inciting internal strife among workers. The group was also accused of attacking "Leninist nationality policy" in Caucasia. Efendiyev claimed that Caucasia had never had such national peace as it then enjoyed precisely because of "Leninist policies." In a speech on "The Opposition and the National Question," Efendiyev stated that as a member of the RCP(b)[5] and as head of the CSC, which "carries out a battle" against nationalists, Trotskiites, and Musavatists, he opposed all displays of nationalist tendencies.[6]

As the battle against nationalists within the party continued, instruments of control were ominously restructured. At the sixteenth All-Union Party Congress (26 June–13 July 1930), Stalin announced the abolition of the WPI-CSC and its replacement by two distinct bodies, one of the party, the Commission for Party Control of the CC RCP(b), and one of the state, the Commission of Soviet Control, which was affiliated with the USSR Sovnarkom. That change was to be made in all republics.[7] An attempt at wide popular mobilization to assist the police in ferreting out traitors, spies, and saboteurs led to "police-aid detachments" in the Caucasian republics, labor unions, Komsomols, factories, farms, and middle schools.[8] "National deviation" was discussed by Sergei M. Kirov, now a member of Politbiuro CC RCP(b), in his address to the CC plenum and Central Control Commission AzCP in November 1930.[9] The plenum affirmed the need to reinforce the Soviet apparatus, the party, and other instruments of the dictatorship of the proletariat. It emphasized the need to mobilize cadres from workers, peasants, the poor and to educate youth and women.

In his memoirs former Musavatist A. Vahap Yurtsever supported information from Soviet sources: Azerbaijan GPU (state security organization) agents in their campaign "to liquidate elements in the CP with nationalist tendencies" worked in all military units, government offices, and AzCP cells. All GPU installations were equipped with facilities for torture. Despite kidnappings, torture, and the "recruitment" of individuals into GPU service,

Yurtsever stated, secret antiregime organizations continued to exist, and the GPU found it hard to break into them.[10]

The purges of this period may have been limited because many national leaders and ADR supporters had already been killed or had fled. Nevertheless, some suspicious deaths were recorded. The governor of Baku, Reshid Akhundov, and Vice-Governor Museyyip Ahijanov were reportedly sent to the firing squad without even being charged.[11] Narimanov died in 1925, officially of heart failure, but it has been suggested that he was poisoned. He died in a Moscow hospital, where, after a quick autopsy by a Kremlin doctor, his body was cremated. Although cremation is not part of either Azerbaijani or Islamic tradition, it did make a subsequent autopsy impossible. Destroying his body and interring his ashes in the Kremlin Wall—one more honor—not only prevented the building of a tomb in Azerbaijan that might become a focus of popular attention but served to associate Narimanov with the regime whose power in Azerbaijan he was said to support. He was denounced in 1937 or 1938 as "a deviationist, traitor, *agent provocateur*, deserter, anti-Communist, and bourgeois nationalist" by Mirza Davud Huseinov.[12]

Musavat Émigrés and Counterrevolution in Azerbaijan

The main object of official wrath in the period before World War II was the Musavat party, the Bolsheviks' bête noire in Azerbaijan. Official organs of the Azerbaijan SSR and the AzCP monitored Musavat émigré publications and, from at least 1925 on, the opposing presses carried on an acrimonious dialogue. But the Soviet side had the power to go beyond rhetoric. The émigré publications' editorials were cited to justify purges in Azerbaijani educational and research institutions, villages, the state apparatus, and even within the AzCP.

Articles on the Musavat in the spring of 1925 continued to criticize wartime and ADR policies. The Tbilisi newspaper *Zaria Vostoka* published a series on the Musavat by Mirza Davud Huseinov, then a member of the CEC TSFSR. Recalling Musavat support for the imperial government during the war and its refusal to criticize tsarist policies specifically in the pages of Rasulzade's *Achik Soz*, Huseinov argued that "neither the Musavat party nor Rasulzade and his comrades promoted any kind of idea about the independence of the Azerbaijani Turks."[13] Similar articles appeared at this time (within weeks of Narimanov's death) commemorating five years of Soviet power in Azerbaijan.[14]

An article published late in 1925 linked Musavat émigré publications to British and Russian monarchists, enemies that, as the writer pointed out, both the Bolsheviks and the Azerbaijan Turks had shared.[15] Many anti-Soviet publications, noted the writer, came from Istanbul, a "haven for Russian monarchists." He argued that counterrevolutionary propaganda was not successful because the people love the revolution and because it is "known" that the proletarian dictatorship is good for the cultural development of the Turks. Still, the need for vigilance exists, the writer warned. Counterrevolutionaries may be hiding under religious or national veils.

The next year attacks on the Musavat became sharper. In a December 1926 speech,[16] Baghirov revealed the existence of anti-Soviet forces inside Soviet Azerbaijan, adding, "This vile work against Soviet power has not for one minute eluded the organs of worker-peasant power." Despite many warnings, some members of "the Turkish intelligentsia, mainly communists, have continued their anti-Soviet, anti-Communist efforts," trying to influence youth by controlling education and publishing. Baghirov claimed that many of these individuals had spoken at the First Turcological Conference in Baku (1926), struggling against "progressive" cultural work by the Communists. Baghirov echoed a warning by Ruhulla Akhundov against "petty bourgeois" attitudes among party members. Baghirov declared a battle against such attitudes and called for all to "liberate" their relatives and acquaintances first.

The Musavat newspaper *Yeni Kavkaziye* (Istanbul) criticized "socialist development": "They have ruined Baku and now they are starting on Ganje."[17] M. Orakhelashvili ridiculed the critics. "Ruining Ganje," he said, meant taking a medieval city, a city half-ruined by counterrevolutionary fighting, cleaning up the remains of Musavat and Dashnaks, modernizing it: "Today the bright eyes of a visitor to Ganje see new factories, stations, clubs, cooperatives, cultural-enlightenment institutions." His words reflected more than the Bolshevik optimism toward industrial development—they were a sign of Soviet power consolidated in a center of national resistance.

In these newspaper attacks few individuals were mentioned, though Rasulzade, once a Hümmetist, was castigated at every turn. Topchibashi and others whose public service was well known had not yet been named by the Soviet press. At this stage, it was perhaps deemed more effective to decry anonymous "khan-bek" circles, oil owners, and Entente collaborators, for they conjured up negative images and suggested unknown enemies.

The anti-Musavat campaign escalated in January 1927 with an article on "Musavatist hairy mongrels," signed S. A.[18] It described Musavat leaders ensconced on the Bosphorus telling fortunes in coffee grounds to estimate how long it would be until Soviet power fell in Azerbaijan. Lately, S. A. wrote, they are no longer content to vent their views harmlessly on the pages of *Yeni Kavkaziye* and to spread ideas around Turkey. Now they want to carry their work inside Azerbaijan. Unable to create a serious social threat opposed by the wide stratum of peasant and worker-Turks, they tried to use a group of chauvinist intellectuals of landowner origin for their anti-Soviet work. In current conditions, the writer argued, there is no real political danger.

> The game of "national" interests of the Azerbaijan people, legends about "red imperialism of the Russian invaders" and cries about "killing of national culture" of the Azerbaijani Turks may find some response in parts of the [Azerbaijani] Turkish bourgeois intelligentsia [or those] connected by their professional interests with national bourgeoisie and feudal landowners of Musavat Azerbaijan or among a few groups of youth who fell into the prison of a chauvinistic mood. But only these.

Toilers, he stated, realize that only Soviet power guards their independence and raises their national culture. Musavatists sow seeds of antagonism and national hatred especially in areas where official work has been weak, mainly in education. But, added S.A., building national industry, irrigation and other aids to the peasantry continues as does the training of Azerbaijani Turkish specialists for all branches of state work. National policy is built on the work of the masses themselves, in sharp contrast to the doubtful "independence" of the bourgeoisie. The writings of *Yeni Kavkaziye* can be opposed inside Azerbaijan, he argued, with the practical work of socialist construction.

This article presents both the threat and the assurance of its insignificance compared with the power of the present regime and its accomplishments. It warned of a hunt beginning for the "chauvinistic intelligentsia" carrying out Musavat work inside Azerbaijan.

Mustafa Kuliyev, in an April 1927 article, "Dreams of the Musavatists,"[19] discussed the émigré journal *Azerbaijan* (Paris):

> Like the [Russian] White Guard newspapers, it printed false information about uprisings in Azerbaijan, about violence, about Red terror and Red imperialism. In the October [1926] number this journal stated that in this period there were 56 various uprisings and that our soviets consisted of a majority of Musavatists who were prepared to sacrifice their own lives for the ideas of the capitalist masters and their Azerbaijani lackeys.[20]

Kuliyev, a career propagandist, stated that *Azerbaijan* "without shame" proclaimed that "'American and European' institutions and circles looked sympathetically upon Azerbaijan." The Azerbaijani peasants, he argued, knew well what English and American support meant from the recent U.S. invasion of Nicaragua and "European rapes and murders in China." Kuliyev ridiculed the assertion that the "Musavat is the sole serious and lawful organization existing in the country, and which gathered around itself the [Azerbaijani] Turkish elements." Kuliyev retorted that "these stupid and shortsighted people suppose that such statements will help them persuade Europe and America 'to free' Caucasia and deliver it to the Mensheviks and

Musavatists. As if it were that simple." Finally, Kuliyev quoted *Azerbaijan*: "A secret organization of the party has its center inside Azerbaijan itself and it sustains numerous departments and cells."

This article justified launching a "witch-hunt" against Musavatists and their supporters on the basis of alleged threats by the émigré publications to overthrow Soviet power and, more damaging, the existence of a large, secret Musavat organization inside the Azerbaijan SSR. Émigré journals' reports of resistance to Soviet power were meant to impress on the West, where anti-Bolsheviks were still a significant political factor, that Communists depended on force to retain power. The dilemma of the émigrés was that publicizing uprisings and anti-Soviet movements in Azerbaijan placed those inside the country at risk, whereas being quiet about violence and expropriation might save lives. The danger of keeping silent was that the world would forget the forcible incorporation of Azerbaijan into Bolshevik Russia and remain ignorant of the usurpation and attacks on culture, the continuing terror, and popular opposition. Western governments could mistake silence for acceptance of Soviet rule and abandon what support they still provided to governments in exile.

Harsh Soviet press attacks continued on the émigré press. Kuliyev,[21] in an article entitled "Musavatists on the 'National Movement,'" referred to an "illiterate political article in the journal *Yeni Kavkaziye* . . . carrying sensationalist 'facts' about the shooting of intellectuals." Kuliyev's article, like others, seemed particularly sensitive to charges of "destroying Turkish culture" and tried repeatedly to refute them. Kuliyev, who was briefly commissar of education, accused the Musavat of trying to turn the intelligentsia against Soviet power by reporting "false news" of the arrests of a thousand citizens. Contrary to *Yeni Kavkaziye* statements, he said, Soviet power had built a "rural intelligentsia" by short-term education courses. Furthermore, the "left wing" of the prerevolutionary intelligentsia, especially the educators, were Communists, he said; only the "far right" was anti-Soviet. As long as most of the intelligentsia support Soviet power, wrote Kuliyev, the Musavat can rant harmlessly.

Workers and peasants support Soviet power, Kuliyev said, so there was no discontent on which an anti-Soviet national movement could build. At the same time, he acknowledged that the New Economic Policy (NEP) and its tolerance of private capital fed national sentiments, thereby criticizing the Musavat and the NEP at the same time. Indeed, attacks on the "rabble," the bazaar merchants and the mullahs, brought back by the NEP were bitter.

Similar newspaper articles appeared in the summer warning of an upsurge in "enemy action."[22] "Machinations of the 'Nationalists,'" by Karayev, and "Legacy of the Cursed Past," by Kuliyev,[23] used harsh tones and language against the Musavat and, by implication, its internal supporters.

Karayev referred to "blood-sucking parasites." Musavat émigrés were said to be taking money from the British who hoped to use locals to overthrow Soviet power in Caucasia, using the words *nation* and *self-determination* as weapons to dupe the workers and peasants and win their support. Individuals were singled out and accused of crimes ranging from "bad faith" to sexual improprieties. Karayev listed the names of representatives (of all nationalities) in the ADR Parliament, arguing that because they were all landowners, this "democratic body" represented only 2–3 percent of the population. He named not just well-known leaders like Rasulzade but ADR-period regional administrators, whom he accused of abusing their power while acting in the name of the popular welfare.

Publications of 1927 laid the groundwork for a frontal assault; the attack came in mid-1928. On 14 September 1928 the newspaper *Kommunist*[24] was devoted almost entirely to a recantation by former Musavatists. The front page proclaimed that "enemies are scattered—but vigilance is still needed." A "declaration" by former Musavatists was printed in full on the second page:

> Azerbaijani Turks' national party Musavat . . . became a tool in the hands of English imperialism and the world bourgeoisie, and turned into the worst enemy of the Turkish people [*Türk halki*].
> This party—the Musavat party—in truth represented the interests of the Turkish bourgeoisie and landowners. Political turncoats like Mehmet Emin Rasulzade, bandits like Hasan bey Sultanov and frauds like Topchibashi . . . became the worst enemies of the Turkish people. . . . The Musavat is selling Azerbaijan. They have nothing to do with the toilers of Azerbaijan. Musavatists are ideologues of the wealthy [Azerbaijani] Turks. . . . Mehmet Emin and company are pickpockets and political prostitutes.

The declaration stated that the present system had brought "peace and brotherhood" to the Caucasus and that the "elevation of the social and cultural level of the Turkish people" had been fulfilled. Agriculture had recovered, Turkish women had been liberated, a new alphabet was coming into use. The Soviet had brought economic progress and a new life to all toilers. Musavat had nothing to do with and no right to speak for Azerbaijani Turks.

The language was familiar to those who had been reading the attacks on the Musavat. Their "confession" not only confirmed the accusations made in the official press against Musavat supporters but affirmed all other claims about the benefits of Soviet power in Azerbaijan. This pattern for confessions would be replayed in the coming years.

Of course, commented *Kommunist*, these individuals might still oppose the worker-peasant government: "Let them prove their desire to work for the toilers of Azerbaijan." Thus confession did not clear these former Musavatists of suspicion.

The *Kommunist* writer warned of other dangers from Musavat efforts. Recently, the Musavat had penetrated the villages and tried to influence local youth. Joining the religious classes, the Musavatists succeeded in entering the lower levels of the *apparat* and in some places were said to have gained influence over young Communists to undermine party work. Schools had been "tainted with nationalist poison. . . . We have said before openly and clearly and we say it again, the workers have no homeland [*vatan*]." *Kommunist* alerted its readers that "our battle is strengthening . . . we must expand our work." The children of the poor must be brought more and more into the school system, and "among them as much political work as necessary must be carried out." As the Communists battle, the writer warned, "our enemies' resistance will increase." The articles ended with a call to carry out the fight against the Musavat and nationalism in every village.

This article called unambiguously for a vigilant search for "enemies" in the party or outside, in the "apparatus," in any village. In the school system, teachers and scholars at all levels were pressured and sometimes purged. Baku University and other institutes were reorganized in the early 1930s, when nationally conscious personnel were replaced by younger people trained in the new communist academies. Even those who recanted were suspect and had to continually prove their devotion "to workers and peasants" by their actions. Musavat leaders were "vile," "butchers," "political prostitutes." Articles published in 1928 "proved" the seriousness of the threat and its extent and at the same time signaled a new and more determined, violent phase of the hunt. Criticism of the Musavat continued.[25]

Campaign against the Countryside

Violence in the villages of Azerbaijan, too, was almost continuous. Soviet works discussing the 1920s and early 1930s mention the battle against "counterrevolutionaries" and "kulaks," so the scope of resistance to Soviet power must have been vast.[26] The WPI-CSC continued its oversight as the party and state urged increased production (though growing more cotton apparently was resisted) and "class warfare" in rural Azerbaijan.

Efendiyev's biographer discussed "class warfare" in the countryside against kulaks which was conducted, as elsewhere, theoretically by the poor and middle peasants but actually by the state and party.[27] Although kulaks had been grudgingly permitted to exist during the NEP, Stalin's call for the collectivization of agriculture in early 1928 signaled an end even to that tolerance. An overt campaign was apparently launched at a joint plenum of the CEC and the CC AzCP in June 1928. Collectivization in Azerbaijan followed the pattern elsewhere in the USSR: an official campaign including propaganda and the use of force, widespread resistance, and official retreat followed by more propaganda and more force.

The first campaigns to collectivize in 1929–1930 created hundreds of new kolkhozy. In January 1930 alone, 591 kolkhozy were established in Azerbaijan. The Soviet press acknowledged that the process had gone "a little too fast," creating "dissatisfaction." The émigré press reported a 1930–1931 uprising that encompassed much of rural Azerbaijan.[28] Official rhetoric softened. (In December 1928 Efendiyev had remarked, "We have the strength to cool the hotheads and put in their places the kulaks who had overstepped their bounds."[29])

Former military intelligence (GRU) officer Ismail Akhundov, who worked in the Caucausus during collectivization, recalled reports on Azerbaijani peasants who fled to the mountains to escape the campaign, where units of the Red Army, border troops, and the security force OGPU hunted them down:

> One [report] I remember indelibly said: "Whole villages are offering desperate resistance. Our units are forced to burn the villages, put to the sword not only men, but also the women and children. When the men were killed fighting our forces, their women, instead of surrendering, threw themselves to death on the bayonets of the Red soldiers." Some of these people, other reports said, had managed to escape across the border to Iran but to no avail. The Soviet troops reported that they crossed the border . . . and wiped them out.[30]

Kolkhoz construction continued, as did resistance. "Brigands" burned a Salyan cotton factory and the Gedebey (Kedabek) *raion* (administrative region) party plenum building. Kulaks in the NKAO and Agham *raiony* were said to have incited conflict among the neighboring villages, and these allegations were used to highlight the "kulak threat." At the twelfth AzCP Congress in January 1934, Efendiyev stated that representatives of the party and soviets had "forgotten their responsibilities" and respect, thereby "making it possible for damage to be done by enemies of Soviet rule."[31]

Yurtsever provided detail on the "dekulakization" of Azerbaijan.[32] Statistics on wealthy peasants previously compiled by the local state and party administrations were based on an estimated percentage of kulaks per village or area. Despite population changes from death and exile, authorities demanded that village soviets surrender that number of kulaks to the GPU. Because village soviets could not produce the quota, they started drawing on middle peasants and *podkulachniki*, that is, those middle or poor peasants who resisted collectivization:

After sunset armed militia or GPU personnel would attack the home of those peasants labeled "kulak." Taking all individuals out of the house . . . , loading them on trucks along with other such individuals from neighboring villages, [they were] taken to the nearest train station and sent to destinations unknown. Not only individuals who were thus treated but their neighbors were thunderstuck with this treatment and did not understand what had happened. Only much later it was understood that these poor farmers were designated "class enemies" and sent to the icy tundra of Siberia and the Urals, to forced labor camps, slowly exterminated.

Yurtsever noted that "dekulakization" was designed to eliminate the most resilient element of free enterprise and to frighten the middle peasantry into turning over their property to the kolkhozy. When the peasants slaughtered their animals instead, the Soviet hierarchy's "surprise and panic was general and complete."

The regime then tried persuasion. Soviet scientists "thought hard and 'discovered' that rabbit meat was more nutritious than beef." Workers had enough trouble feeding their own offspring, however, much less rabbits, and the rabbit-raising campaign failed.[33] Those without property were promised land, fertilizer, and agricultural machinery. Anyone who did not join the kolkhozy was threatened with being classified a kulak. Some people ran away, got false papers with new names, and started new lives, secretly "engaging in commerce," building the famous "second economy." Some tried traditional resistance and joined guerrilla bands in the mountains or forests.

THE "GREAT PURGE" IN AZERBAIJAN

The "great purge" in Azerbaijan was more than an attempt to remove Old Bolsheviks or potential contenders to state power, for many prominent Old Bolsheviks (Narimanov, Azizbeyov) were dead. Those left in power (Efendiyev, Dadashzade, Sultanov, and others) were arrested and exiled or killed. But the wide scope of the purge also encompassed the destruction of the cultural-intellectual elites and became a dragnet for many so-called wreckers. It was during 1937 and 1938 that all these categories of purge victims were pursued simultaneously and with stunning vigor in Azerbaijan.

In the second half of the 1930s, the state and party apparatus was turned against those who had been in the Bolshevik or Hümmet parties long before 1917. The new victims had loyally supported Soviet power, suppressing national resistance to the Red Army and sovietization. The purge began in the Azerbaijan Red Army units and spread from there.[34] Among the accused were men who had formerly denounced fellow Communists for "factionalism." Many held high positions in the local party and government apparatus until the eve of their demise. During 1937 and 1938 surviving former and most current members of the Azerbaijan SSR Sovnarkom, old and young, were executed. Husein Rakhimov, chairman of the Azerbaijan Sovnarkom since January 1935, was executed in 1938;[35] Ruhulla Akhundov, former commmissar of enlightenment and a Marxist theoretician, was removed from the party and executed in 1938 (age 41); Chinghiz Yildirim, commissar of the navy in the first AzSovnarkom, later a member of the AzCEC and the TSFSR CEC, was executed in 1937 (age 47); Dadash Buniatzade, first commissar of education and state control, who later headed several commmissariats and served as president of the Sovnarkom, was executed in 1938 (age 50); Mirza Davud Huseinov, member of the Sovnarkom and the CEC TSFSR in the 1920s, was purged and executed in Moscow in 1938 (age 44); Mustafa Kuliyev, who took an active part in the anti-Musavat campaign of the 1920s, was executed in 1938 (age 45); Ali Heydar Karayev, former commissar of labor, of justice, and the military, was executed in 1938 (age 42); Ghazanfar Musabekov, who had held several commissar posts since 1920 including commissar of land, trade, industry, and food, was executed in 1938 (age 50); and two of the most powerful, Sultan Mejid Efendiyev (51) and Hamid Sultanov (49), were executed in 1938. Among others killed at that time were Isai Dovlatov, M. N. Huseinov, and H. Rakhmanov.

In Azerbaijan political purging in the AzCP began in earnest in 1937. Early that year in Moscow, Azerbaijan communist Husein Rakhmanov, head of the Baku Committeee AzCP, stated: "We have in Azerbaijan pitiful remains of Trotskiite-Zinovievite riffraff and vile Musavatists, Pan-Islamists, Pan-Turkists—Ruhulla Akhundov, Hasan Safarov, party propagandist Mikhail N. Huseinov,[37] and others, striving to damage socialist construction in Azerbaijan."[38] Longtime party leaders were in trouble. Sultan Mejid Efendiyev came under fire shortly afterward. Efendiyev, president of the CEC AzCP in March 1937, opened the ninth All-Azerbaijan Congress of Soviets, which accepted the republic's new constitution. He was also copresident of the CEC TSFSR (from January 1933 until its dissolution in March 1937) and had headed the WPI-CEC and, after their separation, the CEC.[39] But at the twenty-second Baku Party Conference in May 1937, Efendiyev was proclaimed to be a "secret enemy of the Soviet state." Efendiyev's biographer notes that Baghirov's pressure on Efendiyev, Hamid Sultanov, and other Communists was reflected in the stenographic account of that meeting. In June, at the thirteenth AzCP Congress, Baghirov demanded that Efendiyev confess to being a counterrevolutionary. He answered: "For 33 years I have been in the party. During these 33 years, I have worked without blame. Therefore, I cannot be destroyed by any slander or intrigue."[40] Efendiyev, however, was wrong.

Despite the profusion of accusations, only one formerly respected and infuential Communist was actually put on trial—Hamid Sultanov, commissar of communal economics.[41] Sultanov, a Bolshevik since 1907, had been commissar of internal affairs and of trade and in 1925 was appointed president of the Sovnarkom of the Nakhjivan ASSR. He held posts in the CEC of both the TSFSR and the USSR. An article in *Bakinskii Rabochii* of 4 April 1937 criticized the work of Sultanov's commissariat and referred to those who had applauded him at a previous meeting as "fawning." The paper complained that there was no self-criticism in his speech and that his Commissariat of Communal Economics had only fulfilled 88 percent of its plan. It made other accusations, and more criticism followed.

At the twenty-second session of the AzCP Baku Conference in May 1937, two longtime colleagues were criticized along with Sultanov: "The conference especially takes note of the insincere conduct of Sultan Mejid Efendiyev, Hamid Sultanov, and Dovlatov, [who tried] to hide and gloss over their own crude political errors, which they committed until recent days." They were also accused of "crude violations of party regulations and interparty democracy." (The particular actions that constituted these alleged violations apparently were not named.) The conference ordered an inquiry into all "unpartylike conduct" by the three men and, in a resolution, linked Efendiyev, Sultanov, and Dovlatov with "the most vile enemies of the people—counterrevolutionary Trostkiists, on the right, and agents of Japanese-German fascism and their allies, the Musavatists, Dashnaks, and other bourgeois nationalists."[42]

Although Sultanov was elected to the Baku Committee at that meeting, his name did not appear on the list of members the following November, nor did the names of the other "militants"—Efendiyev, Musabekov, and Huseinov. Names that did appear were Husein Rakhmanov, Muzafar Narimanov (nephew of Nariman Narimanov), "Old Bolshevik" Mir Bashir Kasumov, and Baghirov, who by then had added first secretary of the Baku Committee to his titles.[43] Criticism of Efendiyev, Sultanov, Dovlatov, and Kadirli as "bourgeois nationalists" continued at the thirteenth AzCP Congress. By this time, several prominent individuals had already been liquidated after being removed from their posts or, in some cases, while they held them.[44]

Sultanov was arrested in the summer or early fall of 1937. His trial began on 27 October in Shemakhi, where a counterrevolutionary center was allegedly operating. On trial with Sultanov (then 48) were eleven codefendants, among whom were Israfil Ibrahimov (47, former assistant commissar of education), Khalfa Huseinov (45, former AzCP regional secretary), and men who held regional posts from procurator to kolkhoz manager.[45] According to Jeyhun Hajibeyli, Sultanov was the sole member of the "Bolshevik aristocracy of Azerbaijan" present. The charges claimed that a "counterrevolutionary center" intended to overthrow the Soviet regime, separate Azerbaijan from the Soviet Union, and return to capitalism. The center was accused of planning strikes, sabotage, terrorism, and espionage for foreign powers with a "bloc of Trotskiites, Rightists, Musavatists, and Armeno-Georgian bourgeois nationalists."

Interrogated on 10 October 1937, Hamid Sultanov acknowledged the existence of the center and named the members of its bureau who became, in effect, codefendants in absentia: Ruhulla Akhundov, Sultan Mejid Efendiyev, Ghazanfar Musabekov, Dadash Buniatzade, Ayub Khanbudaghov,[46] and Sultanov himself.[47] Sultanov stated that on the orders of Ruhulla Akhundov, several members of the center, including himself, conducted talks with representatives of foreign intelligence services to ask for assistance and passed information of a political and economic nature to them. Finally, Akhundov had planned to assassinate Mir Jafar Baghirov.

The center was to carry out propaganda for "counterrevolutionary nationalism," recruit new members, sabotage the economy and main rail line from Baku to Shemakhi, prepare a general uprising against Soviet power, and mobilize opposition groups in the countryside. That the accused could provide details was used as proof that they had sabotaged the kolkhoz and irrigation systems. The twelve were charged with identical crimes. This process was also identical, according to Hajibeyli, to that conducted in Turkestan, Georgia, and Armenia, where "bourgeois-nationalist saboteurs" were accused of stirring up "discontent with Soviet power among the population."[48]

More confessions were forthcoming. Former Assistant Commissar of Education Ibrahimov confessed on 8 October 1937 to having ordered the creation of "opposition cells" together with Halifa Huseinov, a secretary of an AzCP regional committee. Sultanov and several other accused repeated that they heard about opposition cells from Ibrahimov and Huseinov. They were accused of having been "accessories to the 'counterrevolutionary center' since 1934." Sultanov said that he and Akhundov created political organizations to facilitate the separation of Azerbaijan from the Soviet Union. *Bakinskii Rabochii* wrote of Sultanov: "He spread harm everywhere he could . . . he lost no chance to recruit rebels and saboteurs." Sultanov, like Ibrahimov and Huseinov, refused a defense attorney.

The prosecutor asked Sultanov, "From what time did you begin your ties with the nationalists, with the *Narimanovshchina* [literally, the time of the influence of Narimanov]?" Jeyhun Hajibeyli noted:

This was the first attempt by ruling circles of Azerbaijan to place the first Bolshevik leader, Dr. Narimanov, *who had died in 1925*, on the same docket with the opposition. Prior to this, it is true, there was one speech by M. J. Baghirov, in which he branded *Narimanovshchina* as an incarnation of nationalism, but nothing had yet presaged the use of such pejorative accusations in the Supreme Court of the Azerbaijan SSR against Dr. Narimanov, one of the creators [of Azerbaijan SSR], and the ashes of whose body are next to the Lenin mausoleum. We recall that his nephew was elected *second secretary* of the Baku Committee of the party at the XXII Conference (end of May 1937).

"How could it be," asked Jeyhun Bey, "that the defendant answered this question without commentary: 'Since 1921.'" Sultanov went on to say, "Ruhulla Akhundov said that the Armenian nationalists could supply an armed force. Isai Dovlatov (an Armenian) promised powerful support [by Armenians] within Azerbaijan itself."

In a subsequent interrogation Halifa Huseinov represented the Hümmet as a nationalist party connected with the *Narimanovshchina* and the *Khanbudaghovshchina*. Huseinov also stated that Ali Heydar Karayev, Aghaverdiyev (onetime head of the Azerbaijan Sovnarkom), and Husein Rakhmanov (of the Baku Committee as recently as May 1937) were linked to the conspiracy. Ibrahimov, under questioning, confirmed Rakhmanov's complicity in linking members of separate counterrevolutionary groups to one another, particularly in first putting him (Ibrahimov) in contact with Sultanov. Ibrahimov stated that he could have done worse damage. He denied, however, charges of having prepared an armed uprising. Sultanov, in subsequent questioning, remarked, "I don't know why Ibrahimov denies his guilt. I told him that Ruhulla Akhundov and Hambai Vezirov would give weapons to the Shemakhi rebels."[49] He confirmed the existence of a "reserve center," with members from the party and the state apparatus.

Each defendant's answers seemed to involve yet another member of the AzCP and the Sovnarkom. When the chief prosecutor asked Jabiyev, "Whom did you recruit into the counterrevolutionary organization?" Jabiyev replied, "Many people." Each man accused, like those on trial in October 1937, had been active in the prerevolutionary socialist movement and had held state and party posts since the sovietization of Azerbaijan. Neither prominence, loyal service, nor death shielded individuals from accusation. A kolkhoz director testified that both Ibrahimov and Huseinov instructed him to squander grain and fine the *kolkhozniki* in order to create discontent with Soviet power in preparation for an armed uprising. Jabiyev, in his testimony, accused one of the court prosecutors of spreading religious propaganda for reopening mosques, intending perhaps to take at least one of the opposition down with him.

At the conclusion of the trial, nine defendants, including Sultanov, Ibrahimov, and Huseinov, were sentenced to be shot. The others were sentenced to eight to twenty years of "imprisonment."[50] This trial, according to Jeyhun Hajibeyli, represented the peak of a purge of all the remaining Soviet party leadership except Baghirov. Some had already been liquidated, and others soon would be.

Jeyhun Bey emphasized that he reported these events entirely from Soviet sources to illustrate the similarities to the "Moscow process" of 1936–1938. "What Stalin carried out with Ezhev's help at the center, [Lavrenti] Beria, the secretary of the Transcaucasian party carried out in the Caucasus as his colleagues did in Turkestan, Ukraine, Belorussia and elsewhere." Jeyhun Bey suggested that Stalin and his closest circle were seized by an "omnipotent fear" that was assuaged only by liquidating all those Marxist theoreticians who could prove that "Marxism was something different from Stalinism."[51]

Unlike the Moscow trials, however, most of the accused in Azerbaijan never appeared at trial. Why? Jeyhun Bey admitted,[52]

> one can only suppose: the Caucasians were less "disciplined" with respect to party-ideological matters than their older comrades of the Leninist school and so they never achieved the "spontaneous" confession which was demanded of them by the NKVD specialists. But to go to trial *without prior confessions* might end in unforeseen surprises.

He noted that it was "extremely odd" that Sultanov and two other defendants in his trial had said not one word in their own defense. They could not have acted thus if they had not been certain of saving their own heads, he concluded.

Old Bolsheviks were destroyed, but Mir Jafar Baghirov, a friend of Beria, was spared. Jeyhun Bey, writing in late 1938 or early 1939, did not blame Baghirov for the purges in Azerbaijan but portrayed him as a potential victim saved only by his association with Beria. Were that true, it still would not preclude the possibility that Baghirov, like Rakhmanov in March 1937, used the accusations to destroy and eliminate his rivals in the party and in the republic. Indeed, the "postscript" of the Hajibeyli manuscript indicated that the December 1938 speech of Baghirov before the Baku Committee AzCP accused Karayev, Akhundov, and Mirzoyan (former secretary of the CC AzCP) of "consorting with counterrevolutionary groups for the battle with the party." Baghirov called them "factionalists" and "national deviationists"—rather milder than the charges of 1937, according to Jeyhun Bey.

Efendiyev's biography, however, written after Baghirov's execution, directly accused the former first secretary. Baghirov was said to have testified to Kalinin that Efendiyev had conducted counterrevolutionary activities in Azerbaijan. Efendiyev was executed in 1938.[53] Yurtsever wrote, "Ayub Khanbudaghov, Dadash Buniatzade, Ghazanfar Musabekov were destroyed by his [Baghirov's] hand. Baghirov lasted exactly 30 years in power because he was a slavish follower of Stalin's orders."[54]

Search for Wreckers and Saboteurs

The Baku press carried accounts of sabotage in a wide variety of places conducted by "enemies of the people." *Bakinskii Rabochii* on 29 September 1937 carried a brief story (about 250 words) under the headline "Terrorist Excursion of Bourgeois Nationalists in Aghdam." In a village about eighteen kilometers from the small town of Aghdam, just east of the NKAO, several "enemies of the people," members of an organization of "bourgeois-nationalist, Trotskiite-Bukharinite fascists," attempted "to harm Soviet power, break up kolkhozy, and deprive the kolkhozniki of their joyous, happy lives." Three counterrevolutionaries carried out damaging but unspecified activities. They could not escape the watchful eye of "candidate member of the party Yusuf Mamedov, who fearlessly unmasked the machinations of the enemies." The three attempted to murder Mamedov by shooting into his apartment one night while he slept. Mamedov was wounded.

> Having tried to hide, the criminals could not escape the cadres. The bandits . . . were apprehended by the organs of the Narkomvnudel [People's Commissariat for Internal Affairs]. They now await sentencing by a Soviet court.

The article ended with the assurance that "the workers of the Aghdam *raion* demand the ruthless destruction of enemies of the people." Because the story was published in the Russian-language daily in Baku and not widely read in rural Azerbaijan, it is unlikely that the population of Aghdam was aware of its zeal.

A purge trial in August 1938 at Ganje (Kirovobad since 1934) linked ordinary peasants to officials of the Commissariat of Lands. Among those on trial was the former head of the Commissariat of Lands, Ali Askeroglu Palatzade, who was called the head of a "terrorist and rebel organization." Members of several kolkhozy confessed to damaging harvests and livestock. A veterinarian, Husein Rahimoglu (-ovitch) Shikhaliyev, said that because he had failed to take preventive measures against infectious diseases, more than 120 horses had to be destroyed. The former director of a horse-breeding station who had been a tsarist cavalry officer, Yason Ivanovich Jigitov, confessed to sabotaging his own horse-breeding operation, resulting in gross underfulfillment of the plan for supplying mounts for the Red Army.[55] Other defendants confessed to damaging cattle herds, allowing sheep and goats to become infected with various diseases, and undermining crop expansion programs. In short, all failures were deliberate sabotage by "counterrevolutionary, bourgeois-nationalist, terrorist-rebel, sabotage organizations," or so proclaimed the headlines.[56]

This Ganje purge trial lasted ten days. Ten defendants, including Palatzade, Shikhaliyev, and Jigitov, were sentenced to death and their personal property confiscated. The other four were sentenced to prison for twelve to twenty-five years. Their personal property also was confiscated, suffrage was denied them for five years after their release. According to the report of the sentences, all printed in boldface type, "Workers, kolkhozniki and laboring intelligentsia of Kirovobad present at the trial greeted the just decisions of the court with approval."[57] Workers and kolkhozniki expressed their satisfaction at public meeting; a resolution by textile workers stated, "Our Soviet court has fulfilled the will of the whole people."[58]

Purge of the Intellectual-Cultural Elite

The intellectual-cultural purges touched all strata of the intelligentsia, from the publishers of institutional newspapers to the leading dramatists and poets. An article in *Bakinskii Rabochii*[59] in September 1937, under the headline "Newspapers Hiding Bourgeois Nationalists," informed its readers—and the "enemies" themselves—that

> A band of bourgeois nationalists, enemies, having many times sold the interests of the Azerbaijani people to foreign imperialists, has succeeded in building themselves a warm nest in the Azerbaijan Medical Institute. . . . One occupies a leading post in the institute, another operates under the label "scientific worker," and the third, not without profit to himself, was working as a teacher. [From these positions, the] enemies . . . tried to beat into the heads of the students fascist racial "theories" . . . trying to sow national enmity among the students.

The article accused the institute's newspaper, *For the Medical Cadre*, of "not noticing or, more precisely, not wanting to notice" these transgressions. *Bakinskii Rabochii* quoted current rector Gil'deev as saying that "among the academic workers of the institute there are still people who have thus far not shown a sincere relationship to the policies of the party in the matter of uncovering and unmasking foreign elements." The newspaper commented, ominously for Gil'deev,

> It is not enemies, it seems, not evil bourgeois nationalists that occupied the institute, but people "who have not shown a sincere relation to the policies of the party." Is this not a most vile attempt to mask, to conceal the true face of the enemy? . . . Can this be called something other than direct shelter of enemies?

In the Pedagogical Institute, too, "fascist lackeys tried in every way to interfere with the preparation of young cadres of Azerbaijani pedagogues." The institute's newspaper, *For Leninist Education*, "not only did not notice the vile subversive work of the fascist lackeys, but in essence they had embarked on a path of direct cover-up." The editor, N. Mamedov, "did not want to mobilize the scholarly-pedagogical staff and student body for the liquidation of this danger."[60]

Thus, a seemingly isolated criticism of one institute's newspaper led to the "unmasking" of "counterrevolutionaries" in that and other institutes. The threat to the "training of cadres" was great, for it was clear that the minds of youth were the arena for the ideological struggle. This case revealed the important link between politics, education, and culture.

Cultural figures, too, were purged, but because no reports of trials have come to light, it is impossible to say what happened to them. Many simply disappeared. Some are known to have been sent to Siberian camps where they eventually died. Poet Ahmed Javad, former Musavat party member, was arrested, according to Yurtsever, nine or ten times without being questioned before being sent to exile in Siberia with his family. On another case Yurtsever wrote: "I have personally witnessed Javad Melikyegianeh being imprisoned nine times; [he] was chief of the [Azerbaijani] Turkish labor unions, a member of the Musavat, extraordinary governor of Lenkoran, and an Azerbaijan Parliament member. He completely disappeared during the liquidation."[61] Prose writer Suleiman Sani Akhundov had been head of a local department of the Commissariat of Education in the AONK in the 1920s as well as a member of Baksovet and a candidate member of the CEC of the republic. No information is available on his life after 1930; he died in Baku in 1939.[62]

Nonparty cultural figures also became victims in 1937 and 1938. Husein Javid (1882–1941), one of the most renowned poets of prerevolutionary and early revolutionary Azerbaijan, was born in Nakhjivan and educated at the University of Istanbul, where he wrote and published. He subsequently taught and lived in Nakhjivan, Tiflis, and Ganje, then settled in Baku in 1919. Among his works are dramas and romantic plays in verse form and short poetic works. He enjoyed popularity and official favor, producing his plays in Baku and receiving favorable mention in the contemporary literary journal *Edebiyyat Gazeti*. In March 1937 he and several other writers (Seyid Hussein, Selman Mumtaz, and Atababa Musakhanly) were criticized in *Bakinskii Rabochii* for "ideological errors." In April 1937, at the premier performance of Uzeir Hajibeyli's opera *Köroglu*, Husein Javid was seen for the last time.[63] He was arrested and exiled to Siberia, where he died in 1941. Those named with him—Seyid Husein (1887–1937), Selman Mumtaz (1884–1941), and Musakhanly (1905–1945)—apparently suffered a similar fate. Official biographies provide no information on their lives after the mid-1930s.[64]

Although the fate of the cultural intelligentsia, especially those who never held political posts, is unclear, a large number died between 1937 and 1941; some died a few years earlier or later. Because most of those individuals were born in the 1880s or later, their deaths cannot be attributed to old age and few to disease. There may have been some who died of natural causes during the purges, but given the duration and character of purges, no deaths can be presumed to have been natural. The many elliptical references to cultural figures suggest a need for further investigation.[65]

The destruction of the entire indigenous party-state elite and most of the intelligentsia marked the final consolidation of Soviet power in Azerbaijan. If the purges had been limited to those individuals who had carried out struggles for reform and independence, who had led their community in political and social areas, and who had remembered the old promises and experiments of the Bolsheviks, they would have been bad enough. But the destruction touched all levels of society and the culture. The total number of victims during the entire period is not known, although one source estimated the number of victims in Azerbaijan during 1937–1938 alone at 120,000.[66] This was a devastating figure, on top of collectivization and earlier purges, for a nation whose 1926 population was only 2.6 million.

The more enduring impact was blackening the memories of national and cultural leaders, distorting their words and misrepresenting their intentions, confiscating published writings, and manipulating the content of literature and school curricula. These policies reached beyond the lives of the destroyed individuals to affect later generations in ways that the present generation is only beginning to grasp.

9 World War II and Recovery in Azerbaijan

Those [Turkish] lords who were in China held the Chinese titles and obeyed the Chinese emperor and gave their service to him for fifty years. For the benefit of the Chinese, they went on campaigns . . . as far as the Iron Gate in the west.

Kül Tegin inscription*

The Molotov–Von Ribbentrop Pact of August 1939 delayed the Soviet Union's entry into World War II. While Europe went to war, Stalin's "war against the nation"[1] or, more accurately, against the nations, was winding down. The census of 1939, though revised to conceal the magnitude of losses from post–civil war famine and collectivization, exiles, and purges, indicated that Azerbaijan had a population of 3.2 million, a figure that is certainly inflated but by how much is not known.[2] The census showed that the social composition of the population of Azerbaijan was 57.7 percent workers and 42 percent kolkhozniki. Inequality was proclaimed to have ended; only two "friendly classes" were left.[3] The data showed the physical liquidation of former landowners, intellectuals, merchants, and other "nonproletarian" elements.

---

*Talat Tekin, *Grammar of Orkhon Turkic* (Bloomington: Indiana University Press, 1969).

AZERBAIJAN AND THE "GREAT PATRIOTIC WAR"

On 22 June 1941 the war, which would be known as the "Great Patriotic War," came to the USSR. German war aims included the occupation of Caucasia to acquire Baku oil and to use it as a staging area for further moves against Southwest Asia. The Germans planned to administer Caucasia under a specially created Ostministerium.[4] Azerbaijan was not occupied but, like other republics, made a substantial contribution to the war effort with men, machines, and matériel. Though the war was perhaps the most publicized and glorified era of Soviet history after the revolution itself and a republic's contribution to it granted considerable prestige, Azerbaijan's contribution is rarely mentioned in general accounts of the conflict.

Wartime Administration and Economy

On 30 June 1941 the State Defense Committee (SDC, Gosudarstyennyi Komitet Oborony) was formed. Its offices were established in all republics to oversee wartime production, the evacuation of industrial plants and populations, and the Sovinformbiuro and other agencies. Later in the war, the SDC set up committees for the repatriation and resettlement of reconquered territory.[5] Ironically, it was precisely those committees that permitted the efficient deportation of allegedly "collaborationist" nations—Volga Germans early in the war and Chechen, Ingush, Kabardians, and Crimean Tatars when it was over.

Despite the centralizing effect of the SDC and its branches, the republics were simultaneously given greater discretion to regulate and reassign labor. In February 1944, when the tide of battle had turned against Germany, the USSR Supreme Soviet granted republics the right to expand the sphere of their "sovereignty." They would reorganize their defense establishments on republican lines and conduct direct relations with foreign states including the right to conclude agreements, perhaps as a way of posturing for Western Allies or ensuring multiple points of entry for needed goods. The constitutions of the USSR and of all the republics were amended accordingly.[6]

As in the first World War, the oil fields of Baku were an object of German desire and Russian exploitation. From 1941 Baku became a major fuel-producing and weapons-manufacturing center in the USSR.[7] During the war Azerbaijan produced 75 million tons of oil and 22 million tons of gas and other oil products (70–75 percent of Soviet oil and 85–90 percent of its aviation fuel and lubricating oils).[8]

Like other unoccupied republics, Azerbaijan was ordered to create a "food base" with increases in grain, tea, and animal products as well as cotton and other items. From 1941 to 1943, sown land in Azerbaijan increased by 140,000 hectares.[9] During the war years the republic is reported to have produced millions of pounds of bread, 500,000 tons of cotton, and animal herds of over 1 million head.[10] Women and children were employed extensively, with 25,000 women in the oil industry alone. More than 70,000 young boys and girls worked in all industries of the republic.[11]

Human Contribution

Azerbaijan may have sent as many as half a million men to war, although precise calculations are hard to make because the evidence is fragmentary.[12] Western sources, using reliable 1942 figures, indicate that 45,000 Azerbaijani Turks were serving on the Transcaucasian front and that thousands more were later mobilized. By the end of the war over 30,000 had been decorated. Azerbaijan made a substantial contribution for a population probably under 3 million.

Marshal Andrei A. Grechko stated that "12 large units," meaning a brigade or larger, were formed in the Transcaucasus during World War II.[13] Azerbaijani Turks were recruited into regular army units, partisan units, and national divisions. The latter had been disbanded in 1938[14] but were reestablished at the end of 1941.[15] These units were needed because of rapid German advances that left "a large manpower pool . . . only in Central Asia, the Caucasus and non-Russian areas of the RSFSR."[16]

> [National units] were organized as units of a cadre army, but they were "filled mostly by representatives of the local population of the union and autonomous republics who spoke Russian poorly or not at all. Other representatives of the local population were called up to serve in the usual cadre army." Volunteers apparently constituted a substantial part of the personnel. The non-Russian speakers were presumably encouraged to "volunteer" for the new units.[17]

Between August 1941 and June 1942 three new infantry divisions were created with a large contingent of Azerbaijani men—the 402d, 233d, and 416th. Azerbaijani Turks restaffed the depleted 77th and the ethnically mixed Caucasian 409th. The 125th, the so-called Turkic, division's composition was not specified in available sources.[18] Both the 402d and 416th were half Azerbaijani as of 1 January 1944.[19] Among the Northern Group of Forces of the Transcaucasian front alone, there were 45,000 Azerbaijanis, 20,000 Georgians, and 10,000 Armenians. These figures suggest that all nationalities were not inducted in proportion to their size in the population, for these three were nearly equal.[20] Reportedly, the proportion of Central Asian and

Caucasian peoples in the armed forces was about three times higher than their proportion in the Soviet population. Casualties were high, especially in such pivotal battles as the Caucasus and Stalingrad, where Caucasian and Central Asian troops may have made up as much as half the Soviet forces.[21] The depletion of manpower in these republics was reflected in the changing demographics of both national and regular formations during the course of the war.[22]

A large portion of the recruits were engaged as "partisan" (guerrilla) units in occupied territory. Although precise figures for individual republics are not available, one Soviet Georgian historian stated that at the beginning of the "Great Patriotic War more than 300,000 young troops from Transcaucasian republics joined active service in the Armed Forces of the USSR." He indicated that Georgia contributed 130,000.[23] Units were not adequately armed, and the men made much of their own equipment in special workshops.[24]

Among partisan and underground groups operating in Ukraine was one combined formation with "many Azerbaijanis" under the command of Lieut. Col. M. I. Shukayev. The brigade commander was Izatulla Nasrulayev, the partisan commissar was Alasker Aliyev, the lower-level political commissar was Abdulhalik Magerrov, and the intelligence officers were Akper Aliyev, Gumbat Namazov, and others. This battalion was said to have been composed of men who had escaped from enemy territory. The approximate figures on the destruction they caused are remarkable. They killed 2,500 "fascists," took 500 prisoners, derailed 50 troop trains, blew up 20 railroad bridges, 50 oil derricks, 5 refineries, 50 trucks, 21 military planes, and 1 postal airplane. Their losses were also considerable—of 350 in the battalion, more than 200 were killed.[25]

The partisans from the Caucasian republics were mentioned by Marshal Zhukov in his memoirs[26] in connection with the Battle of the Caucasus (July–October 1943). One famous partisan was D. Mamedov who, in August 1943, succeeded in blowing up a warehouse of aviation bombs and fuel in Stalino (Donetsk). Mamedov and his group were also responsible for disrupting German telegraph and telephone communications on a number of occasions.[27] Partisans from Azerbaijan also participated in operations in Yugoslavia and occupied France.[28]

Despite their effort and their losses, Azerbaijanis were relatively rarely decorated: Only 36,000 Azerbaijanis received medals (perhaps half a million fought), compared, for example, with the 53,500 medals given the numerically smaller Chuvash.[29] According to one general history of the war, the high honor Hero of the Soviet Union was given to "7.9 thousand Russians, over 2,000 Ukrainians, 299 Belorussians, 161 Tatars, 107 Jews, 96 Kazakhs, 90 Georgians, 79 Armenians, 67 Uzbeks, 45 Chuvash, 38 Bashkir, 31 Osetin, 16 Turkmen, 15 Lithuanians, 12 Kirghiz, 8 Kalmyks, and many troops of other nationalities."[30] Although both of its neighbors were mentioned as well as five other Turkish groups, Azerbaijan was not. Stalin spoke of the victories of the great *Russian* people. In a recent history of the republic, however, the authors noted that 121 Azerbaijanis were awarded the Hero of Soviet Union.[31]

Propaganda for Azerbaijan: Mobilization of National Culture

The experienced Soviet propaganda machine employed a wide range of appeals tailored to each nationality. Non-Slavs were told that Nazi designs on all Soviet territory included Reichskomissars for their areas, including Ukraine, Caucasus, and Turkistan.[32] National heroic literature, including dastans, popular songs, stories, and other genre that stressed loving one's homeland and fighting invaders were emphasized.[33] The campaign, orchestrated by the Leningrad-based Oriental Institute (temporarily taking refuge in Uzbekistan), lauded and studied the dastan *Alpamysh* as well as other works of "heroic folk literature."[34]

Films were also used to generate support in Azerbaijan. During the war years films in both Russian and Azerbaijani were produced that glorified the soldiers at the front and mobilized sentiment for them and against the invaders. Among those churned out by the Azerbaijan *kinostudio* were *Son of the Fatherland* (1942), *Bakhtiar* (a man's name) (1942), *Submarine T-9* (1943), and *One Family* (1943). Of these, only *Bakhtiar* was in Azerbaijani.[35] Thus, the emphasis on Russian as the lingua franca and the purported "Russianness" of the war—and the victories—was already implicit in wartime propaganda.

Religious leaders were called on to link the regime's goals to the populace. The old Ecclesiastical Boards, destroyed with bolshevization, were restored. Haji Mullah Aghalizade, sheikh ul-Islam during the independence period, was appointed to head the Shi'i board in Azerbaijan,[36] and, reportedly, mosques were reopened.

The scholarly community was mobilized to support the war effort. One of Azerbaijan's most eminent historians wrote that "the war, which called forth a restructuring [perestroika] in the work of all our industry, agriculture, and cultural institutions, placed serious new issues before the historians of Azerbaijan."[37] History books emphasized battles against foreign invaders. A popular history written in 1941 stopped at the "unification with Russia," which was not, of course, treated as a foreign invasion. The Russian conquest had not been an official conquest since the mid-1930s. In the 1940s it was regarded as "lesser evil," moving rapidly toward being a "positive good," an act of "voluntary unification," which it remained until the 1990s. Thus wartime histories became "patriotic education" rather than scholarship.[38] Among them were works on Babek, Azerbaijan's popular leader, and on resistance to Arab invasions. Some Azerbaijani scholars even produced works about Russian wars against "German aggression" such as the Teutonic Knights. Other books recounted victories by predominantly Azerbaijani units in World War II.[39]

AZERBAIJANI UNITS
ON THE GERMAN SIDE

Many mobilized to fight for the USSR, "for Stalin," had not forgotten how they came to be Soviet citizens. Some remembered collectivization, and even the younger soldiers recalled arrests, trials, and disappearances. Aleksander Solzhenitsyn said that "anti-Stalin feelings"—for non-Russians, one might add antiregime and anti-Russian feelings—were so strong and widespread that the retreat of the numerically superior Soviet forces before the German invasions was a way of "voting with the feet."[40] By the end of 1941 "three and a half million soldiers and officers were taken captive [by the Germans]—the numbers just about matching the strength of the invading army."[41] Many non-Russian soldiers, Azerbaijani Turks among them, wanted to reestablish their homelands as independent states; thus, those captured presented a potential anti-Soviet force.

Initially, the Turks were treated almost as badly as the Jews. Thousands were reported shot by the SS because, being circumcised, they were thought to be Jews. For those who made it to prisoner-of-war (POW) camps, the chances of survival were hardly better: of 100,000 captured Soviet Central Asians in one camp in Poland, only 6 percent survived the winter of 1941. Caucasian Christians fared somewhat better; about half survived.[42] Nazi racial theories placed Asians below Slavs. Nazi ideologues regarded Armenians, though Christian, as "racially inferior because of their . . . parasitic trading practices," whereas Georgians were declared to be Aryans and promised a "dominant position" in a German-ruled Caucasia.[43]

Soon, however, the possibility of mobilizing Soviet prisoners against the communist regime apparently took precedence over racial theories. Specialists on Soviet and Central Asian history at the Ostministerium were probably responsible for the improved treatment of non-Russians. Noting the high desertion rate and the anti-Bolshevik proclivities of Turkish nationalities, these scholars pressed for opportunities to make use of the prisoners. From that idea grew the Eastern Legions, military units formed from the POWs of Central Asia and Caucasia.[44]

The POWs were separated by nationality, placed in camps, and then trained in national formations.[45] By the fall of 1941 the Ostministerium and the Wehrmacht had formed seven companies—six Turkestani and one Azerbaijani—to use behind Soviet lines. Although never used for that purpose, the Azerbaijani company did see action. Another unit formed entirely of prisoners from the Caucasus was deployed in the summer of 1942 on the Caucasian front; it distinguished itself in action and in its ability to attract conationals from the Red Army.[46]

Hitler formally approved creating "national units" from Turkic and Christian Caucasian POWs in December 1942,[47] but several such units had already been formed. "The Balts, Moslems and [Christian] Caucasians were allowed national formations in 1941–42." In December 1941 "a Turkistani, a Caucasian-Moslem, a Georgian and an Armenian battalion" existed in the Wehrmacht.[48] By January 1942 recruiting for regular Eastern Legion battalions began in the POW camps in Poland. Almost all prisoners reportedly volunteered, but only 70 percent were found physically fit for service. From this recruiting drive, fifty-three field battalions from Polish camps and twenty-five more from camps in Ukraine were "turned over to the German Army by 1943."[49] Large numbers of noncombatant units were also formed from the same nationalities. In May 1943 the German army allowed the formation of "an independent Turkic division (the 162nd Infantry Division), which became the largest single unit in the legions." By the end of 1943 the Eastern Legions had reached their peak. Nonetheless, they were perpetually ill-equipped, inadequately trained, and regarded as "second-class" by the German soldiers.[50]

Western scholars note that although the Soviets acknowledge the ability of Germans to recruit captured Soviet troops of all nationalities, they attempt to minimize the phenomenon and discount those who were recruited as a few traitors. Those "traitors," however, were not so few and cannot be so easily dismissed in view of the conditions of their sovietization and their continuing commitment to national independence. (Others were certainly choosing the only alternative to prison camp, where death rates ranged from 30 to 95 percent.)[51] Soviet scholars have linked these units to interwar émigré groups, especially those in Germany. Azerbaijani Turkish émigrés living in Berlin before the war, including the former head of the Musavat, Mehmet Emin Rasulzade, were hardly fascist but, like those in Paris and Istanbul, were certainly anti-Soviet.

Data on those who fought in the German-sponsored units are not complete. The lowest estimates begin at 250,000, but one source, regarded as "fairly reliable," indicated a much larger total including 110,000 Caucasians, though without differentiating nationalities. By May 1943

there were 78 Turkic and Caucasian battalions and additional transport, logistics and construction units, the total of which exceeded 100,000 men. Additional formations included . . . a Turkic Legion and a Caucasian Legion in the Waffen SS. A total estimate of the Moslems and Caucasians in the German forces in World War II ranges from 275,000 to 350,000 men.[52]

Some national groups may have been better represented in the German than in the Soviet army.[53] The magnitude of discontent among these groups may be gauged by comparing these aggregate figures on "Muslim and Caucasian" formations (275,000 to 350,000) with the total of "military collaborators" (600,000 to 1.4 million[54] out of 5.7 million Soviet POWs)[55] or with the number of "Muslim and Caucasian" men in the Soviet armed forces in May 1942 (1.2 million).[56]

Many such men—and countless more who had been innocent of collaboration—rejoined the Soviet forces during the war and were assigned to penal battalions that "were literally used as an offensive weapon, as mine-sweepers and cannon fodder. As pseudonymous Viktor Suvorov wrote, 'the Germans choked on the blood of the penal battalions.'"[57] Those repatriated after the war were sent to prison camps or executed. Others formed sizable émigré communities in Europe, especially in Munich and Paris, and, to a lesser extent, in the United States.

POSTWAR YEARS, 1946–1956

Moscow's greatest need immediately after the war was to reinforce its control. Economic planning was part of this process, but official data indicate only a slight drop in industrial and agricultural production in all commodities in Azerbaijan between 1940 and 1945 and complete "recovery," with production surpassing prewar levels, by 1950. A conference on economic history held in Moscow in November 1951 declared that all republics passed into socialism and commenced building communism in the 1950s.[58]

The loss of the labor of hundreds of thousands of men during the war and the permanent loss of an undetermined number of them afterward severely weakened the republic's economy. The impact of returning males, of females in the labor force during and after the war, and of the ensuing demographics of the nation is not addressed in Soviet sources.

Official Soviet sources stated that greater centralization was needed to rebuild and, ostensibly, to "broaden the rights" of party and state organizations in the republics. The rights of republics were apparently inadequately strengthened because they were still an issue at the 1954 party congress, the first after Stalin's death.[59] The last years of Stalin's reign were a period of high risk. His minions, including Mir Jafar Baghirov in Azerbaijan, still occupied secure positions, and prewar political orthodoxy was reasserted.

Cultural-Intellectual Control

In cultural and intellectual matters, exerting central control over non-Russians meant reasserting the supremacy of Russians. The martial spirit of nationalities that had been awakened during the war now had to be suppressed. Campaigns were launched against individualism, "religious survivals," and "elements of nationalism."[60] Literature was expected to "adjust" to "heal war wounds" and repair the economy.[61] Dastans were now denounced as bourgeois, feudal, and antipopular.[62] Baghirov contributed to the campaign with attacks on Azerbaijan's history. In a 1950 speech he railed against past anti-Russian resistance,[63] denouncing Abbas Kulu Agha Bakikhanli as an idealist, a believing Muslim, and a defender of beks and khans and Mirza Kazembek as a "true servant of tsarism."[64]

Histories written during the war were essentially propaganda. When the war was over, however, Azerbaijani Turkish historians apparently felt the need to place their discipline on a more scholarly footing and, more important, to write the true history of their land and people. Guidelines on writing history, an inherently political subject, came from the CPSU through the USSR Academy of Sciences. As a result, rewriting history placed great emphasis on the primacy of the Russian "elder brother," the "superiority of Russian culture," and the Russian conquest as an "absolute good."[65] History written in these years determined the new, postpurge orthodoxy as postwar historians tried to recover knowledge of their past and still remain within official guidelines.

Many historians[66] took relatively safe paths—archaeology, prehistory, or ancient history—making use of prewar archaeology carried on throughout Azerbaijan.[67] Some examined later local dynasties, such as the Shirvanshahs of eastern Caucasia. Shah Ismail and his Safavid dynasty of Iran were regarded as specifically Azerbaijani,[68] not just "Turkish," in that Ismail's family was from Arbedil in southern Azerbaijan. Furthermore, Ismail's poetry, written under the pseudonym Khatai, was in the Azerbaijan dialect of Turkish and is regarded as an important part of Azerbaijani Turkish cultural history.

The treatment of the "unification" of Azerbaijan with Russia reflected the postwar primacy of all things Russian. Studies of the eighteenth century seem to have been intended to demonstrate the "backwardness" of Caucasia as a prelude to conquest by the Russian army early in the nineteenth century. Works on the conquest frequently refer to the hackneyed "progressive significance" of "unification" in their titles.[69]

Works on this conquest and on Azerbaijan's subsequent history were confined largely to studies of class conflict and the "international proletariat of Baku"; works on the twentieth century were mostly devoted to the "victory of Soviet power in Azerbaijan," or "building socialism."[70]

After the war there was a drive to reestablish schools and communicate new cultural imperatives to future generations. In 1949, at the seventeenth AzCP Congress, yet another call went out to improve the teaching of Russian. Teachers' conferences were held in all regions of the republic "to discuss measures for the improvement of the political instruction of teachers, to liquidate excessive overloading of students with social and extracurricular activities."[71]

At all levels recovery was a huge task. Because a majority of teachers and students in higher education institutions (VUZy) had gone to the front, after the war institutes and programs were reinstituted for the returning troops. Technical training was still emphasized, but suitable instructors had to be demobilized. By the end of the fourth plan period, 14,262 "specialists"—agronomists, engineers, doctors, teachers—had reportedly been trained in Azerbaijan's VUZy.[72]

Publishing had been curtailed during the war because paper and similarly scarce resources were devoted to political purposes. Restoration of some periodicals came slowly.[73]

Films continued to have a political function in the postwar era. In 1945 Uzeir Hajibeyli's comedic operetta, *Arshin Mal Alan* (first produced on the Baku stage in 1915), was filmed;[74] like many other prerevolutionary works by Hajibeyli, it ridicules custom, in this case arranged marriages. In *Arshin*, a young man plans to look over prospective brides by pretending to be a cloth merchant (the title is a call to "those wanting an *arshin* [length] of goods"). The choice of this popular musical by the most prominent national composer (who received a state prize for the film version just two years before his death) was cleverly intended to combat tradition and any residual wartime sentimentality for the past.

10 Recovery and Resurgence after Baghirov (1954–1969)

We know the future is glorious, comrades; it's the past that keeps changing.

Speaker at a conference of socialist historians, Eastern Europe, 1984

THE FALL OF BAGHIROV

By a decision of the Azerbaijan Communist party (AzCP) on 19 June 1953, Mir Jafar Baghirov was expelled from all his posts, including that of chairman of the Azerbaijan Council of Ministers and first secretary of the AzCP. Shortly thereafter, Baghirov and several "accomplices" were arrested. At the twentieth Communist party of the Soviet Union (CPSU) Congress, Baghirov was denounced as a proponent of the cult of personality by Imam Dashdemiroglu Mustafayev, Baghirov's successor as first secretary of the AzCP. Mustafayev stated that those who had perished at Baghirov's hands were innocent, honorable, and loyal party members.[1]

In mid-April 1956 a Soviet Supreme Military Court tried Baghirov and others on charges of "siding with anti-Soviet elements in Azerbaijan" and of cooperating with former Soviet security chief Lavrenti Beria—concealing the fact that Beria had worked for the Musavat intelligence[2] and destroying evidence of that liaison. All defendants were also accused of conspiracy, of attempting to engage in terrorist activities, and of joining a counterrevolutionary organization. Many witnesses provided testimony and documents. The accused confessed and asked for leniency, but they were rebuffed and sentenced to death.[3] Baghirov was executed by firing squad with three others, a Jew from his native Kuba and two Armenians. Two others were given 25-year prison sentences.

In its decision the Military Tribunal stated that "traitor Beria" and Baghirov had conspired together and that Baghirov had worked in Beria's state security apparatus since 1921 and knew of Beria's activities. When Beria's conspiracy was revealed, Baghirov did everything to save him, including destroying all incriminating evidence that Beria had been a member of the Musavat. Baghirov was accused of "employing methods forbidden by Soviet law," liquidating twenty-two prominent officials of Soviet Azerbaijan. The tribunal rehabilitated many of them.[4]

Baghirov's execution stirred many bitter memories among the émigré community, and a host of articles on his bloody career appeared in the émigré press and on Radio Liberty broadcasts. He was called "an enemy of our national thought, our liberation struggle."[5] He had done Moscow's bidding (one émigré asked whether Moscow was really surprised at "revelations" concerning Baghirov) and like many others, he became "inconvenient":

> Now the Soviet administration is changing its clothes to cleanse itself of its past 30 years of history and appear before world public opinion in a civilized and mild face. . . . In June 1953 he was removed from all his positions and by the ruthless hand of historical justice he was thrown into Cheka dungeons which he constructed and for three years was subjected to tortures he instigated before departing for hell.[6]

The period after the fall of Baghirov in Azerbaijan as elsewhere in the USSR was a time of backlash against strong individual leaders and the preeminence of the KGB. Baghirov's successor, Mustafayev (born 1910), who served as first secretary from 1954 until 1959, was a plant geneticist with little significant party experience. Veli Yusifoglu (Yusubovich) Akhundov, who succeeded Mustafayev, was trained as a medical doctor. Neither established a strong public personality. In republican party publications their names were rarely mentioned and their speeches rarely published. According to that written record they maintained a low profile and spoke for the collective leadership. Yet each man acted decisively behind the scenes, and carried out policies that distinguished him but led to his eventual removal from power.

Baghirov had reduced Azerbaijan's "leadership pool" by drinking "the *kaymak* [cream] of the Azerbaijan intelligentsia," as he was rumored to have boasted.[7] By physically destroying the political, intellectual, and social elite that remained in Azerbaijan after bolshevization, he eliminated not only potential rivals but possible successors. World War II losses and the postwar purges and exiles reduced their numbers further. Old men and women, whether inside the country or abroad, were the only ones who recalled the era of independence.

A new generation of leaders matured. The small surviving elite began to reassert itself in politics and cultural matters by rehabilitating purge victims, and by using the native language to ensure its legal place. Their efforts to bolster the economy, however, were constrained by the central party apparatus.

ADMINISTRATION IN
THE POST-BAGHIROV ERA

Apparently moving away from one-man rule, the USSR Soviet of Ministers in May 1955 granted the republican Soviets of Ministers greater latitude "in areas of labor and wages, agriculture, income and expenditures, [and the] allocation of funds for housing and social-cultural construction."[8] The possibilities may have appeared great for Azerbaijan, but the uncertainties remained and the new rules of the game were not known.

Greater republican autonomy was confirmed by the twentieth CPSU Congress in 1956, whose aims were to foster the "friendship of peoples" and expand the sovereignty of the republics.[9] A greater degree of judicial independence was allowed as were laws protecting nature and natural resources. Permission was given to determine internal (oblast' and *krai*) boundaries of a republic, and the Azerbaijan constitution was amended accordingly. Also adopted were several measures ostensibly designed to ensure greater republican participation in all-union decision making. Among these was a provision making the president of each republic's Soviet of Ministers an ex officio member of the USSR Soviet of Ministers.[11] All-union environmental or conservation laws were passed (June 1957). In late 1962, Azerbaijan established an Administration of Energy and Electrification and a Ministry of Water Management.[12]

State policy toward Islam was influenced by broader foreign policy considerations. Soviet-trained "Muslim leaders" were sent on Hajj (pilgrimages to Mecca) and to Islamic congresses to testify to Soviet support of Islam and to spread Soviet political and economic influence in the Middle East. In the mid-1950s these types of Soviet delegations increased simultaneously with the sales of USSR weapons to Arab states. In later decades a small number of Soviet *medresse* (seminary) graduates would be sent to Cairo and become authentic ulema. Yet their position and the position of the entire official Islamic establishment between the Kremlin on one hand and the faithful on the other would continue to be ambiguous.

Mustafayev's Fight for National Recovery

The early Khrushchev years coincided with the tenure of Imam D. Mustafayev as party first secretary in Azerbaijan. Mustafayev, a candidate of science in plant genetics and selection, had made his career in the academic world and in related administrative jobs in Baku, Ganje, and Karabagh. After receiving a candidate degree (1938) at the Azerbaijan Agricultural Institute, he served (1938–1940) as head of its department of selection and seedgrowing. After the war Mustafayev held posts in the Administration of Higher Schools and the Technicums of the Commissariat of Lands of Azerbaijan.[13] His long-standing concern with agriculture, conservation, and rural policies was reflected in his policies as first secretary.

Mustafayev's speech before the twentieth CPSU Congress in February 1956 began with the formulaic acknowledgments of the great work of the party and the leading role of the great Russian people for the development of Azerbaijan as a shining example to the world at large.[14] Mustafayev then moved to economic issues. "Azerbaijan is a republic of oil and cotton," he said. The creation of a Ministry of the Oil Industry (apparently in 1954) had facilitated technical improvement despite a reduction in capital investment from the center, and output had risen "significantly" in the past two years. Related industries such as refining and machine-building had almost all fulfilled their 1955 plan quotas. Mustafayev lauded the development of a synthetic rubber plant and aluminum factory in Sumgait, synthetic alcohol operations, and a cement *combinat* (all of which would contribute to the horrendous pollution of subsequent decades and, because of the high concentration of such enterprises in Sumgait, macabre jokes about its residents being able to survive gas chambers).

Seizing on a theme in Khrushchev's speech, Mustafayev supported the need for rural construction. Although many of Azerbaijan's kolkhozy had adequate funds for construction projects, there was virtually no building going on in any of them, he said. The Ministry of Urban and Rural Construction of the USSR was not providing technical assistance, nor was the barter system they ran operating effectively. Wood, cement, metal, slate, and pipes were in short supply, and rural construction under the existing system, Mustafayev concluded, would take years. The system "limits the initiative of the kolkhozy and kolkhozniki."[15] Such open criticism by Mustafayev and others at this congress must have seemed amazing evidence of the "thaw" of the post-Stalin era.

By contrast, Mustafayev's speech at the twenty-first congress in January

1959[16] was essentially a recitation of growth statistics. He began by referring to the assistance of the "great Russian nation" and ended by noting Azerbaijan's "burning love for the native [Azerbaijani or USSR?] Communist party, the Soviet government."

Another main thesis of his address was his repeated comparison of Azerbaijan with the Turkish Republic and other neighboring states including Iran and Afghanistan. It was perhaps not by chance that the speaker from the illegal Turkish Communist party (located in the German Democratic Republic) spoke immediately before Mustafayev. Mustafayev noted that Azerbaijan had one hundred students in higher education institutions for every ten thousand people, whereas Turkey had only fourteen; that production of cement per capita in Azerbaijan was 4 times greater than in Turkey; and that steel production was 2.4 times greater—all by official Soviet statistics, without reference to quality or content of the education, the cement, or the steel. Mustafayev reiterated Lenin's statement that Azerbaijan must be a model, for it would be "the best agitation, the best propaganda for our affairs throughout this huge multinational East."[17] Mustafayev ended by saying, "It is well known to all that the Soviet Union has never threatened anyone." The first secretary must have relied on his listeners' having forgotten the USSR's 1945 demands to cede Turkish territory and to control the Straits, its occupation of Iranian Azerbaijan until 1946, its blockade of Berlin, and its recent invasion of Hungary.

At home Mustafayev showed himself to be devoted to his nation, pursuing a number of policies that eventually cost him his position. He presided over a large immigration of Azerbaijani Turks into Baku, thereby tipping the population balance in the capital in their favor. Their proportion in Baku's population had been falling since the oil boom of the nineteenth century. By the 1959 census the growing Azerbaijani population in the capital (because of natural increase as well as immigration) was beginning to show. By the 1979 census this demographic "reconquest" of Baku would be an accomplished fact.

Mustafayev struggled to maximize economic autonomy. In a 1988 interview[18] he said that he had opposed Khrushchev's plan to bring republican ministries under Moscow's control. After a "long and heated discussion," he kept the Azerbaijan Oil Ministry, his own creation, from being subsumed under the new structure.

Mustafayev succeeded in amending the republican constitution to make Azerbaijani Turkish the official language of the republic and led the struggle against Moscow's attempt to change education policy on language instruction. The proposed change would have made the study of Azerbaijani Turkish optional in the schools where Russian or another foreign language was the language of instruction. Although his successor, then Prime Minister Akhundov, publicly articulated the official opposition to this change, Mustafayev took the blame. Considered a nationalist, he was removed from office in the middle of the fight over changing language policy[19] (the change was made after his ouster). Mustafayev was given a pension (at age forty-nine) and made head of the section of genetics and selection of grain and legumes at the Institute of Genetics and Selection of the Azerbaijan Academy of Sciences, a post he still held in the summer of 1988.[20]

Mustafayev and other officials were sharply criticized for "mistakes," and the press and Khrushchev raised the matter of "corruption." An "anti-corruption campaign" launched in the wake of the twentieth party congress led to widespread purges (no longer lethal) of the state and party bureaucracy.

Removals for "corruption" become increasingly popular from the Khrushchev era on. Mustafayev's successor would also be removed in connection with corruption charges, and the next first secretary, Heydar Aliyev, would make his career as a fighter against corruption. After his fall he too would be accused of that crime. Accusations of corruption do not tell the complex tale of Azerbaijani politics, loyalties, and exigencies, however. The term *corruption* is convenient and pernicious—it implies much and excludes little. Some kinds, particularly patronage, may be standard operating procedure. In a political system in which accusation or error or both may destroy a career or, in the worst of times, families and human lives, political leaders have every incentive to surround themselves with trusted cadres, especially relatives and friends. Everyone, both those who get jobs when administrations change and those who lose them, is familiar with the practice.

It is the normal "grease in the gears" throughout the entire Soviet system, like the speculation and illegal commerce that provide goods that would otherwise be unavailable. Azerbaijanis have strong entrepreneurial tendencies that in another political system would be unremarkable or even laudatory. But the party and state, articulating Marxist ideas but expressing what seem to be fundamentally Russian values,[22] continued to regard independent economic initiative as both illegal and morally reprehensible. Their attitudes would hinder private enterprise under Gorbachev.

This is not to say that all corruption is acceptable informally. The system has its own tacit rules. Diverting funds from public to private use or striking at an adversary through his children are roundly condemned. At the same time diversion of funds for housing construction or a reduction in cotton acreage, though illegal and antithetical to CPSU dicta, would probably be popular. Nonetheless, revelations about such so-called corruption provide a convenient pretext for the removal of state or party personnel when necessary. There is always evidence to be found, and cleaning up or limiting corruption may mean that a leader has the process under control and can maintain the system discreetly. Corruption cannot be eradicated under the Soviet system; if it were, the state apparatus, perhaps the economy, would grind to a halt.

Akhundov in Power

On 11 July 1959 Mustafayev was succeeded by Veli Y. Akhundov, M.D., who had been minister of health until 1958 and then abruptly elevated to chairman of the Council of Ministers, as if to position him for Mustafayev's job. In his first speech to an all-union party congress, the twenty-second congress in October 1961, Akhundov spent a good deal more time flattering Khrushchev than Mustafayev had done, and referred more often to the "fraternal assistance rendered by the great Russian people." It is difficult to tell whether Akhundov's speech represented the culmination of a trend toward flattery of the leader (relaxation into normalcy) or Akhundov's own propensities. Unlike Mustafayev, Akhundov spoke mostly about industrial development. The address read like a technical report, noting the dependence of Georgia and Armenia on Azerbaijan's oil and gas, citing production statistics, and listing new or expanded operations in synthetic rubber, herbicides, and plastics.

Akhundov, like his predecessor, repeated Lenin's claim that Soviet Azerbaijan would be a model for neighboring countries and all peoples of the East, a theme sounded in party journals.[23] He argued, for example, that the status of women in Soviet Azerbaijan proved their emancipation from pre-revolutionary conditions in "eastern parts of tsarist Russia." Women were doctors, delegates at political party functions, and members in "elected" bodies and were more "emancipated" in Azerbaijan than in the United States. He did not compare numbers of vacuum cleaners and washing machines.

Akhundov's report at the twenty-third CPSU Congress (29 March–8 April 1966) was full of Lenin but nearly devoid of Brezhnev. It affirmed Azerbaijan's support for the decision of the October 1964 plenum that ousted Khrushchev. Several paragraphs were devoted to the friendship-of-peoples theme, particularly to Georgian-Armenian-Azerbaijani relations and to Lenin, the "wise man" who provided a common language (figuratively and literally). This speech, like the previous one, was largely a report on Azerbaijan's industrial production.

Akhundov listed only a few problems, but they were serious: fresh water for Baku and industrial Sumgait (a problem by no means new or limited to that coastal region), living quarters to accommodate the growing work force, land reclamation, and salinization of the soil. Yet the first secretary dispensed with all this in one short paragraph and offered no hint of progress in these areas.[24]

In ideology First Secretary Akhundov adhered to the party line. In a

1968 article in *Azerbaijan Kommunisti*, he had aligned himself with the official doctrine concerning "some issues of our ideological work."[25] At the time of "Prague Spring" in Czechoslovakia, Akhundov emphasized the importance of ideology, highlighting the struggle against bourgeois falsification and the need to give youth proper ideological grounding. Akhundov warned against the subversive influence of "bourgeois propaganda, first of all enemy radio," on young people and urged Soviet propagandists to tailor their message to the intended audience. Little in his message was specific to Azerbaijan; the usual slogans about internationalism and the building of communism simply were repeated. Perhaps by 1968, the eve of his ouster, he had seen the handwriting on the wall.

The Azerbaijan party organization had finally become predominantly Azerbaijani Turks (61 percent by the mid-1960s), but they were still underrepresented compared with their proportion of the population (67 percent in 1959). Russian and Armenian party membership was dropping, but these nationalities were still overrepresented: Russians were 14 percent of the 1959 population (and 10 percent in 1970) but were 15 percent of the AzCP members in 1965; Armenians were 12 percent of the 1959 population (9.4 percent in 1970) but 16.4 percent of party members in 1965. The membership was becoming more educated. Intellectuals predominated, though by "social origin" the AzCP remained a workers' party.[26]

The AzCP thus took on a more national character in that party membership increasingly became the means to career advancement for all professionals, from professors and artists to factory and kolkhoz managers. The regime co-opted many Azerbaijani Turks by making career advancement depend on party membership. Thus many Azerbaijanis became enforcers of central policy and upholders of the regime. Some Azerbaijani Communists strove to serve the legitimate interests of the republic, but they were constrained or opposed by others, including conationals who defended the system to which they owed their careers. Ideology ceased to play a significant role in the AzCP, perhaps as early as the 1960s, but it had to be given lip service. Moscow's—and the Russians'—primacy, however, was intact. The second secretary was always Russian; Russians and Armenians continued to hold many key posts. No political, economic, social, or intellectual life could legitimately take place outside the party's purview.

Akhundov was removed from power in July 1969, ten years after his accession. Several cases of "corruption" were publicized in the Baku press, including charges of private economic activity and laxity by officials.[27] Most of these were apparently not treated with sufficiently strident measures in Moscow's eyes.

Despite official platitudes about "building socialism" and creating the "new Soviet person," widespread crime and violence were reported, especially that committed by youths under eighteen, and drug abuse spread rapidly. Later reports suggested that bribery, influence peddling, and other abuses of power flourished under Akhundov. The economic picture was no better: one report said that 32 percent of Baku's population in 1969 lived in communal apartments of less than ten square meters per person. Illiteracy also persisted.[28] None of these ills was discussed at the time of Akhundov's removal. Official statistics reflected Azerbaijan's relatively weak all-union position with a low per capita income and weak industrial productivity.[29]

It has been suggested that Akhundov (who implemented an unpopular language law making the study of Azerbaijan Turkish optional) was too permissive of national assertiveness by those around him, such as party Third Secretary Sh. Kurbanov, who insisted on addressing even the CC CPSU in Azerbaijani Turkish rather than Russian.[30] Apparently, Akhundov ran afoul of Brezhnev by siding with Ukrainian party boss Alexander Shelepin in a 1965 conflict between the two men "over control of the party-state control organs." Akhundov's support for Shelepin in the 1960s has been attributed to Shelepin's helping Akhundov secure his own series of promotions in the late 1950s. When Shelepin lost, so did his supporters.[31] Akhundov, like his predecessor, was sent to the Academy of Sciences as vice-president though he had been elected to the academy only the previous month.[32] His successor was the energetic and controversial KGB chairman of the republic, Heydar Ali Rzaoglu (Alievich) Aliyev from Nakhjivan.

POLITICS AND HISTORY: REHABILITATIONS

Local efforts to reassert historical identity and dignity included rehabilitating political and cultural figures who had been discredited and often killed in the 1920s and 1930s. The Military Tribunal that had sentenced Baghirov exonerated his victims en masse, and Mustafayev in his twentieth CPSU Congress speech cleared others. Historians working within spoken and tacit party guidelines settled the details.

Poet and dramatist Husein Javid, who had died in a Siberian camp, was rehabilitated in October 1956 in *Bakinskii Rabochii* and in *Kommunist*. After Javid had been denounced for years as a "bourgeois nationalist," "Pan-Islamist," and "Pan-Turkist," his play *Sheykh Sa'nan* was performed in the Azizbekov Dramatic Theater in Baku. Drama critics noted the deep impression of his work "in the spiritual life of his native people," admitting that "for many long years the productions of Javid have not seen the footlights."

Another literary figure, Yusuf Vezirov, exiled and "liquidated" in 1937 as a "bourgeois nationalist," was rehabilitated quietly in 1956 and 1957. Vezirov, a frequent contributor to *Molla Nasreddin*, had been abroad in the early 1920s, was persuaded to return by Baghirov in 1925, and had pursued his writing career and published in Soviet Azerbaijan between 1926 and 1937. In the September 1956 issue of *Literaturnyi Azerbaidzhan*, he was praised as "one of the most talented Azerbaijani writers, famous for his prose, author of numerous stories and novels," by Akbar Agaev. Early in 1957 an announcement was made in the Baku press that the manuscript repository of the Azerbaijan Academy of Sciences had acquired the works of Husein Javid, Ahmet Jevad (another purge victim), and Yusuf Vezirov.³³

Kommunist, on 13 January 1957, rehabilitated Ruhulla Akhundov, an ideologist and former commissar, as part of de-Stalinization. The newspaper printed photos of Ruhulla Akhundov with Kirov and Sultan Mejid Efendiyev, who was also rehabilitated. Other articles lauding Akhundov appeared in *Edebiyyat ve Injesanat*.³⁴ In the early 1960s biographies appeared on Narimanov, Efendiyev, and other communist leaders and on several cultural figures who had been vilified. Short biographies were included in survey histories.

A number of publications were also rehabilitated, the most significant of which was the ancient dastan, *The Book of Dede Korkut*. Professors Hamid Arasli, E. Temirchizade, and docent M. X. Tahmasib discussed in "Poems of *Dede Korkut*" the "remarkable and rich source of the monuments of the history, literature, language, folklore, and ethnography."³⁵

M. E. Rasulzade's prerevolutionary journal, *Tekammul*, was now called a link in teaching the political tactics of Bolsheviks, a propaganda base for revolutionary ideas, and a means of exposing tsarist government actions and capitalists.³⁶ The journal was credited with consolidating democratic forces. Rasulzade, who had died the previous year in Turkey, was mentioned as leader of the Musavat, which had "a majority in Parliament 1918–1920." Noncommunist political leaders were otherwise ignored.

Meaning of Rehabilitation

Literary as well as human rehabilitations were ambiguous. Although formerly taboo names could again be mentioned and people, dastans, or publications could be discussed, such revelations were selective. The motivations of the rehabilitated were imputed to be in line with party ideology—the dead were discovered to have been "loyal Leninists," the dastans now the works of the "toiling masses."

In the case of Husein Javid, for example, two of his plays were left out of rehabilitation discussions. As Jeyhun Hajibeyli, writing in Paris, noted, there was no mention of *Topal Teimur* and *Peygamber*: "Why? Do the [party and state] continue all the same to view these from the epoch of the 'cult of personality'?"[37] Jeyhun Bey demonstrated that much of Ruhulla Akhundov's rehabilitation was actually apologia. Akhundov was said to have been a great supporter of the "Azerbaijani" language (called Turkish while he lived). At the same time, wrote *Bakinskii Rabochii*, "Ruhulla deeply understood the enormous significance of the well-rounded cultural development of our nation [and] emphasized at the same time the significance of the study of the great Russian language."[38]

Another interesting aspect of Ruhulla Akhundov's rehabilitation was the apparent need in 1956 and 1957 to claim that he had supported Azerbaijani Turkish as the state language while acknowledging the importance of Russian. At the same time, First Secretary Mustafayev was ensuring official status for the native language. Although this display of nationalism probably led to Mustafayev's downfall, popular support for the official status of Azerbaijani Turkish was reflected in the Ruhulla Akhundov rehabilitation.

Literary rehabilitations followed the same pattern. An article on *Dede Korkut* acknowledged the 1951 vilification of the dastan as "Pan-Islamic" and "Pan-Turkist." But the dastan was "legitimized" by citations from Marx and references to the Russian "Igor tale," to Christian knights, and Finnish epics. It was thereby removed from the realm of oral history and related to the Western literary, not historical, tradition. Such a rehabilitation laid the groundwork for the argument that dastans were mere "folklore" and were being preserved as such by the Soviet state. In fact, they were reissued in edited, "refined" editions, gutted of their historical message.[39]

Rehabilitations begun in the 1950s were completed in the monographs of the 1960s. These published histories were the major forum for the rewriting of scenarios that rehabilitation required. They reflected official guidelines for the treatment of individuals, works of literature and history, periodical publications, and events. These guidelines would be applied to all fields of history in the ensuing decades.

Most 1960s publications left the last few years of their subject's life to the reader's imagination. They noted only a death date in 1937, 1938, or 1939. In the history of Azerbaijan's Soviet literature, biographies of famous men like Husein Javid, lost in the purges, were by and large left out. Only two apparent purge victims'—Seyid Husein (1887–1937) and Mikail Mirza Kadyroglu Ismailzade (Mushfik) (1908–1939)—biographies were included. Discussion of the work and lives ended in the early 1930s. About Husein's life, it was said simply, "His work continued ten years in all (1927–1937)." The cryptic remarks on Mushfik's life ended, "From 1930 through 1935 he published ten collections of [his own] poetry." Each biography listed numerous works of each writer and gave a positive slant to them. In other cases, however, there were only omissions and implications. Rare individuals took on the extensive rehabilitation of a purge victim; in 1968 a three-volume collection of Husein Javid's works produced by his daughter Turan was published.

Thus, the "rehabilitations" of both people and dastans may be entirely misleading. Information that did not sustain the regime's position was omitted—there is no mention of Husein Javid's play about Timur, and *Dede Korkut* became the "Igor tale of Azerbaijan," truncating the dastan and separating Azerbaijan from its historical antecedents. Although selected individuals could once again be mentioned, only those aspects of their lives that demonstrated their loyalty to Lenin, the party, or Marxist-Leninist principles were acceptable topics for examination, research, and repetition. The limits to revelation were laid down tacitly. Some of those who wrote rehabilitations may have believed that they were making the most of an opportunity, giving at least a half a loaf to society, but they ultimately conveyed a false picture to the nation. The rehabilitations, passing themselves off as products of a "thaw" and instruments of "historical justice," actually co-opted the dead by taking their works out of context or imputing to them intentions that were never there. The same caution used to evaluate these rehabilitations also applies to those of the Gorbachev era.

HISTORY AND POLITICS: REWRITING THE PAST

Several scholarly conferences on historical topics[40] and the dastans *Dede Korkut* and *Köroglu* marked the beginning of an intensive effort to clarify history and historical identity in the late 1950s and early 1960s. The process would culminate thirty years later.

Although reaffirming CPSU resolutions on ideological matters, a 1954 Academy of Sciences Institute of History conference called for better training of scholars and decried "crude distortions of facts" by Baghirov that had disrupted historical studies. Two years later, the twentieth CPSU Congress called for "progress" in scholarly fields of study to match that of economic and cultural development. Specifically, the congress called on historians to write complete general histories of the peoples of the USSR, clearly as part of de-Stalinization's "wiping the slate clean" process.[41] This request coincided with an extensive reorganization of the USSR Academy of Sciences Oriental Institute, the body that made and makes cultural policies for the Turkish, "Muslim" populations of the country. Both dastans and topics in history were reevaluated according to the newly issued guidelines.[42]

The ambitious, three-volume *History of Azerbaijan* was written in this environment. Teams of scholars sought to cover the history of the republic or, more correctly, of the people, governments, societies, cultures, and intellectual life that had developed on the territory of the present-day Azerbaijan SSR, carefully if artificially observing present-day borders,[43] from the first traces of human life until the 1960s. Historians wrote within the requirements of Marxism-Leninism, CPSU resolutions, and Academy of Sciences guidelines and employed the caution born of an era in which people disappeared or died for imprudence, let alone mistakes. The uneven but useful history established the "new orthodoxy" for contemporary and subsequent scholarly publications. Despite its flaws of omission and rigidity, the *History of Azerbaijan* had not been supplanted by any work of comparable scope when the academy planned a new multivolume history in 1990.

The *History of Azerbaijan* addressed the fundamental question of the identity and origin of the "Azerbaijanis" (see chapter 1). The population of Media-Atropatene (4th century B.C.E.–2d century C.E.) was said to be the core of what would later become the "Azerbaijani nationality" (*narodnost'*),[44] with "Turkicization" occuring during the 4th to the 6th centuries. The Khazar element was strong in Caucasian Albania from the 6th century on,[45] and Islam was an important element unifying the population as a prelude to its later development into a nation (*natsiia*).[46] Despite de-Stalinization, the categories of national development (*narodnost'*, *natsii*) Stalin created in his 1913 essay "Marxism and the National Question" remain in use.

The *History of Azerbaijan* explored lesser known issues of social and urban history. Although its framework was Marxist, the result was a relatively coherent picture of the towns, crafts, and commerce of Azerbaijan. Unfortunately, these volumes contain no references notes.

The period from the Russian conquests until the revolution of February 1917 was depicted as a time of "bourgeois capitalist development" and class conflict that led to the "Great October Socialist Revolution." Strikes, the labor movement, the history of the Russian Social Democratic Workers' party and its activities in Baku, and selected "progressive" individuals were overemphasized. The last volume, on the Soviet period, traced the glorious victories of Soviet power and the equally glorious march toward socialism. The Musavat party was a villain; nothing was said about Stalin or the purges. Considerable space was given to the "ideological battle" (resumed zealously after 1945) against individualism, "religious survivals," and "elements of nationalism." Beria and Baghirov were vilified.[47]

Despite the predominance of old interpretations, other scholarly works of this period broke new ground, studying industrial development other than in oil, migrant workers from southern Azerbaijan, trade, the creation of a national bourgeoisie and proletariat, and capitalism in the countryside.[48] Multivolume histories, including surveys of administrative history, literature, and the spread of Marxism in Azerbaijan,[49] laid out the "correct" interpretations, as well as "known" facts from which there was little deviation until the 1980s.[50] There were also obligatory celebrations of the much-resented Transcaucasian Federation and evidence of Azerbaijan's contribution to World War II.

In the 1950s and 1960s some historians were determined to clarify the history of Caucasian Albania, of Babek's movement, and of Shirvan and the various independent states that existed in Azerbaijan between approximately the 6th and the 17th centuries, states that were used later to bolster claims for autonomy and independence. Two pioneers among Azerbaijani scholars were Oktay A. Efendiev[51] and Sara B. Ashurbeyli.[52] Ziya Buniatov's sizable contribution includes political histories, translations, and studies of various primary sources.[53] Minorsky's translation of the *History of Shirvan and Derbent* was republished.[54]

The rewriting of history in the 1950s and 1960s was not an esoteric exercise but a struggle to recover the past, the cornerstone to identity. Authors resisted Russian claims to cultural superiority and to political domination but could not escape the "elder brother" and "new Soviet man" rhetoric of the regime. Historians are still trying to clarify the history of Azerbaijan.

Some academic groups came into conflict with the party. In April 1963 the CC CPSU and the Soviet of Ministers of the USSR passed a resolution on "improving" the academies of sciences in the republics. Like the "restructuring" of the late 1920s to early 1930s, such reorganizations frequently indicate that the republics are pursuing too independent a course. During 1963, numerous departments were added to existing academies and the Azerbaijan Academy of Sciences received eight new departments.[55]

The historians' struggle affected the literary world. Works of literature often drew on history and discussed historical themes and figures, sometimes treading where historians dared not go. Writers could express love for the homeland, not the "Socialist homeland" but Azerbaijan. In the 1960s, literary journals began celebrating literary figures of early Soviet and pre-Soviet times. In 1966 the sixty years since the founding of the journal *Molla Nasreddin* and the 100th anniversary of the birth of its founder and editor, Jelil Mamedkuluzade, were commemorated. A series on music history in the literary journal *Azerbaijan* discussed a famous *ozan* (reciter of dastans) of Shush who died in 1928.[56] The article subtly reminded the reader of the dastans, the fate of many reciters, and of purges for "national deviation."

STRUGGLES OVER EDUCATION
AND IDEOLOGY

Conflict arose over the change in language requirements in republican schools. In November 1958 the CC CPSU and the USSR Council of Ministers approved basic theses for a new education reform law. Thesis 19, which addressed the study of languages in schools in the non-Russian republics, stirred controversy in many republics, especially Azerbaijan. Although it reaffirmed the right of non-Russians to education in their native language, Thesis 19 violated the established practice by which all students in non-Russian republics were required to study Russian and the language of the republic. Now students could choose.

> If a child attends a school where instruction is conducted in the language of one of the union or autonomous republics, he may, if he wishes, take up the Russian language . . . if a child attends a Russian school, he may, if he so desires, study the language of one of the union or autonomous republics. To be sure, this step could only be taken if there is a sufficient number of children to form classes for instruction in a given language.[57]

The future of Russian-language study was not in doubt in that facilities for Russian instruction existed throughout the USSR, and the incentives to study Russian, the all-union language needed for all-union careers, were obvious. Rather, it was the republican languages that were at risk. Thesis 19 seemed to denigrate the indigenous cultures as did the "elder brother" verbiage and the rewriting of history to show the mythical "great friendship." All republics put up some resistance, and Azerbaijan and Latvia put up the most, according to Yaroslav Bilinsky's study. Azerbaijani Turks emphasized the importance of native-language study and tried to take advantage of the official claim that republics themselves would decide the language issue. Each republic wrote its own law, and Azerbaijan's law of April 1959 omitted

> any reference to the parents' right of deciding whether their children should study either Russian or Azerbaijani as a second language. . . . The Azerbaijani Prime Minister [V. Y.] Akhundov explained . . . that for several reasons, political as well as practical, "the knowledge of Azerbaijani as a means of communication [was] vitally necessary. Therefore, the school curricula [would] provide for the study of Azerbaijani in Russian schools as a required subject, presumably."[58]

Only after the removal of First Secretary Mustafayev was the republican law brought into line with the demands of Thesis 19 by an amendment of

November 1959.[59] Akhundov, who voiced official resistance to Thesis 19, came to power during the dispute and oversaw its resolution in favor of the center. In subsequent years the failure of nonnatives in Azerbaijan, even of those born in the republic, to know Turkish would provoke the anger of the native population. By 1966 there were complaints about the inadequate teaching of Azerbaijani Turkish.[60]

Nor was party education neglected. A 1968 article outlined a plan for the "Socialist organization of social labor,"[61] a topic that should have needed no further comment fifty years after the October Revolution. Propagandists were told to teach the basic principles of the socialist organization of labor. (The exhortation suggested that there had been a failure to do so.) Indirect propaganda was perhaps more effective: A woman who had worked for thirty-eight years as a weaver in a textile mill in Ganje complained how sad it was that women no longer wanted to work in such a beautiful profession. As it turned out, there was a shortage of "cadres" at the factory, and it had not fulfilled its plan for several years.[62]

Although there was a "thaw" in Russian literature in the Khrushchev years, control was imposed on culture in Azerbaijan; despite some relaxation after the fall of Baghirov, the conventional accusations about "corruption" or "nationalism" were still employed to discredit and oust political leaders. Even with de-Stalinization, admissions of past errors were limited and "re-habilitations" incomplete. The distinction between form and substance, between the center's rhetoric and its policy, was as crucial as ever. A small, reemerging intellectual-political leadership, symbolized more by Mustafayev perhaps than by his successor, attempted to resume the prewar struggles for local control. The group were few in number and faced greater control and fewer internal supporters than had their fathers. But they laid the foundation on which they and others would build.

11 The Era of Heydar Aliyev (1969–1987)

> Woman: *"I realize I can't be considered a New Englander because I moved here from somewhere else, but my children were born here, so aren't they New Englanders?"*
>
> New England Farmer: *"If your cat had kittens in the oven, would you call 'em biscuits?"*
>
> Old New England anecdote

STATE AND PARTY POLITICS

Heydar Ali Rzaoglu Aliyev (born 10 May 1923) became first secretary of the Azerbaijan Communist party at the July 1969 plenum. He held that post until his 1982 promotion to first deputy chairman of the USSR Council of Ministers. A native of Nakhjivan, Heydar Aliyev's education was interrupted by World War II. According to one report, he was a member of the military counterintelligence group SMERSH on the Ukrainian front.[1] He joined the CPSU and the KGB in 1945; after 1953, he worked in the KGB's Eastern Division, traveling to Pakistan, Iran, Afghanistan, and Turkey. He attended the evening division of the history faculty of Azerbaijan State University and graduated in 1957.[2] During the 1960s he advanced to the rank of major-general in the KGB.

Aliyev's boss in the Azerbaijan KGB was Semyon Tsvigun, a longtime associate and Brezhnev's brother-in-law. Tsvigun reportedly helped Aliyev to succeed him as KGB chief when Tsvigun was promoted by Brezhnev to be deputy KGB chairman in Moscow. Aliyev was the first native head of the Azerbaijan KGB since Baghirov, and he had followed a similar career path, from security forces to first secretary, a coincidence that some no doubt found disquieting. Aliyev became a candidate member of the CPSU Politbiuro in 1976.[3] With the death of Brezhnev, Yuri Andropov brought Aliyev to Moscow and made him a full member of the Politbiuro and first deputy chairman.[4] The promotion was probably a result of Aliyev's own record in the KGB and as first secretary of Azerbaijan, where he was responsible for official increases in industrial and agricultural production, an extensive cleanup of "corruption" in the republic, and strengthening the local party's ideological posture.

A protégé of Brezhnev, Aliyev would also be called an Andropov loyalist, especially as he was entirely beholden to Andropov for his promotion. That he was a member of a national minority, a Turk, and a "Muslim" (an atheist one, to be sure) aroused much speculation in the foreign press at the time of his promotion. Indeed, his liaison with foreign Communist parties in the Middle East and his contacts with the Turkish Republic suggested to many that his appointment signaled a greater Soviet effort in that region. Aliyev, however, never presented himself as a Muslim or a representative of Soviet Muslims but only of the officially atheist Soviet state.[5] Whether he was seen as a Muslim or Turk by foreign states, and what it meant to them if he were, is uncertain.

During the period between Baghirov and Aliyev, reports of republican and all-union party congresses printed in *Azerbaijan Kommunisti* (organ of the AzCP Central Committee) had rarely included speeches by the Azerbaijan first secretary and those that were published were brief. Neither the table of contents nor the annual index of the journal indicated that the speaker/author was the first secretary. Only on the first page of the article itself were his name and title given. Then came Aliyev.

Beginning in the summer of 1970, Aliyev's speeches and reports appeared in full in *Azerbaijan Kommunisti*, sometimes occupying over half the issue. In both the table of contents and the index, his name and full titles were noted, often in boldface, with each speech or report. His speeches, according to these published versions, were frequently interrupted with "applause," "stormy applause," or "stormy and prolonged applause." References to him in other speakers' remarks were often greeted with applause.

Aliyev's speeches set the tone for the era in which he ruled, and his forceful presence reasserted the role of the first secretary as an individual and center of attention, a single leader shaping the affairs of the republic internally and affecting its fortunes within the union. From the economy to the arts, Aliyev emphasized ideology and the central role of the Communist party, especially as ideological leader. He frequently repeated the "new Soviet person" theme. Greater party control and the enforcement of ideology were offered at least as partial solutions to every problem in the republic. Aliyev's first speech to the CC AzCP plenum, in August 1969, named the "guilty" and denounced bribe-taking, blackmail, and patronage.[6] In his address to the twenty-fifth CPSU Congress in 1976,[7] Aliyev pledged greater party control over the economy, the selection of cadres, and the "moral education of the toilers" in the battle against self-interest, petty bourgeois mentality, and acquisitiveness. He pledged further efforts by party and social institutions in creating the "new Soviet person" and thanked the Russian "elder brother" for assistance.

Similarly, Aliyev began his address to the thirtieth AzCP Congress (January 1981) with an extended discussion of the writings of Lenin and Brezhnev and of the moral leadership of the Communist party, which, he said, was to be even more fully exerted over the teachers and schools, the arts and humanities.[8] He suggested a plan for a "thorough restructuring" of higher education.[9]

Two long sections of Aliyev's address were entitled "Organizational-Party Work and Raising the Vanguard Role of Communists" and "Strengthening Ideological Work." Propaganda and agitation had become "more concrete," and the first secretary noted that the party had taken a greater leadership role in the "spiritual life" of the republic.[10] Party membership had grown 27 percent since 1970, bringing it to 330,319.[11] Aliyev did not point out that this represented only about 6 percent of the 1979 republican population or that the proportion of "workers" and kolkhozniki continued to decline; nor did he provide the national composition of the AzCP. Despite the increasing percentage of Azerbaijani Turks, they were still a smaller proportion in the party than in the population (66 percent of the AzCP but 74 percent of the 1979 population). Russians and Armenians, decreasing in number and proportion in both party and population, were still overrepresented.[12]

Aliyev sharply criticized party members accused of inadequately performing their duties. Many of them lost their posts and even their party cards. Aliyev gave no dates for this shake-up in the apparatus, but it must have been some time in the late 1970s. The first secretary of the Kirovobad *gorkom* (city committee) was removed from his post and from the Central Committee; the first secretaries of the Shemakhi and Kazakh *raiony* were removed from their posts and expelled from the party. For errors in the "preparation of cadres," one Central Committee secretary and the *raikom* (*raion* committee) secretaries of Aksu, Julfa, Kutkashen, Dashkesan, and many others were removed.[13] In connection with criticism of the legal apparatus and the policy, Procurator G. Mamedov was removed from his post as were three assistant procurators.[14] Most of those removed seem to have been Azerbaijani Turks; only one or two Russian names appeared.

These removals were nothing new. Aliyev began his tenure with an extensive purge of the party and state apparatus, economic enterprises, and the Komsomol, removing several republican ministers.[15] Among those replaced during his first two years in power were more than a half-dozen ministers and party secretaries and fourteen first secretaries of the republic's fifty-one raiony, including the first secretaries in the NKAO (an Armenian replaced an Armenian) and in Aliyev's own home of Nakhjivan. The new men were all said to be connected with Aliyev through the KGB or some other channel.[16] In the first five years of Aliyev's tenure, two-thirds of the Council of Ministers, eight of ten members of the party bureau, three of four secretaries in the Central Committee, thirteen of fourteen heads of CC departments, and thirty-seven of forty-five district party committee secretaries were replaced.[17] By filling these posts with his own supporters, Aliyev built an extensive republican apparatus under his control. These appointees remained in position under his immediate successor, Kamran M. Baghirov, so that the "Aliyev era" continued as long as his supporters held their posts and Aliyev's personal prestige remained intact. An article in 1983 (the year after Aliyev's promotion) on internal party democracy lauded the achievements in this area during the "past thirteen years," or since 1969, when Aliyev became first secretary.[18]

The era of Aliyev, however, was also the era of Brezhnev in Azerbaijan. Brezhnev visited the republic in 1970, 1978, and 1982 and awarded Aliyev, Baku, and the republic various honors, including the Order of Lenin. Although Aliyev's portrait could be found in party and state offices, it was Brezhnev's face that looked down onto public squares. His 1978 statement "Broadly strides Azerbaijan" became the slogan of the late Aliyev era. Aliyev's position, the free hand he enjoyed in purges and appointments, and apparently his promotions were intimately tied to his support of Brezhnev (some would call it obsequiousness). At the CPSU and AzCP congresses, Aliyev quoted Brezhnev frequently and mentioned his name repeatedly. At the twenty-sixth CPSU Congress, he mentioned Leonid Ilich twelve times in 5½ pages, referring to Brezhnev's "deep analysis" of international affairs and his "powerful" contributions to "Marxist-Leninist sciences."[19] Aliyev was certainly not alone in his flattery of Brezhnev, but he was one of its more energetic practitioners. It may have paid off; by the twenty-sixth congress, Aliyev was a candidate member of the Politbiuro CC CPSU.

Like all strong political personalities, Aliyev evoked strong reactions. To his admirers, he was a dynamic and intelligent leader who breathed life into a sluggish economy and brought renewed prestige to Azerbaijan. He brought an air-conditioning plant to Baku, providing jobs and air conditioners to a republic with seven-month summers and altering, if only slightly, the established pattern in which Azerbaijan provided raw materials but rarely manufactures. He presided over increases in economic and agricultural productivity as Azerbaijan became the major grape-producing republic in the USSR. The exhumation from Siberia and reburial in Azerbaijan of the remains of national poet and dramatist Husein Javid, an act of great symbolic importance, could not have taken place without Aliyev. Finally, Aliyev's promotion meant that Azerbaijan was represented in the Politbiuro for the first time since the fall of Mir Jafar Baghirov, an important event for national prestige and behind-the-scenes political influence.

Aliyev's critics, whose numbers grew considerably after his fall from grace in 1987, point out that much of what Aliyev accomplished for Azerbaijan was a boon to his own career. They admit he is smart—perhaps too clever—but note that he filled the ranks of Azerbaijan's party and state bureaucracies with relatives, friends, and acquaintances from Nakhjivan or the KGB. His supporters answer that protecting oneself in the back-stabbing political atmosphere has less to do with individual style than with the exigencies created by a system that exacts a heavy toll for failure. (The critics also note that Husein Javid was from Nakhjivan.)

Both Aliyev's appointments of personal supporters (those from Nakhjivan rather than the KGB have been singled out) and his acclaimed economic accomplishments have come under attack since his removal from power and retirement at age 64.[20] Accusations by Aliyev's critics, written in Russian-language publications mostly by non-Turks, called Aliyev's rule a period of "mafia" or "clan" domination and "stagnation" associated with the Brezhnev period. Individual instances of personal abuse by Aliyev appointees were recounted in detail, although documentation was lacking.[21] With a complete disregard for history, one writer attributed to Aliyev the distinction of having "invented" favoritism.[22] Attacking the economic record of the Aliyev years, one writer charged that "the harvest of nonexistent cotton had reached one million tons per year."[23] To be fair, the cotton was hardly nonexistent, for deliveries were made, goods were produced, and pesticides used lavishly.

It is too early to draw up an accurate balance sheet on Heydar Aliyev and his career in Azerbaijan, especially in view of his apparent comeback in Supreme Soviet elections in the autumn of 1990. Noteworthy, however, is the language with which Aliyev was criticized, mainly outside Azerbaijan, and the possibility that criticism of him was used in the late 1980s to send messages to the republic. Several articles denounced an Aliyev "cult of personality" in language that recalled de-Stalinization and seemingly drew a parallel between Aliyev's political rule and the disregard for "Socialist justice" that is associated with "personality cults."[24] They seem to say that justice must come from Moscow, for politics in the republics gets too personal.[25] These themes constitute an indirect criticism of Azerbaijan and have to some extent been used with respect to disputes with Armenia.

The demand for the transfer of Nagorno-Karabagh to the Armenian SSR was sounded at the time of Aliyev's fall, and a petition drive in Armenia just preceded the formal announcement (though probably not the decision itself) of Aliyev's "retirement" in the summer of 1987. A speech by Gorbachev's adviser Abel Aganbegiyan advocating the transfer was made in Paris to a group of Armenian war veterans in November. If Aliyev's removal from power in Moscow were interpreted as a loss of power and prestige for Azerbaijan, it would have been an opportune time to advance claims against the republic. It is unlikely, however, that Aliyev's "retirement" was a result of Armenian pressures.[26] Like his promotion, Aliyev's fall probably had more to do with the politics of the center—in this case, with Gorbachev's "house cleaning."[27] Subsequent criticism of Aliyev, like the castigation of Brezhnev and his men, was standard operating procedure. But it was also used to criticize Azerbaijan in general and vis-á-vis the Armenian dispute.

ECONOMY: REAL GROWTH OR ECOLOGICAL DISASTER?

Economic difficulties were acknowledged by V. Y. Akhundov, especially in agriculture, but Aliyev claimed to have overcome them. His reports to the CPSU and AzCP congresses noted increased productivity and a doubling in the output of wheat, cotton, and grapes between 1970 and 1980.[28] For fulfilling the ninth Five-Year Plan, Azerbaijan received the Order of Lenin. Azerbaijan's rate of industrial growth between 1976 and 1980 had been 47 percent, the highest of any union republic.[29]

Aliyev singled out the impressive rates of cotton and grape production. Although cotton production had always been controversial, at the twenty-fifth CPSU Congress, Aliyev claimed to have overcome what he called an "anticotton mood" in the republic. (The problem must have been serious and widely known for him to have mentioned it in a CPSU congress.) In January 1981 at the AzCP Congress, however, he repeated that he had defeated the "anticotton mood of recent years," which suggests that this mood had persisted. At the end of the decade, an outcry was raised against the human and ecological costs of extensive cotton cultivation, the fertilizers used to boost production, and the salinization of the soil from irrigation. The source of the discontent is plain from Aliyev's report. In the 1970s, he stated in January 1981, 5.5 million tons of cotton were produced in Azerbaijan as against 2.4 million tons in the 1960s. Irrigation from the Araz and Kura rivers had been greatly expanded, and the use of mineral and chemical fertilizers—touted as a sign of progress—skyrocketed. In 1980, Aliyev reported 1.53 million tons of mineral fertilizer, nearly 2½ times the amount used in 1970, and "a large quantity of various chemical pesticides, herbicides, and stimulants" were used. During the eleventh plan period the use of these substances was slated to double.[30]

Grapes were the second major target for fertilizers and growth stimulants. In the 1970s, Azerbaijan produced 7.4 million tons of grapes, or 3.6 times more than in the previous twenty-five years. In 1980 the Jeliabad raion alone produced 211,000 tons of grapes (well over the meager 7,000 tons produced in 1970). Aliyev expected the republic to produce 2 million tons in 1985 and 3 million in 1990.[31] Azerbaijan became the USSR's major grape-producing republic, but the impact of chemicals on this food product has not been discussed in Soviet literature. Complaints in the late 1980s focused on the harm to field workers and animals kept near the vineyards rather than to consumers of the grapes. Figures on the use of chemicals, even if imprecise, convey some idea of the ecological damage and the health risks to animals and humans that would later become the focal point of protest.

Even in 1979 there were "voices of conscience" warning against damage by industrialization. Plant geneticist and academician Imam Mustafayev, a former AzCP first secretary, wrote on the need to protect the environment. The Caspian, he said, has shrunk since the 1930s by 53,000 square kilometers. Lower water levels are visible along Baku's waterfront. "Our fathers defended the homeland," he wrote, and we must protect it.[32] Another article called the "Fate of the Caspian" described pollution damage.[33] *Development*, however, was the watchword of the times.

Official statistics showed an improved standard of living in the republic. In 1970, Aliyev stated, the per capita income of Azerbaijan was only 62 percent of the all-union level; by 1980 it had reached 80 percent. He also noted that 98 percent of the residents of the republic had televisions and that 90 percent of those were color. Life, he proclaimed, was "better" for 1.7 million people. On the negative side, plan targets for the construction of new apartments had still not been met.[34] Aliyev did not mention shortages in Baku.

In 1980, despite the rosy statistics, in the republic's capital city meat and butter were in such short supply that for several weeks in the winter even the party stores had none. Reportedly, the shortages had begun in 1978, the year Baku received an Order of Lenin. Talk on the streets was that the decoration "paid" for the meat and butter. Meanwhile, the bazaars and stores in the capitals of the neighboring republics were filled, but Baku's shortages persisted. Rationing was introduced in 1984.[35] One young Azerbaijani said that Moscow would never take food away from Armenia or Georgia because "they'd riot." Asked whether Azerbaijanis would do the same, he replied, "No. There are a lot of troops here. They would shoot us without a thought."

The 1979 census reflected the continued rapid population growth in

Azerbaijan, especially among the indigenous population.[36] The population had grown from 3,697,717 in 1959 to 5,117,081 in 1970 and to 6,028,253 in 1979. For the first time the republic had a larger urban (53 percent) than rural population. More than 1.5 million lived in Baku, and though the 1979 census did not reveal the national composition of cities, the local Azerbaijani Turkish elites believed they had regained their majority in the capital. Indeed, the failure to publish these data was regarded as confirmation of that. Certainly the republic as a whole was more native. In 1959 Azerbaijani Turks were just over 67 percent of the republic's population; according to the 1970 census, they had grown to nearly 74 percent, and by 1979 were over 78 percent. The high birthrate and the emigration of Russians and other nationalities accounted for the shift. In 1979 Russians accounted for only 7.9 percent of the population, the same as Armenians, down from 10 percent each in 1970; in 1959 14 percent were Russians and nearly 12 percent Armenians.[37]

The "re-Turkization" of Azerbaijan has far-reaching implications for politics, social structure, and cultural policy. The "revenge of the cradles" was expected by Western scholars and perhaps by local elites to translate into greater power in politics and the economy and to facilitate the reassertion of cultural dominance.[38]

AZERBAIJANI TURKS IN THE SOVIET MILITARY

In the aftermath of the 1979 census, political and military analysts raised questions about the national composition of future draftees for the USSR's universal male military service. At the root of their concern was the loyalty of "Muslims" (Azerbaijanis, Tatars, Kazakhs, Uzbeks, and others) who had experienced population explosions and whose homelands in many cases bordered Ayatollah-ruled Iran or Soviet-occupied Afghanistan. The anxiety was a tacit recognition of the discriminatory and repressive treatment meted out to these nationalities during the years of Soviet rule. Traditional Russian fears of the descendants of the Golden Horde and Timur (Russia's former rulers and adversaries) came to the fore.

The troubles within the Soviet Armed Forces (SAF) could not be papered over. Azerbaijanis, like other Turkish and traditionally Muslim nationalities, seemed unwilling to serve in the Russian-dominated SAF where they were routinely harassed and injured. Their republics' preinduction programs were weak.[39] Even if the Turks had a good command of Russian (which Azerbaijanis from Baku often do), they were assigned the worst duty, especially in *stroibat* or construction battalions, where conscripts were denied weapons and received no specific military training.[40] These practices recall tsarist-era warnings against training "colonials" to use weapons, for after completing their service, they would form a pool of trained men who were potentially hostile to the regime and who outnumber the active-duty forces stationed in their region.[41] The recruits from these republics were beaten and robbed by senior, or second-year, recruits, were fed substandard food, and received brutal punishments for trivial transgressions.

Specific information from Azerbaijan is lacking in studies of émigrés, probably because of the low rate of emigration by Azerbaijani Turks; émigrés from the republic are usually members of other nationalities. Despite reports of Georgian-Armenian and occasionally Armenian-Azerbaijani violence,[42] several Azerbaijani Turks interviewed in the USSR said there was a tendency for all recruits from Caucasia to band together against Slav officers or noncommissioned officers.[43]

Some Azerbaijanis who had completed Russian-language schooling were assigned to noncombat duties, though they did not lack langauge facility, education, or ability. Other reports of recruits returning from active duty (before 1979) with total hair loss, greatly aged, or impotent fostered rumors that the army was using them for experiments with chemical weapons. These claims were later sustained by the Soviet use of such weapons in Afghanistan. In one case an Azerbaijani recruit was beaten so severely that the victim was hospitalized for several months and never recovered. Despite rumors of the ease of bribing officials to secure exemptions,[44] some Azerbaijanis report the near impossibility of bribing recruiters and the extreme difficulty of securing exemptions even for medical reasons.

REJUVENATION OF NATIONAL CONSCIOUSNESS

Culture remains a theater of ideological struggle in which forces for Russification clash with assertions of native tradition and intellectual elites, as the Communist party fights for dominance in the arts and education.

Education and Language

To Aliyev education meant training technicians and building communist consciousness. At the thirtieth AzCP Congress, he proudly announced that the Academy of Sciences was producing "armies" of researchers for industry, chemistry, and technology. The first secretary blamed the "permissiveness" of some teachers for the improper socialization of future cadres. Aliyev's answer was greater control by the Ministry of Enlightenment, which was overseen by the republican party's Central Committee. The CC planned a thorough "restructuring" of higher education, both teaching and "moral-psychological atmosphere." Practical communist construction was a task to be taken up by all ministries, rectors of educational institutions, and other responsible individuals.[45]

About 1980 bilingual higher-education institutions were urged to expand the number of Russian sectors, apparently because so many students were then studying in the native-language track. Seventy percent of the students at the Azerbaijan State University were studying in Azerbaijani Turkish sectors; 85 percent of the entire student body was Azerbaijani, including half those in the Russian sectors. In contrast, the second-largest higher-education institute in Azerbaijan, the Oil and Gas Institute, conducted class only in Russian,[46] continuing the schism dating from the 1930s that keeps technical education and professions Russian. One study on the use of language in higher education argued for even greater centralization in the use of texts and wider use of Russian materials in all republics.[47]

In scholarship and the arts Aliyev echoed early Soviet policies.[48] To the writers of Azerbaijan the first secretary spoke of the "fruitful process of the internationalization of our lives."[49] To its composers he spoke of the need to borrow from both native and Russian musical traditions, though he devoted far more time in his speech to Azerbaijan's own creative tradition. The distinction between light and serious music existed only for musicians. "To us," he said, "all music is serious."[50] At the thirtieth AzCP Congress, Aliyev reported on 421 new libraries and additional Russian- and Armenian-language journals in the NKAO.[51]

Throughout the Aliyev years, the "friendship-of-peoples" doctrine was applied to formal education, with an emphasis on Russian-language instruction and, therefore, learning Russian in the beginning. A 1974 article in *Azerbaijan Kommunisti* stated that Russian was to be "a second mother tongue."[52] At the precollege level, native-language education was subtly discouraged by emphasizing the "international" character of Russian and the greatness of Russian culture. In Baku, Azerbaijan Turkish-language elementary schools are located far from the residences of Azerbaijani elites. In 1986 Minister of Enlightenment K. N. Rahimov sounded the standard theme of "international education," and asked the party and local soviets to improve education.[53] Like Aliyev he emphasized scientific and technical education. Although he made one statement on the need to improve the teaching of the "Azerbaijan language," along with chemistry, history, and other subjects, Rahimov discussed at length the need to improve and expand the teaching of Russian, beginning in the first grade.

Atheist education continued to have high priority, perhaps because it had never been carried out to official satisfaction. An article published on the eve of Aliyev's fall from power reasserted the need for "scientific atheist education" in Azerbaijan.[54] The failings of the republic's teachers were made clear by the author's beginning by defining the problem: "Scientific atheist education consists in obliterating the concept of religion in the consciousness of students, to educate them in an atheist spirit and to teach them to conduct a sharp ideological battle against religion." The writer cautioned teachers that simply not talking about religion did not constitute an atheist education. Rather, atheism had to be taught in each topic of instruction.

The use of Russian by the population as a whole has been taken to indicate the success not merely of Russian-language instruction but of the friendship-of-peoples policy or even of Russification. Moscow continued to emphasize the acquisition of Russian by non-Russians to facilitate the "drawing closer" (*sblizhenie*) of peoples, especially drawing closer to the Russians.

According to the 1970 census, more than one-third of urban Azerbaijani men and nearly one-quarter of urban women claimed Russian as a second language. Among the rural population, fewer than 10 percent knew Russian. In contrast, only about 10 percent of the Russians and Armenians in the republic claimed to use Turkish as a second language, though many had been born in the Azerbaijan republic. Armenians were far more likely to claim Russian as a second language (over 40 percent of the urban Armenians in Azerbaijan did; over 30 percent in the NKAO) than Azerbaijani Turkish (urban, 10 percent; NKAO, under 4 percent).

Census figures for 1979 reflected little change. About 28 percent of the republic's Azerbaijani population and about 15 percent of the Azerbaijanis in Nakhjivan and the NKAO knew Russian. Most Armenians and Russians did not know the language of the republic where they lived, whereas 43 percent of the Armenians in Azerbaijan (and 31 percent in the NKAO) used Russian as their second language compared with 8 percent of those who used Azerbaijani Turkish (4 percent in the NKAO). Less than 10 percent of Russians knew Azerbaijani (6.5 percent in the NKAO); 25 percent knew some other language, probably Armenian (11 percent in Nakhjivan).[55] If those who speak only their own language are "parochial," then the Russians are the most parochial of all.[56]

These data indicate that national communities can remain separate when members of any one group cannot interact in a meaningful way with most members of another; that a close relationship between the Russians and Armenians is enhanced by their use of Russian (and the Russians' use of Armenian in the NKAO); and that non-Azerbaijanis in the republic enjoy extensive linguistic rights, including apparent Armenian cultural primacy in the NKAO.

Rebirth of National Literature

In the resurgence of history and national literature, journals were the pioneers.[57] A major forum for experimentation was the Azerbaijan Writers' Union monthly *Azerbaijan*. In the early Aliyev years, *Azerbaijan* published many standard items on "progressive" historical or literary figures and on the importance of Russian influence on Azerbaijan's culture. But the journal also published some subtle, ambiguous pieces whose implications for national identity and consciousness were powerful and, to the Azerbaijani accustomed to code words, unmistakable.

In November 1979, for example, *Azerbaijan* published not only a lengthy article called "Brotherhood of Peoples, Brotherhood of Cultures" but also a discussion of an early nineteenth-century English orientalist who wrote on Azerbaijani Turkish literature "from Nizami to Saib Tabrizi."[58] That discussion established international recognition of Azerbaijan's native culture before the Russian conquest.

Markedly less subtle was a poem by Kemala in the next issue of the journal called "My Motherland—Azerbaijan."[59] Other such homeland poems published in *Azerbaijan* about this time used the word *vatan* (homeland); some used the purely Turkish word *yurt*.[60] CPSU rhetoric employs the phrase "Soviet homeland," and vatan has been used in official slogans or documents with that meaning. In contrast, yurt is never used to mean the USSR. In Kemala's "My Motherland," yurt is used in the title, making the context clear.

Baloghlan Shafizade's poem "Vatan" reached far into Azerbaijan's early history:[61]

> You are the flame of the great Zardusht's faith. . . .
> These cliffs, these mountains are my ancestors,
> Their crystal waters flow in my veins . . .
> In my body are grains from their every place,
> It seems I am the sum total of those grains.

Eldar Bakhish's "Vatan" begins[62]

> I eat the bread out of the *tandir* [outdoor oven]
> I eat the fruit brought from the trees
> I eat the honey that runs from the beehive . . .
> In the end, I want from you
> one measure of land
> one handful of soil.

The importance of the land and its natural features are as central to these poets' image of the homeland as is its history.

Poets and prose writers, literary critics, and scholars from various fields expressed the importance of language. Some equated the vatan with the native language.

One powerful expression of the centrality of language as well as of nature and historical themes is Sabir Rustemkhanli's poem "Thank You, My Mother Tongue."[63]

> When I lose my way in a foreign land
> How my name sounds on foreign lips!
> Thank you, my mother tongue,
> You never left me helpless or alone. . . .
>
> Karabagh, Kara dagh [Mountain] . . . [they say] choose, separate,
> I consider the mountains my invincible army.
> Where one of my words lives—
> There I consider my lawful yurt.
>
> Along came the tongues of the Koran
> The voices of the Prophet, the language of law.
> They put you behind the door
> You asked for justice, they robbed you.
> But you were not destroyed, my mother, my dear language,
> You made armies tremble, my hero Tongue!

In addition to the many other images evoked by Rustemkhanli here, the importance of language and thus of ancient culture over Islam was implied. Rustemkhanli is not alone in his devotion to the pre-Islamic past, its history, culture, and values. Poet Yashar Abbas expressed this idea in his poem "I Am a Fire Worshipper."[64] The poet begins by proclaiming "I have no business with holy Jesus Nor with the Prophet Muhammed Nor with the Koran," and states

> I believe in fire [od]
> Like my great ancestors.
> It is such a fire that neither in the sky
> Nor on the earth can anything like it be found . . .
> That fire is in the breast,
> In the heart . . .
>> the fire of art
>> the fire of justice

the fire of love . . .
That fire is my god.

The idea that Islam was a "latecomer" and fundamentally alien to Turkish culture was expressed at this same time by Central Asian writers and had some currency early in the twentieth century.[65] Although the idea cannot be said to have a wide popular following, it has persisted among the cultural elites. By the end of the 1980s it would be more widely discussed by historians, ethnographers, and other scholars as well as by poets and writers in their debate concerning national identity.[66]

Discussion of historical identity is not limited to poetry. The journal *Azerbaijan*, like other publications, carried articles on dastans and serialized several historical novels, including Aziza Jafarzade's *Baku 1501*. Although criticized for placing too much emphasis on Shah Ismail, Jafarzade and her novel received positive reviews, and Ismail was called "Azerbaijan's Peter the Great."[67] Similar daring was exhibited in Central Asia, but the *Azerbaijan* editor Ekrem Eylisli, a prominent novelist, did not lose his job.[68]

A series called "Unopened Pages" reintroduced formerly obscure or taboo historical figures, including Mehmet Emin Rasulzade. In a similar vein, roundtable discussions first published in early 1982 gave a forum to prominent writers, academicians, editors, and poets to raise controversial views, though not all did so. "Standard" remarks were purposely placed alongside more thoughtful comments.

On the nature of citizenship and the intellectual, F. Mustafayev, the first secretary from the Shemakhi raion, confined himself to a repetition of Aliyev's statements. On the definition of *intellectual* he asked, "What can I say?" But People's Writer Mirza Ibrahimov, president of the Governing Committee of the Writers' Union, had a great deal to say. He articulated his society's traditional expectations for the intellectual:

> The people always bear great hopes for the intellectuals. . . . The nation is a great realist. . . . In the depths of its heart . . . it separates bad from good. Therefore, those who in the past have hidden behind the "diploma" of some religious or academic studies, but in reality have sold their consciences for money or career, who are devoid of feelings for their people or homeland, whose words and actions contradict each other, were called "scholars without ideals" and the nation fixed a seal of hatred upon them.[69]

Thus, during the early 1980s a pattern of increasingly frank and substantive discussions of cultural and intellectual issues was established in *Azerbaijan* and other publications such as the *Gobustan* journal (edited by prominent writer Anar [Rzayev]) and the weekly *Edebiyyat ve Injesanat*. By the end of the decade these publications would be the forum for demands for changes in policy and greater local control of economic policy and administration as well as culture.[70] (The party's *Azerbaijan Kommunisti* remained orthodox under Aliyev, and the Russian-language publications reflected the party line.) The implications of the internal discussions in the Azerbaijani Turkish community were momentous. Yet this movement, for it seems to bear the marks of a coordinated and conscious effort, developed under the rule of Heydar Aliyev, a man who vigorously articulated Moscow's line and freely replaced party cadres. Because Aliyev cannot be regarded as weak, uninformed, lax, or obtuse, it can be supposed that he permitted, perhaps encouraged, this upsurge of national self-investigation, this exploration of historic identity, and this expression of national pride. If Aliyev approved of this process, then his era and his legacy are indeed complex.

I 2 "Restructuring" Azerbaijan in the Gorbachev Era

> The Turkish people were about to be annihilated [but]
> Heaven granted strength. . . . My father, the kagan, organized
> and ordered the people who had lost their state and their
> kagan, the people who had turned slaves and servants, the
> people who had lost the Turkish institutions, [he organized
> them] in accordance with the rules of my ancestors.
>
> Kül Tegin inscription, circa 730 C.E.*

THE GORBACHEV-ALIYEV PERIOD

The last two and a half years of Heydar Aliyev's power, from
early 1985 to summer 1987, coincided with the beginning of the Gorbachev
era. Deputy Minister Aliyev chaired two sessions at the twenty-seventh CPSU
Congress in February and March 1986, and Azerbaijan's new first secretary,
Kamran M. Baghirov, spoke at one.[1] Baghirov had nothing new to offer. He
emphasized Baku oil, pledged increases in oil-drilling equipment and support
for the USSR nationalities policy and the "Leninist friendship of peoples." In
two years strikes in Azerbaijan would deprive Siberian oil fields of equipment,
and national clashes would belie the "great friendship."

---

*Talat Tekin, *Grammar of Orkhon Turkic* (Bloomington: Indiana University Press,
1969), p. 265, lines E10–13 of Orkhon stelae.

Evidence of Gorbachev's much-touted "restructuring" (*perestroika, yenidengurma*) was scant inside Azerbaijan, and "openness" (*glasnost', ashkarlyk*) was not heard at all. Indeed, local coverage of CPSU policies emphasized the old, safe themes that came out of Moscow, such as the continued primacy of central party leadership.[2] This is perhaps not surprising in view of the stability of party and state personnel within Azerbaijan and the fundamental caution toward the vicissitudes of party policy. Could not Gorbachev's "thaw" go the way of Khrushchev's? The party journal *Azerbaijan Kommunisti* reported on all party meetings and reprinted major speeches as before. It repeated the rhetoric of "restructuring," as it had all past CPSU policies, but did not apply those exhortations to itself. Some policies—the return of folk music to local radio, the flourishing of Azerbaijani literature, and the study of history—were attributed by Western observers to Gorbachev's "new thinking." In fact, they were phenomena of the Aliyev period.[3]

Not until the middle of 1986 did *Azerbaijan Kommunisti* depart from previous practice.[4] That summer, though its articles on politics remained orthodox, those on culture broke new ground. In the same issue that described the twenty-seventh CPSU Congress and lauded CPSU leadership, an article on literary journals criticized *Azerbaijan* for insufficient expressions of love for the homeland and the native soil.[5]

The official journal of the CC AzCP may have been using the cultural arena to debate the development of historical identity when the political avenues were closed, or it may have reflected an internal party dispute on the appropriate posture toward national aspirations and the articulation of the historic identity. Officially, the AzCP interpreted restructuring as a program for economic improvements, not cultural or political programs.[6] Criticism of bureaucracy was always welcome.[7] Testing the limits of restructuring in 1987, *Azerbaijan Kommunisti* included cultural articles on "Youth and Restructuring" and "From Our Cultural Heritage." It also published a plea to preserve Azerbaijan's historical monuments in Nakhjivan and Karabagh.[8]

Yet *Azerbaijan Kommunisti* devoted much space to conventional matters as well. The head of the CC AzCP Propaganda and Agitation Section, A. Dashdemirov, explained that old propaganda methods were obsolete and that new ones, "closer to life, objective, open," were needed. But his article covered old ground on the importance of properly trained cadres. Religiosity and nationalism were included with drunkenness and drug abuse as social ills.[9] Elsewhere, the report of the twenty-seventh congress droned on about "fraternal friendship" and "international spirit."[10]

The literary journal *Azerbaijan*, one of the most sensitive barometers in the republic, has a relatively freer hand than *Azerbaijan Kommunisti*. That the shift in the contents of both journals was roughly in tandem suggests a freer political climate in 1986–1987. *Azerbaijan*, which had been restrained with respect to culture and identity from 1984 until the end of 1986 under the editorship of poet Jabir Novruz,[11] in November 1986 sent up a "trial balloon." Under the standard heading "Fulfilling the decisions of the 27th CPSU Congress" was an article called "Means to Serve the Homeland [*vatan*]" by Elekber Abbasov.[12] The article began by describing a construction project that had gone "a bit hurriedly." Water pipes lacked the pressure to supply second stories of buildings, but a fracture in one sent a fountain of water gushing into a second-story window. A local man, who identified himself as "rural intellectual," said the water had been gushing for five days. This is just a "drop in the bucket," he remarked, but Abbasov noted that such "drops" are not cheap. To that point, his criticism was fully in line with Gorbachev's rhetoric.

The purpose of this article, however, was not to expose inefficiency but to examine the meaning of the overused term *intellectual*. A true intellectual, argued Abbasov, would not be indifferent to waste and inefficiency but would be concerned about natural resources and the environment, the villages and the cities. In short, being an intellectual starts with love of the homeland. Abbasov was careful to cite Lenin and the central press to support his arguments. At the same time, his tone was ironic. After quoting *Literaturnaia Gazeta* on using Leninist thought to define intellectualism, he offered his own "yardstick." Indians, he said, believe that snakes were God's first creatures, but mountaineers believe the eagle was first. "I think that men were created first; only later some were turned into eagles and others into snakes." The eagles are the real intellectuals, he said. He did not comment on the snakes.

The first serious discussions outside the AzCP and economic circles about the meaning of restructuring appear to have begun more than a year after the twenty-seventh party congress of February 1986. *Azerbaijan* initiated a regular feature, "Restructuring: Problems, Observations," in 1987.[13] An article in the June issue, signed "Sirus," began: "Neither laugh nor cry! Understand!" Asking "Why is our native talent ignored?"[14] the writer pointed out the dichotomy between encouraging words and the cautious, even obstructionist actions of local officials that prevent talented individuals from serving society.

The year 1987 was a turning point in Azerbaijan's venture into open discussion of problems and policies, as well as the year of Aliyev's fall from grace and disappearance from public view. It was at the time of his "resignation," at age 62, that the first demands of the current round were put forward by Armenian spokesmen for the annexation of the Nagorno-Karabagh Autonomous Oblast (NKAO) to the Armenian SSR.

THE STRUGGLE FOR MOUNTAINOUS KARABAGH: THE OPENING SALVOS

This latest conflict over the western portion of historic Karabagh began in the summer of 1987 with a petition drive by Armenians who wished to annex the NKAO to Armenia. At the same time, the Erevan literary newspaper *Grakan Tert* accused Ferida Mamedova of "falsifying Armenian history" in her doctoral dissertation on Caucasian Albania, defended at the Azerbaijan Academy of Sciences.[15] Physicist Andrei N. Sakharov added accompanying "official comments" claiming that Mamedova's dissertation did not reflect familiarity with several major works. Mamedova's dissertation adviser, Ziya Buniatov, answered these accusations in a short article in the Azerbaijan Academy of Sciences quarterly journal entitled "An Apologist Practicing Patronage of the Arts." Buniatov referred to Sakharov's not being familiar with the historical literature relevant to the topic and quoted from the works named by Sakharov to show that they supported Mamedova's positions. Following this tour de force, Buniatov advised, "A. N. Sakharov, if he does not know the ford, he should not enter the river."[16] Thus, the Armenian campaign dates from August 1987 at both the academic and the popular levels. The coincidence of the petition to annex the NKAO and the dissertation controversy suggests coordination and planning.

These issues were raised again in November by Gorbachev's adviser Abel G. Aganbegiyan in a speech made to Armenian war veterans in Paris and reported in *L'Humanité*.[17] Aganbegiyan sounded themes that became pillars of the well-publicized Armenian argument over the following years, referring to both Karabagh and Nakhjivan as "historic Armenian territory" and stating, "I want Karabagh to belong to Armenia. As an economist, I regard Karabagh to be more closely tied to Armenia than to Azerbaijan."

It was subsequently argued that mountainous Karabagh was "given" to Azerbaijan "by Stalin" during sovietization. The term *reunification* was used to suggest that the land had been part of Armenia. The Baku government was accused of "repressions," particularly against Armenian culture, and of inadequate economic development and social welfare provisions in the region. Furthermore, the existence of an Armenian majority in the NKAO, the rationale for its creation in the 1920s, was used to invoke USSR constitutional provisions on self-determination.

In February 1988 *Azerbaijan* published a response by People's Poet and Corresponding Member of the Academy Bahtiyar Vahabzade and Dr. Suleiman S. Aliyarov, head of the kafedra of Azerbaijani history of Azerbaijan State University.[18] Their "Open Letter" outlined arguments that would later be employed by the Azerbaijani Turks in this territorial dispute. Disputing Aganbegiyan's historical argument, Vahabzade and Aliyarov stated that Karabagh is historic Azerbaijani territory (the "Open Letter" was copiously footnoted) and was once an integral part of Caucasian Albania whose inhabitants were ancestors of Azerbaijani Turks.[19] They traced the emergence of Karabagh as an independent khanate populated and ruled by Turks.

On the issue of the current majority in mountainous Karabagh, Vahabzade and Aliyarov noted that the Armenians had been a minority in most of Caucasia at the time of the Russian conquest and were encouraged to immigrate from Iran by the Treaty of Turkmanchai (1828) and Russian state policy until they formed majorities in several pockets.[20] "In this way, under the tutelage of the Russian state, the Azerbaijani people were made to divide their most sacred wealth—their land, their hearths and their homes—with their Armenian brothers."

In this early reply to the Armenian campaign, these two writers placed their arguments firmly within Leninist and Soviet constitutional frameworks. Reviewing the settlement of numerous territorial disputes, including those in Karabagh and Zangezur in the early 1920s, they noted that as Azerbaijan had relinquished its claim to Zangezur, Armenia had relinquished its claim to Karabagh. Vahabzade and Aliyarov stated that Azerbaijan "has not protested these concessions," implying that the Armenian efforts to alter this agreement showed bad faith. They criticized Aganbegiyan for striving to create a republic with a "pure" national composition, an idea that is anathema to Leninist nationality policy. Drawing a parallel to early twentieth-century Armenian claims against Georgian territory, the "Open Letter" ended with a quotation from the Georgian writer Ilya Chavchavadze:

> Are the Armenians really scattered according to our desires? Let exalted God give them strength and skill that they can go and unite themselves at their destination. But let them not covet that which others have, not strive to deprive us of what we have, and not be notorious by defaming our name.[21]

The next phase of the movement began at the same time the Vahabzade-Aliyarov letter appeared. In February 1988 Armenian demonstrations took place in the NKAO and Erevan. Gorbachev met with Armenian leaders of the Karabagh Committee, a small group formed to agitate for the territorial transfer. Within a month (24 March) the USSR Soviet of Ministers passed a resolution calling for faster "socio-economic development" of the NKAO *as part of Azerbaijan*. This resolution employed the same kind of argument that was used in 1923–1924 to create the NKAO, seeming to favor each claimant but fully acceding to the wishes of neither one. Although Gorbachev surely did not wish to open the Pandora's box of boundary redrawing, these acts did nothing to discourage the drive for annexation and implied acceptance of Armenian charges.

At this time violence broke out in the industrial town of Sumgait, just northwest of Baku.[22] Sumgait was built by Azerbaijani Turkish refugees who had been forced out of their villages in Armenia in the late 1940s. In 1988 refugees fleeing from NKAO and Armenia (in early 1988, there were nearly 200,000 Azerbaijani Turks in Armenia) also settled in Sumgait. Some of the recent refugees joined relatives; those without family ties, who often had no jobs, proper housing, or medical care, sometimes struck out at local Armenians. Other Azerbaijanis, apparently longtime residents, hid their Armenian neighbors. Later reports indicated that the police remained passive, suggesting official instigation. The final death toll was thirty-two, of which twenty-six were reportedly Armenian. Gorbachev sent troops to Sumgait, and several Azerbaijanis were arrested for "anti-Armenian" activity. At Armenian insistence, their trials were moved to the RSFSR—a clear slap to the justice system in Azerbaijan. Azerbaijani victims of Armenian attacks were not similarly treated. No "anti-Azerbaijani" trials were ever reported. Soviet and Western news media attributed the incident to "extremism" among the "Muslim" Azerbaijanis.

In the months that followed, strikes and demonstrations took place in Erevan and there was unrest in the NKAO and the neighboring Aghdam raion of Azerbaijan. Azerbaijani Turks living in Armenia fled to Azerbaijan, and Armenians in Azerbaijan fled to Armenia. In late May Moscow removed the first secretaries of both republics. Baghirov was succeeded by Abdulrakhman Kh. Vezirov. Although an Azerbaijani Turk, Vezirov had not built his career in the republic but as a diplomat. His lack of a local power base probably was a plus from Moscow's point of view. He spoke Turkish poorly and was married to a non-Azerbaijani woman. Vezirov seemed to be Moscow's man, but he did not prevent the republican Supreme Soviet from standing its ground. Indeed, the Supreme Soviet seems to have embarked on a course of its own. In mid-June the Armenian Supreme Soviet, with the support of its new first secretary, Arutiunian, passed a resolution insisting on the transfer of the NKAO. The Azerbaijan Supreme Soviet passed a resolution calling the proposed transfer "unacceptable" on the basis of "Leninist principles . . . and the need to preserve the territorial integrity of the Azerbaijan SSR." At the same time the Azerbaijani resolution reaffirmed acceptance of Moscow's resolution of 24 March calling for faster "socioeconomic development" of the NKAO.[23] Azerbaijani officials admitted "errors" by former political leaders,[24] adding that those in the NKAO, like its present leaders, were Armenian. One Azerbaijan Supreme Soviet resolution invoked Article 78 of the USSR Constitution and Article 70 of the Azerbaijan SSR

Constitution, which barred territorial changes without the consent of the republic(s) concerned.[25] President of the Supreme Soviet S. B. Tatliyev emphasized that "the sovereign rights of our republic and our people" were threatened.[26]

At this time the Baku press published letters from Armenians in Shusha and Baku supporting Azerbaijani retention of the NKAO and calling on their fellow Armenians to desist from "illegal demands."[27] Such letters were used to bolster the argument that those who called for annexation of the NKAO, especially those engaged in violence, were an unrepresentative minority of extremists or militants. The party, state, and press in Baku and Moscow always made a careful distinction between this "extremist minority" and the majority of the Armenian people. The call for territorial transfer, however, had widespread support, as evidenced by meetings of Armenians in Erevan and Stepanakert, the NKAO capital.[28]

On 12 July the predominantly Armenian NKAO Soviet unilaterally declared its secession from the Azerbaijan SSR. The Azerbaijan Supreme Soviet promptly declared the act illegal.[29] Within a few days the Presidium of the USSR Supreme Soviet took up the question of the NKAO. The result was a decision on 18 July to establish a "special commission" from Moscow to "observe" conditions in and ostensibly "strengthen and develop the autonomy" of the NKAO. P. N. Demichev, first deputy chairman of the Presidium of the USSR Supreme Soviet, said that the Presidium "emphasized the need to attain the full autonomy of Nagorno-Karabagh, but as part of Azerbaijan." "However," he added, "Article 78 of the USSR Constitution states that no one can change the border of a republic without its consent."[30]

The head of Moscow's commission, Arkadii N. Volskii, acted as the representative of the Presidium and the Central Committee. Volskii had a mechanical-technical education and career. According to Dr. Tofik K. Ismailov, general director of NPO Space Research, "At the time [1988] of our discussions with representatives of the NKAO, Volskii honestly acknowledged that he had no understanding at all of such national relations. You see who was sent to us!"[31] Volskii warmed to his job quickly, imposing martial law in the Stepanakert and Aghdam raiony in late September.[32] Through the Volskii Commission and martial law, the NKAO was taken de facto from direct rule by Baku, despite official statements that it remained part of Azerbaijan. Baku regarded these acts as a defeat and a reprimand.

Azerbaijani Turks regarded the Russian intelligentsia, the Soviet and Western media, and the central government as biased against them. Press coverage drew heavily from sources in Erevan and Stepanakert, rarely from Baku. Azerbaijani refugees and victims were ignored. Russians who spoke before the Presidium expressed sympathy with the Armenian arguments. The staunch support by Sakharov and his Armenian wife for territorial transfer and his ill-informed historical arguments on their behalf embittered those Azerbaijani Turks who had formerly admired his support of human rights.[33] Volskii himself took sides and referred to the "artificial alienation of the Armenian part of the population from Armenia."[34]

The Azerbaijani Turks took exception to such treatment, answering claims that they had discriminated against the NKAO with "social-economic" data. The July issue of *Azerbaijan Agriculture* contained a roundtable discussion on the economy of the NKAO.[35] One set of figures on "Comparative Indicators of Social Development" gave numbers of hospital beds, doctors per ten thousand people, libraries, apartments, and other items in Azerbaijan, Armenia, the NKAO and the USSR. Of the nine indicators, the NKAO ranked above Azerbaijan in eight and above Armenia in seven, including hospital beds and housing space. It ranked above the USSR average in five, including libraries, movie houses, and clubs.[36] Like all Soviet statistics, these must be used cautiously, though commentators did support these conclusions.[37]

Azerbaijanis asked why the less-industrialized Armenia could be a better developer of the NKAO than Azerbaijan could be.[38] The Azerbaijan leadership stated that Armenian party and state workers in the NKAO—who had dominated the apparatus there since 1923[39]—had "facilitated the rousing of a negative mood" toward Azerbaijan.[40] Had Baku withheld funding? According to earlier republican budgets, the NKAO received both a larger share of the republic's budget and more state subsidies than the larger and more populous Nakhjivan ASSR.[41] On the contrary, Azerbaijani Turks said that within the NKAO, it was the Armenians who discriminated against them. Volskii later announced that the 1989 NKAO budget called for only 4 million of the region's 96 million rubles to be devoted to construction in areas of Azerbaijani settlement.[42] The Azerbaijanis did not argue that conditions were good but did say privately that pollution, housing shortages, and the quality and supply of goods and services were worse in Nakhjivan, Ganje, Sumgait, and sometimes in Baku than in the NKAO.[43]

Adding to the pressure were refugees from the NKAO and Armenia, whose numbers reached 75,000 by the fall of 1988.[44] The problem was great enough by July that the CC AzCP created a special commission to oversee housing for Azerbaijani refugees, officially designated as "persons arriving from the Armenian SSR for temporary residence." This commission was headed by the president of the Soviet of Ministers of the republic and was to have branches in all cities and raiony of Azerbaijan. But housing was not enough. The party cadres were called on "to activate mass-political work among persons of Azerbaijani nationality to explain the essence of Leninist nationality policy and the historical significance of the resolution of the Presidium of the USSR Supreme Soviet on the NKAO of 18 July 1988.[45]

On 12 November the Presidium of the USSR Supreme Soviet issued its decision to retain the NKAO in Azerbaijan. Both *Kommunist* (Erevan) and *Sovetskii Karabakh* (the organ of the NKAO obkom [oblast' party committee]) refused to accept this decision and called for a "just" resolution of the issue. *Bakinskii Rabochii* said that a speech made in the Armenian Supreme Soviet "could not fail to create the impression that some individuals in Armenia and the NKAO planned further confrontations."[46] Azerbaijani Turks feared the conflict would drag on.

NOVEMBER ON LENIN SQUARE: A MULTIPLICITY OF GRIEVANCES

Many members of the intellectual and artistic elite, who for over a decade had articulated cultural grievances and national concerns, apparently believed the party and state apparatus were mishandling current problems. On 17 November 1988 a series of mass demonstrations began in front of the government building on Lenin Square. "Tens of thousands of people of various nationalities" were reported by Radio Moscow to gather daily in an area the size of Red Square. Not surprisingly, most speakers were respected academic and literary figures; a worker, Nemat Panakhov, emerged as a popular leader.[47] At the end of the month, Radio Moscow reported that the demonstrations had been peaceful. Work at the vital oil refineries had not stopped, but "life in the city cannot be called normal."[48] A *Bakinskii Rabochii* reporter remained on the square for six days and nights with the participants, who lived in tents and gathered around fires at night.[49] A broad-based, multi-issue mass movement had begun in Azerbaijan. The people had come in part because of anxiety over the Karabagh dispute and the flood of refugees fleeing the fighting.

Other matters were also of passionate concern, notably a scandal concerning the violation of the Topkhana nature preserve in the NKAO. During the summer an Armenian aluminum factory brought in bulldozers and construction equipment to build shops and a holiday hotel for its workers in the preserve near Shusha. Party officials in the NKAO did not take action and construction began.[50] Later it was discovered that a chemical factory in the NKAO, with the support of the party obkom, had made a direct sale agreement with the Armenian SSR, bypassing official channels including Azerbaijan's Trade Ministry. *Bakinskii Rabochii* said the deal reflected the hostility of NKAO's Armenian party leadership toward Azerbaijan. These acts also suggested that quiet steps were being taken, with the collusion of the NKAO party apparatus, to create economic links for an eventual unification through the "back door."

The tens of thousands in Lenin Square, then called Freedom Square, were waiting for answers. People in the crowd passed their questions to the speakers, among whom were the poets Bahtiyar Vahabzade and Sabir Rustemkhanli. (Party and government spokespersons were apparently not present.) The crowd asked why the central government had allowed this crisis to drag on into November when the issues had been clear in February; why Moscow had not fulfilled its constitutional obligations to protect borders; why there were no arrests of militants who agitated for Armenian annexation of the NKAO; and why *Izvestiia* had published such one-sided reports "ignoring the position of Azerbaijanis living in the Armenian SSR." Vahabzade suggested drafting a letter to the Armenian Supreme Soviet asking that it guarantee autonomy like that given Armenians in the NKAO to Azerbaijani Turks living in a compact area of the Armenian republic. Panakhov noted there were as many Azerbaijani Turks in Armenia as Armenians in the NKAO.[51]

During those days Azerbaijan's first "informal groups" strove for legal recognition. One of them was the environmentalist group Varlik (Wealth), which advocated protection of the natural wealth of the republic and the study of its language and history.[52] The pro-environmentalist forces claimed one victory—all construction equipment would be removed from the Topkhana nature preserve.[53] Meanwhile, there was discussion of forming a popular front. According to one participant, demonstrators took control of local television and for at least one full day broadcast all speeches from the square.[54] "Under rain, and in the November nights around camp fires," wrote *Bakinskii Rabochii*, "the crowd waited for a resolution to the Karabagh issue. . . . A quarter of the demonstrators were fasting."

On 23 November it was announced that "special regulations" were to go into effect at midnight. The decree from President of the Azerbaijan Supreme Soviet Tatliyev stated that "from the evening of 21 November in various raiony of Baku there have been hooligan manifestations." Earlier national conflicts had been attributed to "anti-perestroika forces, nationalist elements and hooligans."[55] Disruptions were reported in Nakhjivan city (where "hooligans" attacked some government buildings) and in Kirovobad (Ganje). A curfew was imposed and passport checks instituted; weapons were banned.[56] Nakhjivan city was proclaimed under control the next day.[57] The first secretary of the Kirovobad gorkom was sacked.[58] Bloody clashes broke out between Ganje residents and the army after a small girl was reportedly crushed by an armored vehicle. Official reports blamed "hooliganism" for her death. According to *Komsomol'skaia Pravda*, three soldiers were killed and 160 civilians required medical treatment.[59] *Krasnaia Zvezda* referred to "extremists" in Azerbaijan fighting a "rearguard battle of the time of stagnation."[60]

Despite the "special regulations," the Lenin Square demonstration continued for another full week.[61] A double cordon surrounded the square, soldiers forming the outer ring and demonstrators the inner one. A group of young demonstrators checked identity papers to control access to the square.[62] This process and the efforts of designated groups of students and veterans helped keep order and prevent "provocations" that might lead to violence and give the military an excuse to disperse the group.[63] *Komsomol'skaia Pravda* reporters estimated the nighttime crowd on Lenin Square to be around 20,000 and during the day, a half-million.[64] On 28 November control was tightened. Baku was closed to cars from other cities.[65] The central press noted that the demonstrations remained peaceful.[66]

With military regulations in place, the authorities began a multifaceted, standard psychological warfare campaign to weaken the movement from within. Party and military spokesmen claimed that many demands had been met, that dealing with others would take time, and that everyone should go home.[67] The general director of the republic's Center for Hygiene and Epidemiology, Dr. A. Velibekov, warned of unsanitary conditions and said there was a "dysentery epidemic."[68] *Pravda* quoted two students as saying that "some anti-perestroika forces had attached themselves to our movement."[69] Such language was often seen in press reports but rarely used by ordinary citizens. A *Bakinskii Rabochii* article reported on the "provocative" tone of meetings elsewhere in the republic. The writer A. Dashdemirov wanted to "reevaluate" the movement, for it had some "weaknesses."[70] Dashdemirov, identified merely as "correspondent member of the Academy of Sciences," in 1987 had been head of the CC AzCP Propaganda and Agitation Section when he authored an article on the need for new methods of propaganda. In 1989 he would be head of the CC AzCP section on state law.[71]

The final blow came on 3 December when military authorities published a demand for Lenin Square to be cleared because weapons were reportedly being stockpiled there.[72] On 4 December a "young major" asked several demonstrators, "Why are you sitting on the square? Your demands are known, the issue is being decided." A few people agreed with him.[73] It was the last day of the demonstration.

During the night of 4 December, the demonstrators who remained on the square were rounded up and jailed. Some of those taken into custody were transferred to local prisons and held for several months without trial or without being charged. Some were rumored to be in psychiatric hospitals. Several leaders, including Nemat Panakhov, were in custody until the summer of 1989.[74] The next day there were strikes and demonstrations throughout the republic. In Baku 14,500 workers struck.[75] Local people in Astara blocked the highway to the border and stopped military traffic to show support for the Lenin Square demonstration.[76]

Izvestiia, in a "call to reason," reflected the inability of the central leadership to understand the issues or views of the southern republics that had long ago lost their autonomy. Moscow could talk only of "extremism" as a threat to its plans for "restructuring," forgetting that central policies had established the rules of the game and perhaps prolonged the crisis. The government organs seemed to hope the quandary would resolve itself. The entreaties from the south were just so much bother:

> In Moscow is a torrent of telegrams [with] cries about help, suffering, passion, impatience, demands to intervene immediately and resolve the conflict. . . . Extremism grows, a sizable number of adventurists hang on. . . . There is democracy for you, there is openness.[77]

"Special regulations" or a state of emergency continued for months in much of Azerbaijan. The first secretary of the Baku raikom, A. Jamalov, remarked bitterly, "[We convey] our special gratitude to the soldiers of the Soviet Army for bringing order to our city."[78] *Krasnaia Zvezda* did not seem to grasp the irony of this statement. Violence, especially in the NKAO and along the border with the Armenian republic, continued as did the Armenian campaign to annex the NKAO. Because there was no way to house them or provide medical care, the refugee problem continued to worsen. By the end of December 1988 there were 100,000 refugees in Baku, Kirovobad, Nakhjivan, and more than forty other locations in the republic. At least 50,000 were without housing or relatives to assist them.[79] One year later there would be 160,000 refugees in Azerbaijan.[80] More than 100,000 rubles and clothing for 38,000 people had been collected from citizens throughout the republic for the refugees.[81]

The 7 December earthquake's epicenter was in Armenia, but it affected the neighboring republics as well. The Azelektromash "multinational collective" in Azerbaijan offered material aid to families of earthquake victims in Armenia,[82] and Baku sent relief supplies to eight raiony of western and central Azerbaijan.[83] Azerbaijan received no foreign aid.

The disaster did not end the struggle for the NKAO. An article in *Krasnaia Zvezda* noted that the "disbanded" Karabagh Committee continued to work under the name "Karabagh Movement of Armenia" and that "after the earthquake, it met almost daily in the republican building of the [Armenian] Writers Union.[84]

Moscow decided on its traditional solution—more control. On 12 January 1989 the USSR Supreme Soviet established a "special form of administration" in the NKAO: direct rule by Moscow.[85] Although the decree claimed to be "in accord with suggestions of party and state organs of the Azerbaijan SSR and the Armenian SSR" and with Volskii's Commission, the

AzCP was not consulted.[86] The Volskii Commission, now a committee, replaced the local soviet. It enjoyed plenipotentiary power in the NKAO and answered only to the Kremlin. Moscow and the Western press quickly proclaimed a *pax Russica*. A *Pravda* headline of 15 January read, "Peace to the land of Karabagh; from confrontation to the battle for restructuring."[87] This decree, like others, reaffirmed the NKAO as part of Azerbaijan. Yet, the special form of administration undermined that sovereignty and seemed a possible step to territorial transfer. Thus Moscow did not directly reject Armenian demands, which continued throughout 1989.[88]

After the Lenin Square demonstrations and the consolidation of Moscow's control over the NKAO, the arguments of the Azerbaijani Turks on all issues became bolder. Perhaps the citizens realized that peaceful demonstrations led to special regulations, not openness. Organizations discussed in November 1988 came into being. The Karabagh struggle continued within the framework of a broader movement for economic, political, and cultural autonomy. This movement, the confluence of mass and elite efforts, would come to have direction under the Azerbaijan Popular Front.

THE BIRTH OF POLITICAL ORGANIZATIONS

The first organizations to develop were concerned with cultural issues and refugee relief.[89] One of the latter was Gaighy (Concern) whose president was Imam D. Mustafaev. Throughout the republic, Gaighy distributed aid to refugees though their numbers grew faster than the means to care for them.[90] The People's Aid Committee to Karabagh was created in 1989 to bring supplies to the isolated Azerbaijani Turkish population in the NKAO.

During the spring of 1989 after the release from prison of activists jailed during the November–December demonstration, political groups created the Azerbaijan People's Front (APF), a popular front organization that quickly gained support throughout the republic. The APF, which held its founding congress on 16 July and struggled for recognition until it became legal in October, embodied the politicization of a long process—clarifying cultural and social issues that had been reflected in Azerbaijani Turkish publications in previous decades.[91] The leadership of the APF included the very people who had carried out these earlier debates and studies and their younger colleagues. This educated, articulate elite, sometimes related by blood or marriage, was united by a singleness of purpose and efforts reminiscent of the same coordinated and nationally conscious secular elite active at the turn of the century. Now, as then, political organizations are fluid, with cooperation among some groups and with some individuals belonging to various groups simultaneously. The intellectual leadership strives to understand and articulate the economic, political, and cultural needs of other social strata.

One reason for the long evolution of this movement is the memory of the brutal hand Moscow has extended to the Azerbaijani Turkish intelligentsia since sovietization. Purge losses were extensive among both political and cultural-intellectual leaders. The generation that has begun to speak out on these issues since the late 1970s was born during the 1930s, was not threatened by purges, and did not fight in World War II. Having come of age, the men and women of this generation began where their fathers and grandfathers left off, reclaiming their traditional role in the political arena. The political movement is increasingly in the hands of young colleagues of the postwar generation who are without fear of the bloody past but who are knowledgeable about liberal politics.

The APF is not an elite organization. Its large membership, its many branches, and the "nonelite" among its leaders reflect the degree to which the intelligentsia can express the needs and concerns of workers and peasants. As APF president Abulfez G. Aliyev (Elchibey) noted, a mass movement with a "democratic national" character has emerged in Azerbaijan[92] that could never have come into being without the mass movement as well as the elite. The gulf was not between classes but between the AzCP and the rest of society.

The APF program formulated in the summer of 1989 had several goals: (1) to achieve the democratization of society and ensure human and civil rights for every citizen living in the republic; (2) to gain local control over elections; (3) "to achieve political, economic, and cultural sovereignty for Azerbaijan within the USSR," restoring historic place names and developing economic and cultural ties with Iranian Azerbaijan; (4) to end the exploitation of natural resources, achieving more equality in trade between union republics; (5) to return all land to the peasants and to give them "full freedom" in agricultural policy; (6) to guarantee equal treatment for all nationalities and protect all cultural freedoms; and (7) to end the "barbaric exploitation of the natural resources of Azerbaijan" and adopt a wide range of measures to protect the environment.[93] Supporting arguments were often written and documented by members of the academic community in the APF. Other organizations[94] formed during 1989 were Birlik (Unity), the Azerbaijan Resurgence party (Dirchelish), the Kizilbash People's Front, the Social Democratic Organization of Azerbaijan, and the secessionist National Salvation Organization.[95] These were small and most were short-lived.

During August and September 1989, the APF organized a series of individual then general strikes to press its various demands:[96] officially recognize the APF, convene a special session of the Azerbaijan Supreme Soviet to discuss the NKAO, abolish the Special Administration in the NKAO and restore Azerbaijan's full jurisdiction there, and release imprisoned Birlik members.[97] Strikes in Nakhjivan and among the Azerbaijani Turks of the NKAO were reported.

Railroad workers began to block supply trains to the NKAO, Armenia, and Georgia. Whether this action began under the direction of the APF is unclear, but the APF did negotiate an end to it.[98] The APF said that Nakhjivan had been blockaded by Armenians since June; Azerbaijan's stoppage was retaliatory. Azerbaijani railway workers reported shots fired at them and rocks thrown at engineers or through windows as the trains crossed Armenian territory.[99] By early October Gorbachev proposed special legislation to make strikes illegal for the next fifteen months and to place "Transcaucasian and Azerbaijan railways" under a "special form of management," perhaps like the "special form of administration" in the NKAO. The impact of the stoppage indicated the degree to which both the NKAO and Armenia relied on Azerbaijan's infrastructure and products, including gasoline, heating oil, and gas.[100] It undermined claims, such as that by Aganbegiyan, that the NKAO was economically tied to Armenia.

On 4 October APF leaders met with AzCP representatives, and the APF was registered as a legal organization the next day. It was agreed that the rail stoppage would soon be ended in return for various concessions, including AzCP support for demands that Azerbaijan Turks in the Armenian SSR be granted autonomy comparable with that of Armenians in the NKAO. The APF demanded the withdrawal of AzCP acquiescence in Moscow's "Special Administration" of the NKAO and the security of all trains passing through Armenian territory. A special session of the republic's Supreme Soviet was called, reportedly at APF urging, to approve a new law on sovereignty "asserting the republic's full control of all its natural resources . . . the right to veto laws imposed by Moscow, and the right to quit the Soviet Union." The session was televised at the APF's demand.[101] Bill Keller, one of the few U.S. reporters to go to Azerbaijan, reported on a "remarkable pact" between the AzCP and APF that forced the party into an "effective partnership" with the APF. The subsequent behavior of both parties suggests that Keller's conclusion was premature. If anything, the partnership seems to have emerged between the APF and the Supreme Soviet. "Of all the nationalist movements," wrote Keller, "none has moved from obscurity to power quite so quickly as the Azerbaijani Popular Front."

Within days the trains began to move and attacks on them resumed. *Ogenok* correspondent Georgii Rozhnov rode one of the early trains from Baku via Julfa to Nakhjivan, then to Erevan, describing attacks on his and other trains, including one in which a bomb was found under the tracks in

Armenian Zangezur. The USSR Ministry of Internal Affairs (MVD) officer in Nakhjivan told him that local authorities in Zangezur had done nothing to stop the attacks, which were clearly aimed at disrupting rail transportation. Citizens in Erevan did not know train traffic had resumed.[102]

The NKAO was said to be cut off. The Karabagh Aid Committee's newspaper *Azerbaijan* carried news of its supply convoys being attacked by armed Armenian bands.[103] Armenian organizations succeeded in airlifting supplies to the NKAO. One helicopter chartered by the Armenian organization Mercy contained guns, ammunition, and explosives.[104] Trains were still under fire. There were armed groups on both sides. The degree to which the local Azerbaijani groups' actions were coordinated (or perhaps linked to organizations in Baku) has not been documented. Radio Moscow reported daily clashes despite the presence of Soviet army and MVD troops. TASS called it "the verge of civil war." Those Azerbaijani Turks who remained in the NKAO gathered in Shusha, the historic capital; Armenians in Shusha went to Stepanakert. Each group reported discrimination in the town dominated by the other.[105] At a rally in Stepanakert, Armenians formed "self-defense groups." In Baku the AzCP rejected the APF demand to create a formal republican armed force for the defense of its border and villages.[106]

On 28 November 1989, Gorbachev issued a decree on the "normalization" of administration in the NKAO, including the restoration of the old Armenian-dominated soviet and the continued presence of MVD forces under Moscow's orders.[107] Azerbaijan objected to these two provisions. Within a few days, Armenia declared unilateral annexation of the NKAO. The government in Baku suspended those provisions of Moscow's decree that interfered with Azerbaijan's sovereignty.

INTELLECTUAL UNDERPINNINGS OF POLITICAL ACTION

Whether inside or outside the political arena, the academic and cultural intelligentsia continued to explore the "unopened pages" of history and its restructuring of national literature.[108] Books on historical geography,[109] early history,[110] historical documents or manuscripts,[111] and reprints of Russian scholars' early twentieth-century works[112] were rapidly produced to document Azerbaijan's historical, cultural, and political claims to Karabagh. The region is regarded as a cradle of Azerbaijani art, especially music and poetry, and works on Karabagh's folk art, reciters of dastans, musicians, composers, and modern poets are numerous.[113] Karabagh was the home of the female poet Natevan, composers Uzeir Hajibeyli and Muslim Magomaev, literati such as Firoudin Kocherli, the singer Bülbul and many others over the centuries. Sabir Rustemkhanli, while working as editor for the Karabagh Aid Committee's newspaper *Azerbaijan*, wrote the *Book of Life*, his reflections on his homeland, its art and history.[114] The intelligentsia in the party used AzCP institutions to issue collected documents on the NKAO issue.[115]

As before the activity of intellectual and artistic elites touched a wide range of topics. In the fall of 1988 economic historian Dr. Mahmud Ismailov spelled out the disadvantageous economic position mandated by the State Planning Agency (Gosplan) for Azerbaijan.[116] Azerbaijani cotton growers received 500–700 rubles per ton for their cotton, while finished products made by neighboring republics brought 12–13 thousand rubles per ton. Wool, steel, and grapes were similarly penalized, and Azerbaijan's income remained among the lowest in the USSR. Lenin called it colonialism; Ismailov wrote, "What should we now call an economy that consists of supplying raw materials, resulting in such a low GNP?"[117]

A year later *Seher* (*Morning*), the economic supplement to *Kommunist*, extended Ismailov's point. Republican economists estimated that Azerbaijan produced 50–80 billion rubles of goods annually and provided petroleum products and oil-drilling equipment, cotton, caviar, and carpets to other republics or for foreign export. Despite its disproportionately large contribution, Azerbaijan gets an investment from Moscow of 4.3 billion rubles, compared with 6.3 billion for each neighboring republic. The government, the economists stated, buys Azerbaijani oil cheaper than mineral water.[118] *Seher* later ran a series of economic charts comparing Azerbaijan's exports to and imports from various union republics. On 13 January 1990 the value of trade with Armenia was revealed: Azerbaijan exported 4.5 million rubles worth of goods (including many oil products and gas) to Armenia and received 1.16 million rubles worth (major items were jewelry and pesticides).[119]

Ecology and public health were linked to economic grievances, specifically to the heavy use of pesticides on two major crops—cotton and grapes. To meet plan targets, chemical fertilizers were used in quantities up to twenty times greater (in kilos per hectare) than for the USSR as a whole. Higher rates of cancer, viral hepatitis, tuberculosis, infant mortality, and female sterility resulted, and the data were classified "secret" so that public safety measures were blocked. Chemicals were destroying regional water systems. Combined with wastes carried by the Volga, the Caspian became a "cesspool" for Russia.[120]

In cultural policy, place names were changed and "unopened pages" of history were opened. S. M. Kirov Azerbaijan State University (so named since the 1930s) was renamed Mehmed Emin Rasulzade Baku State University, because M. E. Resulzade's efforts led to its founding in 1919.[121] Kirovobad reverted to Ganje, its historic name,[122] on 1 January 1990.[123] In July 1989

Buniatov called for a return to the Latin alphabet, and in May 1990 the republican Supreme Soviet established a commission to work on Latinization.[124]

Ismailov, Vahabzade, and numerous scholars and literati spoke out against the dominant position of the Russian language in Azerbaijan, despite the official status of Azerbaijani Turkish. Ismailov wrote:[125]

> Is this not disrespect for our language? Some say, "In gatherings there may be five or ten people from other nationalities. If we speak our own language, they can't understand and that would be disrespect toward them." To those people I say, without shame: "Many of those same people were born in Baku, grew up among us, so why do they show such inattentiveness to our language, to the language of the republic in which they live?"

I. D. Mustafayev criticized Azerbaijani Turks who did not use their own language: "Losing one's language, a person begins to lose his own 'face' . . . for communication among Azerbaijans, among ourselves to speak only in Russian . . . constitutes a loss of national dignity, [it is] national nihilism."[126]

More scholars and political figures insist on pre-1937 terminology, calling the language Turkish.[127] Scholars tie Azerbaijan's literary and intellectual traditions to those of Central Asia and point to architectural monuments, workers of statecraft, and poetry of the twelfth century and earlier,[128] thereby defying Russian claims to cultural superiority and elder brotherhood. During the November 1988 demonstrations *Pionir Azerbaidzhana* said: "When the homeland is beset by misfortune, when its land is encroached, the descendants of Babek, Köroglu . . . are prepared for battle and deeds in the name of the people."[129]

As in the past, some have been quick to see in this cultural rebirth the old bogeyman of Pan-Turkism. The Azerbaijani Turks draw an appropriate parallel: The entire English-speaking world, said one scholar, forms a cultural whole and is not regarded as a threat to the rest of the world merely on the basis of that cultural unity. When Turks in Azerbaijan look to *Dede Korkut* or the *Orkhon stelae*, they are like Americans reading Chaucer.[130]

Noteworthy by their absence from political life are religious themes or rhetoric. In keeping with Azerbaijan's long tradition of secular politics and anticlericalism,[131] almost all political groups cast their demands in terms of national needs, economic development, political sovereignty, or protection of the national homeland and its culture. Despite popular media references to a "Muslim-Christian conflict" and the convenient use of Shi'ism to explain unrest, the Azerbaijani Turks have not made religious appeals. Islam, although important in culture and personal life, has not been used for political mobilization, political organization, for unifying the population, or defining any major political platform in Azerbaijan. The APF leadership, which supports religious liberty, has emphatically stated the secular character of its platform. Nemat Panakhov remarked that at one demonstration some people carried green flags (symbolizing Islam) but the front regards these as insignificant fringe elements and does not condone or share Islamic goals.[132] APF coleader Etibar Mamedov noted that Russian reporters admitted to him that they had not seen the reported Islamic banners on Lenin Square in November and December 1988 but had been told of them.[133]

Azerbaijani claims to sovereignty were supported by history. In his discussion of the intimidation used by the Bolsheviks to subdue the ADR, historian Nasib Nasibzade reinforced Azerbaijan's claim to sovereignty on the basis of its independent statehood and the Red Army's guarantees during "unification." Historians have resumed rehabilitations of political or cultural figures who had been purged or vilified, but as in the Khrushchev era, these "rehabilitations" are only partial and old taboos remain. Discussion of ideas is incomplete; political thought is sometimes misrepresented. The eventual fate of those who died in the USSR is not revealed.

The public profile of former First Secretary Imam Mustafayev constitutes another sort of rehabilitation. He lamented the abandonment of formerly prosperous villages as young men took work in Siberia, "where our fathers and grandfathers were exiled." Young women were left without suitable husbands and could not begin families. People should stay on their ancestral land, he said, not move to nearby cities. Mustafayev rejected the "pretensions of Armenia against Azerbaijan," which he said reflect plans to establish a "Greater Armenia." He was not impressed by arguments that Armenians in the NKAO cannot receive television transmissions from Erevan. Perhaps the intervening mountains have more to do with that than evil intent by Baku.

THE CRISIS PEAKS:
WAS MOSCOW LOSING CONTROL?

Events of December 1989 to January 1990 suggest that the national movement in Azerbaijan and the NKAO conflict may have been moving beyond Moscow's ability to restrain or manipulate them. On 1 December the Armenian Supreme Soviet decreed the NKAO part of a "United Republic of Armenia," contrary to many declarations by Moscow.[134] The Karabagh Aid Committee said this resolution "had the smell of blood" and wondered why it took five days for the Azerbaijan Supreme Soviet to rebuff it.[135] In Baku the Supreme Soviet voted on 4 December to establish its own "Organizational Committee" to replace the Volskii Committee in the NKAO and the Orgkom was set up in a few days.[136] Bloody clashes continued in the NKAO and along the border with Armenia. The Karabagh Aid Committee's

Azerbaijan carried photos of bullet-riddled vehicles and wounded civilians reportedly attacked by Armenian bands near the border and the NKAO. Refugee publications described the conditions under which refugees had fled their homes.

By the end of December, violence against the communist regime had broken out in Nakhjivan, Jelilabad, and Lenkoran. Along the Nakhjivan borders with Iran and Turkey residents dismantled frontier fortifications, cutting barbed wire and burning guard towers. They wanted to reclaim about 7,000 acres of fertile land that had been declared a military zone at the border, to visit cemeteries and shrines in this zone, and to have control relaxed along this border, enabling them to visit and trade with neighboring countries.[137] The Soviet press took advantage of Iranian claims that "Islamic zeal" motivated the attacks on the fortifications, and raised the spectre of "Islamic fundamentalism" in Azerbaijan. *Azadlik* accused the government of using the border incident as an excuse to spread disinformation and outright lies about the events. The border was stormed, *Azadlik* wrote, because the Soviet state had ignored petitions for relaxed border regulations, and people took matters into their own hands.[138] Here the APF presented itself as the defender of national rights against the Soviet state.

In Jelilabad troubles had been simmering for at least a year as the local party and state apparatus could not fulfill the center's promises for restructuring. After a party regular defeated the head of a local chemical co-op in a December election for first secretary, people attacked the local raikom building and the local branch of the MVD on 29 December. The local branch of the APF restored order. After a meeting between representatives from the Supreme Soviet and the city, local party and state organs were gradually restored, but the local APF retained some authority.[139]

In Baku the APF held its third conference on 6 and 7 January at the Academy of Sciences.[140] A new Assembly and an Administrative Council were elected. Poet Sabir Rustemkhanli, historian Etibar Mamedov, and dramatist Yusuf Samedoglu (editor of the Writers' Union journal *Azerbaijan* and son of writer Samed Vurgun) were elected to the council. Abulfez Aliyev remained president. Some of APF's goals were "to extinguish the fires of unrest in mountainous Karabagh, to put an end to the activities of armed Armenian bands in that region and along the border," where continued fighting was reported.[141] In the face of official inaction the APF acknowledged "the need for a Military Defense Council." Responsibility for its formation and for establishing relations with the republic's leadership was given to Administrative Council members Etibar Mamedov and Rahim Gaziyev. Thus in conflict resolution and defense the APF seemed de facto to assume the authority of the party and state apparatus.

Disagreement within the Azerbaijan Communist party came out into the open. At a meeting on 8 January, AzCP secretary Hasan Hasanov[142] asked why the destruction of the wall between East and West Berlin was a product of "new thinking" but the attempt of Nakhjivanis to destroy barbed wire separating them from southern Azerbaijan was the "work of extremists." He wondered why the union did not know that the "so-called Karabagh problem" is the work of historical Armenian territorial ambitions and that the first refugees were Azerbaijanis. Where, he asked, does the AzCP stand in relation to these events? He revealed that several central decrees that had ostensibly been arranged in consultation with Baku were unilateral acts by Moscow. The AzCP had been powerless.

In the forty-two days since the end of the "special administration," he said, Armenia had declared its annexation of Nagorno-Karabagh, incorporated NKAO party cells into the Armenian Communist party and the NKAO administration into that of Armenia, and replaced the Azerbaijani flag and republican symbol as well as official signs, inscriptions, and official forms with Armenian ones. He charged that in those forty-two days water pipes and the bridge to the Azerbaijani Turkish enclave at Shusha had been destroyed and that Armenian terrorists had attacked ten Turkish villages in the Lachin raion. All the while, he said, "Armenia screams that we are inflicting damage on them." What had the AzCP done in that forty-two days? Hasanov asked. It had issued one statement in the newspaper. The people look on each member of the administration in Azerbaijan, he wrote, as someone "preferring servility to the center to authority before the people [and] the strength of their own position to defending the interests of the people. They call us, in the full sense of the word, *mankurts*." (*Mankurts* were people in Chingiz Aitmatov's novel *A Day Lasts Longer Than an Age* who, through torture, had lost all memory of their history and identity.)

On 9 January 1990 the Armenian Supreme Soviet with a self-proclaimed national soviet from the NKAO discussed a 1990 republican budget that included the Nagorno-Karabagh region. The Azerbaijan Supreme Soviet called including the NKAO in the Armenian budget a "provocative act" that interfered in the internal affairs of a sovereign republic.[143] Gorbachev agreed. His 10 January statement declared Armenian resolutions of 1 December (on annexation) and 9 January to be violations of his previous decrees, the Soviet constitution, and the sovereign rights of Azerbaijan. He called on the Armenians to reverse themselves. To Baku, however, it was another toothless roar from the Kremlin. The Azerbaijan government merely issued declarations and formed committees.

On 12 January the APF reported helicopters from Armenia landing armed men in the Khanlar raion just northwest of the NKAO boundary. These forces, *Azadlik* reported, armed "with modern weapons," attacked a local Azerbaijani village. Several Turks were killed and many wounded. The

APF concluded that "Armenia is conducting an undeclared war against Azerbaijan."[144] During the fall and winter months, the Popular Front apparently coordinated sporadic and effective rail stoppages against Armenia, depriving that republic of food, fuel, and other supplies. The APF leadership regarded the action as a legitimate retaliatory measure under "wartime" conditions.

In Lenkoran residents expressed their disgust with Moscow's failure to stop Armenian claims on the NKAO. The local branch of the APF took over all functions of the party and state in Lenkoran and created a temporary defense committee. On 12 January the local newspaper *Leninchi (Leninist)* was replaced by the local APF's *Elin Sesi (Voice of the People)*. The APF used an old Bolshevik tactic—controlling the media. The Baku APF, always alert to pretexts Moscow might create and use to intervene, had not known, or approved, of the move by the local APF.[145] Despite meeting with a party-state delegation from Baku, the Lenkoran APF stated it intended to retain power until Moscow "put an end to the so-called Karabagh question." On Saturday, 13 January, bazaars and shops in Lenkoran were open and public transportation was available. The *Bakinskii Rabochii* correspondent, fresh from Jelilabad, went to the party raikom building that snowy morning. It was under APF guard. The young man at the door told him "the raikom no longer exists. No one works here."[146] The description was reminiscent of Petrograd in 1917. Perhaps Moscow thought so, too.

"BLACK JANUARY" 1990

During the weekend of 13–14 January 1990, bloody communal conflict broke out in Baku. Press reports stated that fighting began when "hooligan elements" had tried to evict local Armenians from their apartment and an Armenian killed an Azerbaijani with an ax. During the two days thirty-two Armenians and an unspecified number of Azerbaijanis were killed. Dozens were wounded. Government and party spokesmen as well as the APF appealed for an end to the violence. Etibar Mamedov, in a press conference in Moscow about ten days later, stated that he and other APF leaders had appealed to the Azerbaijan minister of internal affairs to use MVD troops and police to disperse crowds and bring the violence under control. No action was taken; police cars were virtually absent from the streets.[147] Kazakh writer Almaz Estekov, then in Baku, was told by the commander of MVD forces in Baku that he had been ordered by First Secretary Vezirov not to intervene in national conflicts.[148] Azerinform, the official news agency, said the violence was the result of protracted tensions during the previous two years, especially to the presence of tens of thousands of Azerbaijani refugees from Armenia. The catalyst, however, was the latest attempt of the neighboring republic to annex the NKAO.[149]

On 14 January as bloodshed continued, Evgenii Primakov, chairman of the USSR Supreme Soviet's Council of the Union, arrived in Baku.[150] The next day, as clashes ended, the Presidium of the USSR Supreme Soviet announced it was ordering approximately eleven thousand army, navy, and KGB troops to Azerbaijan and Armenia. A state of emergency was declared in the NKAO and along the border between the republics. Azerbaijan was ordered to impose curfews "in Baku, Ganje and other population centers, where the situation had allegedly 'reached the point of attempts at armed overthrow of Soviet power.'"[151] Moscow was preparing to move against the APF and supporters of democratic reform in the Azerbaijan capital. According to Radio Liberty monitoring, a news blackout began on 15 January 1990.[152]

Several sources provide clues to what one reporter termed the "sad mosaic" of events. Some information was later confirmed by an independent commission from the USSR military procurator's office called Shield.[153] Etibar Mamedov reported talks between APF leaders, including himself, and Primakov, who assured the APF that troops would only pass through Baku on their way to the border and that no curfew would be imposed in the capital. Mamedov stated that "it was not clear" why troops and tanks going to the border had to pass through Baku (which would require a detour to the Apsheron Peninsula). Barricades on roads into Baku began to go up on the night of 16 January, according to Mamedov and a Russian journalist on the scene.[154] On 17 January meetings outside the CC AzCP building demanded that troops not enter Baku. On 18 January Primakov appeared before the crowd and said that troops were coming to Baku to protect the people. He was booed down. In a meeting after this incident, Primakov told Mamedov that "they knew" the APF planned to overthrow Soviet power on 20 January and that forces were needed in the city to block the attempt. He also stated that USSR minister of defense Dmitrii Yazov had already issued instructions that armed forces were to open fire if they met any resistance on the road into the capital.[155] Mamedov spoke with General Sokolov, commander of the Baku garrison, who stated flatly that if they were ordered, his troops would not hesitate to open fire on the civilian population.[156]

On 19 January the USSR MVD announced raids by Armenians and Azerbaijanis on each other's villages. Security forces had been blocked in some areas. Armenians had cut off communications with Nakhjivan, and hostages were being taken by both sides. At the same time, an APF spokesman said that a rally of one hundred thousand people outside the CC AzCP building in Baku demanded the withdrawal of Soviet forces from the Baku and Ganje areas. A strike was reportedly planned to press that all forces be removed and that all Azerbaijan's leaders resign.[157]

During these tense days, negotiations were reportedly conducted by various APF leaders and Sheikh ul-Islam Allahshukur Pashazade with the authorities, though sources give few details about their substance. On 19 January, around 6 P.M., Etibar Mamedov reportedly had a last meeting with V. P. Polianichko, AzCP second secretary, in an effort to keep troops from entering Baku.[158] Polianichko told Mamedov "the matter has been decided, nothing can be done." Mamedov was to speak on television that evening, but the radio-television power source was blown up around 7:30 P.M. by individuals who induced the workers to leave by saying they were from the APF and were calling a strike.[159] The Shield investigation subsequently determined that the act was carried out by either Soviet Army special forces or the KGB.[160]

Several other sources implied incitement and organized deception. *Literaturnaia Gazeta* correspondent Andrei Kruzhilin observed that some pickets in downtown Baku, who were ostensibly part of the APF, did not listen to APF leaders who urged them to disperse.[161] A short article in *Bakinskii Rabochii* of 16 January noted seemingly organized attempts to disrupt joint efforts by the APF and "party and law enforcement organs" to calm the political climate in the republic. Its reporter wrote, "And suddenly—disorders. . . . The question presents itself: who benefits?" The writer, a member of the Karabagh Aid Committee, suspected "organizers who undoubtedly were present at recent meetings, but as yet remain in the shadows."[162] Retired KGB men from both Baku and Moscow later agreed there had been instigation in Baku to provide Moscow with a pretext for using force.[163]

Soviet troops received orders to occupy Baku at midnight on 20 January 1990. At 12:20 A.M., the first MVD forces arrived at the barricades on the main roads leading into the city. Lt. Gen. V. S. Dubiniak, "commandant of Baku," reported "returning fire" there and elsewhere in the city for several hours. City residents, who saw tanks coming down the city streets about 5 A.M., said the troops were the first to open fire.[164] The Shield report rejected the military's claims of returning fire, noting there was no evidence that those manning the barricades on the roads leading into Baku were armed. Etibar Mamedov reported that APF offices were surrounded by troops and fired on without warning just after midnight. Several inside were killed. He and several others escaped through a secret exit to the street, where they saw troops firing at windows where lights were burning and at moving vehicles. They later went through town, discovered ambulances and private cars crushed by tanks, and counted bodies in the streets. (Shield listed the vehicle numbers of three crushed ambulances.)[165] More tanks, armored vehicles, and helicopters were coming toward the city. Numerous "extremists" were arrested, including forty-three members of the APF's National Defense Council. APF offices were closed, files seized, and phones disconnected.[166] Etibar Mamedov made his way to Moscow and recounted the events at a press conference of Soviet and foreign journalists on 26 January. He was immediately arrested and charged with violating Article 67 of the criminal code: Inciting National Enmity.[167] He was held incommunicado in Lefortovo Prison in Moscow.

By 6 A.M. on 20 January, according to Shield findings, the military was in complete control of the undefended city. Resistance was reported to have continued in one location, though Shield could find no evidence of civilian possession of firearms. The Salyan barracks on the outskirts of the city had reportedly been "besieged" by the local population, a claim the garrison used to "defend itself" for four full days. The Shield report stated there were no bullet holes in the walls of the Salyan barracks but that civilian buildings opposite were nearly destroyed. Social democratic leader Leyla Yunusova would refer to "techniques of Red fascism," and others would call this "the second invasion of Baku by the Red Army."[168] Military authorities on 20 January reported 83 dead including 14 military personnel and their family members, though family members had supposedly been evacuated several days earlier.[169] Shield reported twelve military dead, 120 civilian dead, and "more than 700 wounded." The journalist Kruzhilin reported more than a hundred civilians shot dead: ninety-eight men, two boys under age 14, a 13-year-old girl, and six women. The Moscow-based newspaper of the "independent Azerbaijan information service," *Umid* (*Hope*),[170] reported a far larger number, but it was not subsequently confirmed;[171] the APF reported 36,000 wounded. Sheikh ul-Islam reported presiding over the burial of 180 people.[172] General Dubiniak "requested" that everyone remain indoors on 20 January. As an APF newspaper wrote, people were thus "prevented from collecting their own dead or from aiding the wounded before their last breath."[173]

Hospitals were crammed. In the aftermath of the bloodshed, several city newspapers published pictures of flattened cars, bullet-riddled apartment buildings, corpses lying in morgues and on streets, and lines of coffins; most telling, however, were published lists of the names and birth dates of the victims. The entire edition of *Seher* of 3 February was devoted to funeral photos and lists of names and birth dates of about two hundred of the wounded and 120 of the dead, both men and women, ranging in age from 14 to over 70. Many charges were documented by video films taken secretly during and in the aftermath of the events by Baku film director Jahangir Zeynaly and others.[174]

First Secretary Vezirov was forced out of office.[175] His successor, Ayaz Niyazi oglu Mutalibov (born 1938), is a Baku native, an engineer trained at the Oil and Gas Institute. A party member since 1963, he began active party work only in 1977, coming up through the ranks under Aliyev. He had been president of the Azerbaijan Council of Ministers since January 1989.[176]

Moscow was ready with a series of justifications for its decision to deploy troops and open fire. The central media repeated the theme of protecting the population, mainly the Armenians. If protection had been the reason, asked two TASS correspondents later, why had troops not been sent the previous weekend when the violence began?[177] Baku reporters asked why locally stationed forces had refused to intervene on 13 January when asked to do so by APF leaders.[178] Several Baku residents, including the half-Armenian chess master Gari Kasparov, confirmed that national clashes had ceased several days before the Soviet Army entered Baku.[179] Shield confirmed this. As for the Russians, Kruzhilin noted that the "Russians left. But who had threatened them?" He believed rumors had been spread to create panic. Many had received calls, apparently the result of a coordinated effort, asking, "Are you Russians? Get out quickly."

There were claims that the unrest in Azerbaijan had been provoked by "Islamic fundamentalism." If the Soviet leadership wished to undercut antic-ipated Western protests about using force to put down a democratic move-ment, then attributing that movement to Islamic fundamentalism would have been a most effective tactic. Iranian leader Khameini provided the initial claim, though Azerbaijan sheikh ul-Islam refused to agree.[180] The president of the United States said he understood Gorbachev's "need to maintain order." Bush's words were received with bitterness in Baku.[181]

The themes of protection and fundamentalism were shrill but short-lived. TASS on 20 January claimed that "Azerbaijani nationalists had called for the 'forceful overthrow of Soviet power, the secession of Azerbaijan.'" That night Gorbachev, in a televised address, justified the use of troops by saying that "extremist forces were attempting to seize power." He identified these "extre-mists" as the leaders of the APF,[182] a characterization he must have known was untrue. The last months' events, however, did reveal the popularity and influence of the APF. Gorbachev sent troops to Baku to shore up communist power there, justifying that act with a barrage of excuses, playing on internal Soviet and Western misinformation and fears of a resurgent Islam. Despite his rhetoric, he acted like a Russian imperial leader preserving power in a colony. He did in Baku what he had not yet dared to do in Lithuania, where the Popular Front had renounced "unification" with the USSR and declared independence. But the West was watching Lithuania, and Gorbachev exer-cised restraint there for another full year until the Western powers were occupied with the war in the Persian Gulf. (Early in the gulf crisis Gorbachev had said, "No dispute, however complicated it might be, justifies the use of force.")[183]

The Azerbaijani Turks were shocked by the use of Soviet troops in Baku, but they were also infuriated. As the body count mounted, President of the Supreme Soviet Presidium E. M. Kafarova on 20 January made a fierce protest against "the crude violation of the sovereignty of the Azerbaijan SSR, [the] brutal action against a peaceful population." She concluded by saying, "The Azerbaijani people will never forgive the tragic killing of their daughters and sons."[184] The next day, the Supreme Soviet went into an extraordinary session. Among those participating were representatives of the APF and other informal organizations. Tragedy had forged a heretofore improbable alliance. At the end of an all-night session, the Supreme Soviet released several decrees, the most significant of which was published in the major newspapers of the capital, both official and unofficial, in Russian and Turkish.[185]

The Decree of the Azerbaijan Supreme Soviet declared that the state of emergency and the sending of troops violated Paragraph 14 of Article 119 of the USSR Constitution because they were undertaken without the agreement of the higher organs of power of Azerbaijan. On that basis the decree labeled the state of emergency "an act of aggression against the sovereignty of the Azerbaijan SSR" and the official decision that led to the death and injury of hundreds, "a crime against the Azerbaijani people." It demanded the immediate lifting of the state of emergency and removal of all troops except those in the NKAO and along the Armenian border. If the all-union (central) government failed to act, the Supreme Soviet pledged to "discuss the utility of maintaining union relations between the USSR and the Azerbaijan SSR." The Supreme Soviet created a special committee to establish the facts of the incident.

With the Soviet troops' invasion of Baku, press, television, radio, and telephone services were suspended. When the first publications resumed on 25 January, they expressed stunned horror over the bloodshed and recounted over and over again what had happened. In later days the press struggled to piece together the events, to clarify the death toll. Most of all it tried to understand why troops had been sent to Baku. Russian correspondents from the central press as well as local reporters, scholars, and writers asked similar questions. Why were the republican state and party organs not consulted as required by the Soviet constitution? When and by whom was "operation Baku" planned and on the basis of what information?[186] Why was a curfew not made known ahead of time in order to minimize civilian casualties? (Shield confirmed that the populace was notified of the curfew only on the morning of 20 January.[187]) Why were families of local military personnel evacuated long before the introduction of forces? And why was the central press claiming that Russians and others were being threatened in Baku?[188] One answer came from Major General A. I. Kiriliuk of the Political Board of the USSR MVD who stated that the military was sent "to crush the

Azerbaijani drive for greater sovereignty in order to discourage similar movements elsewhere in the USSR."[189] The Shield report stated that forces were used in Baku not against any external threat but against the local population.

The rest of the republic responded angrily. Nakhjivan, in the wake of the military occupation of Baku, declared itself independent on 20 January and appealed to the United Nations to recognize its right to self-determination. Soviet troops were ordered to Nakhjivan, and a news blackout again prevented the rest of the world from finding out how perestroika would next be applied. A subsequent Radio Liberty report[190] stated that the republic lasted only eight days under the local APF. The report suggested that a "helicopter full of generals" had presented the APF with an ultimatum that "under the circumstances" they had to accept.

Historic Ganje proved to be, as in 1920, a source of great resentment of the Russian invasion and of powerful national spirit. The official *Vestnik Giandzhi* of 24 January published a decision of the Ganje city soviet "On the crude violation of Paragraph 14 of Article 119 of the USSR Constitution." Supporting the Supreme Soviet's decree and Nakhjivan's secession, it drew the obvious parallel to the April 1920 invasion by the Red Army. The Ganje city soviet called for creating a national armed force and local defense organizations and withdrawal of Soviet forces from the city of Ganje.[191] Ganje's APF newspaper *Vatan*, too, supported Nakhjivan's secession and called for the Azerbaijan Supreme Soviet to consider a similar resolution. The act of 20 January had exposed the Kremlin's "inner face," *Vatan* wrote. "Using the excuses of nationalism, extremism and Islamic fundamentalism, they strove to strangle Azerbaijan's democratic and national independence movement." A cartoon showed Stalin patting a tiny Gorbachev on the head and saying, "Ah, Misha! You are a gifted student."

Despite the arrests of dozens of APF leaders, many branches of the organization survived. An APF special bulletin, *FVChP*, appeared. The meaning of the letters in its name was not given, but it was strident in tone and listed no editorial board.[192] As the APF had anticipated, new parties were formed, some of which, like the tiny Social Democratic party and its newspaper, *Istiglal (Independence)*, criticized Popular Front leadership.[193] The Karabagh Aid Committee's *Azerbaijan* was permitted to appear as was the APF's more conventional newspaper *Azadlik*, though the latter did not receive permission until June 1990. Newspapers and journals dealing with political and cultural issues proliferated in the following months. The scholars and literati, continuing to clarify national identity and loyalty, have published many articles and several books on "Black January."

Epilogue: Azerbaijan after "Black January"

They can kill us, but cannot make us bend.

Azerbaijan, 24 February 1990

The use of troops in January 1990 and the repression of the Azerbaijan Popular Front did not end the struggle over the NKAO, stop the border fighting, or root out support for the democratic movement. Instead, those actions broke whatever bonds of limited trust remained between the rulers in Moscow and their subjects in Azerbaijan, fostered antiregime alliances within the republic, and strengthened bonds between Azerbaijani Turks and Central Asians, who saw the use of force as a lesson meant for them as well. There were demonstrations or shared grief between Azerbaijan and Georgia.[1] Gorbachev seemed to have made Nicholas II's error—shooting people who made political demands, arresting the moderate leadership, and leaving society radicalized and angry. Symbolically, people changed their family names, dropping the Russian -*ov* ending and replacing it with the Turkish -*oglu*.

Critics became more outspoken. Members of the republican Supreme Soviet's investigatory commission gave interviews concerning their efforts to gather information on the January events. Commission member Dr. Tofik Ismailov charged that there had been instigation by people "directly connected with party and state power."[2] Until April official and unofficial publications reflected the republic's lingering state of collective shock, covering the invasion with eyewitness accounts and foreign press reports. The newspaper of the Karabagh Aid Committee, *Azerbaijan*, on 24 February published stories about the victims of January and a full front-page photo of a mass funeral with tens of thousands marching across Lenin Square in Baku, under the headline "They can kill us, but cannot make us bend."

Signs that the republic's party organization had lost its authority and credibility were plain in December and January in Nakhjivan, Jelilabad, and Lenkoran. The obvious impotence of the AzCP in the face of Moscow's decision to send troops to Baku led to the public burning of party cards throughout Azerbaijan.[3] Gorbachev contributed to the destruction of AzCP authority by ordering troops to Baku and keeping them there over republican protests. The AzCP leadership's public posture was utterly out of touch with popular sentiment. When the Azerbaijan Supreme Soviet expressed its outrage at the deaths of hundreds of innocent people, the AzCP expressed sympathy but called for a return to work.[4]

First Secretary Ayaz Mutalibov had to give the party new direction. To reassert AzCP leadership over the population, he had to embrace popular goals or, more to the point, appear to do so.[5] Independent Communist parties had never been tolerated by Moscow, and the AzCP leadership was not about to become one. Influential party members had a personal stake in the continuation of the system that provided their security and, for those who skimmed profits from cotton and other industries, vast illegal wealth. In any case, the presence of the army, KGB, and MVD forces meant that real power was in the hands of the military. Popular authority rested with the Popular Front and opposition publications; the Academy of Science's *Elm*, the Karabagh Aid Committee's *Azerbaijan*, and the Vatan society's *Odlar Yurdu* were "the real people's tribunals."[6]

Mutalibov's dilemma was steering a course between the center and his own people, either of which could remove him from power (the people by undercutting his authority). His first speeches in February reflected his need to accept popular goals as the Communist party's own. He blamed Moscow's failure to rebuff Armenian demands for the NKAO for protracted tensions and noted the all-union press's prejudicial treatment of Azerbaijan in its coverage of the disputes with Armenia. He called for the withdrawal of troops from Baku, an end to the special regime in the capital and the NKAO, and a purge of "unprincipled party members."[7] Creating credibility was not an immediately successful process. In April 1990 the Karabagh Aid Committee's newspaper *Azerbaijan* argued that there existed between the people of Azerbaijan and the government, both in Baku and in Moscow, a "bitter ideo-political, economic-legal crisis."[8]

By late May plans for elections were under way throughout the USSR, including Azerbaijan. Despite the continued state of emergency, Baku was made to appear normal—soldiers and tanks were no longer in the streets. Mutalibov, without opposition, was elected president of the republic.[9] For republican Supreme Soviet elections, the AzCP tried, through a "new" program, to present itself as the representative of national interests, hoping to usurp leadership of the popular democratic movement, for many APF leaders were in jail and the state of emergency obstructed all opposition activity. The AzCP program was in fact the early Popular Front program combined with opposition goals as articulated in the unofficial press and couched in Communist party rhetoric.[10]

The new AzCP platform stated that the "sovereign will of the Azerbaijani people, the toilers of the republic, is the sole source of power in the Azerbaijan SSR." It called for guarantees of territorial integrity, security of borders, equitable prices for Azerbaijan's products, and enhancing the official position of the native language (which the party program continued to call "Azerbaijani"). The NKAO and Nakhjivan ASSR were affirmed as inalienable parts of Azerbaijan; in keeping with their autonomous status, the program assured their rights to determine their own "economic and social development and cultural construction." The party, however, would "carry out a decisive and uncompromising battle against any attempts at creation of unconstitutional organs of power" in those regions.

This was still the Communist party program, written by men whose careers had been shaped by the party and whose future was intertwined with the fate of the party. The program affirmed its commitment to a "Leninist conception of socialism" and claimed political leadership for the AzCP as guarantor of restructuring. In Mutalibov's first presidential speech he welcomed "political pluralism," pledged that the AzCP would contend in elections with other parties using democratic methods, but warned that "unruliness" would not be permitted.

The Popular Front and other opposition groups continued to press for the removal of troops, an end to the state of emergency and the NKAO crisis, and genuine political change. The expanding opposition press debated every issue.[11] Branches of the APF were not bound by the Baku leadership's policies or party discipline, and Popular Front newspapers of raiony or cities outside Baku reflected that diversity. Official groups including the Academy of Sciences and the Writers' Union issued their own opposition newspapers. In the Social Democrats' *Istiglal*, party leader Leyla Yunusova castigated APF leaders' lack of political acumen in "not expecting" Moscow to use troops in Baku: did they really think that a regime that shot Hungarians in Budapest, Czechs in Prague, Afghans in Kabul, and Georgians in Tbilisi would hesitate to shoot Azerbaijanis in Baku?[12]

Although some disputes were pointed and occasionally personal, the critics shared basic goals. Opposition forces won a postponement of elections until September, arguing that no legitimate campaign could take place under a state of emergency that banned public meetings. The parties and groups united under a bloc called "Democratic Azerbaijan" and campaigned as best they could.

Key APF leaders were still in prison as elections approached. As of early September, Etibar Mamedov had been permitted to see his brother once during his seven months of incarceration. No Western human rights organizations inquired about his case or those of his colleagues.[13] He and Rahim Gaziyev, also a member of the APF Military Defense Council, were granted a hearing on 1 November—after the elections—and released. Others were still being held.

By September, a new Popular Front platform had been formulated that served as a basis for the Democratic Azerbaijan bloc. Although the AzCP platform had usurped many of the Popular Front's original planks, the new APF platform reflected a significant evolution in political thought. In the new platform, the Popular Front no longer defined itself with respect to the Communist party or the old order, a sign of its political maturity and its decisive opposition to the regime in Moscow and the entire Soviet system.

The platform urged the Azerbaijan SSR Supreme Soviet to adopt a resolution proclaiming the creation of the Azerbaijan Soviet government an illegal act carried out by an occupying Red Army. Other articles stated that relations between Azerbaijan and the union must be changed in accord with the Azerbaijan constitution and that provisions contrary to the economic, political, and cultural interests of the Azerbaijani people would be eliminated. The republic would maintain its own foreign policy.

Regarding domestic policy the platform stated a willingness to fight for sovereignty, territorial integrity, and the security of all citizens; it affirmed the need for self-defense and internal security. The platform also argued for the development of a concept of independence and the creation of an independent state. The state, legal system, and information structures should be "de-partyized" and the civil society should be "de-ideologized." Freedom of speech, conscience, and religion should be guaranteed; the passport regime should be dismantled, and cultural development of all citizens regardless of their nationality should be protected. To secure the territory, the NKAO should be dissolved.

On economic issues the platform called for creating a free market and conditions for foreign investment and foreign trade and encouraging tourism. In social policies it called for reconsidering the existing social welfare system and for valuing the work of mothers raising children as highly as other labor. The section on human rights demanded their guarantee and pledged to fight for a "democratic government (majority government)." The legal system and prisons should be reformed: in litigation, the accused would be presumed innocent; acts not prohibited by law would be regarded as legal. The program called for a new administration in "culture and education," the return of national-cultural wealth illegally taken from the republic, alphabet "reform," and the restoration of religious buildings seized or damaged by the state or party. A final section on ecology restated the APF commitment to environmental protection and called for the current Council of Ministers committee for environmental protection to be dissolved and a comparable commission created under Parliament.[14]

The proponents of this program clearly stood for nothing less than the complete destruction of the Soviet system in Azerbaijan. The communist leaders could therefore not permit them to win any substantial representation and resorted to traditional Communist party practices, obstructing candidates trying to register and closing local APF branches in some parts of the republic. Several APF candidates were jailed and two were murdered a few days before the elections.[15] During the elections, voting fraud was apparent. The Democratic Bloc charged the local authorities and the AzCP with intimidation and illegal actions. Not surprisingly, AzCP candidates won most seats; the Democratic Bloc got 26 of 350. In several districts runoffs were held on 14 October, but opposition candidates did no better. Aside from denouncing the illegal practices, the Popular Front could do little.[16] Opposition continues in the spoken and printed word.

Azerbaijani commentators said in late 1990 that prolonged repression and failed elections contributed to growing political indifference among the population.[17] One man stated, "The tanks are not seen on the streets, but the people have anger in their hearts." Baku commemorated Black January in Kirov Park (now without the statue of Kirov) overlooking the sea. The park, once the burial place for the victims of the March Days of 1918, now holds the graves of victims—of all nationalities—of January 1990. The commemoration was made more poignant by similar military actions, though with fewer fatalities, in Lithuania and Latvia. Despite Azerbaijani sympathy for the Balts, the Azerbaijanis were embittered to see the world press criticize Gorbachev (now holder of the Nobel Peace Prize) for his actions in the Baltics and asked where were those voices of outrage a year earlier when their blood was being shed.

By mid-1991, more than a year after Black January, the state of emergency was finally lifted but fighting continued in Karabagh and along the Armenian border. Refugees were still in need of housing, medicine, clothing, and other supplies. The Communist party had failed to resolve political, economic, ecological, or cultural problems. In the debate on a new union treaty, opposition forces regarded any treaty written by the center rather than the republics as unsatisfactory. One commentator argued that protection of territorial integrity was given to the center in 1922 but that Moscow had given bits of Azerbaijan to its neighbors over the last seventy years: Azerbaijan was 97,000 square kilometers in 1922 but 86,600 square kilometers today.[18] Economic critics argued that power must be given by the republics to the center (not the reverse) and that the proposed union agreement relied too heavily on organs of coercion and would not develop infrastructure in the republics, "freezing" them at current relative levels (to Azerbaijan's detriment).[19] Although President Mutalibov accepted the draft treaty, the APF continued to oppose it. Western analysts spoke of Azerbaijan as a republic content to remain in the USSR.

The postwar generation has begun to play an increasingly active role. Etibar Mamedov noted that the older literati and scholars had made important contributions to the current democratic movement but that the time had come for the younger generation to assume responsibility.[20] Perhaps because the political leadership is the intellectual elite, restoring historical memory is often stressed. Both People's Poet Bahtiyar Vahabzade, in his 60s, and Mamedov (a historian in his mid-30s) compare the events of the 1980s and 1990s with the turn of the century and the period of Azerbaijan's independent statehood and warn against forgetting the lessons of history.[21] Among those lessons are that Russian imperial rule in Azerbaijan was not less prejudicial than Soviet, merely less efficient. A new postcommunist Russian empire may not bear the promise of liberty for Azerbaijan (or the de facto colonies in Central Asia), which it is presumed to carry for the Russians. Former APF leaders Mamedov, Rahim Gaziyev, and Nemat Panakhov criticized APF leaders including its president, Abulfez Aliyev (Elchibey), for failing to adhere to the Front's stated goals and for acquiescing to AzCP maneuvering. The critics stress the need for agreement on a viable plan for national liberation. Mamedov left the Front in the summer of 1991 and founded the National Independence party.[22]

Uncertain about the meaning for Azerbaijan of changing politics in Russia, Azerbaijani Turks continue to rely on their own traditions and values as expressed in their oldest art form, poetry. After Black January, Fikret Goja, one of Azerbaijan's premier poets, expressed the trauma of bloodshed. His poem "Azerbaijan" also displayed the spiritual resilience linked, like so much other poetry, to images of the land:

> Let the stones of the Homeland (Yurt) rise up,
> Let my soul die and arise a thousand times!
> Triumphantly, I rub my face with soil
> And say, may good fortunate be yours, my Azerbaijan.[23]

Appendix:
Unofficial and Opposition
Publications, 1988–1991

(Published in Baku unless noted otherwise.)

Ädalät
Published by the Union of Jurists of Azerbaijan beginning in July 1990.

APF Bulletin
This first publication of the Popular Front began May 1989 but was superseded by other publications. It explained the basic program, emphasized human and civil rights and the refugee problem, and reasserted Azerbaijan's historic claim to the NKAO. Its first issues accused "Armenian nationalists" of violating the "sovereign rights of Azerbaijan" and advocated declaring 28 May Independence Day.

Akhïn
Published by the Academy of Sciences branch of the APF beginning in January 1990. Appeared for the first time when the Soviet army stormed Baku.

Aydïnlïg
Published by the Gayghï Society for refugee relief beginning in August 1990. Appears regularly, focuses on political issues.

Azadlïk

This Azerbaijan Popular Front weekly (bilingual) began December 1989 and has become one of the major papers in Baku. Editor in chief is Najaf Najafov.

Azärbayjan

This People's Aid Committee to Karabagh weekly (bilingual) began in October 1989. Its stated main goal was to draw attention to the difficulties of Azerbaijani Turks living in Karabagh but it also included "varied and interesting issues concerning our nation yesterday, today and tomorrow . . . in short, whatever interests or disturbs us all." It proclaimed its desire to follow the "beautiful and significant traditions" of its namesake, the *Azerbaijan* newspaper of 1918–20. It came out irregularly until 19 January 1990, the day before the Soviet Army moved into Baku. It resumed publication on 25 January. One of the major papers in Baku with political and cultural articles, its editor in chief is poet Sabir Rustemkhanli.

Dedem Gorgud/
Dedem Korkut

This independent literary-arts weekly began in the summer of 1991 and seemed to concentrate on arts only.

Dirchelish

The Dirchelish (Resurgence) party produced only a few mimeographed copies in the spring of 1989. The first issue of 27 May 1989 employed a forceful tone: "While Angola develops, Azerbaijan remains behind. . . . They want to scatter the last drop of [our] blood. They want to condemn us to death. Aren't these indicated by the blow against Karabagh, stillborn children, mothers whose milk has gone dry, the death of Sumgait and the dying Caspian?" The piece ended with an affirmation that no more concessions should be made.

Elm

Azerbaijan Academy of Sciences newspaper (bilingual) begun 1984 is not affiliated with any unofficial group, but has taken positions opposing the AzCP.

FVChP

This special bulletin of the Azerbaijan Popular Front, begun in the spring of 1990, was especially incendiary, castigating the AzCP and governments of both the republic and the USSR for use of troops.

Feryad

This publication of the Ministry of Oil and Gas and the Ministry of Chemical and Oil Refining Industries began in October 1990.

Gala	(Town of Masally) This independent literary-arts newspaper began in January 1991.
Ganjlik/Moldost'	This monthly magazine of the CC Azerbaijan Komsomol publishes one issue in Russian and one in Azerbaijani Turkish. Although published by an official body, in the first year (1988) of its appearance, it covered formerly taboo topics.
Garabagh	Begun in 1990 by the AzCP oblast' Organization Committee, this Azerbaijani Turkish-language newspaper of the NKAO presented the Azerbaijani view of conflicts there. Although official, it represented local opposition to the AzCP.
Ilham	Begun in November 1990, this publication was put out by "Ittifagteatr" Creative Production Union, Azerbaijan branch of USSR Theater Union.
Istiglal	Begun in the spring of 1990, this assertive, mimeographed paper of the Social Democratic party of Azerbaijan (bilingual) was produced almost entirely by the leaders of the SDP, Leyla Yunusova and Zardusht Alizade. Most of the articles were in Russian. Few issues appeared.
Meydan	(Square, probably a reference to the Lenin Square demonstrations.) Only a few issues of this publication by the Azerbaijan Popular Front, October region (Baku) branch, seem to have appeared. Issue no. 2 (October 1989) published the official recognition of the APF on 5 October, the number of the APF bank account, and its first congress on 28–29 October. On the front page was an agreement between APF and the republic's leaders in which the APF agreed to end the rail stoppage in return for APF recognition, end the curfew in Baku, and form a commission to investigate all changes in the republic's territory since sovietization.
Mübariza	This publication of the Union of Afghanistan Veterans for Azerbaijan Republican Territorial Unity began in November 1990.
Panorama Azerbaidzhana	(Moscow) This publication of the Plenipotentiary Representatives of the Azerbaijan Republic, begun in January 1991, is official but opposes the slow pace of change and prejudicial treatment of Azerbaijan by Russians in government and media.

Respublika	Begun by the Soviet of Ministers of AzSSR in July 1990.
Sähär	This daily economic supplement to *Kommunist*, begun in 1989, although official, opposed inequitable economic policies of the center toward Azerbaijan. It ran the series "What We Give, What We Get" on Azerbaijan's trade with other republics.
Shusha	This publication of Shusha raikom (regional committee AzCP) and the regional soviet of people's deputies was begun in 1932.
Tanïdïm	The slogan of this publication of the Tanïdïm Charitable Society, begun in April 1991, is "Know Yourself, Know the World, Be Known in the World." It regards knowledge of history and culture as essential to this goal.
Tarikh	This supplement to *Elm* put out by academy historians involved in the Popular Front was begun in September 1990.
Ümid	(Moscow) This mimeographed bulletin of "the independent Azerbaijan information center" is run by T. (Tofik?) Ismailov. Despite the title, it was in Russian; begun in the spring of 1990, it was devoted to coverage of January 1990 events and responses to them in the world press.
Vätän	(Ganje) This publication of Ganje section of the Azerbaijan Popular Front, begun in late 1989 or January 1990, was outspoken in the aftermath of the January 1990 events, calling for Azerbaijan's secession.
Vätän säsi	This publication of the Azerbaijani Society of Refugees, begun in April 1990, has become a regular weekly dealing with various political issues but mainly refugee problems. It reflects the anger of the refugees at official inaction.
Vestnik Giandzhi	(Ganje) Although long the official paper of the Ganje gorkom (city committee AzCP) and city soviet of people's deputies (since 1922), it has been vitriolic in criticism of the AzCP and republican and central governments since January 1990.
Yurt	Issue no. 4 of this organ of the "Yurt birligi" or Yurt (homeland) union is dated May 1990; perhaps monthly since February 1990.
Yurtdash	The Union for Ties to Co-nationals Living Outside the Union has been publishing this since January 1991.

Notes

CHAPTER 1

1. *Istoriia Azerbaidzhana/Azärbayjan Tarikhi*, 3 vols. (Baku: Academy of Sciences, 1958–1963), 1:36–43. (Hereafter cited as *Ist. Az.*)

2. Ibid., pp. 62–67, on the Roman invasions of Albania. The stone is surrounded by a stone and iron fence near the archaelogical dig of Gobustan. In 1980 when I visited that site it was in good repair.

3. Keith Hitchins, "The Caucasian Albanians and the Arab Caliphate in the Seventh and Eighth Centuries," in *Bedi Kartlisa; revue de kartvélologie*, vol. 42 (Paris, 1984), pp. 238–40, which is based on C. J. F. Dowsett's translation of *The History of the Caucasian Albanians by Movses Dasxuranci* and Soviet secondary sources; *Ist. Az.* 1:109.

4. Other etymologies of Azerbaijan are "land of fire" (*azer* meaning fire), or are related to the Zoroastrian "fire worshippers" or the "eternal flames" caused by the seepage of natural gas and oil. Faruk Sumer, "Oğuzlara Ait Destani Mahiyetde Eserler," in *Dil, Tarih, Coğrafya Fakültesi Dergisi* (Ankara: Ankara University, 1959), citing folio 379B of *Tarihi Cihangüsa*, ed. Kazvini (Leiden, 1916), stated the name is Turkish, from *azer* meaning "high" and *baygan* signifying a "place for the wealthy and exalted."

5. *Istoricheskaia geografiia Azerbaidzhana*, Ziya M. Buniatov, ed. (Baku: Elm, 1987), p. 6. The book manuscript was completed in late 1986 but was not issued until late 1987.

6. Farida Mamedova, "O nekotorykh voprosakh istoricheskoi geografii Albanii I

v. do n. e. - VIII v.," in *Istoricheskaia geografiia Azerbaidzhana*, pp. 10–11; *Ist. Az.*, 1:52.

7. *Ist. Az.*, 1:60–62; Sara Balabeigyzy Ashurbeili, *Gosudarstvo Shirvanshakhov; VI–XVI vv.* (Baku: Elm, 1983), p. 24.

8. According to Ptolemy (2d century C.E.), Albania was bound on the North by the Sarmatians (Central Asian nomads), on the West by the Iberians, on the South by Atropatene and part of Armenia, and on the East by the Caspian Sea. *Ist. Az.*, 1:50, and Mamedova, "O nekotorykh voprosakh," pp. 7–8. See also Vladimir Minorsky, "Caucasica IV: Sahl ibn Sunbat of Shakki and Arran. The Caucasian Vassals of Marzuban in 344/955," in *The Turks, Iran and the Caucasus in the Middle Ages* (London: Variorum Reprints, 1978), from the *Bulletin of the School of Oriental and African Studies* 15, no. 3 (London, 1953).

9. Cited in Ashurbeili, *Gosudarstvo*, p. 24; *Syriac Chronicle known as that of Zachariah of Mitylene* 12, 7 (London, 1899), p. 327.

10. Minorsky ("Caucasica IV," p. 504) says "Aran" is Arabic "ar-Ran"; S. S. Äliyarov ("Redaksiya pochtundan," *Azärbayjan* [September 1988]) says Aran is Turkish, citing G. Geibullaev, *Toponimiia Azerbaidzhana* (Baku, 1986), pp. 27–28; Ashurbeili, *Gosudarstvo*, pp. 56–58.

11. Hitchins, "Caucasian Albanians," pp. 235–36, says that "Albania was a semi-independent principality ruled by the native dynasty of the Mikhranids."

12. Hitchins, "Caucasian Albanians," pp. 235–38; *Ist. Az.*, 1:104–7, on arrival of the Arabs.

13. Babek is now regarded as an Azerbaijani "national liberation" leader against the Arabs. See *Ist. Az.*1:117–25, and Minorsky, "Caucasica IV," pp. 505–10.

14. Ashurbeili, *Gosudarstvo*, p. 44. On the Khazars, see Peter B. Golden, *Khazar Studies* (Budapest: Hungarian Academy of Sciences, 1980).

15. Ashurbeili, *Gosudarstvo*, pp. 20, 25, citing Armenian sources and more recent secondary works by J. Marquardt and Minorsky (his translation of *History of Sharwan and Darbend* in Russian and English). Minorsky ("Caucasica IV," pp. 505–6) discussed "the considerable Muslim principality of Sharvan, a survival from Sasanian times, but now [9th century] ruled by the family of the Yazidis of the Shaybani tribe." *Ist. Az.*, 1:98, stated that the Shirvan state evolved in the 7th century. Another group of autonomous states was ruled by *atabeks* in the 12th and 13th centuries; Buniatov, *Gosudarstvo Atabegov Azerbaidzhana* (Baku, 1978); his "Et-nopoliticheskie rubezhi Azerbaidzhana v period pravleniia Ildenizidov," in *Istoricheskaia geografiia Azerbaidzhana*, includes a map for the period.

16. Quoted in Ashurbeili, *Gosudarstvo*, p. 42.

17. Ibid. p. 42. The author cites a 9th-century text by Ibn Khordadhbeh, *Kitab al-Masalik Wa'l-Mamalik*.

18. Ashurbeili, *Gosudarstvo*, p. 86, noted that in circa 1025, attempts to revive Sasanian rather than Arab Muslim names became evident. She suggested this may have been linked to the declining fortunes of the Abbasid caliphate.

19. Ashurbeili, *Gosudarstvo*, pp. 42–55; Minorsky, *A History of Sharvan and Darbend* (Cambridge, 1958), pp. 22–23; *Ist. Az.*, 1:128, gives dates only for the Mazyadids.

20. Ashurbeili, *Gosudarstvo*, p. 109. In 982 c.e., Shirvan occupied Barda (ibid., p. 78, quoting Minorsky). The name Albania had been used at least as late as the 9th century according to *Ist. Az.*, 1:129.

21. Ibn Hauqal, *Kitab al-masalik wal-mamalik*, cited in Minorsky, "Caucasica IV," pp. 518–19; also noted in Ashurbeili, *Gosudarstvo*, p. 92, citing various sources.

22. Ashurbeili, *Gosudarstvo*, p. 107; *Ist. Az.*, 1:147.

23. Ashurbeili, *Gosudarstvo*, pp. 235–37, 240–44, citing Persian and Arabic sources.

24. Ibid. pp. 272–74.

25. Shi'i religious doctrines represent what Marshall G. S. Hodgson (*Venture of Islam* [Chicago: University of Chicago Press, 1974]) called "pietistic opposition" to early Muslim dynasties. Central is the issue of legitimate succession, with many arguing that only descendants of Ali and Fatima could be legitimate rulers of the Muslim community. See also Fazlur Rahman, *Islam*, 2d ed. (Chicago: University of Chicago Press, 1979) and Moojan Momen, *An Introduction to Shi'i Islam: The History and Doctrines of Twelver Shi'ism* (New Haven: Yale University Press, 1985).

26. In 1510 Ismail killed Shibani Khan in battle. In true Central Asian nomad fashion, Ismail is said to have made a drinking vessel out of his victim's skull, stuffed the skin with straw, and sent it to Ottoman sultan Bayezit II.

27. As secretary to the ambassador from Holstein in the 1650s, the German scholar Adam Oleari recorded that Turkish held a commanding place in Isfahan, the Iranian capital. The French traveler Jean Batiste Tavernier testified that "the language of the members of the court is Turkish." German traveler Engelbert Kempfer noted that "Turkish which is the mother tongue of the Safavid dynasty has spread from the court to the homes of high-ranking and faithful individuals" (Aliyarov, "Pochtundan").

28. *Ist. Az.*, 1:169–72.

29. Ashurbeili, *Gosudarstvo*, pp. 18–22.

30. According to Mamedova, "O nekotorykh voprosakh," p. 7, the Kura was described in ancient sources as running through Albania; the left bank was the northwest side, the right bank the region toward the Araz. She quoted Strabo's statement that this territory was part of Albania.

31. Aliyarov, "Pochtundan," p. 182, citing Abu Muhammad Abdulmalik ibn Hisham, *Kitab ut-tijan fi-muluk himyar* (Haydarabad, 1347 a.h.), pp. 312–487.

32. Äliyarov, "Pochtundan," p. 182.

33. Ibid., p. 182. Äliyarov, like Ashurbeili and other scholars, bases his arguments in part on toponyms. In this article, for example, Äliyarov stated that the words Alban and Aran were both Turkish, citing G. Geibullaev, *Toponimiia Azerbaidzhana* (Baku, 1986), pp. 27–28; Ashurbeili, *Gosudarstvo*, pp. 56–58. Dastans are used here; *Dede Korkut* was cited earlier; *Manas* is one of the oldest Central Asian Turkish dastans.

34. Äliyarov, "Pochtundan," p. 181, citing *Alban tarikhi*, pt. 2 (St. Petersburg, 1861). Citation is given in Azerbaijani Turkish.

35. Peter B. Golden, "The Turkic Peoples and Caucasia," in Ronald Grigor Suny, ed. *Transcaucasia: Nationalism and Social Change* (Ann Arbor: University of Michigan Slavic Publications, Department of Slavic Languages and Literatures, 1983), pp. 45, 49.

36. I thank Professor Golden for discussing these points with me; see also his forthcoming monograph, *An Introduction to the History of the Turkic Peoples*.

37. I. P. Petrushevskii, *Azärbayjanda vä Ermenistanda feodal münasibätlärinin tarikhinä dair ocherklär* (Leningrad, 1949), p. 52; though cited in Turkish, the work is in Russian; cited by Vahabzadä and Äliyarov in "Redaksiya pochtundan" *Azärbayjan*, February 1988. *Ist. Az.*, 1:109, stated that the Arabs tried to Arabize Albania but failed.

38. Hitchins ("Caucasian Albanians") noted the importance in historiography of Islamization and Arabization and, citing Buniatov, made this point about the ease of later Turkicization. *Azerbaidzhan v VII–IX vv* (Baku, 1965).

39. Hitchins ("Caucasian Albanians") reviewed the literature on both sides of this debate as well as the current political animosity.

40. B. Allahverdiyev (*Kitablar haggïnda kitab* [Baku: Ganjlik, 1972], p. 8) cites an Armenian-language manuscript found by I. V. Abuladze in 1937 in the Armenian SSR.

41. Hitchins, "Caucasian Albanians."

42. *Istoriia agvan Moiseia Kagankatvatsi* (St. Petersburg, 1861), pp. 239–40, cited by Äliyarov, "Pochtundan," p. 181.

43. Muriel Atkin, *Russia and Iran, 1780–1828* (Minneapolis: University of Minnesota Press, 1980), pp. 11–13.

44. Ibid., pp. 12–13.

45. Ibid., p. 6

46. Ibid., p. 24; see also chap. 3.

47. Rahman, *Islam*, p. 68.

48. Ashurbeili, *Gosudarstvo*, p. 237.

49. Omeljan Pritsak ("Moscow, the Golden Horde, and the Kazan Khanate from a Polycultural Point of View," *Slavic Review* 26, no. 4 [December 1967]) made this point in connection with the reign of Ivan IV (1533–84) and his elevation of Simeon Bekbulatovich, a Chinghizid prince.

50. A. A. Pakhmani, "Azerbaidzhana: granitsy i administrativnoe delenie kontse XVI–XVII vv," in *Istoricheskaia geografiia Azerbaidzhana*, citing *Tadhikrat al-muluk: A Manual of Safavid Administration (circa 1137/1725)*, Persian text, trans. V. Minorsky (London: n.p., 1943), Persian text, pp. 107–13, English translation, pp. 100–115.

51. Atkin, *Russia and Iran*, p. 14–15.

52. *Islam Ansiklopedesi* (Istanbul: Maarif, 1940–1960), pp. 966–67, entry for Baku; and *Ist. Az.*, 1:133, 143–4.

53. *Ist. Az.*, 1:239–42.

54. Atkin, *Russia and Iran*, p. 14–15.

55. The wall built by Shah Abbas Safavid (1587–1629) now demarcates the Inner City, or central portion of Baku.

56. A survey of several structures, with photographs, is found in *Ist. Az.*, 1:153–59. A monograph by A. V. Salamzade (Sälamzadä), *Arkhitektura Azerbaidzhana XVI–XIX vv.* (Baku: n.p., 1964), includes drawings, photographs, and even sketches of Azerbaijan; cities by foreign travelers. See also Sälamzadä and K. M. Mämmädzadä, *Arazboyu abidälär* (Baku: n.p., 1979), and Davud Aghaoglu Akhundov, *Arkhitektura drevnego i rannesrednevekogo Azerbaidzhana* (Baku: Azerneshr, 1986).

57. A Säfärli and Kh. Yusifov, *Gädim vä orta äsrlär Azärbayjan ädäbiyyatï* (Baku: Maarif, 1982).

58. Collections of his works, some without any biographical information, include *Üräk Döyünütüläri* (Baku: Ganjlik, 1979) and *Khagani Shirvani; Sechilmish äsärläri* (Baku: Azerneshr, 1978).

59. To commemorate the 840th anniversary of his birth, the publishing house Yaziji issued each part of the *Khamsa* as a separate volume between 1981 and 1983, all listing Nizami Ganjevi as author. In 1983 the Academy of Sciences' *Elm* issued, in Azerbaijani Turkish, his *Iskendername*, part of the *Khamsa*.

60. In the late 1950s, in honor of the 400th anniversary of his death, several collections of Fuzuli's work as well as books about him were published. A two-volume set of his writing appeared in Azerbaijani Turkish (*Äsärlär* [Baku: n.p., 1958]), and one volume appeared in Russian (*Izbrannoe sochinenie* [Baku: n.p., 1958]); H. Araslï, *Böyük Azärbayjan shairi Fuzuli* (Baku: n.p., 1958). Much of his work has been published in the Turkish republic. On his life and work, see Hitchins, "Fuzuli" in the *Modern Encyclopedia of Russian and Soviet Literatures*, vol. 8, pp. 75–80.

61. These and other poets are also discussed in Yusuf Seyidov and Samet Älizadä, *Klassik Azärbayjan shairleri söz hagginda* (Baku: Ganjlik, 1977).

62. Husein Taghiyev, *Azärbayjanda kitabkhanajilig ishi* (Baku: n.p., 1964), pp. 8–9. The early 20th-century Azerbaijani Turkish writer M. S. Ordubadi described Nizami's personal library in his novel *Gilinj vä gäläm* (*Sword and Pen*).

63. Taghiyev, *Kitabkhanalar*, pp. 10–11. Noting varying reports on the Maragha library, he concludes that 400,000 was "entirely believable."

64. Taghiyev, *Kitabkhanalar* pp. 15–24. The manuscripts from Shusha were, as of 1964, distributed among libraries in Georgia, Armenia, Moscow, Leningrad, and, finally, Azerbaijan.

65. Bakhmaniar al-Azerbaidzhani, *At-Takhsil (Poznanie)*, 3 vols. (Baku: Elm, 1983) was part of the Classic Heritage of Azerbaijan series published by the Institute of Philosophy and Law of the Azerbaijan Academy of Sciences.

66. For example, Khaji Nasreddin Tusi, *Akhlagi Nasiri* (Baku: Elm, 1980), is a translation, with annotations and notes, from Persian into Azerbaijani Turkish of a

major manuscript from the Azerbaijan Academy of Sciences' manuscript repository. Nasreddin Tusi, *Tansugnameyi Elkhani (Javahirname* (Baku: Elm, 1984), also from the manuscript repository, is a slim volume on precious gems. Like the other volume cited, it is in Azerbaijani Turkish.

67. H. B. Paksoy, *Alpamysh: Central Asian Identity under Russian Rule* (Hartford, Conn.: Association for the Advancement of Central Asian Research, 1989), pp. 1–2. This study of the *Alpamysh* dastan discusses both the importance of the dastan genre and the Russian imperial and Soviet efforts to destroy and subvert *Alpamysh*. An English translation of the dastan is included. The only other dastans to appear in English are A. Hatto's translation of *Kökötöy* from the large *Manas* dastan and Lewis's *The Book of Dede Korkut.* "The Tale of Bamsi Beyrek of the Grey Horse" in *Dede Korkut* is a variant of *Alpamysh*.

68. *The Book of Dede Korkut*, pp. 103–5.

CHAPTER 2

1. Muriel Atkin, *Russia and Iran*, 1780–1828 (Minneapolis: University of Minnesota Press, 1980).

2. Iran's success or failure to get French or English aid against Russia depended on the shifting alliances of the Napoleonic Wars; see Atkin, *Russia and Iran*, chap. 8. "The Great Game" has been examined in detail in two monographs by Edward Ingram: *The Beginning of the Great Game in Asia 1828–1834* (Oxford, Eng.: 1979) and *Commitment to Empire: Prophecies of the Great Game in Asia 1797–1800* (Oxford, Eng.: Clarendon Press, 1981).

3. J. F. Baddeley, *The Russian Conquest of the Caucasus* (New York: Russell and Russell, 1969), pp. 61–62, quoted in Atkin, *Russia and Iran*, p. 73.

4. Atkin, *Russia and Iran*, p. 73. Her assessment is overwhelmingly negative and carefully documented.

5. Erevan was not annexed to Russia until the second Russo-Iranian War.

6. Atkin (*Russia and Iran*, pp. 143l–44) says the Talysh area, later the Lenkoran district south of the river, was ceded "in essence," though border negotiations were deferred to a later time.

7. The treaty lowered tariffs for Russian goods imported into Iran and provided exemption from internal tariffs. Russia secured the sole right to maintain a navy on the Caspian. Russian subjects were exempt from Iranian law. This treaty constituted the framework for Russo-Iranian relations until 1917. London received comparable privileges in 1841.

8. One of the few known revolts was the 1837 uprising in Kuba, caused at least partly by men resisting conscription for duty in Warsaw. A. S. Sumbatzade, *Kubinskoi vosstanie 1837 g.* (Baku: Elm, 1961).

9. Atkin (*Russia and Iran*, pp. 146–47) does not specify the makeup of the boards.

10. Nicholas I appointed Vorontsov in 1844; a law of 1846 officially created the viceroyalty.

11. *Ist. Az.* 1:88–92; A. Mil'man, *Politicheskii stroi Azerbaidzhana v XIX- nachale XX veka* (Baku: Azerneshr, 1966), pp. 123–41, for detail and documentation; L. H. Rhinelander, "Viceroy Vorontsov's Administration of the Caucasus," in Ronald G. Suny, ed., *Transcaucasia: Nationalism and Social Change* (Ann Arbor: University of Michigan Slavic Publications, Department of Slavic Languages and Literatures, 1983).

12. Mil'man (*Politicheskii stroi*, pp. 135–36) cites published laws and archival documents.

13. In 1832 regulations were adopted for the resettlement of Old Believers into Caucasia and within the first five years, 672 Old Believer families were resettled in Karabagh and Shirvan *provintsii* (Mil'man, *Politicheskii stroi*, p. 10). By 1900 there would be thousands.

14. *Svod zakonov rossiiskoi imperii* 1857, vol. 14, chap. 3 concerns Caucasus. I thank Mariana Tax Choldin at the University of Illinois for providing a copy of this chapter.

15. Tadeusz Swietochowski (*Russian Azerbaijan 1905–1920; The Shaping of National Identity in a Muslim Community* [Cambridge, Eng.: Cambridge University Press, 1985], p. 40) describes both Golitsyn and Vorontsov-Dashkov, viceroy from 1905 to 1915.

16. On the issue of the Muslim religious establishment in the Caucasus, see Audrey L. Altstadt, "The Forgotten Factor: The Mullahs of Prerevolutionary Baku," in *Passe Turco-Tatar, Present Sovietique*, ed. C. Lemercier-Quelquejay, G. Veinstein, and S. E. Wimbush (Paris: Louvain, 1986). Other such policies were applied throughout non-Russian territories. See George J. Demko, *The Russian Colonization of Kazakhstan, 1896–1916* (Bloomington: Indiana University Press, 1969); Altstadt, "Nationality Education Policy in the Russian Empire and Soviet Union," *Journal of the Institute of Muslim Minority Affairs* (JIMMA) 10, no. 2 (1989); Z. V. Togan, *Türkili Türkistan*, 2d ed. (Istanbul, 1981); H. B. Paksoy, "Basmaci Movement from Within: Account of Zeki Velidi Togan" (a paper read to the 3d International Central Asian Conference in Madison, Wis., 27–30 April 1988); Isabelle Kreindler, "Ibrahim Altsynsaryn, Nikolai Il'minskii and the Tatar National Awakening," *Central Asian Survey*, vol. 2, no. 3 (1983) on the manipulation of languages as part of education policy and missionary work.

17. Ministry of Finance, *Obzor Vneshnei torgovlii*, 1831–1863 (St. Petersburg: n.p.); these figures are adjusted to compensate for the introduction in 1839 of the ruble *asignats*.

18. "White" in this context probably refers to nontaxed as opposed to taxed ("black") land. Later, two *mahalle* (quarters) were built east of the town center called White Town and Black Town, but this seems to have related to the physical appearance—the latter was black with factory soot; the former was relatively clean.

19. Alexandre Dumas, *Adventures in Caucasia* (Westport, Conn.: Greenwood Press, 1962), p. 154.

20. John McKay, "Entrepreneurship and the Emergence of the Russian Petroleum

Industry, 1813–1881," *Research in Economic History: A Research Annual,* vol. 8, ed. Paul Uselding (Greenwich, Conn.: Jai Press, 1983), pp. 49–51. The tax-farming (monopoly contract) system was called *otkup*. Mirzoev expanded production fivefold between 1863 and 1868, though a decline set in during subsequent years.

21. Ibid.

22. S. Gulishambarov, *Ocherki fabrik i zavodov Bakinskoi gubernii* (Tiflis: n.p., 1890), p. 25.

23. Ibid., pp. 70–71. The largest was owned by Haji Z. A. Taghiyev and produced over 1 million barrels in 1888. The total amount extracted in Baku that year was just over 18 million barrels.

24. Ibid., pp. 113–16. Among the largest refineries, after the huge operations of Nobel, Gukasov, and Rothschild, were those of Shamsi Asadullayev, Musa Naghiyev, and a few others.

25. McKay, "Entrepreneurship," pp. 63–64; Robert W. Tolf, *The Russian Rockefellers: The Saga of the Nobel Family and the Russian Oil Industry* (Stanford: Hoover Institution Press, 1976).

26. In 1866 there were 1,431 workers in Baku according to K. A. Pazhitnov "Entreprenuership," *Ocherki po istorii bakinskoi neftedobyvaiushchei prómyshlennosti* (Moscow-Leningrad, 1940), p. 104, note 2.

27. See McKay, "Entrepreneurship," on Nobel's marketing network, transportation planing, and production and refining strategy.

28. McKay, pp. 77–78, 86.

29. These figures were converted from puds, at 9.5 puds/bbl., from Pazhitnov, *Ocherki po istorii* p. 95; M. Musaev, "Razvitie torgovli goroda Baku v period kapitalizma (1860–1917 gg.)" (unpublished Ph.D. diss., Baku, Academy of Sciences, 1970, p. 50).

30. Pazhitnov, *Ocherki po istorii,* p. 89.

31. *Kaspii,* 30 December 1908.

32. *Kaspii,* 4 May 1908.

33. Essad Bey (Lev Nisinbaum), *Blood and Oil in the Orient,* trans. Elsa Schuster (New York: Simon and Schuster, 1937), p. 1.

34. A. Umaev and A. M. Kasumov, "Rol' bankskogo i rostovshchicheskogo kapitala v ekonomicheskom razvitii dorevoliutsionnogo Azerbaidzhana," in *Materialy po ekonomicheskoi istorii Azerbaidzhana* (Baku: n.p., 1970), pp. 38–46. (Hereafter cited as *Materialy ekon. ist.*)

35. Ministry of Finance, *Ezhegodnik,* vol. 25 (1899), pp. 552–53.

36. *Ist. Az.* 2:234; D. Guseinova, "Razvitie morskogo transporta, formirovanie kadrov rabochikh moriakov Azerbaidzhana i ikh revoliutsionnye (Ph.D. diss., Academy of Sciences, 1975), p. 17. By 1907 most ships had been built in the empire.

37. Among the shipping magnates were some oilmen (Taghiyev, Naghiyev, Manafov, and the Huseinov family); many were involved in oil only secondarily or not at all (the Dadashev brothers, Ashurov, Zeinalov, Buniatov).

38. *Ist. Az.* 2:257, 440; Guseinova, "Razvitie," pp. 21–22.

39. Gulishambarov, *Ocherki fabrik,* p. 99. Although oil companies had their own oil tank cars,, there was a market for rental.

40. Sh. S. Fatullaev, *Gradostroitel'stvo Baku, XIX-nachale XX vekov* (Leningrad: Stroizdat, 1978). He described and provided photos of major buildings in Baku along with street plans. Of the more than forty architects and civil engineers who designed buildings and parks in Azerbaijan, a rough compilation suggests there were twenty-one Russians (four uncertain), seven Turks, two Jews, two Armenians, and nine with European names.

41. M. A. Ismailov, "Gornaia promyshlennost' i mekhanicheskoe proizvodstvo Azerbaidzhana v period kapitalizma," in *Materialy ekon. ist.,* pp. 81–85.

42. On the textile industry, see L. M. Alieva, *Rabochie tekstil'chskhiki* (Baku: Elm, 1969). For a good overview of all industries, see M. A. Ismailov, *Promyshlennost' Baku v nachale XX v.* (Baku, 1976).

42. Gulishambarov (*Ocherki fabrik,* pp. 193, 257) provides names of owners.

44. *Ist. Az.,* 2:159, 171. Madder from the Kuba *uezd,* which increased nearly four times from 1860 to 1868, went from Baku to the Nizhnyi Novgorod fair and an international fair in London in 1862.

45. Richard E. Wright, "On the Origins of Caucasian Village Rugs," *Oriental Rug Review* 10, no. 4 (April/May 1990).

46. *Ist. Az.,* 2:172–74. One pud is 36 pounds.

47. Musaev, "Razvitie torgovli," p. 32, 52. On Baku's trade, see Musaev's two monographs: *XX äsrin ävvälärinä Bakï shähärinin tijareti (1900–1917)* (Baku: Elm, 1974) and *XIX äsrin sonlarinda Bakï shähärinin tijareti (1883–1900)* (Baku: Elm, 1972).

48. Musaev, "Razvitie torgovli," pp. 36–46, on trade between Baku and the Azerbaijan hinterland, and with Russia and Iran in the late nineteenth century.

49. Mil'man (*Politicheskii stroi,* p. 208) said the provision was extended to the Caucasus only in 1878 because the government thought the area "too backward" for urban self-rule. However, the *Entsiklopedicheskii slovar* (vol. 17, N. Brokgauz and I. A. Efron [St. Petersburg: Semenov Typo-Lithograph of I. A. Efron, 1890–1904], p. 326) stated that the reform was phased in throughout the empire gradually and extended to the Caucasus in 1874 after it was applied to the capitals in 1872.

50. For detail on the legal provisions and the working of the Baku City Council in the early twentieth century, see Altstadt, "Baku City Duma: Arena for Elite Conflict," *Central Asian Survey* 5, no. 3/4 (1986).

51. *Entsiklopedicheskii slovar,* 17:327; in a guberniia capital, the Uprava could have three members; in a city with a population over 100,000, it could have four.

52. Ibid., 17:326–28, and 18:429.

53. Mil'man, *Politicheskii stroi,* pp. 238, 248, 264–65.

CHAPTER 3

1. George Bournoutian, "The Ethnic Composition and Socio-Economic Condition of Eastern Armenia in the First Half of the Nineteenth Century, in Ronald G. Suny, ed., *Transcaucasia: Nationalism and Social Change* (Ann Arbor: University of Michigan Slavic Publications, Department of Slavic Languages and Literatures, 1983), pp. 77–79.

2. *Spiski nasel'ennykh mest' rossisskoi imperii*, vol. 65, pt. 1 (Tiflis: Kavkazskii statisticheskii komitet, 1870), pp. 84–85.

3. *Naselenie imperii po perepisi 28-go ianvaria 1897 goda po uezdam* (St. Petersburg: S. P. Iakovlev, 1897) (hereafter cited as *Naselenie imperii*) and *Pervaia vseobshchaia perepis' naseleniia rossisskoi imperii, 1897 g.* (vol. 61, Bakinskaia guberniia: vol. 63, Elizavetpolskaia) (St. Petersburg, 1905) (hereafter cited as *Perepis'*, 1897).

4. *Ist. Az.*, 2:159.

5. *Perepis', Naseleniia gor. Baku, 1913*, vol. 3, pt. 2 (Baku: n.p., 1916) (hereafter cited as *Perepis'*, 1913), p. 87.

6. Next in size were Shusha (in Karabagh) with 25,600, Nukha with 24,800, and Shemakhi at 20,000.

7. Ukrainians, Belorussians, and Poles totaled only 2,400 in Baku in 1897, but thousands more lived throughout the Baku and Elizavetpol gubernii. Many Ukrainians and Poles were in the armed forces; most Belorussians were Old Believers.

8. M. A. Musaev, "Ravitie gor. Baku v period kapitalizma (1860–1917 gg.)" (Ph.D. diss., Academy of Sciences, Baku, 1970) pp. 91–92. Armenians were 19.5 percent of the population and owned 27.2 percent of the trade establishments. Russians were 36 percent of the population and owned 9.4 percent of the trade establishments.

9. Categories for social structure formulated for Russian society did not match society in Caucasia. The *soslovii* (sing: *soslovie*, social groups) included Christian clergy but not their non-Christian counterparts; *meshchane* (townspeople) meant shopkeepers, professionals (doctors, lawyers, journalists), and craftspeople. For Baku the category was used to encompass the numerous bazaar merchants (*bazari*) who bore little resemblance to the European shopkeeper. More than half the Tatar-speaking community was classified as *meshchane*.

10. *Goroda Rossii* (St. Petersburg; Statistical Committee of the Ministry of Internal Affairs, 1904) provided data for 1904 but was not reliable. Much of the data is at variance with the 1903 city census. It recorded 17 Orthodox churches, 2 Roman Catholic, 2 Protestant, 3 Armeno-Gregorian and 1 synagogue, but no mosques, though the contemporary press and materials of the Ecclesiastical Boards (and physical remains) indicate there were four large (cathedral) and several smaller mosques then in Baku.

11. *Perepis' naseleniia gor. Baku, 1903* (Baku, 1905). (Hereafter cited as *Perepis'*, 1903); *Perepis'*, 1913. The introduction explains that only portions of the 1903

census were ever published and that what remained of the raw data was destroyed in the "disturbances" of 1905.

12. The data in the 1903 city census were categorized by place of residence, indicating data for populations of the town proper, outlying districts (*prigorod*), and the oil districts (*promysla*), which had been peasant villages. The combined city and suburban figures are comparable to the 1897 and 1913 censuses.

13. The borders of the mahalle are shown in the 1913 census but not in the 1903 census. Although police districts seem to have been renumbered between 1903 and 1913, it is likely that the mahalle did not change boundaries significantly if at all.

14. These numbers are taken from the 1903 census data on place of birth. In the 1913 census, data on language and nationality allowed a distinction between Iranian Azerbaijanis and Persians. In 1913 there were 5,830 fewer Persian speakers than there were Persian citizens and 5,290 more "Azerbaijani Turkish" language speakers (this label was used in 1913 census) than there were Azerbaijani Turks.

15. *Perepis'*, 1903, vol. 1, pt. 2, pp. 12–13. In the city and suburbs 67,912 individuals were employed, and nearly 80 percent of these were engaged in some industry or trade; 10,048 were in professions and services, nearly 30 percent of which were "police and armed forces."

16. In the microfilm copy of the 1903 census that was available to me, the pages with the Russian and Armenian employees in administration, the judiciary, and banking and commodity trading were missing. Other sources, however, including the 1897 and 1913 census and M. Musaev's monographs on Baku's trade history, show large numbers of Armenians engaged in trade. The 1897 census and the *Kavkazskii Kalendar* for the early twentieth century show a preponderance of Russians in administration and law enforcement.

17. The number of Azerbaijani Turks in education more than doubled from 50 in 1897 to 138 in 1913; in "art, science, literature," it increased form 0 to 49; in the judiciary, from 12 to 55. The influx of Iranian Azerbaijanis appeared with 133 "Persians" in administration, 24 in education, 21 in "art, science, literature," and 122 clerics.

18. As early as the 1820s, shipowners of Baku had 60 ships with a total tonnage of 2,160 tons (*Ist. Az.* 2:20–25). Lists of merchants are found in the Ministry of Foreign Trade publication, *Obzor vneshnei torgovli.*

19. Musaev, "Razvitie torgovli," pp. 96–97; M. A. Musaev, "Milli kapitalïn takamülü," in *Azärbayjan igtisadi tarikhinin aktual problemläri* (Baku: Elm, 1978), pp. 67–70. Taghiyev was one of the few to purchase oil lands in the 1873 auction. They promptly yielded several gushers.

20. Musaev, "Razvitie torgovli," p. 97, and "Milli kapitalïn," pp. 70–71.

21. Musaev, "Razvitie torgovli," p. 97, and "Milli kapitalïn," pp. 71–72.

22. Altstadt, "The Azerbaijani Bourgeoisie and the Cultural-Enlightenment Movement in Baku: First Steps toward Nationalism," in Suny, *Transcaucasia.*

23. The Muslim Charitable Society, founded by Taghiyev, was headquartered in a

building donated by Naghiyev in memory of his son. It now belongs to the Azerbaijan Academy of Sciences.

24. There was a famine in Ganje in 1906, and Taghiyev's wife and the wives and daughters of other prominent Azerbaijani businessmen organized a relief effort (*Baku*, 16 December 1906).

25. For an overview of the press of this era, see Alexandre Bennigsen and Chantal Lemercier-Quelquejay, *La Presse et le Mouvement Nationale Musulman de Russie avant 1920* (Paris: Mouton, 1964).

26. Musaev, "Razvitie torgovli," p. 91.

27. Ibid., pp. 91–92.

28. *Naselenie imperii*, p. 16.

29. *Ist. Az.* 2:180–181.

30. Ibid. Peasants used 1,882,000 *desiatina* (1 desiatina = 2.7 acre); 604,000 desiatina were arable (328,000 required irrigation); 1,121,000 desiatina were pasture or unusable. Nearly half of all peasants had 2 desiatina or less. Without knowing the type of land, the claim cannot be evaluated.

31. Ibid., pp. 182–187.

32. Ibid., p. 184.

33. I. M. Gasanov, "Is istorii krest'ianskogo dvizheniia v Azerbaidzhane v gody pervoi russkoi revoliutsii," in *Azerbaijan v gody pervoi russkoi revoliutsii* (Baku: Elm, 1966), pp. 164, 170.

34. *Ist. Az.* (2:187–88), quoting a report from Lenkoran.

35. According to the 1897 census, 7.25 percent of the population of Baku guberniia (nearly 60,000) and just over 4 percent in the Elizavetpol guberniia (more than 35,000) were day laborers.

36. Different categories are used by different writers. K. A. Pazhitnov (*Ocherki po istorii bakinskoi neftedobyvainshchei promyshlennosti* (Moscow-Leningrad: Gospotekhizdat, 1940) for example, reportedly derived his figures from the 1897 census. That census lacks the "oil worker" category. "Extractive industries" and "chemical production" categories include workers in industries other than oil.

37. Aleksandr Mitrofanovich Stopani was a member of the RSDWP. In 1913 he was assistant head of the Statistical Bureau of the Congress of Oil Industries. His data were republished, with analysis, by A. D. Bok, "Usloviia byta rabochikh-neftianikov g. Baku," in N. K. Drunkhin, ed., *Usloviia byta rabochikh v dorevoliutsionnoi Rossii (po dannim biudzhetnykh obsledovanii)* (Moscow: Sotsekon, 1958).

38. S. S. Aliiarov (Äliyarov), "Trud A. M. Stopani 'Neftepromyshiennyi rabochii i ego biudzhet' kak istochnik," *Uchenye zapiski*, no. 7, Series on History and Philosophy, Azerbaijan State University (1978): 23–29. He noted that Stopani used information sheets about the workers filled out through a system of special registers then being used in the United States. Stopani's findings were released in 1910, but his work was not published until 1916.

39. Stopani's sample included 1,666 "single" and 578 married men.

40. Oil worker wages averaged 429 rubles annually, without bonuses, compared with 276 for the average male worker in Moscow and 375 for metalworkers in the western provinces. In Batum (with a large oil-related work force), unskilled male laborers earned 90 to 150 rubles annually. But oil workers had the highest accident, injury, and death rates. *Goroda Rossii,* p. 253; Bok, "Usloviia," pp. 66, 71. On the accident rate, see Pazhitnov, *Ocherki po istorii,* pp. 100–101.

41. According to Stopani's figures, a cash wage constituted 74 percent of the income of the average workers. Pay for overtime, continuous work, and bonuses added another 10 percent. The remaining 16 percent was in the form of housing or housing allowance, fuel, bath facilities, soap, or allowances for these expenses.

42. Either single workers' expenditures were a higher portion of their more modest incomes or the wives of married men would take care of the clothing, possibly making some of it themselves (sewing machines were listed under household expenditures). Bok, "Usloviia," p. 87.

43. Ibid., pp. 90–91. Only 17 percent of "single" workers spent anything on cultural demands, as opposed to 63 percent of the married workers.

44. Ibid., pp. 89–91.

45. Ibid., p. 73. Bok reported disbursed income for "single workers" as 94 percent (average per worker) and for married workers, 93.4 percent. Then he included an "undisbursed" category. On pp. 92–93, he rearranged the categories so as to produce a deficit in accounts of the "average worker," even though he included a line item called "savings."

46. Aliiarov, "Trud A. M. Stopani." He used Stopani's original data, not simply Bok's synopsis.

47. Eva Broido, *Memoirs of a Revolutionary,* Vera Broido, trans. (London: Oxford University Press, 1967), pp. 68–69, 71.

48. Essad Bey was one pseudonym of Lev Nisinbaum. Born in Baku in 1905, his family fled the Bolsheviks in 1920 and moved to Berlin, then to Vienna and subsequently to Italy, where he died in 1940 after a brief illness. He published more than 12 books between 1926 and his death, including the novel *Ali and Nino* under the pseudonym Kurban Said. (Isfendiyar Vahabzade, *Odlar Yurdu* [August 1989, Latin script edition]).

49. Essad Bey (Lev Nisinbaum), *Blood and Oil in the Orient,* Elsa Schuster, trans. (New York: Simon and Schuster, 1937), p. 23. This book was translated from German; it had been published in Berlin in 1934.

50. Perhaps the word should be *kochu* from *koç,* meaning "ram," but alluding to a sturdy and brave young man.

51. Broido, *Memoirs,* p. 71.

52. According to Isfendiyar Vahabzade, Essad Bey's mother was Azerbaijani. The marriage of a Muslim woman to a Jewish man would have been extremely rare, suggesting perhaps a secular upper-class family. The Nisinbaums reportedly were a wealthy merchant family.

53. The *passazh Tagieva* was a series of shops under one roof and is now a department store in central Baku.

54. The *chaykhana (chay*—tea; *hana/hane*—Persian for house) is an important social institution across Central Asia: to render the word literally as "tea house" conjures up a misleading image of the Far East. In Azerbaijani chaykhanas, like those in Turkey, tea (and coffee) is served in glasses and men (only) may sit for hours and talk, read the newspaper, or play backgammon.

55. Tadeusz Swietochowski, *Russian Azerbaijan, 1905–1920* (Cambridge, Eng.: Cambridge University Press, 1985), p. 41.

56. Newspapers from January to March 1905 were not available at the Historical Archives in Baku, so it is not possible to determine whether the February clashes were connected to the Erevan area fighting.

57. Gasanov, "Iz istorii krest'ianskogo dvizheniia," pp. 171–72.

58. Swietochowski, *Russian Azerbaijan*, p. 41–42.

59. In 1897 Zangezur and Shusha uezdy had nearly equal Armenian and Azerbaijani populations. Major population shifts appear to have taken place after the 1905 fighting and may have influenced demands between 1918 and 1920.

60. *Baku*, 7 September 1905.

61. *Baku*, 8 September 1905.

62. *Baku*, 18 October 1905 (commentary signed "M.S." in Latin letters); 12 November (by commentator Orest Semin); 29 November (report on Social Democrats' meeting against the outbreak of communal violence); 3 December (Social Democrats blame the Pan-Islamism of Muslims and nationalism of Armenians); 14 December (Aleksandr Novikov on the sudden development of class consciousness among the "Tatar proletariat").

62. For example, Gasanov ("Iz istorii krest'ianskogo dvizheniia" p. 189) cited a case of twelve Azerbaijani Turks protecting eighteen Armenians and their property. He also pointed out that the majority of both groups did not engage in violence.

64. *Rabochee dvizhenie v Baku*, docs. 87, 88, pp. 99–102, and Tsentral'nyi Gosudarstvennyi Istoricheskii Arkhiv (Central State Historical Archive, Azerbaijan; hereafter cited as TsGIA Az.), f. 486, op. 1, ed. khr. 23–26, l. 192. (The abbreviations refer to the Archive's internal classification system.)

65. *Baku*, 21 September 1905.

66. Gerard J. Libardian, "Revolution and Liberation in the 1892 and 1907 Programs of the Dashnaktsutun," and Anahide Ter Minassian, "Nationalisme et socialisme dans le mouvement révolutionnaire arménien (1887–1912)," both in Suny, ed., *Transcaucasia*; Louise Nalbandian *Armenian Revolutionary Movement* (Berkeley: University of California Press, 1963).

67. Work of the Peace Committees was detailed in *Baku*, 21 July; 5, 11, 26, 27, 28, 30 August; 4, 6, 7, 8, 11, 13, 14, 16, 18, 21, 22, 23 September; 5, 18 October; 19, 26, 29 November; and 1, 3, 6 December 1905.

68. *Baku*, 15 September 1905.

69. Altstadt, "Muslim Workers and the Labor Movement in Pre-war Baku," in Sabri M. Akural, ed., *Turkic Culture: Continuity and Change*, Indiana University Turkish Studies Series, no. 6 (Bloomington: Indiana University Press, 1987). Testimony given to local authorities is cited using contemporary press, and Swietochowski (*Russian Azerbaijan)* corroborates (p. 41), citing Vorontsov-Dashkov (*Vsepoddanneishaia Zapiski po upravleniiu Kavkazskim Kraem* [St. Petersburg: n.p., 1907], p.n.) and published documents of the Azerbaijan Academy of Sciences.

70. Meshadi Azizbekov (1876–1918) was best known in secondary sources as one of the 26 Baku commissars who formed the Bolshevik committee (so-called Baku Commune) of Baku in 1918.

71. TsGIA Az., f. 486, op. 1, ed. khr. 23–26, ll. 192.

72. Swietochowski, *Russian Azerbaijan*, pp. 40–42.

73. D. B. Seidzade, *Iz istorii Azerbaidzhanskoi burzhuazii* (Baku, 1978); Ronald G. Suny, *Baku Commune* (Princeton: Princeton University Press, 1972). Even Swietochowski (*Russian Azerbaijan*, p. 39) refers to Armenians posing "ruinous competition." On Seidzade's misuse of data, see Altstadt, "Critical Essay-Review of D. B. Seidzade's *Iz istorii Azerbaidzhanskoi burzhuazii*," *Kritikia*, no. 4 (1984) (Publication of the Harvard U. History Department).

74. *Ist. Az.* 2:193–95; Gasanov, "Iz istorii krest'ianskogo dvizheniia."

75. From *gachmag (kaçmak)*, "to run."

76. On the gachags and Nabi in particular, see *Ist. Az.* 2:196–99; Gasanov, "Iz istorii krest'ianskogo dvizheniia," pp. 176–77, 192–99.

77. The following is a summary of *Ist. Az.* chap. 14, vol. 2 by I. Ibrahimov; Gasanov, "Iz istorii krest'ianskogo dvizheniia."

78. Gasanov, "Iz istorii krest'ianskogo dvizheniia" pp. 173–76. Official Soviet guidelines required that the peasant movement be treated as "class warfare" or "anticolonial." National clashes are traced solely to diversionary instigation by officials, certainly an important part of the story, but without acknowledging causes for antagonism. Evidence itself suggests that the main thrust of peasant action was anti-colonial, not class warfare.

79. Gasanov ("Iz istorii krest'ianskogo dvizheniia," pp. 177–78) describes the Burjalar movement, citing Ragim Guseinov, *Ocherki revoliutsionnogo dvizheniia v Azerbaidzhane* (Baku: Elm, 1926) and documents in the Georgian SSR historical archive.

80. Gasanov, "Iz istorii krest'ianskogo dvizheniia," p. 193, citing TsGIA Georgian SSR, f. 13, op. 15, d. 178, l. 44.

81. Ibid., pp. 182–83; on the use of the army, pp. 183, 189–91.

82. Suny's *Baku Commune* provides a detailed and thorough examination of the labor movement in Baku, focusing on Russian and Armenian workers and their political organizations.

83. This agreement established the nine-hour work day, abolished systematic daily overtime, set the length of work shifts, established a wage schedule and settled various other issues of contention between labor and management. Subsequent strikes pre-

sented demands for the observance of these terms. The agreement is in *Rabochee dvizhenie v Baku* doc. 30, pp. 34–36.

84. *Baku*, 6 September 1905.

85. *Baku*, 14 September 1905. The Technical Society proposed resettlement of workers and urged the police to close all gathering places such as the *kebabkhanas* (kebab restaurants), *chaykhanas*, and bars; it urged the state to grant workers the right to organize and strike "as in Europe" and called for the reorganization of the police.

86. This viewpoint was reflected in *Neftianoe delo*, the newspaper of the Congress of Oil Industrialists, and in various documents in *Rabochee dvizhenie v Baku*.

87. *Rabochee dvizhenie v Baku*, doc. 85, pp. 95–96, a letter from the Congress to the Ministry of Lands and State Properties.

88. The press discussed whether to participate and what guarantees they would require. Ronald Suny, "A Journeyman for the Revolution: Stalin and the Labor Movement in Baku, June 1907–May 1908," *Soviet Studies*, no. 3 (1971): 384.

89. Ibid., p. 388.

90. In the 1950s, Soviet Azerbaijani scholars worked on this cross-border connection in the prewar period. Professor Nariman Hasanov published a book (*Täbriz Üsiyanï* [Baku: Elm, 1989]) on the Tabriz rebellion (1909–1910) in 1989.

91. TsGIA Az., f. 509, op. 1, ed. khr. 268, ll. 1–6.

92. The full list was published in the newspaper *Baku* on 30 July 1913 and in A. N. Guliev, *Bakinskii proletariat v gody novogo revoliutsionnogo pod'ema* (Baku: Azerneshr, 1963), pp. 100–101.

93. Regulations published in John Mitzakis, *A Handbook of the Russian Oil Industry* (London: Allen and Unwin, 1913), pp. 95–96, discussed precautions against fire and established a schedule of fines mostly equivalent to wages for one or two days.

94. Leopold Haimson, "Social Stability in Urban Russia, 1905–1917," *Slavic Review* 23, no. 2 (December 1964), and 24, no. 1 (March 1965).

95. Three days after the beginning of the general strike on 25 July 1913, the oil industrialists offered salary increases from 10 to 20 percent, the setting of a minimum wage, and restructuring of the bonus system. Guliev, *Bakinskii proletariat*, pp. 98–105, 107.

96. Ibid., pp. 104, 107–8.

97. In a meeting of 31 July 1913, Baku's *gradonachal'nik* Martynov forbade the industrialists to carry on talks with workers or any representatives that were not from their own firms. He also forbade them to discuss or accept noneconomic demands or to agree to pay directly or indirectly for the days of the strike. He suggested that owners make noon on 1 August the deadline for all workers to be back on the job. Guliev, *Bakinskii proletariat*, pp. 108–9.

98. Ibid., pp. 104, 107–8, citing a letter of 31 July from the minister of trade and industry to the president of the Council of Ministers in St. Petersburg.

99. *Rabochee dvizhenie v Baku*, doc. 13, pp. 16–18.

100. *Rabochee dvizhenie v Baku*, doc. 145, pp. 154–55.

101. *Rabochee dvizhenie v Baku*, doc. 398, pp. 372–3; doc. 401, p. 374.

102. Guliev, *Bakinskii proletariat*, p. 105; TsGIA Az. f. 509 (Factory Inspector Reports), op. 1, ed. khr. 268, ll. 1–6.

103. There was apparently a confrontation (widely believed to be historically accurate) after the revolutions of 1917 between Nariman Narimanov (M.D., later chairman of the Sovnarkom of the new Azerbaijan SSR) and Taghiyev, who had provided the stipends that allowed Narimanov to attend medical school. Taghiyev said Narimanov was ungrateful. Narimano replied, "Because you paid for our educations, do you think it means you bought our thoughts as well?"

104. Lenin's correspondence with Armenian Bolshevik Stepan Shaumian provided insights into Shaumian's perceptions and Lenin's concerns. The correspondence is disucssed in Suny, *Baku Commune*, pp. 48–59.

105. Suny's term was *Journeyman*.

106. E. H. Carr, *The Bolshevik Revolution 1917–1923*, vol. 1 (New York and London: W. W. Norton, 1985), p. 30.

107. For a brief description of the origins of Hümmet, see Altstadt, "The Azerbaijani Turkish Community of Baku." Swietochowski has described the Hümmet in detail in his *Russian Azerbaijan*.

108. On the early days of Adalet in Baku, see Sadulla S. Aslani, "Obrazovanie Iranskoi partii 'Edzhtimaiiun-e Amiiun (Mudzhakhid)'" Ph.D. diss., Azerbaijan State University, 1975), pp. 9–10.

109. *Rabochee dvizhenie v Baku*, doc. 389, pp. 366–67.

110. *Rabochee dvizhenie v Baku*, doc. 393, pp. 369, and doc. 398, pp. 372–73.

111. *Rabochee dvizhenie v Baku* doc. 396, p. 371; doc. 421, pp. 388–92; doc. 555, p. 491; and doc. 559, pp. 494–96.

112. TsGIA Az., f. 486, 11. 122, 187, 192; and f. 46 (Baku *guberniia* Gendarme Admin.), op. 3, ed. khr. 231–3, various listovki. See *Ist. Az.* 2:721–75 for an overview.

113. TsGIA Az., f. 486, op. 1, ed. khr. 23, l. 49.

114. Ibid., ll. 85, 101.

115. Ibid., ll. 134, 167, 169.

116. Ibid, ed. khr. 24, ll. 187, 190.

117. Aliiarov, "Internatsional'nyi sostav i edinstvo proletariata Azerbaidzhana (kanun i period pervoi mirovoi voiny)" in *Uchenye Zapiski*, Series in History and Philosophy, Azerbaijan State University, no. 6, p. 110.

118. TsGIA Az., f. 486, op. 1, ed. khr. 23–26, ll, 192.

119. Ibid., ll. 198, 203.

120. TsGIA Az., f. 486, op. 3, ed. khr. 231, l. 201, op. 1, ed. khr., 26, ll. 177 (for 26 June 1914) and 184 (for 27 June 1914).

121. A tobacco concession to an Englishman evoked public anger at foreign control over a product of consumption. The ulema declared a religious ban on tobacco that

eventually forced the shah to rescind the concession. See Nikki Keddie, *Religion and Rebellion in Iran: The Tobacco Protest of 1891–92* (London: Frank Cass, 1966).

CHAPTER 4

1. Kazembek, a native of Derbend and a convert to Christianity, worked with Orientalists B. Dorn and Mirza Jafar Topchibashi (an Azerbaijani Turk at St. Petersburg University) on a Persian-Arabic-Turkish-Russian dictionary. *Istoriia Azerbaidzhana/Azärbayjan Tarikhi* (Baku: 1958–1963) (hereafter *Ist. Az.*) 2:101–12, 116–19.

2. All books published in Azerbaijan (or published in Caucasia concerning Azerbaijan) are listed in *Azärbayjan kitabï (Bibliyografiya)*, vol. 1, 1780–1920 (Baku, 1963). Other volumes, though three were planned, do not appear to have been issued.

3. On Akhundzade, see *Ist. Az.* 2:122–29, 363–69; *Encyclopedia of Islam*, 1st ed., 2:83; *Islam Ansiklopedesi* (Istanbul: Maarif, 1940–1960), 4:577–81.

4. The verb *ekmek* means to sow seed. *Ekinji* has been reprinted in book form in Cyrillic orthography with a brief introduction on Zardabi. *Äkinji, 1875–1877 (Tam mätni)* (Baku, 1979).

5. *Ziya (Light)* was published 1879–1881, *Ziya-i Kafkasiyye*, 1881–1884, and *Kashkül (Dervish Bowl)*, 1884–1891. Tadeusz Swietochowski, *Russian Azerbaijan, 1905–1920* (Cambridge, Eng.: Cambridge University Press, 1985), p. 29. He notes that these three publications used a language more like Ottoman and less like the spoken vernacular which had been the hallmark of *Ekinji*.

6. Alexandre Bennigsen and Chantal Lemercier-Quelquejay, *La Presse et le Mouvement Nationale Musulman de Russie avant 1920* (Paris: Mouton, 1964). The chapter on Azerbaijan was written in collaboration with Jeyhun Hajibeyli who was living in Paris at the time this book was written.

7. Soviet Azerbaijanis have lionized this journal and its editor. Gulam Mämmädli (*Molla Näsreddin* [Baku, 1984]) reported on worldwide translations of journal items; also see H. B. Paksoy, "Elements of Humor in Central Asia: The Example of the Journal *Molla Nasreddin* in Azerbaijan," *Turkestan; als historrischer Faktor und politische Idee*, ed. Erling von Mende (Cologne: Studienverlag, 1988).

8. *Kaspii*, 7 February, 19 March, 30 October, 1908; various editions in 1910.

9. The phrase was Jeyhun Hajibeyli's, used in his later accounts of his brother's work.

10. In *Arshin*, staged in French translation by Jeyhun, a young man pretends to be a cloth merchant so he can get a look at single girls; *Meshtibad* is a classical story of a young couple whose plans for marriage are disrupted by the girl's father's plan to marry her to a fat, ugly, middle-aged merchant. The Hajibeylis added twists to the plot by making the merchant, Meshtibad, a religious conservative and by substituting

the young man for the young girl in the wedding ceremony. The lyrical arias are well known.

11. Shöket Hanim Memedova recounted the incident in a film interview on Uzeir Hajibeyli's life.

12. *Baku*, 18 November 1906; *Kaspii*, 9 January and 28 May 1909.

13. Bakikhanli's "Project for the Establishment of a Muslim School" was presented to High Commissioner of Caucasia Baron Rosen on 20 February 1832. It is reproduced by the Azerbaijan Academy of Sciences in *Abbaskuluaga Bakikhanov* (Baku: Elm, 1983), pp. 251–54.

14. *Kavkazskii kalendar*, 1910, pp. 234–36.

15. *Baku*, 7 August 1906, 13 January 1907.

16. *Baku*, 12 September 1906; *Kaspii*, 9 October and 17 December 1908.

17. *Kaspii*, 5 September, 4 November 1908; 28, 29 August, 1, 3 September 1909.

18. *Baku*, 13 January 1907; *Kaspii*, 23 September and 7 October 1909.

19. *Kaspii*, 24 May 1908; 18, 25 July, 1 August 1910; 3, 30 May 1913.

20. *Kaspii*, 17 December 1908. The issue is well documented in Azade-Ayşe Rorlich, *Volga Tatars: Profile in National Resilience* (Stanford: Hoover Institution Press, 1986).

21. On adult education, see *Kaspii*, 9 August, 8 September, and 5 November 1909; N. Tairzade, "Vechernie kursy prosvetitel'nogo abshchestva 'Nijat' (1908–1914)," *Izvestiia*, Series on History, Philosophy and Law, Academy of Sciences of Azerbaijan, 1976, no. 1. Participation in other charitable work is also discussed in *Kaspii*, 5 November, 16 December 1908; 1 July 1909; and 3 June 1913; and *Baku*, 24 February 1907. See also Altstadt, "The Azerbaijani Bourgeoisie and the Cultural-Enlightenment Movement in Baku: First Steps Toward Nationalism," in Ronald Grigor Suny, *Transcaucasia: Nationalism and Social Change* (Ann Arbor: University of Michigan, 1983).

22. *Kaspii*, 19 September, 18 November 1908; 9 August, 12 December 1909.

23. *Kaspii*, 18 September, 18 November 1908; 1 July, 8 September, 5 November 1909 listed teachers in the evening courses.

24. *Kaspii*, 30 May 1908.

25. *Kaspii*, 21 October 1908.

26. A reading room was opened by Narimanov with his own money and carried journals and newspapers from countries in the Middle East and Asia. Sh. A. Taghiyeva, "Näriman Närimanovun 1905–1911–ji illär Iran ingilabï ilä älagädär fäaliyyäti hagginda," *Izvestiia*, Series on History, Philosophy and Law, Academy of Sciences of Azerbaijan, no. 3, 1973, pp. 38–50; M. A. Kaziev, *Nariman Narimanov (Zhizn' i deiatel'nost')* (Baku: 1970), p. 12.

27. Most Sunnis apparently lived near Daghestan. According to the imperial Survey of Settled Places of 1870, there were no Sunni Muslims at all in the Baku uezd. As late as the 1900s, despite immigration from Daghestan and the Volga, Baku had no Sunni schools.

28. Tsentral'nyi Gosudarstvennyi Istoricheskii Arkhiv (Central State Historical Archive), Azerbaijan (hereafter cited as TsGIA Az), f. 291 (Sunni Ecclesiastical Admin.), op. 11, ed. khr. 51, ll. 83–84. (Abbreviations refer to internal categories of the archive.)

29. Ibid., ll. 49–82 provide regulations and jursidiciton of religious classes.

30. TsGIA Az, f. 290 (Shi'i Ecclesiastical Board), op. 14, ed. khr. 9165, l. 128; and op. 16, ed. khr. 10460, ll. 123–4.

31. I have had access only to materials in the Azerbaijan Historical Archive from the early twentieth century. Secondary sources do not provide the necessary detail to state confidently when these regulations were enacted. Because the state had experience with the Orenburg Board, it is likely that the Caucasian Boards were well developed at their creation.

32. The "modernization" of *mekteps* often meant reintroducing subjects that had been taught in earlier centuries, including mathematics and geography. As in secular education, reformers faced inadequate facilities, textbooks, and qualified teachers. The *jadid* method is associated with these reforms and phonetic reading.

33. *Ist. Az.* (2:318–19) stated that literary circles developed in these schools. This information is not the sort usually found in this work, which upholds the standard Soviet interpretation of "backward" religious education.

34. Ibid.

35. The Shi'i ulema were trained in Iran or Shi'i centers of Ottoman Iraq. The Sunni ulema, who ministered to pockets of Sunni living near the mountains and in western zones, might be trained in the Ottoman Empire or in Bukhara which, although it was a Russian protectorate, was always referred to as a foreign state. Even religious books from Bukhara were governed by the same censorship provisions as those coming from the Ottoman Empire.

36. TsGIA Az., f. 290, op. 14, ed. khr. 9165, l. 127.

37. The 1910 data are from TsGIA Az., f. 291, op. 11, ed. khr. 51, ll. 49–82.

38. Figures on income and expenditures of these mosques are given in Altstadt, "The Azerbaijani Turkish Community of Baku before World War I" (Ph.D. dissertation, University of Chicago, 1983), pp. 225–27.

39. TsGIA Az., f. 290, op. 21, ed. khr. 14024, ll. 33–35.

40. Many mullahs taught privately or in mekteps or *medreses*. Wages in those institutions were not recorded in available archives.

41. TsGIA Az., f. 291, op. 11, ed. khr. 51, ll. 83–4.

42. Noted in the proceedings of the first two congresses.

43. Narimanov referred to his own translation of the RSDWP party program (not stated whether for Azerbaijan or for Iran) in which he omitted the item on the separation of church from state and of schools from the church. Described in S. S. Aslani, "Obrazovanie Iranskoi partii 'Edzhtimaiiun-e Amiiun (Mudzhadkhid),'" (Ph.D. dissertation, Baku, Azerbaijan State University, 1975), p. 18.

44. The leaflet entitled "What Does the Worker Need?" was dated Hijra 1324.

45. *Baku*, 7 October 1908. *Baku* noted this support; the mullahs were, after all, outnumbered.

46. *Kaspii*, 5, 10, 15 January 1908.

47. *Kaspii*, 8 January 1908.

48. A few years later, a similar conflict developed over the replacement of the mufti of Orenburg. That dispute seemed to center around the appointee himself rather than the selection process; A. Arsharuni and Kh. Gabdullin, *Ocherki panislamizma i pantiurkizma v Rossii* (Moscow: Bezbozhnik, 1931), p. 22.

49. *Kaspii*, 29 May 1908; the proposal mentioned here was for additions to the Russian Orthodox and Armenian Gregorian churches, which the Muslim representatives supported.

50. *Baku*, 3 August 1905.

51. *Kaspii*, 6 June 1908.

52. *Kavkazskii kalendar*, 1910, pp. 231–234.

53. *Kaspii*, 14 March, 20 March, 29 March, 2 May 1913. The new mayor, L. L. Bych', suggested forming committees to handle the work load.

54. Akhundzade, the "father of Azerbaijani theater," stated that "the purpose of the dramatic art is to improve people's morals and to teach." Akhundov, *Äsärläri* 2:223, cited in Swietochowski, *Russian Azerbaijan*, p. 27.

55. The name of the group apparently came from a newspaper it published from fall 1904 to early 1905.

56. Soviet sources (*Ist. Az.*, Sh. A. Taghiyev, S. Sh. Aslani, and others) as well as one of the group's founders, Bolshevik Sultan Mejid Efendiyev, contend that the Hümmet was founded in 1904 "with the active participation" of members of the Baku Committee, Japaridze, Stopani, Fonshtein, and Efendiyev himself. Western scholars including Bennigsen and Lemercier-Quelquejay (*Islam*); Edward J. Lazzerini ("Hümmet," MERSH 14:55–57), and Swietochowski argue that the Hümmet was formed in 1903 as a study circle by Azerbaijani intellectuals, some of whom had had experience in the RSDWP. The group was accepted into the social democratic movement in Baku in 1904, a year after its formation.

57. *Rabochee dvizhenie v Baku v gody pervoi russkoi revoliutsii: Dokumenty i materially* (Baku: Academy of Sciences, 1962).

58. Only the last two points on a popular militia and redistribution of land were not part of the reformist petitions being written throughout the empire, including Caucasia, in 1905. Their inclusion does demonstrate the widespread popularity of socialist demands and can be found in the literature of people not associated with the Hümmet. Cited in E. Bor-Ramenskii, "Iranskaia revoliutsiia 1905–1911 gg. i bol'sheviki Zakavkaz'ia," *Krasnyi Arkhiv*, no. 5 (1941), pp. 51–52.

59. M. A. Kaziev, *Meshadi Azizbekov (Zhizn i deiatel'nost)* (Baku, 1976), p. 44.

60. Their first newspaper was *Hümmet* in 1904. *Täkamül* was published in 1906–07, edited by Mehti Hajinskii, who also wrote for *Kaspii*.

61. Firuddin Köcherli, *Marksizm-Leninizm vä Azärbayjanda demokratic ijtimai fikir* (Baku, 1976), pp. 23–24, 52.

62. Ibid., p. 49.

63. Topchibashi wrote that people had "fallen asleep" to their own history and had "fallen into a bewitched land of darkness." B. Seidzade, *Iz istorii Azerbaidzhanskoi bruzhuazii* (Baku: Elm, 1978), pp. 46–47, citing *Kaspii*, 1 and 23 January 1905.

64. Seidzade, *Azerb*, pp. 49–50, citing *Kaspii*, 20 February and 5 March 1905.

65. *Kutadgu Bilig*, the Orkhon-Yenisei inscriptions. This tradition is mentioned in the discussion of Bakikhanli and in Altstadt, "Rewriting of Central Asian History in the Gorbachev Era," *Journal of Soviet Nationalities* (forthcoming).

66. This and many such commentaries appeared in *Irshad* (in 1907) under the pseudonym Filankes, meaning "Someone." The series was called "Ordan burdan," meaning "From here and there." These essays were published in a small book: Uzeir Hajibäyov, *Ordan Burdan*, comp. Mirabbas Aslanov (Baku: Yaziji, 1981); quotation, pp. 37–38.

67. The movement employed only legal means. At the second congress (January 1906), Ittifaq became a political party and agreed to unite with the Kadets for elections to the State Duma. The Azerbaijanis began to withdraw from the all-Russian Muslim movement and focus on local issues. Topchibashi was one of the few Azerbaijani Turks who continued to maintain close ties to the all-Russian movement. At the third Congress (August 1906), Topchibashi was chairman of the Presidium; ten of its fourteen members were from the Ural-Volga region. The final estrangement between the two groups would come at the Muslim congresses in 1917–18. A fine and detailed account of all congresses can be found in Rorlich, *Volga Tatars*, chap. 9.

68. These are the terms used for the 1897 imperial census. The city censuses for Baku do not use Azerbaijani Turk until 1913.

69. The "Turkish Revolutionary Committee of Social Federalists" reportedly existed in February 1905. Its legacy was limited to this slogan, later used by *Gayret* (Perseverance) in Ganje and by Social Democrats.

70. The following account is based on Naki Keykurun [Sheyhzamanli], *Azerbaycan istiklal mücadelesinin hatıraları* (Istanbul: Azerbaycan Gençlik Derneği, 1964) except where otherwise noted.

71. Swietochowski, *Russian Azerbaijan*, pp. 44–45, cites Keykurun, *Azerbaycan istiklal* and adds Ismail Ziyatkhanov and Shafi Rustambekov.

72. Swietochowski, *Russian Azerbaijan*, p. 44.

73. Keykurun, *Azerbaycan istiklal*, notes their activities ceased, but does not say why. This was the time of the antirevolutionary crackdown and greater vigilance on the part of the viceroy, which may explain it.

74. Yusufbeyli (Ussubekov) would later become prime minister of the independent Azerbaijan republic (April–June 1919, December 1919–March 1920) and proved

especially wary of plans to compromise with the Bolsheviks. He would be assassinated by them in 1921.

75. The National Committee's greatest effort, Keykurun reported, was assisting fugitives from the Russian Administration. The Committee maintained a Ganje Youth Organization and its head was Keykurun himself. Keykurun, *Azerbaycan istiklal*, pp. 23, 28–29.

76. Ibid., pp. 73–74; no date for the meeting was given.

77. Names and speeches are found in the stenographic accounts of the Dumas. After the change in election laws in 1907, Muslim representation was radically reduced. Only Aliakper Khasmemetli represented the region in the Third Duma. Swietochowski, *Russian Azerbaijan*, p. 51.

78. Topchibashi attempted to organize the Muslim fraction, as he would later in 1914. In 1906 he signed the Vyborg Manifesto.

79. The restoration of the 1876 "Midhat" Constitution was the result of the Young Turk coup of summer 1908.

80. Aghayev (*Kaspii*, 5, 18, 19 September 1909) reported that the Ottoman sheikh ul-Islam was one religious leader who made this argument.

81. For example, *Kutadgu Bilig* had been translated twice before World War I by Vambery partially into German in Innsbruck, 1870, and by Radloff into German in Petersburg, 1910. Various manuscripts were known at that time. One located in Cairo was "found" in 1896 by German scholar Moritz (discussed in the introduction to the modern Turkish translation of *Kutadgu Bilig* by Resid Rahmeti Arat [Ankara, 1974] and by Dankoff in his English translation).

82. *Kaspii*, 5 September 1909.

83. "Evidence" supporting claims of his "Pan-Islamic" posture often consists of references (without quotations or details) and allusions taken out of context, as in Seidzade, *Azerb. burzhuazii* (see Altstadt, "Critical Essay-Review of D. B. Seidzade's *Iz istorii Azerbaidzhanskoi burzhuazii*," *Kritika*, no. 4 [1984]). Swietochowski, *Russian Azerbaijan*, p. 34–36, described what he called the "pro-Persian and anti-Ottoman" writings of Aghayev's student days, but then also called him a Pan-Islamicist. These passages represent at least a too-casual use of Pan-Islamic.

84. Pan-Islamism was a doctrine of political unity and anti-colonial action. The leading light of the movement was Jamal al-Din al-Afghani; see Nikki Keddie, *Sayyid Jamal al-Din al-Afghani; A Political Biography* (Berkeley, 1972); Nikki Keddie "The Pan-Islamic Appeal: Afghani and Abdulhamid II," *Middle East Studies* 3 (October 1966), Niyazi Berkes, *The Development of Secularism in Turkey* (Montreal: McGill Press, 1964); Bernard Lewis, *Emergence of Modern Turkey*, 2d ed. (Oxford, Eng.: Oxford University Press, 1976).

85. *Baku*, 28 July 1905.

86. Köcherli, *Marksizm-Leninizm*, p. 52.

87. *Baku*, 8 December 1905, 17 September 1906.

88. In other letters, Aghayev described "The National Question in Turkey" and Turkish reformers committed to the idea of liberty, "united against despotism without

distinction of faith or nationality, status or class"; *Kaspii*, 21 and 22 July 1909; 28 July, 12 August 1909 (on national relations).

89. Hüseinzade employed Ahmet Kemal and Abdulla Cevdet who had come with him from Turkey at *Füyuzat* (another Taghiyev-owned newspaper).

90. "Turan" antedated a poem of the same name by Ziya Gökalp, the "Father of Turkism of the Ottoman Empire." Gökalp acknowledged his intellectual debt to Hüseinzade.

91. Arminius Vambery, *Travels in Central Asia* (London, 1865).

92. Mim Kemal Öke, "Prof. Arminius Vambery and Anglo-Ottoman Relations 1889–1907," in *Turkish Studies Association Bulletin*, vol. 9, no. 2 (1985), makes use of British FCO documents.

93. Sir Denison Ross, *Manual on Turanians and Pan-Turanianism* (British Admiralty: Naval Staff Intelligence Dept., 1918). The author adapted this work from Arminius Vambery's *Türkenvolk* (Leipzig, 1885). Sir Denison told this to Bashkurt leader Zeki Velidi Togan, who recorded it in his *Bugünkü Türk Ili Türkistan ve Yakin Tarihi*, 2d ed. (Istanbul, 1981).

94. Mandal'shtam wrote the introduction and Kerensky published an incendiary anti-Turkish work by an Armenian couple named Nalbandian, writing under the pseudonym Zarevand, called *Turtsiia i panturanizm* (Paris, 1930).

95. After 1920 émigrés fled the Red Army conquests and took refuge in Europe or Turkey. Some saw Pan-Turkism as a possible means to drive the Russians from their homeland. The Turkish republican government, however, regarded such political movements as anathema and treated the ideas as extremist and their proponents as dangerous. Most were jailed.

96. Quoted in Swietochowski, *Russian Azerbaijan*, p. 32.

97. Iranian Azerbaijan had been the province ruled by the heir apparent to the throne and occupied something of a privileged position. Southern Azerbaijani Turks had played a leading role in the Iranian Constitutional Movement. Finally, until the brutal "Persianization" policies of the Pahlavi dynasty (from the 1920s), Azerbaijan's Turkish language culture had not been threatened as it had in the North under Russian rule. Many ruling Iranian dynasties, such as the Safavids and, some would say, also the Pahlavis, had in fact been Turks.

98. *Kaspii*, 20 April 1913.

99. *Trudy* ("Works") of the first All-Union Conference of Historian-Marxists (December 1928–January 1929), vol. 1 (Moscow, 1930). The discussion on the Musavat, pp. 501–20, here citing the main speaker on this topic, IA. Ratgauzer, pp. 501–8.

100. Ibid., pp. 509–12; speaker was S. Sef (whose name, ironically, means "mistake" in Azerbaijani Turkish), the main opponent of Ratgauzer's position.

CHAPTER 5

1. Tadeusz Swietochowski, *Russian Azerbaijan, 1905–20* (Cambridge, Eng.: Cambridge University Press, 1985), p. 76, citing Ronald G. Suny, *Baku Commune* (Princeton: Princeton University Press, 1972), p. 19, and Serge Zenkovsky, *Pan-*

Turkism and Islam in Russia (Cambridge, Mass.: Harvard University Press, 1960), p. 124; Suny, too, cites Zenkovsky. Taghiyev supported building a war hospital, and some accounts say he offered volunteer units to fight at the German front; Naki Keykurun, *Azerbaycan Istiklal mücadelesinin hatıraları* (Istanbul: Azerbaycan Gençlik Dernegi, 1964), suggested that no volunteers were accepted until 1916.

2. S. S. Aliiarov, "Izmeneniia v sostav rabochikh Baku v gody pervoi mirovoi voiny," *Istorii SSSR*, no. 2 (1969), pp. 51, 53, 54.

3. Suny, *Commune*, pp. 58–59, 62–4, citing Shaumian's collected works; on strikes, V. V. Pokshishevskii, *Polozhenie bakinskogo proletariata nakanune revoliutsii (1914–1917 gg)* (Baku, 1927).

4. Aliiarov ("Iz istorii gosudarstvenno-monopolisticheskogo kapitalizma v Rossii: Osoboe soveshchanie po toplivu i neftianye monopolii," *Istoriia SSSR*, no. 6 [1977], p. 54), noted that this led to a rise in oil company stock values. The discussion below is drawn from this article. Much of Dr. Aliyarov's information is based on *Neftianoe delo (ND)*, the newspaper of the Congress of Oil Industrialists, *Obzor bakinskoi neftianoi promyshlennosti* for 1915 and on historical archives in Azerbaijan and Moscow.

5. Aliiarov ("Iz istorii," p. 55) noted that the committee, "the first state organ of regulation of its kind," was made up mostly of representatives of ministries: fourteen from Communication, three from Internal Affairs, and three from Finance; one each from Trade and Industry and Lands, and several others as well as representatives of industries (*ND*, 1915, no. 7). The Nobels were absent, he suggests, because of a rumor that there was too much German influence in their company.

6. Aliiarov, "Iz istorii," p. 55, citing again *ND*, 1915, no. 7.

7. The oilmen at the first of three meetings included major exporters Nobel, Gukasov, Lianozov, and others.

8. Aliiarov, "Iz istorii," pp. 57–59; more committees were created in August 1915, including a Special Commission on Fuel, *Osobyi Soveshchanie po toplivu (Osotop)*, directed by the Ministry of Trade and Industry.

9. Aliiarov, "Iz istorii," p. 55, citing *ND*, no. 9 (1915). Later *ND* announced that this rate applied only to shipping and that railroad, city, and private companies were excluded from the agreement. Other oil companies then agreed to provide Volga customers at 38 k/pud.

10. Suny, *Commune*, p. 62, citing Pokshishevskii, *Polozhenie*.

11. Ibid., pp. 64–66, and S. E. Sef, *Bor'ba za oktiabr' v Zakavkaz'i* (Tiflis, 1932).

12. Swietochowski, *Russian Azerbaijan*, p. 83, citing *Kaspii*, 1917, no. 7, stated the Baku press criticized the 1916 Central Asian uprising against conscription.

13. On factors affecting this decision by the Ottoman government see Stanford Shaw and E. K. Shaw, *The History of the Ottoman Empire and Modern Turkey*, vol. 2 (Cambridge, Eng.: Cambridge University Press, 1977) pp. 310–13; A. B. Kadishev (*Interventsiia i grazhdanskaia voina v Zakavkaz'e* [Moscow: Min. Oborona, 1960], p. 41) noted the Ottoman forces acted on the Caucasus front within "the general strategic plan of the Germans."

14. This is discussed in Swietochowski, *Russian Azerbaijan*, pp. 80–81. Enver

Pasha was one of the ruling triumvirate of the Committee for Union and Progress that took power in Istanbul in 1908. See Shaw and Shaw, *History of the Ottoman Empire*, vol. 2, pp. 311–14.

15. Shaw and Shaw, *History of the Ottoman Empire*, pp. 313–15; Swietochowski, *Russian Azerbaijan*, pp. 76–78.

16. Shaw and Shaw, *History of the Ottoman Empire*, p. 316. The question of the extremely heavy civilian casualties suffered by Armenian populations in connection with the deportation and other wartime actions and by the Turkish population during the war has been the object of much anguished rhetoric by members of both nationalities and by scholars. The works of Richard Hovanisian, Christopher Walker, David Lange, and many others represent well the Armenian side. Few extant works in English present Turkish views or arguments.

17. A. P. Steklov, *Revoliutsionnaia deiatel'nost' bol'shevistskikh organizatsii na kavkazskom fronte, 1914–1917 gg* (Tbilisi: Sabchota Sakartvelo, 1969), p. 14.

18. Swietochowski, *Russian Azerbaijan*, pp. 79–80, using W. E. D. Allen and D. Muratoff, *Caucasian Battlefields* (Cambridge, Eng.: Cambridge University Press, 1953); W. Bihl, *Die Kaukasuspolitik der Mittelmächte* (Vienna, 1975), and G. Jäschke, "Der Turanismus der Jungtürken," *Welt des Islams* 32, nos. 1–2 (1941).

19. Quoted in Swietochowski, *Russian Azerbaijan*, p. 81, from *National Question in the Russian Duma* (London, 1915).

20. D. (Mirza Davud?) Huseinov, "Ideia nezavisimosti Azerbaidzhana i partiia mussavat; I. Do fevral'skoi revoliutsii," *Zarya Vostoka* (hereafter *ZV*), 28 April 1925.

21. Ibid., citing *Achik söz*, 9 October.

22. Ibid.

23. The following account is extracted from N. Keykurun, *Azerbaycan Istiklal Mücadelesinin Hatıraları* (Istanbul: Azerbaycan Gençlik Derneği, 1964), pp. 24–28.

24. Swietochowski, *Russian Azerbaijan*, pp. 114–16; Suny (*Commune*, p. 216, fn. 5), cited Sef saying that officers were Russian "like in most Muslim divisions" and sided with the Muslims over the Soviets. Names of officers like Talyshkhanov are clearly Turkish names with Russian endings. Swietochowski (p. 113) also suggested officers were "Muslims" and noted that in fall 1917, "training native officers began in the cadet school in Baku."

25. Detailed English-language works on this period have been published. Each makes a valuable contribution, but each excludes certain issues. Richard Pipes, *Formation of the Soviet Union, 1917–1923*, rev. ed. (Cambridge, Mass: Harvard University Press, 1964), has the least detail. Swietochowski, *Russian Azerbaijan* deals less with social than political issues and relies heavily on religion as an explanation for national action. Suny's *Commune* focused on labor issues with little attention to Azerbaijanis. A stereotyped image emerges, marred by unconcealed bias. He refers to "the likelihood of Moslem treachery," p. 198; "danger from Moslem bands around Baku," p. 200; and a "Moslem menace," p. 202.

26. Swietochowski, *Russian Azerbaijan*, p. 84.

27. Bych was a Russian Kadet. List in Suny, *Commune*, p. 73, n. 11, citing Popov, p. 282.

28. Suny, *Commune*, pp. 74–75, 77, 81.

29. The following discussion is from Keykurun, *Azerbaycan Istiklal*, pp. 19–20.

30. Keykurun notes that all had completed university education.

31. Nalbandian, *Armenian*, chap. 5, described the Hunchak's origins and program.

32. When the membership of the Executive Committee was forwarded to the capital, Kerensky responded with a request for further information on the Difai. Keykurun complied.

33. Keykurun, *Azerbaycan Istiklal*, p. 21.

34. Keykurun, *Azerbaycan Istiklal*, pp. 118–21, citing Rasulzade; also in Pipes, *Formation*, p. 99; Swietochowski, *Russian Azerbaijan*, pp. 89–90.

35. In congresses and the all-Russian Muslim movement, Tatars and some others supported extraterritorial "cultural autonomy," for communities without a clearly defined territory or with a large diaspora. "Muslim unity" was stressed, but the degree to which this meant religious unification varied greatly; some clearly used the term in a political or cultural sense. Azade-Ayşe Rorlich, *Volga Tatars: A Profile in National Resilience* (Stanford: Hoover Institution Press, 1986).

36. Keykurun, *Azerbaycan Istiklal*, pp. 118–121, quoted Resulzade on the alliance and mentioned *Achik söz*. Keykurun, in his own narrative (p. 52), noted that the two leaders, Yusufbeyli and Rasulzade, decided to merge the parties since both had independence as their goal.

37. Swietochowski, *Russian Azerbaijan*, pp. 93–95.

38. In September two religious parties, one from Baku and one from Ganje, would merge. The Rusyada Musulmanlik (Islam in Russia) and the Ittihad-i Islam (Union of Islam) would become Rusyada Musulmanlik-Ittihad (Ittihad). It rejected national identity in favor of an all-Russian Muslim union and "freedom from European capitalism and imperialism." Ittihad's electoral victories for the Constituent Assembly reveal support in the villages of the Apsheron Peninsula. The Musavat won most of the Azerbaijani votes. Swietochowski, *Russian Azerbaijan*, pp. 88–89.

39. Ibid., p. 88.

40. Suny (*Commune*, pp. 139, 155–56, citing *Izvestiia* and *Kaspii*) and Swietochowski, l. 147 (p. 95) gave the same figures: Musavat–8,147; SRs–6,305; Dashnaks–5,289; Bolsheviks–3,883; Mensheviks–687.

41. Suny, *Commune*, pp. 191–93; Swietochowski, *Russian Azerbaijan* pp. 103–4.

42. Pipes, *Formation*, p. 103; Swietochowski, *Russian Azerbaijan*, pp. 106–7.

43. Pipes, *Formation*, pp. 100, 105–6, stated this 30 percent was equal to the Muslim population. The 1897 census, however, shows that nearer to 40 percent of the population in Transcaucasia was Azerbaijani or other Muslim. The vote might reflect "under-participation" by Azerbaijanis because of past disenfranchisement.

44. The Azerbaijani national parties received the most votes, but in the City Council, Azerbaijani Turks were outnumbered by Armenians, probably because of

Armenian representation in parties other than Armenian national parties. The Bolsheviks had 16 percent of the Duma seats. The soldiers had supported the Bolsheviks (2,675 of 3,093 who voted); Suny, *Commune*, pp. 160–61 (figures on election results), 171–81, 195; Swietochowski, *Russian Azerbaijan*, pp. 101–3.

45. Suny, *Commune*, pp. 158–60, 161–66 on SR split; Swietochowski, *Russian Azerbaijan*, pp. 101–2 on Musavat proposal of 7 November.

46. Suny, *Commune*, pp. 201–2, citing *Znamia truda*, no. 9 (1918).

47. Ibid., pp. 190–91, 196–200.

48. Keykurun, *Azerbaycan Istiklal*, p. 53, and Swietochowski, *Russian Azerbaijan*, p. 112, noted Kerenskii's failure to supply arms though he agreed to do so.

49. Suny (*Commune*, p. 198) referred to Azerbaijani fears of the armed Armenians.

50. Ibid., n. 72.

51. Keykurun, *Azerbaycan Istiklal*, pp. 21–22, 47–51.

52. Suny (*Commune*, pp. 199–200) without source, referred to the "tragic and confused events at Shamkor"; Swietochowski (*Russian Azerbaijan*, p. 113), citing Shaumian, Sef, and two others, to a "Shamkhor massacre."

53. Keykurun, *Azerbaycan Istiklal*, pp. 51–52.

54. Tiflis Soviet failed to take power in November 1917. Pipes, *Formation*, p. 106.

55. Suny, *Commune*, p. 204.

56. Ibid., pp. 203–4; Swietochowski, *Russian Azerbaijan*, pp. 113–15.

57. Suny, *Commune*, pp. 210, 215.

58. On the "March Days," Pipes, *Formation*, pp. 199–201; Suny, *Commune*, pp. 215–26 called the Azerbaijanis "rebel Moslems" and by the end of the narrative refers to "Moslem insurrection" as if against a legitimate power; Swietochowski, *Russian Azerbaijan*, pp. 116–18.

59. Keykurun, *Azerbaycan Istiklal*, p. 22; he added that the so-called Tatar regiments included men from the North Caucasus.

60. Swietochowski (*Russian Azerbaijan*, p. 116) quotes Narimanov and Shaumian's own collected works. He treats the Narimanov-Shaumian discussions and the approaches to Japaridze as though they were part of one effort; Suny (*Commune*, p. 217) treated them as separate.

61. Swietochowski (*Russian Azerbaijan*, p. 116) described these terms; the full text of the ultimatum is found in Suny, *Commune*, pp. 222–23.

62. Swietochowski, *Russian Azerbaijan*, p. 116.

63. Suny, *Commune*, p. 224.

64. McDonnell's report to the War Office, cited in A. J. Plotke, "We Must Trust to What We Can Improvize: The British Empire and the Intelligence Operations in North and South Russia, 1918" (unpublished manuscript), p. 327. I am grateful to Professor Plotke for permitting quotation.

65. The soviet nationalized the oil industry in June (apparently against Lenin's orders), intending to facilitate deliveries to Russia. The result was a drop in production. Pipes, *Formation*, p. 201; Swietochowski, *Russian Azerbaijan*, p. 135.

66. Suny, *Commune*, pp. 227–28 and p. 231, n. 43, citing *Bakinskii Rabochii* (hereafter, *BR*) indicated 23 Musavat members in the Baku Soviet in mid-April 1918.

67. A. Mikoyan, *Memoires of Anastas Mikoyan; The Path of Struggle*, vol. 1 (Madison, Conn.: Sphinx Press, 1989), pp. 437–39. The book, originally published in Russian in Moscow during the 1970s, had the usual claims: all opponents were "counter-revolutionaries," or puppets of England, the national government of Azerbaijan was an "anti-populist regime" (p. 311).

68. Suny, *Commune*, pp. 206–7, citing *BR*; massacres of Muslim communities by Armenians were noted in intelligence reports to Ottomon Gen. Kazim Karabekir, and in the newspaper *Azerbaijan*, 2 April 1920, reproduced in *K istorii obrazovaniia nagorno-karabakhskio avtonomnoi oblasti Azerbaidzhanskoi SSR, 1918–1925; Dokumenty i materialy* (Baku: Az Gos. Izd, 1989), pp. 40–41 (hereafter cited as *Obrazovanie*).

69. Suny, *Commune*, pp. 206–7; Swietochowski, *Russian Azerbaijan*, pp. 114–15, quoting Shaumian and Soviet sources.

70. Shaw and Shaw, *History of the Ottoman Empire*, pp. 184, 188, 190–91; Pipes, *Formation*, chap. 2 on the Diet.

71. Pipes, *Formation*, pp. 106–7; Garash Madatov, *Pobeda sovetskoi vlasti v Nakhichevani i obrazovanie Nakhichevanskoi ASSR* (Baku: Academy of Sciences, 1968), p. 46, stated that as early as December 1917, Turkish forces insisted that Transcaucasian representatives speak for an independent government.

72. Detail is given in Pipes, *Formation*, pp. 106–7, 193–95.

73. Ibid., p. 107; Suny, *Commune*, pp. 208–11, quoted Shaumian in March 1918 calling the act "forsaking Europe for Asia."

74. Pipes, *Formation*, pp. 193–95; Swietochowski, *Russian Azerbaijan*, pp. 125–26, 129.

CHAPTER 6

1. Näsib Näsibzadä, *Azärbayjan demokratik respublikasi* (Baku, 1989), pp. 43–44; English translation is in Tadeusz Swietochowski, *Russian Azerbaijan, 1905–1920* (Cambridge, Eng.: Cambridge University Press, 1985), p. 129.

2. Näsibzadä, *Azärbayjan*, p. 11.

3. Swietochowski, *Russian Azerbaijan*, pp. 130–31; G. A. Madatov, *Pobeda sovetskoi vlasti v Nakhichevani i obrazovanie Nakhichevanskoi ASSR* (Baku: Academy of Sciences, 1968), pp. 47–59. N. Keykurun, *Azerbaycan Istiklal mücadelesinin hatıraları* (Istanbul: Azerbaycan Gençlik Derneği, 1964), pp. 70–71, described his own visit to Istanbul in early 1918 and discussion with Enver at the time he (Enver) appointed Nuri as commander of forces to enter Caucasus.

4. Swietochowski, *Russian Azerbaijan*, p. 131, citing Mirza Bala's history of the Musavat and Soviet sources, such as Madatov, *Pobeda Nakhichevani*, pp. 47–49. Näsibzadä, *Azärbayjan*, p. 12, claims Nuri did not interfere but upheld the story that

he referred members of the ADR government to his advisor Ahmet Aghayev (see chapter 4), who urged the change in the cabinet.

5. Madatov, *Pobeda Nakhichevani*, p. 50, quoted Azizbeyov in the spring of 1918 as saying that Mensheviks (Georgians) and the Musavat would rather have Turkey rule Transcaucasia than the Bolsheviks. ADR preferred independence.

6. Swietochowski, *Russian Azerbaijan*, pp. 132–33.

7. Ibid., p. 134, cites Mirza Bala's history of the Musavat, according to which Rasulzade and several colleagues had been invited to Istanbul to remove them from the scene of action. One must wonder about Rasulzade's political judgment in leaving Baku for an extended period during such critical times.

8. I wish to thank Dr. A. J. Plotke for permission to cite here her "The Dunsterforce: Military/Intelligence Mission to Northern Persia in 1918" (UMI, 1987). The following is based on chaps. 6–7.

9. Marshall pointed out that oil fields consisted of 2,000 concrete reinforced wells and would not even speculate on the quantity of explosives needed. Plotke, "Dunsterforce," pp. 295, 162, citing Marshall's *Memoirs of Four Fronts* (London, 1929), p. 304.

10. Discusssed by Plotke, "Dunsterforce," pp. 312–321. Goldsmith succeeded in establishing a wireless link with Baku and Baghdad.

11. According to E. A. Tokarzhevskii (*Ocherki istorii Sovetskogo Azerbaidzhana v period perekhoda na mirnuiu rabotu po vosstanovleniiu narodnogo khoziaistva (1921–1925 gg)* [Baku, 1956], pp. 12–13), in May the fourth Moscow Airborne Revolutionary Unit was sent to Baku and in July land forces were sent.

12. See Reginald Teague-Jones (alias Ronald Sinclair) (*The Spy Who Disappeared: Diary of a Secret Mission to Russian Central Asia in 1918* [London: Victor Gollancz, 1990]) concerning the conditions of the "invitation."

13. C. H. Ellis, former British colonel and participant in the intervention, discussed the missing arms (*The Transcaspian Episode, 1918–1919* [London: Hutchinson, 1963], pp. 36–37); Suny (*Commune*, p. 321) omitted the weapons as a reason for the Bolsheviks' being turned back.

14. Swietochowski (*Russian Azerbaijan*, p. 138) gave no precise numbers, but stated this force was smaller than Baku expected. Ellis (*Transcaspian*, p. 34) said Centro-Caspian dictatorship representatives had been told not to expect a large British force; he noted (p. 38) they apparently "looked to" Dunsterville to provide both troops and equipment for the city's defense. He referred (p. 39) to "Dunsterville's 900 troops."

15. Ellis, *Transcaspian*, p. 39. Further details of the same view were provided by Capt. R. Harrison, a Dunsterforce officer, in his report, which is located in the Public Archives of Canada, RG 9111, vol. 3096, 0-11-36. I thank Professor Plotke for providing me with a copy.

16. Alfred Rawlinson (*Adventures in the Near East 1918–1922* [New York, 1924]), who was on the scene, stated he loaded a ship of "best explosives and arms," from the Baku military stores, sailed with Dunsterville's "fleet," to Enzeli.

17. Swietochowski, *Russian Azerbaijan*, pp. 138–39; Ellis, *Transcaspian*, pp. 36–40.

18. Swietochowski, *Russian Azerbaijan*, pp. 139–40. Ottoman forces successfully occupied Iranian Azerbaijan.

19. The Committee for Union and Progress (CUP) government, which had taken power in 1908 and conducted the war, was overthrown. Its leading triumvirate, including Enver Pasha, fled. The new sultan agreed to Allied peace terms and occupation, provoking resistance from successful generals who started a national movement.

20. Richard H. Ullman (*Britain and the Russian Civil War*, vol. 2 in a series on Anglo-Soviet Relations, 1917–1921 [Princeton: Princeton University Press, 1968], p. 50) says 1,200 British and 800 Indian troops landed "on the heels of the departing Turks"; D. B. Guliev, *Bor'ba Kommunisticheskoi partii za osushchestvlenie leninskoi natsional'noi politiki v Azerbaidzhane* (Baku: Azerneshr, 1970), pp. 83–88; A. Raevskii, *Angliiskaia interventsiia i musavatskoe pravitel'stvo* (Baku, 1927), chaps. 1–2; Swietochowski, *Russian Azerbaijan*, pp. 141–57.

21. Communications between the Musavat leadership and Thomson are in Raevskii (*Angliiskaia*, pp. 32–34, 36, 39–40). He stated telegrams to Khan Khoiskii seemed to suggest de facto recognition of Azerbaijani independence by Thomson; see also Swietochowski, *Russian Azerbaijan*, pp. 140–41.

22. Näsibzade, *Azärbayjan*, pp. 15–17.

23. Stalin informed Shaumian (summer 1918) that it was imperative that the Germans accept the problems of Armenia and Azerbaijan as internal Russian matters. Pipes, *Formation*, p. 202; Swietochowski, *Russian Azerbaijan*, pp. 133–34.

24. Raevskii, *Angliiskaia*, p. 37.

25. Ullman (*Britain*, p. 219) cites a report by Maj. L. H. Torin (Batum) to General Staff Intelligence, 15 September 1919.

26. Ibid., pp. 220 and 224; Raevskii, *Angliiskaia*, chap. 1; Edward Ingram, *In Defense of British India* (London, 1984).

27. Ullman (*Britain*, p. 124) cites a Foreign Office (British) report by W. J. Childs and A. E. R. McDonnell, 31 May 1921, file E 8378/8378/58; FO 371/6280.

28. Swietochowski, *Russian Azerbaijan*, pp. 141–42.

29. Guliev, *Bor'ba*, pp. 89–90; Näsibzadä, *Azärbayjan*, p. 17.

30. Guliev, *Bor'ba*, p. 88, citing Tsentral'nyi Gosudarstvennyi Arkhiv Oktiabrskoi Revoliutsii (Central State Archive of the October Revolution, Azerbaijan) (hereafter TsGOAR), f. 894, op. 7, d. 11, l. 20; and f. 970, op. 1, d. 36, l. 48 (abbreviations refer to internal classification of archive); and on Yusufbeyli's complaints about interferences, citing documents of the party archive.

31. Guliev, *Bor'ba*, p. 160–62; Swietochowski, *Russian Azerbaijan*, pp. 143, 152–53.

32. Näsibzade, *Azärbayjan*, p. 52, notes the policy.

33. Swietochowski (*Russian Azerbaijan*, pp. 142–44) cited British Foreign Office records and recent Armenian sources that Sultanov was regarded as "anti-Armenian"; the Russian-language newspaper *Bor'ba* reported in April 1919 that the Armenian government protested the fact that he was an Azerbaijani.

34. Swietochowski (*Russian Azerbaijan*, p. 159; Tokarzhevskii, *Ocherki*, p. 16) stated that Thomson appointed an American governor general of Nakhjivan but gave no name or source.

35. For details see Guliev, *Bor'ba*, pp. 94–103.

36. These included the Muslim Charitable Society, the Baku Russian Charitable Society, the Baku Armenian Cultural Society, and a Baku Jewish home (Guliev, *Bor'ba*, pp. 118–59).

37. Other members named by Swietochowski (*Russian Azerbaijan*, p. 154), based on British Foreign Office records, were "Hajinskii [apparently not Mehmet Hasan who was in the Cabinet], Mekhtiyev, Muharramov and Aghayev and . . . Jeyhun Hajibeyli." They left Baku in December 1918 but were held up in Istanbul waiting for visas. Aghayev was detained for his role in the Young Turk government and sent to exile on Malta. The rest of the delegates arrived at the Peace Conference in April or May 1919.

38. Swietochowski, *Russian Azerbaijan*, pp. 165–68; Tokarzhevskii, *Ocherki*, pp. 16–19. Swietochowski noted the Bolsheviks lost support when, in early 1919 they tried to introduce the slogan "All Power to the Soviets."

39. Guliev, *Bor'ba*, p. 79, citing *Azerbaijan*, 11 November (29 October) 1918.

40. Swietochowski, *Russian Azerbaijan*, pp. 148–49, citing Soviet and émigré sources.

41. Ullman, *Britain*, p. 225, citing War Office telegram from Milne; Denikin, *Ocherki russkoi smuty*, vol. 4 (Paris and Berlin, 1921–26), pp. 132–34; F. Kazemzadeh, *The Struggle for Transcaucasia (1917–1921)* (New York: Philosophical Library, 1951); George A. Brinkley, *The Volunteer Army and Allied Intervention in South Russia, 1917–1921* (South Bend, Ind.: University of Notre Dame Press, 1966), pp. 162–63.

42. The Armenians were reportedly not prepared to oppose any Russian force. Swietochowski, *Russian Azerbaijan*, pp. 143–44, 152–53, 158.

43. Ibid., p. 156. Thomson protested the withdrawal.

44. By July 1919, Mikoyan led the Baku Committee of the RCP(b) in calling for a split in the Hümmet to incorporate the "left wing" into the RCP(b). Several "left" Hümmetists, including Karayev and Huseinov, rejected these pressures, but others followed this first step of Mikoyan's plan. They established an Azerbaijan Communist party—Hümmet. The rest of Hümmet would resist absorption. Swietochowski, *Russian Azerbaijan*, pp. 166–67, partly citing Guliev, *Bor'ba*, p. 405.

45. Pipes, *Formation*, pp. 219–22; Swietochowski, *Russian Azerbaijan*, pp. 170–71.

46. Swietochowski, *Russian Azerbaijan*, pp. 165–66; Tokarzhevskii, *Ocherki*, p. 22, reported that fighting units were created.

47. Swietochowski, *Russian Azerbaijan*, p. 177; cited also by Näsibzadä, *Azärbayjan*.

48. This account was given by Näsibzadä, *Azärbayjan*, pp. 30, 35–41.

49. Pipes (*Formation*) documents the process region by region.

50. The Red Army entered Baku on an armored train that day and Soviet power was officially established on 28 April.

51. Pipes (*Formation*, pp. 224–27) makes this argument.

52. Swietochowski, *Russian Azerbaijan*, p. 177.

53. Pipes, *Formation*, p. 226, and Swietochowski, *Russian Azerbaijan*, p. 177.

54. Suggested by Näsibzadä, *Azärbayjan*, p. 69. He gives details of an Armenian attack on the ADR garrison at Khankend (now Stepanakert) on the Novruz Bayram holiday (late March) 1920.

55. Swietochowski, *Russian Azerbaijan*, p. 181.

56. Ibid., p. 178.

57. Manaf Suleiman, "Dni minuvshie," *Vyshka*, 10 February 1990.

58. Quoted in Swietochowski, *Russian Azerbaijan*, p. 182.

59. The ultimatum demanded surrender of authority within twelve hours; Pipes, *Formation*, chap. 5, and articles published in the émigré journal *Azerbaycan Yurt Bilgisi*, published in the 1930s in Turkey.

60. *Bor'ba za pobedu sovetskoi vlasti v azerbaidzhane 1918–1920; dokumenty i materialy* (Baku, 1967) (hereafter cited as *Bor'ba za pobedu*), doc. no. 641, pp. 461–62; English translation, Swietochowski, *Russian Azerbaijan*, p. 182.

61. Karabekir was chief of the Intelligence Division of the Ottoman General Staff (1912–1914) and became a general in 1918 at age 36. Enver Pasha, his classmate at the Military Academy, apparently resented Karabekir and, to get him out of Istanbul, promoted him and had him transferred. In 1919, after the armistice, when the weak sultan accepted draconian peace terms, Karabekir, one of the most successful Turkish generals, became an early leader of the Nationalist Movement. He remained on the eastern frontier, directing intelligence and military activities until 1924. Kazim Karabekir, *Istiklal harbimiz* (Istanbul, 1960); biography precedes text.

62. Karabekir, *Istiklal Harbimiz*, p. 621, quoting a telegram of 12 April 1920. Karabekir's analysis of intelligence reports (p. 605) showed that Az aijan could not successfully fight the Armenians in Zangezur and Karabagh unless it came to terms with the Bolsheviks.

63. Karabekir, *Istiklal harbimiz*, p. 633, quoting a telegram of 18 April 1920.

64. Swietochowski's argument (*Russian Azerbaijan*, p. 163), that Mustafa Kemal proposed Turkish-Bolshevik action against Azerbaijan if the ADR should refuse to act as a conduit for supplies from Moscow and instead create a pro-British "Caucasian wall" completing the encirclement of the Turkish National forces, is flawed on two counts. First, it cites a telegram from Kemal (Karabekir, *Istiklal Habimiz*, pp. 466–67) that is more ambiguous than Swietochowski's translation. It is not clear from the

passage whether the "joint action" was to be directed against the Caucasian republics themselves or, perhaps more likely given the context, against the British. Second, supplies from Moscow to Turkey went via the Black Sea, not through the Caucasus.

65. Näsibzada, *Azerbayjan* pp. 46–48, 51–52.

66. Pipes, *Formation*, chap. 5; Richard G. Hovanissian, "Caucasian Armenia between Imperial and Soviet Rule: The Interlude of National Independence," in Suny, *Transcaucasia*. Also *Obrazovanie*; Madatov, *Pobeda Nakhichevani*.

67. *Atlas Azerbaidzhanskoi SSR* (Moscow, 1979); Pipes, *Formation*, p. 210.

68. Population estimates are given by George Bournoutian, on the basis of Russian military statistics. Of approximately 143,000 in the Erevan and Nakhjivan khanates in 1826, only 25,151 (under 20 percent) were Armenian. He states that many Armenian historians had overestimated the Armenian population in the region by using post-1830 figures ("The Ethnic Composition and Socio-Economic Condition of Eastern Armenian in the First Half of the Nineteenth Century," in Suny, *Transcaucasia*).

69. Madatov (*Pobeda Nakhichevani*, p. 13) noted these were changed by tsarist fiat without regard to economic ties or ethnic composition.

70. *Azerbaijan*, 1 November 1918, in *Obrazovanie*, pp. 11–12.

71. Ibid., p. 12.

72. *Bor'ba*, 21 March 1919, reporting on news in the Armenian newspaper *Ashkhatavor*; reprinted in *Obrazovanie*, p. 13.

73. *Bor'ba*, 5 April 1919, reprinted in *Obrazovanie*, pp. 13–14.

74. Such charges were frequent. *Azerbaijan* of 6 July 1919, for example, carried an editorial stating, "We notice recently a strengthening on all fronts of the aggressive work of Armenian activists against the legal rights of the Azerbaijani Turks. 'Build our own good fortune on the misfortune of the Turks' is the motto of the Armenians." Reprinted in *Obrazovanie*, pp. 19–21.

75. This according to Näsibzadä, *Azärbayjan*, pp. 50–51.

76. *Bor'ba*, 18 April 1919, carried a Russian translation of a story published in the Armenian newspaper *Zhogovordi Dzain*, as reproduced in *Obrazovanie*, pp. 14–16.

77. S. M. Kirov, *Stat'i rechi, dokumenty*, vol. 1 (Moscow, 1936), pp. 143–45, reproduced in *Obrazovanie*, pp. 14–16.

78. Harry N. Howard, *The King-Crane Commission* (Beirut, 1963), pp. 241–42, and *Papers Relating to the Foreign Relations of the United States, 1919*, vol. 2 (Washington: U.S. Government Printing Office, 1934), p. 827 (hereafter cited as *Foreign Relations*). All Entente representatives were asked to cooperate. In December 1919 (vol. 9, pp. 167–68) at Haskell's request, his authority was extended over relief operations in Azerbaijan and Georgia.

79. *Bor'ba*, 2 September 1919, reprinted in *Obrazovanie*, pp. 25–27. Haskell reflected an Anglo-French plan to interpose troops in such a corridor both to "contain" Turkish forces and to direct the attention of the Caucasian republics toward fighting Bolsheviks. Also in Guliev, *Bor'ba*, p. 116.

80. *Bor'ba*, 5 September 1919, cited in *Obrazovanie*, pp. 27–28.

81. *Foreign Relations 1919*, vol. 9, pp. 606–7.

82. Report by Mikoyan to Lenin, dated 22 May 1919, reproduced in *Obrazovanie*, p. 16. Furthermore, Suny points out in "Tiflis," in Michael F. Hamm, *The City in Late Imperial Russia* (Bloomington: Indiana University Press, 1986) that Tiflis not Erevan had been the center of the Armenian national movement in Caucasia.

83. The newspaper *Daily Telegraph* (London), 24 May 1920, in a report from a special correspondent in Baku.

84. Swietochowski, *Russian Azerbaijan*, p. 177, Näsibzadä *Azärbayjan*, p. 39; *Azerbaijan*, 26 March 1920, in *Obrazovanie*, pp. 39–41. Details on these and similar attacks were provided in intelligence reports sent to Karabekir from sources throughout the region. Karabekir, *Istiklal Harbimiz*, p. 605.

85. Madatov, *Pobeda Nakhichevani*, pp. 26–28, on election violations reported in petitions to the governor of Erevan guberniia.

86. Ibid., p. 39, citing *Novyi Vostok*, 1922, no. 1, pp. 336–37.

87. Madatov, *Pobeda Nakhichevani*, pp. 29–31, citing documents from TsGAOR Arm f. 39/13, on seizing grain; TsGAOR Geo, f. 723, on peasants' seizing irrigation systems and refusing to pay taxes; and TsGAOR Arm f. 39/103, on workers and peasants in Nakhjivan, with the slogan "Don't submit to the Provisional Government"; the uezd commissar and local "national committee" sent against the meeting a "punitive detachment," which led to bloodshed.

88. Madatov, *Pobeda Nakhichevani*, p. 38.

89. Ibid., p. 25; later in the summer of 1917 he states peasants' deputies also joined the soviet.

90. Ibid., pp. 36–37, 43, 45, had to admit this, noting the absence of proletarians in Nakhjivan, the "political immaturity of peasants," and the "sharpness and complexity of the national question."

91. The town of Maku is located about 65 km west-northwest of Nakhjivan city in Iran.

92. *Lenin milli siyasätinin yetirmäsi; Nakhjivan MSSR'in 50 illiyi* (Baku, 1974), p. 23 (hereafter cited as *Nahkjivan MSSR*), claimed Nakhjivan had a soviet.

93. Madatov, *Pobeda Nakhichevani*, p. 43, citing, respectively, telegram to Erevan governor on 2 February 1918 in TsGAOR Armenia, f. 39/103; documents in Tsentral'nyi Arkhiv Sovetskoi Armii (Central State Archive of the Soviet Army; hereafter cited as TsGASA), f. 195; and, on the garrison fighting "khans' bands," TsGAOR Georgia, f. 1.

94. Madatov, p. 45, and *Nakhichevani MSSR*, pp. 23–24, cited *Novyi Vostok* 1922, no. 1, p. 339.

95. During the early summer of 1918, Nakhjivan was attacked by Andranik's units. Defeating Azerbaijani peasants, Andranik took the territory of Ordubad, Julfa station and surrounding villages. By mid-June, his units besieged Nakhjivan city and defeated its defenders. Madatov, p. 51, citing Tsentral'nyi Gosudarstvennyi Istori-

cheskii Arkhiv (Central State History Archive of Nakhjivan ASSR; hereafter cited as TsGIA Nakh ASSR), f. 1.

96. Described in Näsibzadä *Azärbayjan*, p. 50.

97. *40 let Nakhichevanskoi ASSR*, p. 20. *Nakhjivan MSSR* seems to have been translated from *40 let*.

98. *Nahkjivan MSSR*, pp. 25–26, citing documents in TsGAOR Arm, f. 200. This text maintained that Colonel Ray "conducted secret negotiations" with the Musavat, Dashnaks, and Turkish representatives. A decree over Ray's signature (in Russian "Rei," so the spelling given here is presumed) was printed in *Bor'ba za pobedu*, pp. 313–14; his name could not be found in the multivolume *Foreign Relations* for 1919.

99. *40 let*, p. 23, citing TsGASA, f. 109, noted the arrival of British forces in Nakhjivan in late June to early July 1919; Haskell's report and Daily's announcement are described in *Nahkjivan MSSR*, p. 26, citing TsGAOR Arm, and *Azerbaijan*, 23 October 1919; the letter and decrees were reprinted in *Bor'ba za pobedu*, pp. 263–65, 313–16. Daily's name could not be found in *Foreign Relations* for 1919.

100. Karabekir, *Istiklal Harbimiz*, p. 65. In 1919 he sent four officers and seven enlisted men to reestablish a regiment in Nakhjivan.

101. Curzon was the most forceful spokesman for the view that India's defense perimeter ran through Caucasia. Balfour argued that intervention was not worth the cost, that Transcaucasia was not an approach to India, though the General Staff moved these "vital approaches" farther and farther from India all the time.

102. Whether Russia would reemerge as a major power was one point of debate. Ullman, *Britain*, pp. 11, 13–14, 16, 69, 76, 119, 221, 331–32.

103. Churchill early on supported fighting Bolshevism wherever it did not currently exist. Most of the British army thought the "buffer states" around Russia could serve as bulwark against future Russian strength whether Bolshevik or not. Ibid., p. 223.

104. Kadishev (*Interventsiia*, p. 238) states the officer's name was Sagatelian.

105. Ullman, *Britain*, pp. 333–34. Churchill made this remark in January 1920 with de facto recognition of Azerbaijan and Georgia.

106. Ibid., p. 73. Ullman also notes that support for the creation of an Armenian state was part of the planned partition of Turkey.

107. The U.S. posture was discussed in Ullman, *Britain*, and *A History of the Peace Conference of Paris*, vol. 6, ed. H. W. V. Temperley (London: Henry Frowde and Hodder Stoughteon, 1924).

108. Frederick Stanwood, *War, Revolution and British Imperialism in Central Asia* (London: Ithaca Press, 1983), p. 9.

109. Ullman, *Britain*, pp. 119, 221.

110. Ibid., pp. 77–78.

111. Ibid., p. 79, Balfour on p. 72; Sir Henry on p. 324.

112. Ullman, *Britain*, p. 68; Sir Henry's diary entry, 18 January 1920, p. 336.

113. Ullman (*Britain*, p. 323) noted that the delegates deferred recognition of

Armenia until settlement of Turkish territory planned in the summer of 1920. Daghestan was considered economically unviable.

114. Ibid., pp. 344–45.

CHAPTER 7

1. A. Sh. Mil'man, *Azerbaidzhanskaia SSR—Suverenoe gosudarstvo v sostave SSSR* (Baku: Azerneshr, 1971) p. 42.

2. V. E. Malanchuk, *Istoricheskii opyt KPSS po resheniiu natsioinal'nogo voprosa i razvitiiu natsional'nykh otnoshenii v SSSR* (Moscow: Vyshaia Shkola, 1972), p. 91. The *Narodnyi kommissariat po delam natsional'nostei*, Narkomnats, was established immediately after the Bolsheviks' seizure of power and had only one commissar until superceded in 1924 by the Soviet of Nationalities—Stalin. See Stephen Blank, *Stalin and the Narkomnats: Sorcerer as Apprentice* (forthcoming); Richard Pipes, *Formation of the Soviet Union*, 2d. ed. (Cambridge, Mass.: Harvard University Press, 1964), chaps. 2 and 4.

3. D. B. Guliev, *Bor'ba Kommunisticheskoi partii za osushchestvlenie leninskoi natsional'noi politiki v Azerbaidzhane* (Baku: Azerneshr, 1970), p. 521, n. 1; 534–37; 585; some decrees of May and July 1920 were issued over Huseinov's signature in Narimanov's absence. Decrees in *Bor'ba za poedu, Sovetskoi vlasti v Azerbaidzhane, 1918–1920* (Baku: Academy of Sciences, 1967), pp. 484, 487, 488.

4. Mil'man, Guliev, and some others state the Sovnarkom was created on the first day of soviet power by the Azrevkom (most of whose members were not on the scene). S. V. Kharmandarian (*Lenin i stanovlenie zakavkazskoi federatsii, 1921–1923* [Erevan: Aiastan, 1969], p. 88) stated the Sovnarkom was elected at the first All-Azerbaijan Congress of Soviets, 6–19 May 1921.

5. *Bor'ba za pobedu*, doc. nos. 543–44, pp. 462–63.

6. Mikoyan was also on this soviet. Guliev, *Bor'ba*, p. 532.

7. A. Vahap Yurtsever, "Azerbaycan İstiklal Savaşında Saheler," *Azerbaycan* (Ankara), multipart article, July–August 1956. Yurtsever was a Musavatist who remained in Baku after the fall of the republic.

8. According to Mil'man (*Azerbaidzhan SSR*, p. 54, citing *Izvestiia Vremennogo Revolutsionnogo Komiteta Azerbaidzhana*, no. 1, 29 April 1920), the head of the AzCheka was added to the Azrevkom. Yurtsever ("Istiklal Savasaşinda") stated AzCheka was staffed by Russians.

9. Guliev, *Bor'ba*, p. 537.

10. Quoted in Blank, "Bolshevik Organizational Development in Early Soviet Transcaucasia: Autonomy vs. Centralization, 1918–1924" (hereafter cited as "Centralization" in Ronald G. Suny, *Transcaucasia: Nationalism and Social Change* (Ann Arbor, 1983), p. 326.

11. For example, one 1920 meeting of the Bureau CC AzCP(b) included ten

members, of which five were Azerbaijani Turks. Among the other members were Mikoyan and Ordzhonikidze.

12. *Zaria Vostoka* (hereafter *ZV*), 5 December 1925, indicated 43 percent natives in the AzCP.

13. A. B. Kadishev, *Interventsiia i grazhdanskaia voina v Zakavkaz'e* (Moscow: Voennoe Press, 1960), pp. 291–92, provides a list of units and areas they were ordered to occupy between 11 and 18 May 1920.

14. Tadeusz Swietochowski, *Russian Azerbaijan, 1905–1920* (Cambridge, Eng.: Cambridge University Press, 1985), p. 190, notes resistance into 1924.

15. Kadishev, *Interventsiia*, p. 289.

16. Ibid., pp. 289–90.

17. Ibid., pp. 292–93.

18. According to Colonel Kazimbekov who fought there, the rising began on 22 May, not 26 May, and lasted until 4 June 1920.

19. He died in Berlin. This information was contained in an obituary of Jihangir Kazimbekov by Jeyhun Hajibeyli.

20. Kadishev, *Interventsiia*, p. 298.

21. Ibid., pp. 293–98, also includes a map of the region and shows where forces were deployed.

22. Ibid., p. 300.

23. Kadishev provides details on all these clashes, pp. 300–311.

24. Anatolii Aleksandrovich Karenin, *Sultan Mejid Äfändiyev*, trans. M. Taghizadä (Baku, 1963), pp. 79–81. Efendiyev had been in Astrakhan, was sent to Crimea in February 1920, returned to Baku on 10 May.

25. Ibid., pp. 82–84.

26. Mil'man, *Azerbaidzhan SSR*, p. 48, citing K. N. Ragimov (dissertation, Baku, 1967).

27. Mil'man, *Azerbaidzhan SSR*, p. 51; Kharmandarian, *Lenin*, p. 88.

28. Kadishev, *Interventsiia*, p. 291.

29. Mil'man, *Azerbaidzhan SSR*, p. 47.

30. "Protokol zasedaniia konferentsii otvestvyennykh rabotnikov Karabakha sovmestno s chlenami Orgbiuro Tsk AKP(b)," 21 October 1921, in *K istorii obrazovanii Nagorno-Karabakhskoi avtonomnoi oblasti Azerbaidzhanskoi SSR: Dokumenty i materialy* (Baku: Azerneshr, 1989), pp. 99–101 (hereafter cited as *Obrazovanie*).

31. These included light industry. L. G. Alieva, "Iz istorii razvitiia legkoi promyshlennosti Azerbaidzhanskoi SSR," in *Azärbayjanin igtisadi tarikhinin aktual problemläri* (Baku: Elm, 1978) (hereafter, *Az igtisadi*), pp. 134–35, citing Tsentral'nyi gosudarstvennyi arkhiv oktiabrskoi revoliutsii (Central State Archive of the October Revolution, Azerbaijan, hereafter cited as TsGAOR, Az.), f. 130, 133 (abbreviations refer to the internal categories of the archive); Azerbaijan Soviet of Agriculture, *Otchet o deiatel'nosti za 1920 g* (Baku, 1921), pp. 1, 37–39.

32. The foreign trade monopoly of 1 June precluded private sales outside the

republic. A state monopoly was created on the purchase, sale, and distribution of cotton; see A. K. Dil'bazov, "Nachalo sotsialisticheskogo preobrazovniia promyshlennosti Azerbaidzhane," *Az igtisadi*, pp. 80–81, 83.

33. Dil'bazov, "Nachalo," p. 78, citing TsGAOR Az., f. 2511.

34. Dil'bazov, "Nachalo," p. 78, citing Kh. Rustamova, "Iz istorii natsionalizatsii neftianoi promyshlennosti Azerbaidzhana (1920 g)," *Uchenye zapiski* (Azerbaijan State University), no. 7 (1963).

35. S. M. Kirov, *Stat'i, rechi i dokumenty*, vol. 1, p. 19 (Moscow, 1936), cited in Dil'bazov, "Nachalo," p. 76.

36. Decree of 15 May. A commission would control record keeping, protection of the enterprise from sabotage, and preparation for turning it over to state control. Dil'bazov, "Nachalo," pp. 77–78.

37. Ibid., pp. 81–82; even the smallest workshops were seized.

38. Ibid.

39. Ibid., p. 83, citing Party Archive, TsGAOR Az., f. 1, f. 130.

40. G. Y Abdulsälimzadä, "Azärbayjan SSR-in igtisadi inkishafinda yeni märhälä vä geläjäk yuksälish perspektivläri," in *Az igtisadi*, pp. 159–60. According to *Istoriia Azerbaidzhana* (Baku, 1979) (hereafter cited as *Ist. Az.* [1979]), p. 157, oil output in 1920–21 was 2.4 million tons compared with 7.3 million in 1913.

41. Karenin, *Äfändiyev*, pp. 159–60, for example, stated that crafts and textile industries did not recover until 1930.

42. Nazar A. Pashaev (*Pobeda kulturnoi revoliutsii v sovetskom azerbaidzhane* [Moscow: Nauka, 1976], p. 97) noted that in June 1920, a Baku department of "Kavrost" (a telegraph agency) was established. It was reorganized into AzTag (Azerbaidzhanskoe telegrafnoe agenstvo) at the end of 1921.

43. Mil'man, *Azerbaidzhan SSR*, p. 58.

44. Pashaev, *Pobeda Kulturnoi*, p. 98.

45. Abdulsälimzadä, "Igtisadi inkishafindä," p. 160.

46. *Ist. Az.* (1979), p. 157.

47. Dil'bazo, "Nachalo," p. 81.

48. Mil'man (*Azerbaidzhan SSR*, pp. 51–52) noted only poor and middle peasants had voting rights in the *kombedy*. Courts were discussed on pp. 52–53.

49. Karenin, *Äfändiyev*, p. 89.

50. Ibid., pp. 92–93.

51. Kharmandarian, *Lenin*, pp. 280–81; other areas also produced refugees. The issue has not been adequately studied.

52. Kharmandarian, *Lenin*, pp. 277–78.

53. *Papers Relating to the Foreign Relations of the United States, 1921*, vol. 2 (Washington, D.C.: U.S. Government Printing Office, 1936), p. 782.

54. *Istoriia natsional'no-gosudarstvennogo stroitel'stva v SSSR, 1917–1926*, vol. 1 (Moscow: Mysl', 1972, p. 359) (hereafter cited as *Nats-gos*).

55. *Nats-gos*, 1:316, citing Lenin, *Polnoe Sobranie sochineniia* (hereafter *PSS*), vol. 52, p. 136.

56. This account is drawn principally from Kharmandarian, *Lenin*, pp. 127–38. His main sources are documents of the Institutes of Marxism-Leninism and CP archives in appropriate republics.

57. Kharmandarian, *Lenin*, p. 129.

58. *Bakinskii Rabochii* (hereafter *BR*), 2 March 1922, reported relief efforts for over 80,000 starving in four uezdy; a report at the Second Congress of Soviets in April noted 500,000 going hungry. Since the 1926 population of the republic was given as about 2.6 million, this figure represents about 20 percent of the population; *Obrazovanie*, pp. 106–7, 117–18.

59. Kharmandarian, *Lenin*, p. 131.

60. Ibid., p. 132. Kaderli's real name was Israfilbekov.

61. *Nats-gos*, 1:316, citing Lenin, *PSS*, V. 52, p. 153.

62. Nats-gos, 1:362, citing *Obozrenie SSSR; Sbornik Dokumentov, 1917–1924 gg* (Moscow-Leningrad, 1949), p. 273.

63. *Nats-gos* 1:362. Curiously, Malanchuk (*Istoricheskii opyt*, p. 108) reports this dissent in nearly the same language as in *Nats-gos*.

64. Kharmandarian, *Lenin*, p. 146. After the meeting, he noted, the plan met opposition in Azerbaijan and Georgia.

65. Ibid., pp. 147–49.

66. Narimanov, "K istorii revoliutsii v okrainakh," dated Moscow, 24 December 1923; published in *Khäbärlär/Izvestiia*, Azerbaijan Academy of Sciences series in History, Philosophy and Law, 1989, no. 4, pp. 71–77, quotation on p. 73.

67. A series of decrees of CP committees supported Azerbaijani possession of Karabagh (*Obrazovanie*, pp. 49–54) and may be traced to the continued existence of Dashnak rule in Armenia.

68. Mil'man, *Azarbaidzhan SSR*, p. 233.

69. Ibid., pp. 233–34; Kharmandarian (*Lenin*, p. 99) added that mountainous Karabagh's peasants had a right to self-determination. Later reports indicate that they voted to remain in Azerbaijan.

70. Pipes (*Formation*, p. 233) provides a translation of the treaty.

71. Mil'man, *Azarbaidzhan SSR*, p. 234, citing G. A. Madatov, *Pobeda sovetskoi vlasti v Nakhichevani i obrazovanie Nakhichevanskoi ASSR* (Baku: Academy of Sciences, 1968), p. 95.

72. Mil'man, *Azarbaidzhan SSR*, p. 234, citing Madatov, *Pobeda Nakhichevani*, p. 95.

73. Kazim Karabekir, *Istiklal Harbimiz* (Istanbul, 1960), p. 328, wrote in September 1919 that it was "impossible to incorporate Nakhjivan into our national borders, but I favor its incorporation into Azerbaijan's territory."

74. The two treaties represented the short-lived "friendship" between two revolutionary movements that were not recognized by the Allied powers. Stanford J. Shaw

and Ezel Kural Shaw, *History of the Ottoman Empire and Modern Turkey*, vol. 2 (Cambridge, Eng.: Cambridge University Press, 1977), pp. 344, 351, 355; memoirs of Ambassador to Moscow general Ali Fuad Cebesoy, *Moskova Hatırları* (Ankara, 1982), pp. 343–352; on pp. 337–39, Cebesoy wrote that at the time of the Kars Treaty neither Georgia nor Armenia asked for border adjustments, nor had they objected to the Moscow Treaty.

75. Mil'man (*Azerbaidzhan SSR*, p. 235) noted that the Moscow Treaty called Nakhjivan "an autonomous territory under the protectorate [*protektorat*] of Azerbaijan"; the Kars Treaty used the words "under the protection [*prodkrovitel'stvo*] of Azerbaijan."

76. Kharmandarian (*Lenin*, p. 101) noted that Rasulzade was on this commission. Because he does not give first names, whether this was Mehmet Emin or the M. D. Rasulzade mentioned on p. 260 is not known. Mehmet Emin Rasulzade did, according to one Soviet specialist on this period, play some political role in Soviet Azerbaijan for the first year or two of its existence. He is not mentioned in Soviet sources, but he left the USSR in 1922, from Moscow via Finland. He lived thereafter in Berlin and Istanbul, writing on Azerbaijani history and politics.

77. Kharmandarian (*Lenin*, pp. 102–3) did not suggest that Azerbaijan had not agreed to the transfer. A document in *Obrazovanie*, pp. 88–90, recorded Huseinov's telling Narimanov that "Armenian comrades" insist that Azerbaijan agreed to the transfer. The Armenian plenipotentiary was Askanaz Mravian.

78. *Obrazovanie*, pp. 86–87, 88–90, for texts of decisions of 27 June; Kharmandarian, *Lenin*, p. 103.

79. Four issues were voted upon: (1) Karabagh in entirety should go to AzSSR (for: Narimanov, Makharadze, Nazaretian; against: Ordzhonikidze, Miasnikov, Kirov, Figatner); (2) Plebiscite held throughout Karabagh, both nationalities (for: Narimanov, Makharadze; against: not given); (3) Moutainous part of Karabagh to Armenia (for: Ordzhonikidze, Miasnikov, Kirov, Figatner); (4) Plebiscite only in mountainous Karabagh (i.e., among Armenian population) (for: Ordzhonikidze, Miasnikov, Kirov, Figatner, Nazaretian). Resoutions 3 and 4 were carried; Kharmandarian, *Lenin*, pp. 105–7; on p. 200 he noted that Miasnikov's real name was Miasnikian. Resolution in *Obrazovanie*, pp. 90–91. Full vote was not given in either source.

80. Kharmandarian, *Lenin*, pp. 105–7.

81. Also on 5 July, Narimanov and Makharadze signed an agreement on Azerbaijan-Georgian border. Ibid., p. 110.

82. Ibid., p. 108, stated these were passed "without disagreement," but the document itself, in *Obrazovanie*, p. 92, shows the vote was four for with three abstentions, though nine were present, ten including Stalin.

83. Ibid., p. 77; *Obrazovanie*, document of 19 July, pp. 92–94, lists Kirov as "Secretary CC AzCP"; Malanchuk (*Istoricheskii opyt*) stated Kirov became head of AzCP immediately after the Narimanov-Ordzhonikidze fight over economic integration, in July 1921. *Nats-gos* incorrectly placed the appointment in October 1922.

84. Blank, "Centralization," provided related details.

85. Mil'man (*Azerbaidzhan SSR*, p. 249) quoted a report to the Presidium of AzCEC, 19 July 1921. Narimanov stated: "Mountainous Karabagh remains an inseparable part of Soviet Azerbaijan with the right of internal self-rule within the framework of the Soviet Constitution with an oblast' executive committee at its head."

86. *Obrazovanie*, pp. 95–96.

87. *Obrazovanie*, pp. 101–3; members of the fact-finding commission (Protocol of Orgbiuro CC AzCP, 6 October 1921, on pp. 97–98) were "comrades Muradian, Erganjanian, Ahmed Nadirshina, Lifshits, Habib Ismail and Ishkhanov [also called Ishkhanian])."

88. Mil'man, *Azerbaidzhan SSR*, p. 249, citing TsGAOR Az, f. 379.

89. *Obrazovanie*, p. 103, dated 10 December 1921.

90. *Nats-gos*, chap. 3, part 2.

91. Kharmandarian, *Lenin*, pp. 202–3, 208–9; *Nats-gos* 1:363, citing *Obozrenie SSSR*, p. 280.

92 Kharmandarian, *Lenin*, p. 216; they wrote their criticism during 15–17 November 1921.

93. *Nats-gos*, 1:363–4.

94. Kharmandarian, *Lenin*, pp. 207, 218.

95. Ibid., pp. 226–28.

96. The same might be said for the initial occupation of Baku in 1920, and Narimanov's consistent position raises the suspicion that he went to Moscow from Makhachkala on the eve of that invasion to argue against it.

97. During Narimanov's absence, several matters of trade and security and the "Higher Economic Soviet" were discussed by the TSFSR soviet; Kharmandarian, *Lenin*, pp. 206–63.

98. The pieces of this puzzle are scattered throughout Kharmandarian, *Lenin*, pp. 228–30, 238, 302–3, 306. Published AzCP(b) resolutions from March 1922 from Baku (in *Obrazovanie* 1989 and *Khäbärlär/Izvestiia* 1990 issues of the Azerbaijan Academy of Sciences) do not report Narimanov in attendance, suggesting he stayed in Moscow.

99. Armenian Bekzadian went to Genoa; Kharmandarian, *Lenin*, p. 302.

100. *Nats-gos*, 1:365, quoting 1924 Constitution.

101. Ibid. The structure worked out by year's end was little different from the plan; *Nats-gos* 1:475–76, citing *Istoriia Sovetskoi Konstitutsii (v dokumentakh), 1917–1956*, pp. 499–500.

102. *Nats-gos* 1:357–8 noted the CC AzCP agreed to permit free exporting to Iran. RSFSR Foreign Trade Commissariat successfully stopped it.

103. The plan to make non-Russian areas "autonomous regions" of the RSFSR with few legal guarantees; see Pipes, *Formation*, chap. 6.

104. *Nats-gos* 1:370–79, Pipes, *Formation*, chap. 6.

105. *Nats-gos*, 1:327, 377.

106. Ibid., 1:446.

107. Ibid., 1:476. Each republic's Soviet of Commissars (Sovnarkom) included commissars for agriculture, labor, internal affairs, justice, worker-peasant inspection, education, public health, social security, finance, and a plenipotentiary of the TSFSR Commissariat for Internal Trade.

108. Ibid.

109. Ibid., 1:452–53, 459, 462–63.

110. Karenin, *Äfändiyev*, p. 93, citing *BR*, 15 December 1922; *Bor'ba za pobedu*, p. 524.

111. Ghazanfar Musabekov is listed as Sovnarkom president in a 1925 document in *Obrazovanie*, p. 316, but Narimanov vacated that post and assumed his post in the CEC USSR in Moscow in 1923 or 1924, so Musabekov probably replaced him at that time; Karayev's election was reported in *BR*, 20 November 1927.

112. *Obrazovanie*, pp. 287–88.

113. R. G. Bagirova, "Razvitie transporta Azerbaidzhana v period postroeniia fundamenta sotsialisticheskoi ekonomiki (1926–1932 gg)," *Az igtisadi*, p. 97.

114. Ibid., p. 100.

115. A. Karimbekov, "Razvitie sotsialisticheskogo sorevnovaniia na Azerbaidzhan-skoi zheleznoi doroge v gody predvoennykh piatiletok," in *Az igtisadi*, pp. 123–24.

116. Ibid., pp. 124–25.

117. Bagirova ("Razvitie transporta," p. 100, citing TsGAOR, Azerb, f. 412, op. 1, d. 612, l. 3) refers to a rapid increase of passenger and freight traffic on the "Aliat-Julfa" line between 1928 and 1931. (Aliat is the terminus where the line south from Baku meets the westbound lines, both to Tiflis and Nakhjivan.) The émigré journal *Kurtuluş* (Berlin) discussed this rail link in 1930s, however, as if it were still not complete.

118. See *Atlas Azerbaidzhanskoi SSR* (Moscow, 1979), p. 6.

119. Karenin, *Äfändiyev*, pp. 96–98, 100–101.

120. *ZV*, 5 December 1925.

121. *BR*, 28 March 1926.

122. Alexandre Bennigsen and Chantal Lemercier-Quelquejay (*Islam in the Soviet Union*, G. Wheeler, trans. [London: Pall Mall, 1964], p. 135) note the policy was inaugurated in 1921.

123. There were only 98 Georgians, less than 1 percent. Figures for the Caucasian party and for Azerbaijan for 1925 from *ZV*, 5 December 1925.

124. *Tsentral'yi Komitet Azerbaidzhanskoi Kommunisticheskoi Partii (bol'shevik) Otchet VI s'ezdy Azerbaidzhanskoi Kommunisticheskoi Partii (bol'shevik)* (Baku, 1924), p. 94, reproduced in *Obrazovanie*, p. 146.

125. His name appears as Karakozian in *Kommunist* (hereafter, *Kom*) (Baku), 12 May 1920; *Obrazovanie*, pp. 43–44.

126. Published resolutions and decrees reflect other nonnatives: e.g., Gikalo (deputy commissar of internal affairs, Inozemtsev in CC AzCP in 1923; Pleshakov, Sorokin and Poluyan in Presidium CC AzCP in 1922.

127. Blank ("Centralization," pp. 333–34) agrees with this idea.

128. Narimanov's position on these matters, similar to that of Tatar M. Sultangaliev, has been documented in Soviet sources which denounced, then rehabilitated him.

129. Azerb. Academy of Sciences, *Khäbärlär/Izvestiia*, 1989, no. 4.

130. On these language policies, see H. B. Paksoy, *Alpamysh* (Hartford, Conn.: Association for the Advancement of Central Asian Research), chap. 2; Stefan Wurm, *Turkic Peoples of the USSR: Their Historical Background, Their Languages and the Development of Soviet Linguistic Policy* (Oxford, Eng.: Central Asian Research Centre with St. Antony's College, 1954), p. 50; the argument is developed further in Wurm's *The Turkic Language of Central Asia: Problems of Planned Culture Contact* (Oxford, Eng.: Central Asian Research Centre with St. Antony's College, 1954). The latter is Wurm's translation, with a commentary, of N. A. Baskakov, "Razvitie iazykov i pis'mennosti narodov SSSR," *Voprosy iazykoznaniia*, 1952/53.

131. Wurm, *Turkic Peoples*, p. 48, quoting Baskakov, "Razvitie iazykov," p. 41.

132. For example, M. Kuliyev, "Imdiki Türk edebiyati hakkinda," *Kom* [n.s., n.d., circa 1928] from J. Hajibeyli, private archive.

133. Pir (pseud.), "Pervye lastochki proletarskoi liberatury," *BR*, 8 July 1927.

134. "Konferentsiia azerbaidzhanskogo uchitel'stva," *BR*, 13 February 1925.

135. "Mearif sistemin äsas prinsipleri," *Kom* (10 October, no year, circa 1927) said that teachers had been indifferent to the class principle in culture. Therefore, the newspaper was calling them (presumably Azerbaijani Turks in Baku) to a large conference to discuss these "Basic Principles of the Education System."

136. *Obrazovanie*, pp. 104–112, 126–29.

137. *BR*, 20 December 1922; *Obrazovanie*, p. 137.

138. Armenak Nikitich Karakozov, born 1890 in a village of Zangezur, had been a party member since 1917. *Bor'ba za pobedu*, p. 540, and document no. 494, p. 421.

139. CC AzCP(b) protocol, 17 December 1922; *Obrazovanie*, pp. 134–35.

140. On Karakozov's posts, *Obrazovanie*, p. 105. *Bor'ba za pobedu*, p. 540; lists of party workers, see *Obrazovanie*, pp. 104, 134–35, 145, 147–48, 158–59.

141. According to *Nats-gos*, 1:326–27, the recommendation, made on 20 June 1923, was "to separate both the mountainous and lower portions of Karabagh into one single administrative unit." Inclusion of lower Karabagh had not previously been mentioned, so this recommendation was either a departure from previous plans or is reported in this source incorrectly.

142. *Obrazovanie*, pp. 149–50.

143. Decrees of AzCEC of 4 July, of the border commission of 7 July, of CC AzCP of 16 July, and allotment of funds of 28 July, 8 August, 5 September in *Obrazovanie*, pp. 151–55, 159, 176, 186–87.

144. *Nats-gos*, 1:326–27; document in *Obrazovanie*, pp. 268–70.

145. Protocol of CC AzCP, 22 October 1923; *Obrazovanie*, pp. 208–9.

146. In 1924–25, AONK received 596,523 rubles and NahkSSR, 525,931; in 1925–26, figures were 827,818 and 848,580, respectively. "General budget figures," AzCP Congress, 1925, *Obrazovanie*, p. 273.

147. Letter from Commissar of Education M. Kuliyev to CC AzCP dated 13 May 1925, *Obrazovanie*, pp. 287–88.

148. On decree and implementation, *Ist. Az.*, 3(1):305–6. Decree published in *BR*, 26 November 1924, in which each town and village to be included was listed.

149. In March 1925 Chairman of AzSovnarkom Musabekov reviewed continued difficulty of Azerbaijani Turkish nomads denied access to traditional *yaylaks*; *Obrazovanie*, pp. 279–80.

150. For example, at the March 1925 Fourth Congress of Soviets in Baku; text in *Obrazovanie*, pp. 279–80.

151 *Nats-gos*, 1:326–27, citing Party Archive of the Institute of History at the CC AzCP, f. 1.

152. Mil'man, *Azerbaidzhan SSR*, pp. 236–39; its constitution would not be complete until April 1926 and is described on pp. 240–48.

153. *Nats-gos*, 1:475, 477.

154. Ibid., 1:491–98; Azerbaijan constitution of 1937 discussed in Mil'man, *Azerbaidzhan SSR*, pp. 82–84.

155. Ratification was on 14 March 1937, *Nats-gos*, 1:492. The draft was published in *BR*, 24 February 1937. Karenin (*Afändiyev*, p. 118) listed members of the constitutional committee: G. Aghaverdiyev, N. Narimanov, H. Rahmanov, Efendiyev "and others." By 1935, however, Nariman Narimanov had been dead for ten years. The reference either is to a relative or reflects the Narimanov "mystique."

156. Based on the draft copy, *BR*, 24 February 1937.

157. Mil'man, *Azerbaidzhan SSR*, p. 82.

CHAPTER 8

1. Mir Said Sultangaliev was a leading Tatar "national communist" who argued that all members of "oppressor nations" (including Europe and Russia) equally oppress all members of "proletarian nations" (including Central Asia, the Volga, Azerbaijan, etc.). Thus the Russian proletariat was just as oppressive to the Central Asians as was the tsarist "bourgeois" regime. Alexandre Bennigsen and S. Enders Wimbush, *Muslim National Communism in the Soviet Union* (Chicago: University of Chicago Press, 1979); Azade-Ayşe Rorlich, *Volga Tatars: A Profile in National Resilience* (Stanford: Hoover Institution Press, 1986).

2. Baghirov was born in Kuba. Although it is likely he was an Azerbaijani Turk, some have suggested he was not. The biographical information on Baghirov is taken from various newspapers during and after his tenure of office. Some sources call him head of the AzCheka or AzGPU; documents in *K Istorii obrazovnii Nagorno-Karabakhskoi avtonomnoi oblasti* (Baku, 1989) (hereafter cited as *Obrazovanie*) show that he was commissar for internal affairs at least from 1921 to 1923.

3. "Rech' tov. Bagirova," *Bakinskii Rabochii* (hereafter, *BR*), 31 December 1926.

4. *Bor'ba za pobedu sovetskoi vlasti v Azerbaidzhane, 1918–1920; Dokumenty*

i materialy (Baku, 1967), pp. 536–37 (hereafter cited as *Bor'ba za pobedu*). According to this source, Khanbudaghov was head of the AzCheka "after the fall of the Musavat regime."

5. All-Union Communist party, but "ACP" was avoided for possible confusion with "AzCP."

6. Anatolii Aleksandrovich Karenin, *Sultan Mejid Äfändiyev*, M. Taghizadä, trans. (Baku, 1963), pp. 105–7, in the last instance, citing documents: Marxist-Leninist Institute, Azerbaijan filial party archive.

7. *Istoriia Azerbaidzhana/Azärbayjan tarikhi*, 3 vols. (Baku: Elm, 1958–1962) (hereafter cited as *Ist. Az.*), 3(1):494.

8. "Kavkaz GPU'ya Yardim" (reported by Ost Express telegraph agency, dated Moscow, 13 November 1934), in *Kurtuluş* (Berlin), no. 1 (November 1934).

9. *Ist. Az.* 3(1):397.

10. A. Vahap Yurstsever ("Azerbaycan İstiklal Savaşında Saheler," a multipart article in the journal *Azerbaycan* [Ankara], July–August 1956) stated that since 1921 secret groups with nationalist and socialist goals had existed in Soviet Azerbaijan.

11. Yurtsever ("İstiklal Savaşında") gave no date.

12. Alexandre Bennigsen and Chantal Lemercier-Quelquejay (*Islam in the Soviet Union*, Geoffrey Wheeler, trans. [London: Pall Mall, 1964], p. 160) cite *BR*, 8 December 1938. Huseinov was named in the 1937 purge trials and was executed in 1938. The date of *BR* may have been reported incorrectly.

13. Mirza Davud Huseinov, "Ideia nezavisimosti Azerbaidzhana i partiia mussavat," *Zaria Vostoka* (Tiflis) (hereafter, *ZV)*. The first article in the series was "I. Do fevral'skoi revoliutsii," 27 April 1925. This may have been the basis for Huseinov's 1927 monograph on the Musavat.

14. Baghirov, "Piat' let pobed i dostizhenii," and G[hazanfar] Musabekov, "Pod Znakom neuklonnogo rosta," *ZV*, 28 April 1925.

15. "Türk-Tatar Äksinkilabchilar," *Kommunist* (Baku) (hereafter, *Kom.*), 24 December 1925.

16. "Rech' tov. Bagirova," *BR*, 31 December 1926.

17. M. Orakhelashvili, "Im slezy—trudiashchimsia radost'," *ZV*, 17 December 1926; it was dated Ganje 12 December.

18. S. A. [pseud.], "Musavatskie shavki," *BR*, 3 January 1927.

19. "Mechty musavatistov," *BR*, 13 April 1927.

20. Mustafa Zakariaoglu Kuliyev, born in 1893 in Nukha, had been a Bolshevik since 1918. He edited major ideological journals. Z. B. Geiushev ([Göyüshev], *Filosofskaia mysl' v sovetskom Azerbaidzhane; kratkii ocherk* [Baku: Elm, 1979], pp. 26–27) gave no death date.

21. M. Kuliyev, "Musavatisty o 'natsional'nom dvizhenii'," *BR*, 23 May 1927.

22. Gh[azanfar] Musabekov, "Dusman kara kahinda janlanma," *Kom*, 3 June 1927; an Azerbaijani [pseud.], "Musavat-Ittihad Fa'aliyeti," *Kom*, 17 June 1927; A.

H. Karayev, "Ne tez unuttunuz biz ki unutmamishig," *Kom*, 11 August 1927, accused them of stirring up a "new provocation" about peasant taxation.

23. Karayev, "Makhinatsii 'nationalistov'," *BR*, 13 July 1927. Within two weeks Kuliyev would write "Nasledie prokliatogo proshlogo," *BR*, 25 July 1927.

24. "Dushmanlar daghilir—dahada ayik olmali," *Kom*, 14 September 1928.

25. Kerimov, "Musavat firkasy kechmishde ve Imdi," *Kom*, October 1928; A. H. Karayev, "Musavatcilarin yal da'vasy; Deterding köpekleri bogushurlar," *Kom*, 29 January 1929; and Mustafa Kuliyev, "M. E. Resulzadenin jeni manevrasi," *Kom* 31 August; 2, 3, September 1931.

26. *Ist. Az.*, 3(1):370, 376–79; Karenin, *Äfändiyev*, pp. 108–13.

27. Karenin (*Äfändiyev*, p. 112) discussed Efendiyev's support for cotton and his work in trying to convince peasants to grow it.

28. "Azerbaycan askerleri," *Kurtuluş*, November 1934.

29. *BR*, 21 December 1928. Karenin, *Äfändiyev*, p. 108, citing.

30. John J. Dziak, *Chekisty: A History of the KBG* (New York: Ivy Books, 1988), pp. 60–61.

31. Karenin, *Äfändiyev*, pp. 109–11.

32. Yurtsever, "İstiklal Savaşında," *Azerbaycan*, May–June 1955.

33. Ibid., July–August, 1955.

34. Radio Liberty script no. 1284, 28 April 1956, by A. Sultanzade.

35. *Ist. Az.*, 3(1):504, 534.

36. *Ist. Az.*, 3(1):534, contains only one paragraph on the purges in the entire volume, stating merely that they were victims of the "cult of personality." For short biographies of these men and other key figures, see *Bor'ba za pobedu*, pp. 511–46.

37. Mikail Namazoglu Huseinov, born in 1900 in Ganje. After 1925, he began a long career as propagandist, including, in 1930–31, head of dialectical materialism (diamat) kafedra at one institute in Baku. Although Geiushev (*Filosofskaia mysl'*, pp. 24–25) gave no death date, he gave no information after 1932.

38. *BR*, 14 March 1937, quoted in Jeyhun Hajibeyli's manuscript "Nekotorye otgoloski chistki 1937-go goda v Azerbaidzhane"; manuscript in private archive. Jeyhun Bey compiled the information from the Soviet press.

39. *Ist. Az.*, 3(1):505; Karenin, *Äfändiyev*, p. 118.

40. Karenin, *Äfändiyev*, p. 121.

41. The account of the trial is taken from Hajibeyli, "Nekotorye otgoloski."

42. Reported in *BR*, 30 May 1937; cited by Hajibeyli, "Nekotorye otgoloski."

43. Hajibeyli made this point in "Nekotorye otgoloski" but gave no citation for the publication of the November list.

44. Hajibeyli, "Nekotorye otgoloski," citing *BR*, 4, 5, and 6 June 1937.

45. Hajibeyli, "Nekotorye otgoloski," p. 2.

46. Khanbudaghov was the only one of this group to have been accused of wrongdoing before, in 1924, after which he was not even removed from the party.

47. Also named were Haydar Vezirov and Hasan Safarov, about whom no information was provided in this manuscript.

48. Hajibeyli, "Nekotorye otgoloski," gave these and other details of the confessions, citing *BR*, 28 October 37.

49. Vezirov was identified as "commander of an Azerbaijan Division" by Hajibeyli.

50. *BR*, 28 October–3 November 1937, cited by Hajibeyli. He did not specify whether this was to be hard labor.

51. Jeyhun Bey argued this was accomplished by the end of 1937; because he apparently wrote this article at the beginning of 1939, he could not have known of subsequent purges, such as those in the Red Army. In contrast, the NKVD purges were clearly a case of purging the purgers.

52. Hajibeyli, "Nekotorye otgoloski," pp. 5–6 of conclusion.

53. Karenin, *Äfändiyev*, p. 121. Karenin is silent on Efendiyev's fate.

54. Yurtsever, "İstiklal Savaşında," *Azerbaycan*, May–June 1956.

55. *BR*, 14 August 1938.

56. *BR*, 15 August 1938; all other headlines for this trial also included this litany— 14, 15, 18, 20 August.

57. *BR*, 20 August 1938.

58. Ibid.

59. "Gazety pokryvaiushchie burzhuaznykh natsionalistov," *BR*, 29 September 1937.

60. Ibid.

61. Yurtsever, İstiklal Savaşında," *Azerbaycan*, July–August 1956.

62. *Ocherk istorii Azerbaidzhanskoi sovetskoi literatury* (Moscow, 1963), a publication of the USSR Academy of Sciences; short biography on pp. 165–73 (hereafter cited as *Az Sov Lit*).

63. Gulam Mämmädli, comp., *Javid—Ömrüboyu; häyati vä yaradijilig salnamäsi; 1882–1941* (Baku: Yaziji, 1982), p. 292.

64. According to an English-language anthology of Azerbaijani poetry (*Azerbaijanian Poetry: An Anthology*, ed. Mirza Ibrahimov [Moscow: Progress Publishers, 1969?], p. 255), Haji Kerim Sanili (1878–1937?) was "slandered and arrested on false charges" in 1937. His work was still sensitive when the anthology was published, for it included only one short selection from his voluminous works.

65. Among other major cultural figures who died in this period were prose writers and dramatists Suleiman Sani Akhundov, 1875–1939, Sultan Mejid Ganizade, 1863–1938, Ibrahim Musabekov, 1879–1936, Jafar Jabarly, 1899–1934 (officially of "heart disease"), Buyuk Agha Talybly, 1897–1939, Hajibaba Nazarly, 1895–1937; poets Jelil Memedkuluzade, 1866–1932, Mikail Mushfik (Mikail Mirza Kadyroglu Islamzade), 1908–1939; composer Muslim Magomayev, 1885–1937.

66. Zbigniew Brzezinski, *The Permanent Purge: Politics in Soviet Totalitarianism* (Cambridge, Mass.: Harvard University Press, 1956), p. 189, citing A. Uralov (A. Avtorkhanov), *Staline au pouvoir* (Paris), pp. 163, 170.

CHAPTER 9

1. The phrase is from Adam Ulam, *Stalin: The Man and His Era* (New York, 1973).

2. *Istoriia Azerbaidzhana* (Baku, 1979) (hereafter cited as *Ist. Az.* [1979]), p. 172. This single-volume work was meant as an update to the Academy of Science's three-volume work published during 1958–1962.

3. *Istoriia natsional'no-gosudarstvennogo stroitel'stva v SSSR.* Vol. 1, *1917–1936* (Moscow: Mysl', 1972) (hereafter cited as *Nats-gos*), p. 173. Among "workers" were both blue and white collar, *rabochie i sluzhashchie.*

4. Details on these plans and the actual occupation of portions of the North Caucasus are provided by Alexiev and Wimbush, *Ethnic Minorities in the Red Army: Asset or Liability?* (Boulder: Westview Press, 1988), pp. 95–100.

5. *Nats-gos*, 2:78–81, describes in detail these and other administrative changes.

6. *Nats-gos*, 2:94, 99–100.

7. *Ist. Az.* (1979), p. 172; *Nats-gos*, 2:90.

8. *Ist. Az.* (1979), pp. 171–72.

9. *Nats-gos*, 2:91.

10. *Ist. Az.* (1979), p. 171; *Nats-gos*, 1:182.

11. *Ist. Az.* (1979), p. 178.

12. According to *Ist. Az.* (1979), p. 182, "over half-million went to the front" from Azerbaijan and "many" gave their lives.

13. Susan L. Curran and Dmitryi Ponomareff, *Managing the Ethnic Factor in the Russian and Soviet Armed Forces*, paper no. R-2640-1 (Santa Monica, Calif.: Rand Corporation, July 1982), pp. 31–32, citing Garish Ali Madatov, *Azerbaidzhan v Velikoi Otechestvennoi voine* (Baku: Elm 1975), p. 106; and Nikolai A. Kirsanov, *Partiinye mobilizatsii na front v gody Velikoi otechestvennoi voiny* (Moscow: Moscow State University, 1972), pp. 168–69. The revised paper (hereafter cited as "Managing") was included in Alexiev and Wimbush, ed., *Ethnic Minorities.* Coverage of Azerbaijan was weak.

14. Teresa Rakowska-Harmstone, et al., *The Warsaw Pact: A Question of Cohesion*, Phase 2, vol. 3. An Operational Research and Analysis Establishment Extramural Paper of the Canadian Department of National Defense, no. 39 (Ottawa, 1986), pp. 21–24.

15. *Nats-gos*, 2:99.

16. Rakowska-Harmstone, *Warsaw Pact*, p. 24.

17. Ibid., p. 25, quoting Kirsanov, "Kommunisticheskaia partiia—organizator

dobrovol'cheskikh formirovanii Krasnoi Armii v gody Velikoi Otechestvennoi voiny," *Voprosy istorii KPSS*, no. 11, 1976, p. 9.

18. Curran and Ponomareff, "Managing," p. 58, in Alexiev and Wimbush, *Ethnic Minorities*. They stated the division had a "Turkic-named officer" and cited Madatov, *Azerbaidzhan v Velikoi*, p. 174.

19. Curran and Ponomareff, "Managing," p. 57.

20. Ibid., pp. 55, 57–58, 61. Only 1.33 percent of the USSR population was Azerbaijan; 1.33 percent Georgian; 1.27 percent Armenian.

21. This point was noted by Christopher Jones and is elaborated in Rakowska-Harmstone, *Warsaw Pact*, Phase 2, vol. 1, chap. 5; Jones was a participant in and coauthor of this study.

22. Rakowska-Harmstone, *Warsaw Pact*, pp. 26–28.

23. K. Tskitishvili (*Zakavkaz'e v partizanskoi voine, 1941–1945 gg* [Tiflis, 1973], p. 116) cites Communist party archives (hereafter, Partarkhiv) of Georgia. In this book Azerbaijan was covered least of the three republics, using mainly *Bakinskii Rabochiii* (hereafter, *BR*). *Nats-gos*, 2:95–97, provided some information on the activity of partisan units in Ukraine, Belorussia, and RSFSR.

24. Tskitishvili, *Zakavkaz'e*, pp. 156–57, citing Partarkhiv in Azerbaijan.

25. Tskitishvili, *Zakavkaz'e*, p. 127.

26. Ibid., p. 155.

27. Ibid., pp. 175–76.

28. Ibid., pp. 207–9. He described other partisans in Slovakia (pp. 215–16, 223, 24) and in France (p. 228), citing *BR*.

29. *Nats-gos*, 2:87. Among those receiving relatively few decorations were the Tajiks with 14,000 and Turkmen with 15,000; the bulk went to those Slavs whose territories were occupied. The Balts, victims of both the Nazis and the Soviets, received few decorations: 11,500 for Estonians; 11,000 to Latvians, an 6,000 to Lithuanians.

30. *Nats-gos*, 2:87.

31. *Ist. Az.* (1979), p. 182.

32. *Nats-gos* 2:77.

33. P. Äfändiyev (*Azärbayjan shifani khalg ädäbiyyati* [Baku: Maarif, 1981], pp. 343–51) described themes and works.

34. H. B. Paksoy, *Alpamysh: Central Asian Identity under Russian Rule* (Hartford, Conn.: Association for the Advancement of Central Asian Research, 1989), chaps. 1–2.

35. Nazar A. Pashaev, *Pobeda kulturnoi revoliutsii v sovetskom Azerbaidzhane* (Moscow: Nauka, 1976), p. 149.

36. A. Vahap Yurtsever, "Azerbaycan İstiklal Savaşında Saheler," *Azerbaycan* (Ankara), May–June 1956.

37. A. S. Sumbatzade, *Azerbaidzhanskaia Istoriografiia XIX–XX vekov* (Baku: Elm, 1987), p. 100.

38. Ibid.

39. *416-ia Krasnoznamennaia Taganrogskaia strelkovaia diviziia: Sbornik doku-mentov* (Baku: Azernshr, 1944). Sumbatzade, *Istoriografiia,* p. 101, cited this and many other such works.

40. Quoted in Rakowska-Harmstone, *Warsaw Pact,* p. 30.

41. Ibid.

42. Ibid., p. 34, citing A. Alexiev, "Soviet Nationalities in German Wartime Strategy 1941–1945," Rand Corporation, R-2772-NA (Santa Monica, Calif.: August 1982). This Alexiev paper was the basis for his article in Alexiev and Wimbush, *Ethnic Minorities.*

43. Alexiev, "Soviet Nationalities in German Wartime Strategy," in Alexiev and Wimbush, *Ethnic Minorities,* p. 73.

44. These were combat units, not the *Hilfswillige* auxiliary units used for noncombat functions and made up overwhelmingly of Ukrainians and Belorussians—men freed once their native lands had been occupied. See Alexiev, "Soviet Nationalities in German Wartime Strategy," pp. 108–9.

45. Tskitishvili (*Zakavkaz'e,* pp. 179–80) provided extensive detail on the creation of Georgian and Armenian units.

46. Alexiev, "Soviet Nationalities in German Wartime Strategy," p. 114.

47. Ibid. This may be an error, for context suggests 1941.

48. Rakowska-Harmstone, *Warsaw Pact,* pp. 30, 32, 34, the last citing Alexiev, *Soviet Nationalities in German Wartime Strategy,* Rand Corporation paper.

49. Alexiev, "Soviet Nationalities in German Wartime Strategy," citing Hoffman, *Die Ostlegionen,* pp. 38–39, 76.

50. Alexiev, "Soviet Nationalities in German Wartime Strategy," pp. 115–16.

51. Rakowska-Harmstone (*Warsaw Pact,* pp. 30–45) articulates these points. Tskitishvili (*Zakavkaz'e,* pp. 177–200) conforms to the official line that men were recruited under duress, hunger, and torture. Once in these units, he says, men from the Caucasian republics formed secret "underground organizations" that planned to flee the German forces once in action and join partisan or regular units of the Red Army against the Germans.

52. Rakowska-Harmstone, *Warsaw Pact,* p. 34.

53. Alexiev, "Soviet Nationalities in German Wartime Strategy," p. 115, citing Patrik von zur Muehlen, *Zwischen Hakenkreuz und Sowjetstern: Der Nationalismus der sowjetischen Orientvoelker im Zweiten Weltkrieg,* vol. 5 (Dusseldorf; Droste Verlag, 1971). Figures for other groups are as follows: 110,000–180,000 Central Asians; 35,000–40,000 Volga Tatars; 20,000 Crimean Tatars.

54. Rakowska-Harmstone, *Warsaw Pact,* p. 33, citing Alexiev, *Soviet Nationalities in German Wartime Strategy,* Rand Corporation paper.

55. Ibid., p. 254, note 69, citing Alexander Dallin, *German Rule in Russia, 1941–1945: A Study of Occupation Policies* (London and New York: Macmillan and St. Martin's Press, 1957).

56. Rakowska-Harmstone, *Warsaw Pact*, p. 27.

57. Ibid., p. 42, quoting Viktor Suvorov (pseud.), *Inside the Red Army* (London: Hamish Hamilton, 1982).

58. On this conference, trends in postwar economic history, and an overview of the works on economic history written in the postwar period, see Y. Hasanov, "Müharibädän sonraki dövrdä Azärbayjanda igtisadi tä'lim," *Azärbayjanïn igtisadi tarikhinin aktual problemläri* (Baku: Elm, 1978) (hereafter cited as *Az igtisadi*).

59. *Nats-gos*, 2:103–4, 115–16.

60. *Istoriia Azerbaidzhana/Azärbayjan Tarikhi*, 3 vols. (Baku: Elm, 1958–1962) (hereafter cited as *Ist. Az.*, followed by volume and part numbers), 3:(2):214–15.

61. Äfändiyev, *Azärbayjan shifahi khalg ädäbiyyatï*, p. 352.

62. Alexandre Bennigsen, "The Crisis of Turkic National Epics, 1951–1952; Local Nationalism or Internationalism?" in *Canadian Slavonic Papers* 17, nos. 2–3 (1975), and Paksoy, *Alpamysh*, chap. 2.

63. Bennigsen and Chantal Lemercier-Quelquejay, *Islam in the Soviet Union*, Geoffrey Wheeler, trans. (London: Pall Mall, 1964), pp. 219–20.

64. Described by A. N. Guliyev in his address to the Azerbaijan Academy of Sciences in 1954; reported in M. A. Ismailov, "Nauchnaia sessiia v Institute istorii i filosofii Akademii Nauk Azerbaidzhanskoi SSR," *Trudy* (Institute of History) 4 (1955). A year earlier, Baghirov had called both men "progressive."

65. Lowell Tillet, *The Great Friendship* (Chapel Hill: University of North Carolina Press, 1969), p. 83, contrasted treatment of wartime and immediate postwar histories. The Kazakh history was attacked, others were not. Tillet noted that the Ukrainians, Armenians, and Tajiks fought "Poles, Turks, Persians, Arabs and Mongols. The Kazakhs, in their modern history at least, had specialized in fighting Russians."

66. The following discussion is taken from Sumbatzade, *Istoriografiia*, chap. 4.

67. Digs in Mingechevir in central Azerbaijan and in Nakhjivan and Karabagh were reported in the Azerbaijani press during the 1920s and 1930s; at that time "learned societies" were formed to popularize the findings, and links to the university were fostered.

68. *Ismail Safavi (Azerbaidzhanskii polkovodets XV-XVI vv.)* (Baku, 1942), cited in Sumbatzade, *Istoriografiia*, p. 113.

69. Not least are Sumbatzade's own works: "O razoritel'nom kharaktere iranskikh nashestvii na Azerbaidzhan v period prisoedineniia strany k Rossii (1801–1828)," *Uchenye zapiski* (Azerbaijan State University), no. 2 (1955); "Progressivny ekonomicheskie posledstviia prisoedineniia Azerbaidzhana k Rossii v XIX v.," *Trudy* (Institute of History and Philosophy, Azerbaijan Academy of Sciences) 5 (1954).

70. Description and citations in Sumbatzade, *Istoriografiia*, pp. 119–22.

71. Pashaev, *Pobeda kulturnoi*, pp. 24–25.

72. Ibid., pp. 44–46.

73. Ibid., pp. 86–87.

74. Ibid., p. 150.

CHAPTER 10

1. In 1954 Baghirov was expelled from the CC AzCP. For Mustafayev's speech, see *XX s"edz Kommunisticheskoi Partii Sovetskogo Soiuza, 14–25 fevralia 1956 g; Stenograficheskii otchet* (Moscow, 1956), p. 544. The title commissar was changed to minister during World War II.

2. A charge corroborated by N. Keykurun (Seyh Zamanli); *Azerbaycan* İstiklal mücadelesinin Hatıraları (Istanbul, 1964), pp. 88–100, describes meetings and conversations between Keykurun and Beria.

3. *Bakinskii Rabochii* (hereafter, *BR*), 26 May 1956.

4. A. Vahap Yurtsever, "Bagirof'un İdami," *Azerbaycan* (Ankara), May–June 1956, pp. 8–12, and A. Azertekin, "Bir adamdan alinacak ders," *Azerbaycan*, May–June 1956, pp. 19–20.

5. Radio Liberty scripts 1379–80 of 1956.

6. Yurtsever, "Bagirof'un İdeami," p. 11.

7. Naturally sweet, *kaymak* rises to the top when whole milk is boiled and among nomads may constitute a main staple in the diet. So the "*kaymak* of the Azerbaijani intelligentsia" is more than "best," it is its sustaining force.

8. *Istoriia natsional'no-gosudarstvennogo stroitel'stva v SSSR*, Volume 2, *1936–1972* (Moscow: Mysl', 1972) (hereafter cited as *Nats-gos*), p. 117. This policy statement left out specifics as well on the origin of funds that the republic now had the right to spend and whether and how this reform was enacted.)

9. The following comes from *Nats-gos*, 2:117–32, citing, inter alia: "Dikrety KPSS i Sovetskogo pravitel'stva po khoziaistvennym voprosam, 1917–1957 gody," *Sbornik dokumentov* 4 (1953–1957):674–77.

10. *Nats-gos*, 2:130; it was also adopted by Uzbek, Tajik, Moldavian, and Armenian SSRs. Article 16 of Azerbaijan's 1937 constitution stated that "territorial change" could not be made without the approval of the republic. The 1956 amendment was more specific.

11. *Nats-gos*, 2:129–30; Khrushchev initiated his Seven-Year Plan at this time and his famous (or infamous) "territorial" system of economic organization.

12. *Nats-gos*, 2:150–51.

13. These biographical data were given in an interview with Mustafayev, "Sluzhit' narodu—schast'e!" *Gänjlik/molodost'*, no. 6 (1988). *Gänjlik* is the organ of the Azerbaijani Komsomol.

14. *XX s"ezd kommunisticheskoi partii sovetskogo souiza, 14–25 fevralia 1956 g; Stenograficheskii otchet* (Moscow, 1956), I:538–44.

15. It was in this speech that Mustafayev criticized his predecessor and stated that

Baghirov's victims—among whom he named Narimanov—were "honorable . . . fighters for the revolution."

16. *Vneocherednoi XXI s"ezd Kommunisticheskoi Partii Sovetskogo Soiuza: 27 Ianvaria–5 Fevralia 1959 g. Stenograficheskii otchet* (Moscow, 1959), I:455–62, morning session of 31 January.

17. Ibid., p. 461; Mustafayev was actually quoting Sergei M. Kirov, AzCP first secretary in the 1920s.

18. Mustafayev, "Sluzhit' narodu—schast'e!"

19. Yaroslav Bilinsky ("The Soviet Education Laws of 1958–59 and Soviet Nationalities Policy," *Soviet Studies* 14, no. 2 [October 1962]: 138–57), partly citing Jeyhun Hajibeyli, argued that Mustafayev's opposition to the change led to his removal. Azade-Ayşe Rorlich ("Not by History Alone: The Retrieval of the Past Among the Tatars and the Azeris," *CAS* 3, no. 2 [1984]) suggested Mustafayev's removal was part of a broad purge. The two possibilities are not mutually exclusive.

20. An article commemorating his 80th birthday (*Elm*, 19 May 1990) listed more than 300 articles and five monographs, suggesting his scholarly credentials were legitimate.

21. Rorlich, "Not by History Alone"; also Steven E. Hegaard, "Nationalism in Azerbaidzhan in the Era of Brezhnev," in G. W. Simmonds, ed., *Nationalism in the USSR and Eastern Europe in the Era of Brezhnev and Kosygin* (Detroit, 1977). Despite a lack of Turkish-language materials and the often uncritical treatment of information, Hegaard does relay some useful information.

22. Even in imperial Russia, the merchant ranks were filled with non-Russians—Jews, Tatars, Armenians, Germans, and others.

23. "Iranda antikommunizm ideologiyasïnïn bä'zi jähätläri," *Azärbayjan Kommunisti* (monthly journal of the AzCP CC) (hereafter cited as *Az Kom*), no. 7 (1965), concerned U.S. anti-Communist propaganda in Iran; Dr. Prof. M. Gaziyev, "V. I. Lenin Shärg khalglarïnïn dostudur," *Az Kom*, no. 10 (1968), was an article reviewing a two-volume collection of documents (*V. I. Lenin—drug narodov Vostoka* [Baku, 1967]), noting Lenin's intent to make the Soviet East a model for "liberation, movements" elsewhere.

24. Hegaard ("Nationalism") described an exchange between Akhundov and Brezhnev at the March Plenum in which Akhundov explained lowered cotton output by soil depletion, saying cotton needed to be "taken out" for the sake of soil recovery. Brezhnev reportedly acknowledged this as an "objective" problem. No source cited.

25. Y. Akhundov, "Ideolozhi ishimizin bä'zi mäsäläläri haggïnda," *Az Kom*, no. 5 (1968); quotations from pp. 13–15.

26. "Azärbayjan kommunist partiyasï rägämlärdä (1961–1965-ji iller)," *Az Kom*, no. 9 (1965); 40–50. There were 198,539 full and candidate members, 19–20 percent women in 1961–65. Members with higher education increased from 16.7 percent of members on 1 January 1962 to 17.8 percent on 1 January 1965. Those with middle education went from 25.2 percent to 29 percent, whereas those with only elementary education dropped from 7.6 percent to 5.9 percent. The largest single

group were the "intellectual" or artistic group at 29.8 percent; 23 percent were in technical-engineering or agriculture. There were 41.3 percent "workers," 19.6 percent *kolkhozniki,* and 26.6 percent technical and agricultural "specialists."

27. Two cases are cited in Hegaard, "Nationalism," p. 191.

28. Ilya Zemtsov, *Partiia ili mafia?* (Paris, Les Editeurs Reunis, 1976), pp. 43–44, citing "secret party statistics," pp. 9, 44. This exposé was by a former sociologist in the office of the Azerbaijan first secretary who served under Akhundov, and in the early Aliyev years. Despite his access to sensitive material, he was allowed to emigrate. His writings have not been corroborated by any other source and must be used with caution.

29. Even compared with other republics of Central Asia from 1960 to 1975, Azerbaijan's position continued to slip. According to data compiled by Martin McAuley, Azerbaijan's "real per capita total income" in 1960 ranked above only the Kirgiz and Tajik SSRs. Figures for 1965, 1970, and 1975 show Azerbaijan ranked higher than Tajikistan only among Central Asian republics. Martin McAuley, "The Soviet Muslim Population: Trends in Living Standards, 1960–75," in Y. Ro'i, ed., *The USSR and the Muslim World* (London: George Allen & Unwin, 1984), p. 99.

30. Rorlich, "Not by History Alone," p. 92.

31. Hegaard, "Nationalism," makes a persuasive case here, pp. 193–94.

32. Ibid., p. 194.

33. From handwritten manuscript by Jeyhun Hajibeyli, signed "Azeri"; private archive.

34. *Ädäbiyyat vä Injäsänät,* 20 January 1957.

35. Hamid Araslï, E. Temirchizadä, and M. X. Tahmasib, "Dädä Gorgut'un she'iri," *Kommunist* (Baku) (hereafter cited as *Kom*), 26 March 1957.

36. *BR,* 29 December 1956.

37. Jeyhun Hajibeyli in a manuscript signed "Azeri"; private archive.

38. Ibid., citing unnamed article by Mirza Ibrahimov in the literary weekly news-paper *Ädäbiyyat vä Injäsänät,* 20 January 1957.

39. This is documented in the case of the *Alpamysh* dastan by H. B. Paksoy (*Alpamysh: Central Asian Identity under Russian Rule* [Hartford: Association for the Advancement of Central Asian Research, 1989]). Such manipulation would be more difficult to accomplish with *Dede Korkut* because manuscripts and translations have long been available in the West. It may have been partially achieved with *Köroglu*; further study is needed to clarify the issue.

40. M. A. Ismailov, "Nauchnaia sessiia v Institute istorii i filosofii Akademii Nauk Azerbaidzhanskoi SSR," *Trudy* (Institute of History) 4 (1955). This article described a conference of March 1954. The case of the Alpamysh dastan, which was "rehabi-litated" at such a conference but then replaced with a "sanitized" version touted as the "most complete," is detailed in Paksoy, *Alpamysh*, chap. 2. It is suggestive for *Köroglu*, less so for *Dede Korkut*. All are shared by Turks in several areas and can not truly be considered "national" in the narrow sense.

41. *Istoriia Azerbaidzhana/Azärbayjan tarikhi* (hereafter cited as *Ist. Az.*), 3 vols. (Baku: Elm, 1958–1962), 1:xi.

42. On the Oriental Institute reorganizations, see N. A. Kuznetsova and L. M. Kulagina, *Iz istorii sovetskogo vostokovedeniia* (Moscow: Nauka, 1970), and Wayne Vucinich, "Structure of Soviet Orientology," in Wayne Vucinich, ed., *Russia and Asia; Essays in the Influence of Russia on Asian Peoples* (Stanford: Stanford University Press, 1972). On dastans, see Alexandre Bennigsen, "The Crisis of Turkic National Epics, 1951–1952; Local Nationalism or Internationalism?" in *Canadian Slavonic Papers* 17, nos. 2–3 (1975), and Paksoy, *Alpamysh*, chap. 2.

43. This tendency to follow current borders predominated into the 1980s. Thus even ancient monuments are placed only in the territory of the present-day Azerbaijan SSR omitting, for example, Zangezur, now in the Armenian SSR.

44. *Ist. Az.*, 1:44–49.

45. *Ist. Az.*, 1:94–95; on the Khazars, see Peter B. Golden, *Khazar Studies* (Budapest: Hungarian Academy of Sciences, 1980).

46. A. S. Sumbatzade, *Azerbaidzhanskaia Istoriografiia XIX-XX vekov* (Baku: Elm, 1987), pp. 132–33.

47. *Ist. Az.*, 3(2):214–15.

48. Sumbatzade, *Istoriografiia*, pp. 199–201, listed his own works: *Sel'skoe khoziaistvo Azerbaidzhana v XIX v.* (Baku, 1958); *Promyshlennost' Azerbaidzhana v XIX v.* (Baku, 1964); *Sotsial'no-ekonomicheskie predposylki pobedy sovetskoi vlasti v Azerbaidzhane* (Baku, 1972) and I. A. Talybzade's Azerbaijani Turkish-language work (cited in Russian): *Agrarnaia reforma v Azerbaidzhane v 1912 gody* (Baku, 1965).

49. *Ocherki istorii Azerbaidzhanskoi literatury* (Moscow: Nauka, 1963). Iu. Samedov, *Rasprostranenie marksizma v Azerbaidzhane*, 2 vols. (Baku, 1966), and Kamal Talybzadä, *XX äsr Azärbayjan ädäbi tängidi* (Baku, 1966).

50. This is corroborated by Rorlich in "Not by History Alone."

51. Efendiyev, *Obrazovanie azerbaidzhanskogo gosudarstva Sefevidov v nachale XVI v.* (Baku, 1961).

52. See her *Ocherki istorii srednevekovogo Baku, VIII - nachalo XIX vv.* (Baku: Academy of Sciences, 1964) and her 1983 work on the Shirvanshahs cited above and in the bibliography.

53. Among Ziya Buniatov's major works are *Azerbaidzhan v VII-IX vekov* (Baku: Elm 1965); its Azerbaijani Turkish translation is *Azärbayjan VII-IX äsrlärdä* (1989); translations on the history of Azerbaijan from Arabic are Abu Muhammad Ahmad ibn A'sam al-Kufi, *Kitab al-futuh* (tenth century) as *Kniga zavoevanii* (Baku: Elm, 1981), and from Turkish, Ibrahim Efendi Peçevi, *Peçevi tarihi* (seventeenth century) as *Istoriia* (Baku: Elm, 1988).

54. Cited in Sumbatzade, *Istoriografiia*, p. 194. This volume was also published in English by Cambridge University Press in 1963.

55. *Nats-gos*, 2:152.

56. *Azärbayjan* (Baku), no. 11, (1966):198–201.

57. Quoted in Bilinsky, "Soviet Education Laws," p. 139.

58. Ibid., p. 146, quoting *BR*, 27 March 1959.

59. Ibid., note 57.

60. Report of Radio Liberty Munich, 18 August 1967, on an article in *Azärbayjan müällimi* of 20 June 1967.

61. A. Zeynalov (candidate of economic sciences), "Ijtimai amayin sosialistjasina täshkili," *Az Kom*, no. 1 (1968).

62. Keramet Taghiyev, "Onun hayat yolu belädir," *Az Kom*, no. 12 (1968), had interesting aspects and was not merely a propaganda item.

CHAPTER 11

1. Ilya Zemtsov, *Partiia ili mafia?* (Paris: Les Editeurs Reunis, 1976), p. 70; post-1987 accusatory articles against him sometimes suggest he "sat home" during the war.

2. Zemtsov (*Partiia ili mafia?* pp. 72–74) stated he went to the Senior Party school. R. D. Laird (*The Politburo: Demographic Trends, Gorbachev and the Future* [Boulder, Colo.: Westview Press, 1986], p. 118) stated that Aliyev joined the party in 1945 and that his education was in history. This is confirmed by interviews in Baku; he studied in the Evening Division of Azerbaijan State University. The formal name of SMERSH was Chief Directorate for Counterintelligence of the People's Commissariat for Defense; it was a Special Department of the NKVD.

3. Laird, *Politburo*, p. 118, gave Aliyev's record of promotions and titles. On Tsvigun, see John Dziak, *Chekisty: A History of the KGB* (New York: Ivy Books, 1988), pp. 174–75.

4. According to Alexander Rahr ("The Composition of the Politbiuro and the Secretariat of the CC of the CPSU," *Radio Liberty Research* [Munich], 236/87 [26 June 1988]), Aliyev was named chairman, Bureau of the Politbiuro Commission for Direction and Control of Working Out Complex Programs of Development of Consumer Goods Production and System of Consumer Services in 1983, and had been chairman, Bureau of Council of Ministers for Social Development, since November 1986.

5. That he was primarily an Andropov protégé and a skilled party manipulator was convincingly argued by S. Enders Wimbush in "Why Geidar Aliev?" *Central Asian Survey* (hereafter cited as *CAS*) 1, no. 4 (April 1983). Wimbush discussed the other popular interpretations and their many weaknesses. For example, if the Kremlin wanted a "Muslim" to parade before the Islamic world, why choose a member of a Shi'i people rather than a Sunni like Uzbekistan's Rashidov?

6. Steven E. Hegaard, "Nationalism in Azerbaidzhan in the Era of Brezhnev," in

G. W. Simmonds, ed., *Nationalism in the USSR and Eastern Europe in the Era of Brezhnev and Kosygin* (Detroit, 1977), citing *Bakinskii Rabochii* (hereafter cited as *BR*), 7 August 1969.

7. *XXV s"ezda kommunisticheskoi partii Sovetskogo Soiuza (24 fevralia–5 martaa 1976 goda), Stenograficheskii otchet* (Moscow, 1976), vol. 1, pp. 209–15.

8. *Materialy XXX s"ezda kommunisticheskoi partii Azerbaidzhana (28–30 ianvaria 1981 goda)* (Baku, 1981), p. 76. The long introduction described is found on pp. 7–14.

9. Ibid., pp. 80, 83, 85.

10. Ibid., pp. 113–21. Numerous conferences, seminars, and "political days" had been held and meetings arranged for writers and artists to meet with kolkhoz workers. In 1980 alone more than 330,000 lectures were given in the republic on ideological topics including the works of Lenin and Brezhnev.

11. Ibid., pp. 87–89. In the 1981 party, there were 36.2 percent workers, 10 percent kolkhozniki—down from 1965 levels of 41.3 and 19 percent—12 percent "technical intelligentsia," and 17 percent "those engaged in science, literature, art, education, health services, etc."

12. In 1970 Armenians were 13.7 percent of the AzCP but 9.4 percent of the population, and Russians were 12.4 percent of the AzCP and 10 percent of the population. Institut Istorii Kompartii Azerbaidzhana, *Kommunisticheskaia partiia Azerbaidzhana v tsifrakh; statisticheskii sbornik* (Baku, 1970), p. 12.

13. *Materialy XXX s"ezda* listed names of individuals removed (pp. 93, 97, 101, 106–7, 111), including ministers, heads of international enterprises, first secretaries of the Salyan, Kubatli, and Zangelan raikomy, and many others.

14. Arkadii Vaksberg ("Burnye aplodismenty," *Literaturnaia gazeta* 21 September 1988) reported Gambai Mamedov's statements that he had criticized Aliyev's administration in a party session for ignoring abuses of justice. Mamedov attributed his removal from his post as retaliation by Aliyev for public criticism.

15. Hegaard ("Nationalism"), citing *BR* and *Pravda*, listed the ministers of internal affairs and industrial construction among others purged by November 1969. For economic crimes, at least two individuals were reportedly executed in 1973.

16. Zemtsov, *Partiia ili Mafia?* pp. 89–92.

17. John Patton Willerton, "Patronage and Politics in the Soviet Union" (Ph.D. dissertation, University of Michigan, 1985), cited in R. G. Suny, "Transcaucasia: Cultural Cohesion and Ethnic Revival in a Multinational Society," in Lubomyr Hajda and Mark Beissinger, eds., *The Nationalities Factor in Soviet Politics and Society* (Boulder, Colo.: Westview Press, 1990), p. 230.

18. R. Mehdiyev, "Partiya dakhili demokratiya vä partiya intizamïnïn möhkäm-ländirilmäsi," *Azärbayjan Kommunisti* (hereafter cited as *Az Kom*), no. 3, 1983. This journal is the monthly organ of the Central Committee AzCP.

19. *XXV s"ezda*, pp. 210–11; *XXVI s"ezd kommunisticheskoi partii Sovetskogo Soiuza (23 fevralia–3 marta 1981 goda), Stenograficheskii otchet* (Moscow, 1981), vol. 1, pp. 180–85.

20. *Sovetskaia kul'tura*, 4 February 1989, announced that Aliyev retired "last year." This fifteen-line item was "from Novosibirsk."

21. Vaksberg, "Burnye aplodismenty," began with examples of the sycophancy toward Aliyev, then moved to the discussion of the Mamedov case. The article had little material on Aliyev himself. L. Polonskii ("Tri priezda," *BR*, 14 August 1988) described Brezhnev's visits and Aliyev's promotion of Brezhnev's "cult of personality" in Azerbaijan. The article was more anti-Brezhnev than anti-Aliyev. Vladimir Sinitsyn ("Chernaia pamiat'," *Sel'skaia zhizn'*, 21 October 1988) tried to draw a strained parallel between Baghirov's killings and Aliyev's nepotism, including misplaced sympathy for the brutal Ordzhonikidze.

22. Javanshir Melikov, "V zalozhnikakh u klana," *Sotsialisticheskaia industriia* 23 October 1988. From the name one might guess this writer to be at least partly Azerbaijani, but the name Melikov is ambiguous.

23. "V zalozhnikakh u klana."

24. "Tri priezda"; "Chernaia pamiat'" ended in this vein.

25. "V zalozhnikakh u klana."

26. Suny ("Cultural Cohesion," pp. 245–47) claimed Aliyev's removal was part of a "trade" in which the Armenian first secretary was also removed. Not explained is why the Azerbaijanis would agree to trade their bishop for a pawn, or why they would think they had to trade anything.

27. Thane Gustafson and Dawn Mann ("Gorbachev's Next Gamble," *Problems of Communism* 36, no. 4 [July–August 1986]) confirmed this pattern even before the fall of Aliyev.

28. *XXVI s"ezda*, pp. 182–83.

29. *Materialy XXX s"ezda*, p. 19.

30. Ibid., pp. 40–49 on cotton, pp. 55–58 on irrigation, and pp. 59–60 on chemicals.

31. Ibid., pp. 40, 50–51, on grapes.

32. I. D. Mustafayev, "Här sheyin äväli," *Azärbayjan*, no. 10 (1979). This is the organ of the republican Writers' Union.

33. Emil Aghayev, "Khäzärin taleyi," *Azärbayjan*, no. 10, 1979.

34. *Materialy XXX s"ezda*, pp. 18, 73–74.

35. Observed by the author during research trips in Baku, 1980–81 and 1984–85. In 1984, with rationing in place, two kilograms of meat (excluding sausage and chicken, which were not rationed) and one kilogram of butter were allowed per month per person.

36. *Chislennost' i sostav naseleniia SSSR; Po dannym vsesoiuznoi perepisi naseleniia 1979 goda* (Moscow, 1984); some percentages from Suny, "Cultural Cohesion."

37. Comparable statistics for neighboring Georgia and Armenia, cited partly by Suny in "Cultural Cohesion," pp. 236–37, show that these two republics had a higher proportion of natives than Azerbaijan. Among the Azerbaijani Turks in the USSR, 84–86 percent resided in Azerbaijan between 1959 and 1979.

38. One of the first and most spectacular discussions of these demographic changes and their possible implications was presented by Hélène Carrère d'Encause, *L'Empire éclaté* (Paris, 1978) (English translation: *Decline of an Empire* [New York: Newsweek, 1979]).

39. Even Aliyev did not try to make false claims about the program in Azerbaijan, noting merely its importance in "internationalist and patriotic education." *Materialy XXX s"ezda*, p. 123.

40. A survey of the Soviet and Warsaw Pact military establishment is in Teresa Rakowska-Harmstone, et al., *The Warsaw Pact: A Question of Cohesion*, phase 2, vol. 3, Extra-Mural Paper of the Canadian Department of National Defense, no. 39 (Ottawa, 1986). See S. Enders Wimbush and Alex Alexiev, *The Ethnic Factor in the Soviet Armed Forces*, Rand Corporation R-2787/1, March 1982; and S. Enders Wimbush, *Soviet Nationalities in Strategic Perspective* (London: Croom Helm, 1985).

41. Alex Alexiev and S. E. Wimbush, eds., *Ethnic Minorities in the Red Army: Asset or Liability* (Boulder, Colo.: Westview Press, 1988), pp. 16–17. This is based on the Rand study cited above.

42. Alexiev and Wimbush, *Ethnic Minorities in the Red Army*, p. 188.

43. Interviews cited here were conducted by this writer during field research in Baku between 1980 and 1985.

44. Alexiev and Wimbush, *Ethnic Minorities in Red Army*, pp. 128–30.

45. *Materialy XXX s"ezda*, pp. 80–82.

46. "Azerbaidzhanskii iazyk v sfere vysshego obrazovaniia," *Razvitie natsional'nykh iazykov v sviazi s ikh funktsionirovaniem v sfere vysshego obrazovaniia* (Moscow: Nauka, 1982), p. 34–35, reported that ten faculties of the university provided "parallel" sectors in Russian and Azerbaijan Turkish, though the latter were more numerous. The portion of Azerbaijanis were 96 percent in the oriental faculty, 78 percent in history, 90 percent in geology, 85 percent in economy, 67 percent in chemistry, 70 percent in juridical faculty.

47. "Azerbaidzhanskii iazyk v sfere," pp. 29–63.

48. "Milli azadlïg häräkatï vä müasir antikommunizmä garshï mübarizä mäsäläläri," *Az Kom*, no. 12 (1971).

49. Gasïm Gasïmzadä, "Garshïlïglï ädäbi tä'sir problemi," *Azerbaijan*, no. 1 (1980).

50. "Bästäkarïn yüksäk väzifäsi vä amalï," *Azerbaijan*, no. 11 (1979).

51. *Materialy XXX s"ezda*, pp. 130–34.

52. M. Shiräliyev, M. Mämmädov ("Dilimizin sälisliyinä diggäti artïrag," *Az Kom* no. 9 [1974]) claimed that Azerbaijanis learned about world culture through Russian; Z. Äliyeva, F. Süleymanov, A. Hüseynzadä ("Khalg Maarifinin Väzifäläri," *Az Kom* no. 1 [1978]) emphasized "communist education."

53. K. N. Rähimov, "Mäktäb islahatï vä respublikada khalg maarifinin ughurlu addïmlarï," *Azärbayjan mäktäbi* no. 1 (1986).

54. Hajï Novruzov, "Mäktäb ateistlär yetishdirir," *Azärbayjan mäktäbi*, no. 6 (1987).

55. In contrast Azerbaijani Turks living in Armenia are more likely to use Armenian as second language than Russian: among urban men, 26 percent know Armenian, 18 percent know Russian; among women, 23 percent know Armenian, 5 percent Russian; among the rural population, fewer than 10 percent know a second language. In Georgia the Turks are more likely to speak Russian than Georgian (calculated from 1970 census). Figures for 1979 were calculated from *Chislennost'*.

56. A category used by Brian Silver, "Methods of Deriving Data on Bilingualism from the 1970 Soviet Census," *Soviet Studies* 27, no. 4 (October 1975).

57. Frank Huddle, Jr. (*Handbook of the Major Soviet Nationalities*, ed. Z. Katz, R. Rogers, and F. Harned [New York: Free Press, 1975]) noted that the number of Azerbaijan Turkish periodicals dropped in the 1970s, but their circulation was more than four times that of Russian-language periodicals. The drop is less important than their content.

58. Vilayät Guliyev, "Nizamidän Saib Täbriziyä gädär (İngilis shärgshunasï G. Auslinin (1790–1845) ädäbiyatïmïz haggïnda gejdläri)," *Azärbayjan*, no. 11 (1979).

59. Kämalä, "Ana Yurdum—Azärbayjan," *Azärbayjan*, no. 12 (1979).

60. Yurt was the mark left in the ground by the round tent used by Central Asian nomads, and came to be used by foreign observers for the tent itself. By the late nineteenth century, the word came to mean the homeland, though it retains even today its connotation of historic homeland, of antiquity. The word *vatan*, though commonly used, is of Arabic origin (*watan*).

61. Baloghlan Shäfizadä, "Vatan," *Azärbayjan*, no. 7 (1970).

62. Eldar Bakhïsh, "Vätän," *Azärbayjan*, no. 3 (1980).

63. Rüstemkhanlï, "Sagh ol, ana dilim," *Azärbayjan*, no. 6 (1982).

64. Yashar Abbas, "Atäshpärästäm," *Azärbayjan*, no. 3 (1980). The word *atesh-perest*, literally "lover of fire," was used for "Zoroastrian." I have translated it here literally because of the emphasis in the poem on fire, using the Turkish word *od*.

65. A striking example is Ali Shir Ibadin(ov), "Kuyas ham Alov," which appeared in the periodical *Gülistan* (published in the Uzbek SSR), no. 9 (1980); annotated translation in H. D. Paksoy, "Sun Is Also Fire," *Central Asian Monuments*, ed. H. D. Paksoy (forthcoming.).

66. E.g., Paksoy, "Central Asia's New Dastans," *CAS* 6, no. 1, (1987).

67. Early criticism of *Baku 1501* was heard at a congress of writers and seconded by Akif Hüseinov, "Näshrimiz vä kechmishimiz," *Azärbayjan* no. 10 (1982). This novel and historical novels as a whole were later praised by Bäkir Näbiyäv, "Epik zhanr vä müasir häyat," *Azärbayjan*, no. 7 (1986), who called Ismail the "Peter the Great" of Azerbaijan.

68. In the early 1980s changing editors in two waves with apparent political intent was discussed in Paksoy, *Alpamysh*, chap. 4. The Uzbek case was detailed by John Soper, "Shakeup in the Uzbek Literary Elite," *CAS* 1, no. 4 (April 1983).

69. "Vätändashlïg fäallïghï, fädakarlïg äzmi," *Azärbayjan*, no. 2 (1982); quotations on pp. 5, 8–9. A two-part discussion on related topics was published in *Azärbayjan*, no. 1 (January 1982), and no. 3 (March 1982).

70. The development in this direction was not a simple linear progression. From July 1983 to October 1987, *Azärbayjan*, under editors Isa Ismailzade and Jabir Novruz, was less bold.

CHAPTER 12

1. *XXVII s"ezd kommunisticheskoi partii sovetskogo soiuza; 25 fevralia–6 marta 1986 goda; Stenograficheskii otchet* (Moscow: Politlit, 1986), vol. 1, pp. 275–80.

2. S. Gändilov, S. Ähmädova, "Partiya häyatïnïn äsas ganunu," *Azärbayjan Kommunisti* (hereafter cited as *Az Kom*), no. 6 (1986).

3. Rarely noticed was the publication of Arabic script Turkish-language books, apparently for export to Iran. On Soviet Azerbaijan's propaganda effort toward Iranian Azerbaijan, see David B. Nissman, *The Soviet Union and Iranian Azerbaijan: The Uses of Nationalism for Political Penetration* (Boulder, Colo.: Westview, 1987).

4. Ä. Abbasov ("Tarikhi hünär," *Az Kom*, no. 1 [1983]), for example, on the Battle of Stalingrad, made only one mention of Azerbaijan's contribution to the battle, but dutifully recited numbers of tanks and troops, airplanes and artillery.

5. "Kommunizm gurujulughu täjrübäsi vä ädäbi-bädii näshrlär," *Az Kom*, no. 6 (1986).

6. R. Allahverdiyev, "Bashlïja istigamät üzrä," *Az Kom*, no. 9 (1986). It ended with a plea for better working conditions and more apartments.

7. Kh. Mämmädov, "Dövlät statistikasï yenidängurma yolunda," *Az Kom*, no. 12 (1986). He discreetly criticized party and state personnel without revealing actual problems.

8. N. Häsänäliyäv, "Abidälär layejd münasibät," *Az Kom*, no. 4 (1987). A short biography of S. M. Efendiyev (Kh. Räfiyev, "Khalgin gälbindä," no. 5 [1987]) as usual ended with 1927.

9. Ä. Dashdämirov, "Ideolozhi ishin bä'zi aktual problemläri," *Az Kom*, no. 4 (1987).

10. Dr. Prof. Bähruz Abdullayev, "Milli Münasibätlärin inkishafïnda aparïjï güvvä," *Az Kom*, no. 3 (1987).

11. Jabir Novruz had not previously been listed as a member of the Editorial Board when he became chief editor in October 1984. His predecessor Isa Ismailzade, a longtime member of the Editorial Board and chief editor from July 1983 to October 1984, became assistant editor and remained on the board. Ismailzade's predecessor, Eylisli, also remained on the board. Novruz's tenure of office was marked by relative quiescence in terms of national literature, with little on history or politically sensitive issues. Yet, during his last year as editor, there was a sudden upsurge in political material in connection with "restructuring" discussions. When Norvuz ceased to be editor in October 1987, his name completely disappeared from the journal.

12. Äläkbär Abbasov, "Vätänä Khidmät Demäkdir," *Azärbayjan*, no. 11 (1986).

13. *Azärbayjan* started the series "Yenidängurma: problemlär, mülanhizälär," no. 2 (1987) in February. The first item was a piece of some 9,000 words by writer Mestan Aliyev written during 1985–86 in the old format. It contained the familiar call for social justice and greater services and the usual complaint that economic development is stalled.

14. Sirus (pseud.), "Chaiji Jälal vä Köroghlu," *Azärbayjan*, no. 6 (1987).

15. Ferida Mamedova, "Politicheskaia istoriia i istoricheskaia geografiia Kavkazskoi Albanii, III v. d.n.e.–VII v. n.e." (Ph.D. dissertation, Baku Academy of Sciences, 1987).

16. *Khäbärlär/Izvestiia* (Azerbaijan Academy of Sciences Series on History and Philosophy), no. 4 (1987) (hereafter cited as *Khäbärlär/Izvestiia*).

17. Agabegiyan's speech was reported in *L'Humanité*, 18 November 1987. He reportedly repeated similar arguments in December to an Armenian group in London.

18. English translation in *Journal of the Institute of Muslim Minority Affairs* (London) 9, no. 2 (July 1988).

19. Bahtiyar Vahabzade and Suleiman S. Aliyarov cited Russian Caucasologists who argued along these lines. The interpretation has been debated in academic circles in Azerbaijan.

20. The Armenian minority is confirmed in Russian surveys (one survey of 1832 showed that in the whole of Karabagh 34.8 percent were Armenians and 64.8 percent were Azerbaijanis) and by George Bournoutian, "The Ethnic Composition of and Socio-Economic Condition of Eastern Armenia in the First Half of the Nineteenth Century," in Ronald Grigor Suny (ed.), *Transcaucasia: Nationalism and Social Change* (Ann Arbor, 1983).

21. Vahabzade and Aliyarov cited the source as follows: Ilya Chavchavadze *Ermeni alimläri vä feryad goparan dashlar* (Tiflis, 1902), pp. 80, 123. Although cited in Turkish, the work is in Russian.

22. The following is a composite from coverage by *Bakinskii Rabochii* (hereafter cited as *BR*), *Kommunist* (Erevan) (hereafter cited as *Kom* [Erevan]), *Sovetskii Karabakh,* and *Radio Liberty* (Munich) (hereafter cited as *RL*) *Daily Reports*. Subsequent press coverage during the trials in October and November clarified some issues. On the refugees of the 1940s, see Rauf A. Huseinov, "A Survey of Karabagh's History" (paper delivered during speaking tour in United States during the winter of 1991).

23. The resolutions were printed in native- and Russian-language newspapers in the respective capitals; the Armenian resolution on 17 June, the Azerbaijani on 18 June.

24. "Spravedlivoe reshenie," by a Russian, *BR*, 12 November 1988.

25. Reference to resolutions of 13 and 17 June in later resolution of 12 July, published in *BR*, 14 July 1988.

26. "Informatsiia predsedatelia presidiuma verkhovnogo soveta Azerbaidzhanskoi SSR Tatlieva S. B.," *BR*, 18 June 1988. "Konstitutsii vopreki," *BR*, 17 June 1988, was an interview with the director of the judicial department of the Presidium of the

Supreme Soviet Azerbaijan, Abdulla Hajibaba oglu Ibrahimov, elaborating the legal and constitutional arguments advanced by Azerbaijan.

27. "Obrashchenie armian zhivushchikh v Shushinskom raione," *BR*, 17 June 1988; "Ispolneny trevogi i volneiia," *BR*, 21 June 1988.

28. Among the many reports in the Baku press were "Za razumnyi treznyi podkhod," *BR*, 24 June 1988; an item from *Sovetskii Karabakh* of 23 June was also reprinted.

29. *BR*, 14 July 1988. Both resolutions bear the same date.

30. The press conference, held 19 July, was carriéd in *Argumenty i fakty*, no. 30 (July 1988).

31. "Tofik Ismailov: S nadezhdoi smotriu," *Vyshka* (Baku), 25 February 1990. Volskii had been head of the department of machine construction in the CC CPSU under Andropov.

32. "Obraschenie predstavitelia TsK KPSS i Prezidiuma Verkhovnogo Soveta SSSR v Nagorno-Karabakhskoi avtonomnoi oblasti," *Kom*, 25 September 1988. In this decree Volskii traced the strikes in Stepanakert that led to his taking "decisive steps."

33. A group of Azerbaijani academicians wrote to *Moskovskie novosti* to answer a letter by Sakharov supporting "reunification" of the NKAO to Armenia "in the interest of *every* people [*narod*]" involved. The Azerbaijanis pointed out that he was ignoring Azerbaijani interests and rights as well as constitutional provisions.

34. Broadcast on Radio Moscow, 1 December 1988; reported on the same date by *RL* as "Sotsial'no-ekonomicheskii mery v otnoshenii nagornogo Karabakha okazalis' deval'virovannymi."

35. "Ekonomika Nagorno-Karabakhskoi avtonomoi oblasti Azerbaidzhanskoi SSR: Problemy i perspektivy," *Azärbayjan Khalg täsärrüfati/Narodnoe khoziaistvo Azerbaidzhana*, no. 7 (1988), pp. 8–16.

36. Both Azerbaijan and Armenian SSRs had more doctors per 10,000 people— 29.1 in the NKAO as against 38.4 in Azerbaijan and 38.6 in Armenia. For children in preschool, a practice not condoned by Azerbaijani Turks, the NKAO had 35 percent of its preschool children in "day care" versus 39 percent in Armenia and 20 percent in Azerbaijan. Apparently the proportion of Armenians in the NKAO is the reason for the similarity of this pattern.

37. Imam D. Mustafayev would repeat these findings in his interview, "Sluzhit' narodu—schaste!" *Gänjlik/Molodost'*, no. 6 (1988).

38. The following arguments were made in privately circulated letters and articles during 1988 and 1989 and were stated in telephone interviews during that period. Some were openly expressed in the demonstrations of November–December 1988 and subsequently.

39. The 1920s are discussed in chapter 6; in 1955 NKAO: First Secretary Grigoryan, Secretaries K. M. Nikolaev, S. A. Abramyan; Industry Section: Ayrapetyan (*BR*, 14 December 1955). In 1988, at the Third Central Asian Conference (Madison, Wisconsin), Michael Rywkin gave a report on the party cadres in the NKAO and noted that all top posts were held by Armenians.

40. "Informatsiia predsedatelia presidiuma."

41. *Altïnjï Charghïrïsh Azärbayjan SSR Ali Sovetinin Ijlaslarï, 9-ju sessiya (21–22 dekabr 1965-ji il); Stenografik hesabat* (Baku, 1966), pp. 107–11.

42. "K sobytiiam v Nagornom Karabakhe," *Pravda* (hereafter cited as *Pr*), 10 May 1989.

43. These were still discussed in the press; *Trudy*, 25 August 1988, reported harmful effects of pesticides in Azerbaijan.

44. Radio Moscow on 1 December 1988 reported "thousands" of refugees. The text was reproduced in "Soviet Media Actualities," *RL*, 1 December 1988. "Vremia otvetstvennykh deistvii," *Pr*, 5 December, gave figures of 75,000 Azerbaijani refugees from Armenia and NKAO.

45. *BR*, 24 July 1988.

46. E. Abaskulieva and R. Mustafa, "Trevozhnye dni i nochi," *BR*, 23 November 1988; the article was dated 21–22 November.

47. R. Lynev and A. Stepanova, "Razgovor na ploshchadi," *Izvestiia* (hereafter cited as *Izv*), 28 November 1988. One participant stated that most speakers were from the university and the Academy of Sciences. Anyone who wished to speak was permitted.

48. Radio Moscow, 30 November 1988; text reproduced by *RL* Media Actualities.

49. Abaskulieva and Mustafa, "Trevozhnye dni i nochi."

50. The "Topkhana" controversy received much press coverage, and the removal of equipment was reported by TASS on 27 November in a story from Baku and Stepanakert. The issue was mentioned only briefly by Abaskulieva and Mustafa, "Trevozhnye dni i nochi."

51. Lynev and Stepanova, "Razgovor na ploshchadi."

52. Abaskulieva and Mustafa, "Trevozhnye dni i nochi."

53. "Topkhana obretaet pervozdannyi vid" apparently appeared in *Izv*, 28 November 1988; from *RL Features Digest*, 5 December 1988.

54. Private communication with participant.

55. Such was the list of troublemakers given by Gen. Iu. V. Shatalin, commander of internal forces in the Caucasus, in an interview in *Pr*, 24 November 1988.

56. *BR*, 24 November 1988.

57. "Soobshchenie Azerinforma," *BR*, 25 November 1988.

58. R. Lynev and A. Stepanova, "Vchera, 29 noiabria, Baku," *Izv*, 20 November 1988.

59. "Baku, Erevan: trevozhnaia osen'," *Komsomol'skaia Pravda* (hereafter cited as *Kom Pr*), 27 November 1988.

60. "Dni, polnye trevogi," *Krasnaia Zvezda* (hereafter cited as *KZ*), 27 November 1988. A later report (Lt. Col. N. Burbyg, "Na nochnykh ulitsakh Kirovobada," *KZ*, 30 November 1988) told of incidents from Ganje, including an especially poignant one in which a woman of unspecified nationality approached the writer, a Soviet Army lieutenant colonel, and asked, "Are you on our side or theirs?"

61. R. Lynev and A. Stepanova, "Baku, 26 noiabria," *Izv*, 27 November 1988.

62. A. Romanov and A. Tepliuk ("Slukhi i fakty," *Kom Pr*, 29 November 1988) wrote, "On the square, zealous young people were endlessly checking documents."

63. Lynev and Stepanova clarify in "Baku, 26 noiabria."

64. Romanov and Tepliuk, "Baku, Erevan: trevozhnaia osen'," *Kom Pr*, 27 November 1988.

65. Romanov and Tepliuk, "Baku," *Kom Pr*, 30 November 1988.

66. "Trevogi pogranichnoi Astary," *KZ*, 1 December 1988; "Obstanovka slozhnaia," *Pr*, 1 December 1988.

67. Konstantin Mikhailov, "Trevozhnye dni Apsherona," *Sobesednik*, no. 3 (January 1989).

68. Romanov and Tepliuk, "Men'she emotsii, bol'she mudrosti! *Kom Pr*, 1 December 1988.

69. "Obstanovka slozhnaia," *Pr*, 1 December 1988.

70. A. Dashdemirov, "Otdelit' zerna ot plebel,"*BR*, 3 December 1988.

71. In this post, Dashdemirov granted an interview to the new youth magazine *Gänjlik/Molodost'* in June 1989. He was still a correspondent member of the Academy.

72. *BR*, 3 and 16 December 1988.

73. Mikhailov, "Trevozhnye dni Apsherona."

74. Some participants described the military action against them; on Panakhov, Mirza Khazar, "The *Birlik* Society in the Azerbaijani Democratic Movement," *RL* report 23 (August 1989).

75. Mikhailov, "Trevozhnye dni Apsherona."

76. "Trevogi pogranichnoi Astary," *KZ*, 1 December 1988.

77. Mikhail Shatrov, "Prizyvaiu k pazumu i vole," *Izv*, 28 November 1988.

78. Col. O. Falichev, "Pravda sil'nee vsego," *KZ*, 22 December 1988.

79. *Pravda* ("Obstanvoka slozynaia," 1 December 1988) reported 22,000 refugees from Azerbaijan in Armenia and more than 55,000 refugees from Armenia and the NKAO in Azerbaijan. "Soobshcheniia Azerinforma," *BR*, 3 December 1988; N. Demidov and Z. Kadymbekov, "Vremia otvetstvennykh deistvii," *Pr*, 5 December 1988. "Okazat' posil'nuiu pomoshch'," 7 December 1988, reported more than 100,000 throughout the republic.

80. From the Committee for the Defense of the Rights of Azerbaijani Refugees from Armenia, as reported in the republican press, see *BR*, 27 May, 2 June 1989. First Secretary of the Apsheron *raikom* S. N. Murtuzayev described a plan to resettle 1,170 refugee families on the Apsheron peninsula; *BR*, 28 May 1989.

81. "I snova o slukhakh," *BR*, 7 December 1988.

82. *RL* Soviet Media Actualities, 9 December 1988, on Radio Moscow report.

83. "O merakh po likvidatsii poledstvii zemletriaseniia v riade raionov Azerbaidzhanskoi SSR," *BR*, 9 December 1988.

84. Maj. O. Vladykin, "Aktivisty razdora," *KZ*, 16 December 1988.

85. *BR*, 15 January 1989; also in *Chernyi ianvar; Baku—1990. Dokumenty i materialy* (Baku: Azerneshr, 1990), pp. 30–32.

86. This would be revealed by AzCP secretary Hasan Hasanov in January 1990.

87. "Mir zemle Karabakha; Ot konfrontatsii—k bor'be za perestroiku," *Pr*, 15 January 1989.

88. At the May 1989 Congress of People's Deputies in the Kremlin, an Armenian deputy renewed calls for the annexation of the NKAO to Armenia; "Obrashchenie gruppy predstavitelei Azerbaidzhana v adres s"ezda narodnykh deputalov SSSR; Ne dopuskat' razhiganiia strastei," *BR*, 30 May 1989, p. 1.

89. Political activist Leyla Yunusova, "Pestraia palitra neformal'nykh dvizhenii v Azerbaidzhane," *NRS*, 19 September 1989.

90. "I snova o slukhakh," *BR*, 7 December 1988.

91. That these issues were discussed mainly in Azerbaijani Turkish-language publications was lamented in an article about the Azerbaijan Writers' Union Russian-language monthly *Literaturnyi Azerbaidzhan* in *Literaturnaia Gazeta* (Moscow), 31 May 1989.

92. *Azadlïk*, no. 1 (24 December 1989). Aliyev, then age 52, had studied at the oriental faculty at Azerbaijan State University and received his bachelor's degree in 1962. He worked as an Arabic-language translator in Egypt 1963–64 and taught at the university's history faculty but spent a year in prison in 1975–76 for "nationalism." He had worked at the Academy of Sciences Manuscript Institute since 1977.

93. A full English translation is in *Caucasus and Central Asian Chronicle* (London) 8, no. 4 (August 1989), formerly *Central Asian Newsletter* (Oxford and London).

94. See Appendix.

95. Yunusova mentions Turan, Shebeke, Azadlik, "and other" groups but provides no information on these, nor have I seen mention of them. See *RL Daily Report*, 19 December 1989.

96. The following account of political events is compiled from *RL* Daily Reports for August–September 1989.

97. Another demand at this time was the recall of Azerbaijan's deputies to the Congress of People Deputies on the grounds that elections had been manipulated by the authorities.

98. When the stoppage began, the APF indicated that workers acted on their own. Later reports suggested that the APF was coordinating the strike. The authorities in Baku and Moscow certainly behaved as though the APF controlled it.

99. Georgii Rozhnov (*Ogenok* correspondent), "Doroga bez kontsa," *Vyshka* (Baku), 11 February 1990.

100. "Nä veririk, nä alïrïg? Azärbayjan-Ermänistan," *Sähär*, 13 January 1990. This was one of several balance sheets published by the newspaper *Sähär* on Azerbaijan's trade with other republics.

101. William Keller, "Nationalists in Azerbaijan Win Big Concessions from Party Chief," *New York Times*, 12 October 1989.

102. Rozhnov, "Doroga bez kontsa."

103. *Azärbayjan* (weekly newspaper, organ of the Committee for Aid to Karabagh, (hereafter cited as Azärb [n]), 2 October 1989, showed a truck and car convoy to Karabagh riddled with bullet holes. The first issue (one week earlier) had noted that many relief supplies for Armenian earthquake victims had not been sent to the victims but to armed bands in the NKAO.

104. Reuters news wire report from Moscow, 9 October 1989; the MI-26 helicopter had "hunting rifles, 52 grenades, more than 150 detonators and fuses, and several hundred rounds of ammunition."

105. "K sobytiiam v Nagornom Karabakhe," *Pr*, 10 May 1989. A "Letter to the Editor" published in *Kom*, 26 April 1989, stated that Azerbaijanis in Stepanakert were prevented from receiving mail and sending telegrams in Turkish.

106. Keller, "Nationalists in Azerbaijan."

107. *Izv*, 30 November; reprinted in *Chernyi ianvar'*, pp. 32–33.

108. Historical series are published in the Writers' Union journal *Azärbayjan*, the Karabagh Aid Committee's newspaper *Azärbayjan*, the Vatan Society's newspaper *Odlar Yurdu*, and a few other Baku periodicals.

109. *Istoricheskaia geografiia Azerbaidzhana* (Baku, 1987).

110. Ziya Buniatov's *Azerbaidzhan VII-IX vv.* was issued in an Azerbaijani Turkish translation, *Azärbayjan VII-IX äsrlärdä*, in 1989. One thousand copies of the earlier version were printed; 35,000 copies of the 1989 translation were printed.

111. *Garabaghnamälär* (Baku: Yazïjï, 1989); *K istorii obrazovanii Nagorno-Kara-bakhskoi avtonomnoi oblasti, 1918–1925; Dokumenty i materialy* (hereafter cited as *Obrazovanie*) (Baku: Azerneshr, 1989) is a set of documents on the formation of the NKAO.

112. V. L. Velichko, *Kavkaz: Russkoe delo i mezhduplemennye voprosy* (St. Petersburg, 1904; reprinted Baku: Elm, 1990).

113. Mostly short works in literary journals; "Firrudin Bey Shushaly," *Odlar Yurdu*, no. 1 (January 1990).

114. Sabir Rüstemkhanlï, *Ömür kitabï* (Baku: Gänjlik, 1989); 10,000 copies printed.

115. *Nagornyi karabakh: razum pobedit; Dokumenty i materialy* (Baku, 1989) issued by the Institute of Party History of the Marxism-Leninism Institute. The Kommunist publishing house issued *Daghlïg Garabagh: häyäjanlï sätirlär*, 1989, with extracts from the newspaper *Kommunist*, February 1988 to September 1989.

116. Mahmud Ismailov formerly wrote in Russian; since 1988 he has been writing cultural pieces in Azerbaijani Turkish.

117. *Caucasus and Central Asia Chronicle* 8, no. 3 (July 1989).

118. "Respublikanïn igtisadi müstägilliyi; Onu nejä heyata kechirmäli?" *Sähär*, 4 August 1989. This was a powerful opening salvo on the front page of the new paper's first issue.

119. "Nä veririk, nä alïrïg? Azärbayjan-Ermänistan," *Sähär*, 13 January 1990. The series showed that Azerbaijan was a net exporter to almost all republics.

120. J. D. Peterson, "Killer Mushrooms," special report for *RL*, 17 May 1990. He noted that Azerbaijan is the republic suffering the highest DDT concentrations in the USSR.

121. Stated in a June 1989 meeting of Academy of Sciences; reported by APF spokesman, historian Mehdi Mamedov, of the university. In 1990, several writers in *Azärb* (n) were identified as members of the faculty of "Baku State University, named for M. E. Rasulzade."

122. Ismailov was one of the first to demand, in a public forum, the restoration of Ganje's historic name; *Azärbayjan*, no. 6, (1988):159.

123. The Azerbaijan Supreme Soviet passed a resolution changing the city's name on 30 December 1989.

124. *Cumhuriyet* (Istanbul) 26 May 1990; during the spring and summer, 1990, several Baku newspapers discussed the proposed alphabet change.

125. *Azärbayjan*, no. 6 (1988): 159.

126. "Sluzhit' narodu—schaste!"

127. As early as 1983, one influential monograph (T. I. Hajiyev, K. N. Väliyev, *Azärbayjan Dili Tarikhi: Ocherklär vä materiallar* [Baku: Maarif, 1983], p. 9) on language history stated that "the Azerbaijani language spoken by today's Azerbaijanis was not historically known by that name; from antiquity to the 1930s, it was called the Turkish language [Türk dili]."

128. In addition to the historical series appearing in *Azärbayjan* during 1988, see Nizami Jafarov, "Azärbayjan mädäniyyäti," *Ädäbiyyat vä Injäsänät*, 17 March 1989.

129. Romanov and Tepliuk, "Baku."

130. A later essay, "Tiurkskii vopros: puti vykhod iz krizisa," by Tatar Giyaz Malikhov (*Azärb* [n], 24 March 1990), also denounced accusations of "Pan-Turkism" in urging renewed study of all Turks' history, language, and literature, as well as attempts to coordinate alphabet reform.

131. The literature of the late nineteenth and early twentieth centuries shows little support for Islamic-based unity in any form. Bennigsen and Chantal Lemercier-Quelquejay were perhaps the first Western scholars to point out this strong secular tendency in Azerbaijan.

132. William Reese ("Religious Revival and Nationalism in Caucasian Events," *RL* Report, 5 December 1988) did not clearly differentiate national from religious allegiance.

133. "Pravda sil'nee vsego," *KZ*, 22 December 1988.

134. *RL* Daily Report for 4 December 1989.

135. *Azärb* (n), 9 December 1988.

136. *RL* Daily Reports, 5, 8 December 1989.

137. *BR*, 4, 7 January 1990. Both reprinted in *Chernyi ianvar'*, pp. 59–64.

138. *Azadlïk*, 14 January, recapitulated the demands: to visit graves of relatives, not by special *propusk* (permit) but at any time, and local farmers wanted to recover land in the border zone, which they needed more than ever for refugees who had fled Armenia and for Meskhetian Turks from Central Asia.

139. The APF "organizational committee," headed by engineer Nagi Nagiyev, whose loss in the election for first secretary seems to have triggered the outbreak, was still in existence on 8 January, a week after the incidents ended. Z. Dzhapparov, "Protivostoianie, kotoroe mozhet zavesti v tupik reshenie problem," *BR*, 12 January 1990.

140. *Azadlïk*, 14 January 1990.

141. *Elm*, the bilingual weekly of the Academy of Sciences, 6 January 1990.

142. The speech was reported in *Azadlïk*, 14 January 1990, and *Vestnik Giandzhi*, 20 January; reprinted in *Chernyi ianvar'*, pp. 51–59.

143. Passed on 10 January, published *BR*, 11 January 1990; reprinted in *Chernyi ianvar'*, pp. 33–34.

144. *Azadlïk*, 14 January 1990; reprinted in Russian translation in *Chernyi ianvar'*, pp. 49–50.

145. This problem was discussed in the Baku press in January 1990; confirmed in conversation with Etibar Mamedov, May 1991.

146. Dzhapparov, "Trevozhnyi ianvar' v Lenkorane," *BR*, 17 January 1990; reprinted in *Chernyi ianvar'*, pp. 70–74.

147. "Zaiavlenie chlena pravleniia NFA Etibara Mamedova na press konferentsii v Moskve," *Akhïn*, no. 3 (March 1990); publication of the Academy of Sciences branch of the APF.

148. Almaz Estekov, "Politicheskaia otsenka sobytii v Baku," *Turkestan* (supplement to *Obozrevatel'*), no. 1 (January–February 1990): 1. Produced by Estekov in Riga, it was reproduced in the *AACAR BULLETIN* (Amherst, Mass.) 3, no. 2 (Fall 1990).

149. *BR*, 16, 17 January 1990; APF statements in *Azadlïk*, 18 January 1990.

150. Radio Moscow broadcast, 14 January 1990; reported in *RL Daily Report*, 15 January.

151. *RL Daily Report*, 16 January 1990, quoting unnamed source in Moscow.

152. *RL* continued to report on Radio Moscow news about "militants" in Azerbaijan and the calming effect of Soviet troops on the local situation. *RL* also reported the accusations from Radio Erevan.

153. The commission Shchit (Shield) examined evidence 12–22 July 1990; its report was in *Moskovskie novosti*, 12 August 1990, and *BR*, 17 August, entitled "Ianvar' v Baku." References are from *BR*.

154. Andrei Kruzhilin, "Baku: do i posle prikaza," *Literaturnaia Gazeta*, 7 February 1990; reprinted in *Chernyi ianvar'*, pp. 108–114.

155. According to Etibar Mamedov, Primakov left Baku the afternoon of 19 January. According to Sheikh ul-Islam (private conversation in September 1990), Primakov was in Baku during the invasion, and negotiations continued.

156. "Zaiavlenie chlena pravleniia NFA Etibara Mamedova."

157. *RL Daily Report*, 19 January 1990.

158. Rähim Äliyäv, "Gyrkh gün düsünjäläri," *Azärb* (n), 2 March 1990.

159. "Zaiavlenie chlena pravleniia NFA Etibara Mamedova."

160. "'Ianvar' v Baku," *BR*, 17 August 1990.

161. Kruzhilin, "Baku: do i posle prikaza." Kruzhilin apparently did not witness all the events he reported, given the distance between them.

162. Eldeniz Ibrahimov ("Nuzhno trezvo otsenit' situatsiiu," *BR*, 16 January 1990; reprinted in *Chernyi ianvar'*, p. 80) urged each individual to adhere to the law, and members of the media not to fan the flames by one-sided reporting.

163. Retired KGB Gen. Oleg Kalugin suggested KGB instigation in an interview with the West Berlin daily *Tage zeitung*, 25 June 1990; reported in *RL* Daily Report, 26 June 1990.

164. Reported by TASS special correspondents P. Siniakov, B. Fomin, "Pochemu pogibli eti liudi?" *Molodezh Azerbaidzhana*, 3 February 1990; reprinted in *Chernyi ianvar'*, pp. 118–19.

165. One instance is detailed in "On vypolnial sluzhebnyi dolg," *Vyshka* (Baku), 2 February 1990. Others are mentioned in subsequent press reports. Etibar Mamedov noted the deaths of numerous Azerbaijani doctors and one Russian and one Jewish doctor.

166. *RL* Daily Report of 25 January 1990.

167. *Akhïn*, no. 2 (29 January 1990).

168. Leyla Yunusova, "Mera otvetstvennosti politika," *Istiglal*, no. 4 (April 1990):5.

169. Reported by *RL*, 22 January; earlier evacuation of residents of the area is a sign that this move was planned well in advance.

170. "Natsional'nyi tragediia," *Umid* (Moscow) (the organ of "the independent Azerbaijan information center"), January 1990.

171. *Umid* reported by 6 P.M. on 20 January, the APF had given military authorities a list of 567 persons killed ("whose bodies had been found"). According to the rumor mill, thousands had been killed. Although this belief may have contributed to the panic and anger at the time, it has not been confirmed by subsequent accounts.

172. Lecture delivered at the Fourth International Conference on Central Asia (Madison, Wis., September 1990).

173. *Akhïn (Torrent)* (the organ of the Academy of Sciences branch of the APF), 20 January. This was its first issue.

174. Zeynaly's film was shot on the streets and in hospitals during the night of the military intervention and in the following days. He showed the film at the Fourth International Conference on Central Asia (Madison, Wis., September 1990).

175. It was suggested that Vezirov was later expelled from the CPSU. This is either incorrect or he was reinstated by fall.

176. Mutalibov worked from 1959 to 1974 in the Baku electrical equipment factory, eventually becoming director. He holds two Orders of the Red Banner. *Kom*, 27 January 1990, did not identify any other candidate.

177. P. Siniakov, V. Fomin, "Pochemu pogubli eti liudi?" *Molodezh Azerbaidzhana*, 3 February 1990; reprinted in *Chernyi ianvar'*, pp. 118–119.

178. This issue was raised in *Chernyi ianvar*, p. 140.

179. The Kasparov interview was broadcast in the United States on NBC News about a week after the invasion.

180. Kruzhilin, *Chernyi ianvar'*, p. 113.

181. Some newspapers reported foreign press accounts under the heading "Let us know who are our friends and our enemies." One private letter stated: "In America, it seems, everything is solved . . . there remains only Karabagh."

182. *RL*, Daily Report, 22 January; speech published in *BR*, 25 January 1990; reprinted in *Chernyi ianvar'*, pp. 85–87.

183. Gorbachev's statement was made on 2 August 1990 concerning Iraq's invasion of Kuwait of that date. The Soviet ambassador remarked on 6 August that "new thinking" allows no double standards. This was said with respect to Soviet support of U.N. sanctions against Iraq despite many years of good Soviet-Iraqi relations.

184. Printed in *Chernyi ianvar'*, p. 89.

185. The decree was dated 22 January 1990 and appeared in Russian in *BR* and in *Seher* in Turkish on 25 January and in *Akhïn* (Turkish) on 29 January. A synopsis was carried in *Odlar Yurdu* in its late-January issue in Cyrillic script. The Russian version was reprinted in *Chernyi ianvar'*, pp. 91–92.

186. *RL*, Daily Report, 20 February 1990; *New York Times* reporter Keller in mid-February reported the widely held belief that Russian second secretary Polianichko assisted Moscow in planning the move.

187. Gorbachev imposed a curfew for 20 January, but the announcement dated 19 January was not known in Baku. An announcement may have been planned on *Vremia*, but the bombing of the radio-television center earlier that evening by special forces prevented it. In any case, *Vremia* aired at 10 P.M. in Baku, which would give short warning that a curfew was about to be imposed.

188. Issues were reported in *RL*, Daily Report, 20 February 1990 and more fully in *Chrenyi ianvar'*, pp. 138–140.

189. His article and one by film director Stanislav Govoukhin came to the same conclusions. Both appeared in *Moskovskie novosti*, no. 7, reported in *RL*, Daily Report, 20 February 1990.

191. *RL*, Daily Report, 12 March 1990.

191. *Vestnik Giandzhi*, 24 January 1990.

192. *FVChP*, which apparently began in January 1990, may stand for "Fövgeladä Väziyetden Chïkhmag Programi" (Program for Ending the State of Emergency). Only a few issues appeared.

193. Abulfez Aliyev noted in an interview in *Azadlïk*, 24 December 1989, that various parties would and should evolve and that eventually either the APF would be supplanted by strong parties or a new front would be organized by the parties.

EPILOGUE

1. *Azärbayjan* (weekly newspaper, organ of the Committee for Aid to Karabagh; hereafter cited as *Azärb* [n]), 7 April 1990, featured memorial ceremonies in Baku and Tbilisi for more than a dozen unarmed people killed by troops there in April 1988.

2. The point was raised by Tofik K. Ismailov in his interview in *Vyshka*, 25 February 1990. He was a member of the USSR Supreme Soviet and general director of the NPO space research institute. Another interview was published in *Elm*, 17 February 1990, with the commission's co-chair, Tamerlan Karayev.

3. *Edasi* (Estonia), 9 February, told a journalist that Nakhjivanis reported that the smell of burning party cards was horrible; *RL*, Daily Report, 12 March. Baku papers had photos of piles of party cards on the streets.

4. *Bakinskii Rabochii* (hereafter cited as *BR*), 30 January 1990; reprinted in *Chernyi ianvar'*, pp. 142–43.

5. The problem of AzCP credibility was discussed in the March 1990 issue of *Azärbayjan Kommunisti* (hereafter cited as *Az Kom*).

6. Aydïn Mikayilov, "Garabagh 'problemi' vä milli mänlik shüurumuz," *Azärb* (n), 20 April 1990.

7. *Az Kom*, no. 3 (1990): 13–14, 32–34.

8. Aydïn Kärimov, "Ali Sovetin än yakhïn gonshusu—shähidlär khiyabanï," *Azärb* (n), 20 April 1990.

9. Ädäbiyyat vä Injäsänät, 25 May 1990, pp. 1–2, published Mutalibov's acceptance speech.

10. *BR*, 22 May 1990, pp. 1–2.

11. These included newspapers of existing, registered organizations, which proliferated in 1990–91. These are listed in the Appendix.

12. "Mera otvetstvennosti politika," *Istiglal*, no. 4 (April 1990): 20, quotation.

13. *Azadlïk*, 11 August, published an article by reporter Chinghiz Sultansoy who went to Lefortovo Prison to speak with the prosecutor for Mamedov's case. Sultansoy was not permitted to see him. According to private communications of March and June 1990, Helsinki Watch (New York and Washington offices) had been considering investigating events in Azerbaijan. It sent a staff member in December and issued a report during the summer of 1991.

14. *Azadlïk*, 8 September 1990.

15. Interview with Hikmet Hajiyev, an APF leader, was conducted by Chinghiz Sultansoy on 7 August 1990 and circulated as manuscript; it may have been published later in the month.

16. Although observers were kept out of Baku, the staff of the U.S. Congressional Commission on Security and Cooperation in Europe along with members of the U.S. embassy (Moscow) were permitted to observe elections and to interview members of the government and opposition groups. The published report was dated 25 October 1990; I am grateful to the staff for providing it.

17. One commentary on this topic was "Hakimiyyät vakuumu, yahud ikitäräfli üchbujag," *Azadlïk*, 22 November 1990, p. 6.

18. Tofik Gandilov, *Azärb* (n), 4 May 1990.

19. Saleh Mämmädov (doctor of economics), "Ittifag programï bizä nä vä'd edir?" *Azadlïk*, 22 November 1990.

20. Meeting with Etibar Mamedov, May 1991.

21. Bahtiyar Vahabzade, "Shänbä gejäsindä gedän yol," *Azärbayjan*, no. 9 (1990); Mamedov statement on Baku television, January 1991, reported by Voice of America, Azerbaijan service, 29 January 1991.

22. *Aydïnlïg*, 2 August 1991.

23. Fikret Goja, "Azärbayjan," *Azärbayjan*, no. 2 (1991):11.

Bibliography

ESSAY ON SOURCES

A study spanning imperial and Soviet rule in Azerbaijan necessarily draws on two very different groups of sources and secondary literature. For the imperial period, the revolution, and Azerbaijan's years of independence, available materials include published documents, reliable and detailed imperial statistics including the 1897 imperial census and two Baku city censuses, the periodical press, collected works of principals, memoirs, diplomatic and intelligence reports, and archives and libraries in the Soviet Union. There are a large number of secondary sources, though on only a few topics. Much is available in the United States, including imperial statistics in major research libraries, part of the prerevolutionary periodical press at the University of Chicago and Columbia University, and foreign diplomatic reports. Papers and publications of some principals, especially those regarded as "progressive" (prolabor, pro-Bolshevik, pro-Russian) have been published in the USSR and are readily available. Accounts by travelers or journalists (some of whom were "observers" for British intelligence) are of limited value because they saw the local population as backward colonials and were interested mainly in the economic or strategic benefit of the area for the West. An antidote to these are memoirs of Turks such as General Kazim Karabekir and Ali Fuat Cebesoy.

Sources on Soviet Azerbaijan are more difficult to obtain and must be used with caution, realizing the political intent of works produced throughout the USSR. The dearth of reliable secondary sources and the continued unavailability of archives (into 1991) require use of contemporary writings for each period, published party congress proceedings and resolutions, analytical or historical writings by émigrés, and other material from which patterns must be gleaned. The periodical press has been used in the present volume, as have published speeches and works of literature. The Soviet press of the 1920s and 1930s, when available, provided detail on policies and disagreements on politics and culture that were weeded out of subsequent narratives. In some cases, those press accounts belie official Soviet claims that were formulated in the post–World War II era. Although the Soviet government consistently denounced émigrés and their publications, the revelations of the 1980s and 1990s show that many émigré reports were true.

When Soviet publications are available, more than the usual caveats must be kept in mind. Aside from the obvious touting of the party line, works on nationalities convey other messages such as the inferiority of the native culture and the "progressive significance" of Russian/Soviet rule. Thus, in Soviet sources, Soviet (and to some extent Russian imperial) rule is equated with industrialization, increased literacy and education, and a higher standard of living. Discontent may have a nationalistic, cultural, or religious ("fanatical") basis, which is to be expected as "backward" people evolve toward the internationalism espoused by the regime. Nation-minded behavior, however, is not considered justifiable on the economic grounds regarded as essential to a Marxist view and stressed by Moscow. Because few historians have focused on Soviet Azerbaijan and even fewer have used Azerbaijani Turkish-language materials, there has been little exploration and much speculation on the Soviet history of Azerbaijan.

Significant changes in Azerbaijani scholarship on the history of Azerbaijan, starting in the 1970s, have helped radically reinterpret the standard Soviet history of that land. The diversity of economic and political affairs has begun to be explored; former taboos—of individuals and publications—have begun to be described, though not fully. Some daring individuals have challenged the "historic friendship" and the "voluntary unification" of Azerbaijan with Russia, imperial and Bolshevik. Disclosures and rehabilitations are incomplete; they continue to reflect conventional categories and parameters or the political issues of the day. As new materials are produced, the best research tools of the historian remain familiarity with the issues and a sharp critical eye.

Abbreviations

Journals (all but Central Asian Survey are in Turkish)

Az Kom	Azärbayjan Kommunisti (CC AzCP monthly)
Azärbayjan	Azärbayjan (Writers' Union monthly)
Azerbaycan (Ankara)	Azerbaycan (émigré, 1950s)
Azerbaijan (Paris)	Azerbaijan (émigré, 1920s)
CAS	Central Asian Survey (London)

Newspapers (Russian, unless otherwise indicated)

Azärb (n)	Azärbayjan (People's Aid Committee to Karabagh weekly, bilingual)
BR	Bakinskii Rabochii (CC AzCP daily)
Kom Pr	Komsomol'skaia Pravda (Komsomol daily)
Izv	Izvestiia (USSR daily)
Kom	Kommunist (AzCP, evening daily, in Azerbaijani Turkish)
KZ	Krasnaia Zvezda (Soviet armed forces daily)
NRS	Novoe Russkoe Slovo (New York, émigré)
PN	Posledniaia Novosti (Paris, émigré, 1920–30s)
Pr	Pravda (CPSU daily)
ZV	Zaria Vostoka (Tiflis, GCP daily)

Archives (Republic designated in note references)

TsGAOR: Tsentral'nyi Gosudarstvennyi Arkhiv Oktiabrskoi Revoliutsii (Central State Archive of the October Revolution)

TsGASA: Tsentral'nyi Gosudarstvennyi Arkhiv Sovetskoi Armii (Central State Archive of the Soviet Army)

TsGIA: Tsentral'nyi Gosudarstvennyi Istoricheskii Arkhiv (Central State Historical Archive)

SELECTED BIBLIOGRAPHY

Azerbaijan Communist Party Meetings and Statistics

Altïnjï Chaghïrïsh Azärbayjan SSR Ali Sovetinin Ijlaslarï, 9-ju sessia (21–22 dekabr 1965-ji il); Stenografik hesabat. Baku, 1966.

"Azärbayjan kommunist partiyasi rägämlärdä (1961–1965-ji iller)," *Az Kom*, 1965, no. 9.

Kommunisticheskaia partiia Azerbaidzhana v tsifrakh; statisticheskii sbornik. Baku: Institute of Party History, 1970.

Materialy XXX s"ezda kommunisticheskoi partii Azerbaidzhana (28-30 ianvaria 1981 goda). Baku, 1981.

CPSU Congresses

[Dvadtsatyi] *XX s"ezd kommunisticheskoi partii sovetskogo soiuza, 14–25 fevralia 1956 g; Stenograficheskii otchet.* Moscow, 1956.

[Dvadtsat' sedmoi] *XXVII s"ezd kommunisticheskoi partii sovetskogo soiuza, 25 fevralia–6 marta 1986 goda; Stenograficheskii otchet.* Moscow: Politlit, 1986. Vol. 1.

[Dvadtsat' piat'yi] *XXV s"ezd kommunisticheskoi partii Sovetskogo Soiuza, 24 fevralia–5 marta 1976 goda; Stenograficheskii otchet.* Moscow, 1976.

[Dvadtsat' shestoi] *XXVI s"ezd kommunisticheskoi partii Sovetskogo Soiuza, 23 fevralia–3 marta 1981 goda; Stenograficheskii otchet.* Moscow, 1981.

Vneocherednoi XXI s"ezd Kommunisticheskoi Partii Sovetskogo Soiuza, 27 ianvaria–5 fevralia 1959 g; Stenograficheskii otchet. Moscow, 1959.

Primary Sources, Published Documents, Works of Literature

Abbas, Yashar. "Atäshpärästäm," *Azärbayjan* No. 3, 1980.

Abbaskuluaga Bakikhanov. Baku: Elm, 1983.

Azärbayjan kitabi (Bibliyografiya). Vol. 1, Baku, 1963.

Azerbaidzhanskii Sovet Narodnogo Khoziaistva. *Otchet o deiatel'nosti za 1920 g.* Baku, 1920.

Bakhmaniar al-Azerbaidzhani, *At-Takhsil (Poznanie).* Baku: Elm, 1983. 3 vols. Classic Heritage of Azerbaijan series of the Institute of Philosophy and Law of the Azerbaijan Academy of Sciences.

Bakikhanli (Bakikhanov), Abbas Kulu Agha, *Gülistan-i Irem* (Turkish). Baku: Academy of Sciences, 1951.

———. (Persian) *Gülistani-Irem.* Baku: Academy of Sciences, 1970.

———. (Russian) *Giulistan-Iran.* Baku: Obshchestvo obsledovaniia i izucheniia Azerbaidzhana, 1926.

The Book of Dede Korkut. Translated by G. L. Lewis. London: Penguin, 1974.

Bor'ba za pobedu sovetskoi vlasti v Azerbaidzhane, 1918–1920; Dokumenty i materialy. Baku: Academy of Sciences, 1967.

Chislennost' i sostav naseleniia SSSR; Po dannym vsesoiuznoi perepisi naseleniia 1979 goda. Moscow, 1984.

Chernyi ianvar; Baku—1990; Dokumenty i materialy. Baku: Azerneshr, 1990.

[Chetyristashest'nadtsataia] *416-ia Krasnoznamennaia Taganrogskaia strelkovaia diviziia: Sbornik dokumentov.* Baku: Azerneshr, 1944.

Daghlïg Garabagh: häyäjanlï sätirlär. Baku: Kommunist, 1989.

Fuzuli, *Äsärlär.* Baku, 1958.

————. *Izbrannoe sochinenie.* Baku, 1958.

Garabaghnamälär. Baku: Yaziji, 1989.

Gulishambarov, S. I. *Obzor fabrik i zavodov bakinskoi gubernii.* Tiflis, 1890.

Ismayil, Mämmäd. "Vätän." *Azärbayjan,* no. 11 (1981).

Jäfär Jabbarlï; Äsärläri. Baku, 1968.

K istorii obrazovaniia nagorno-karabakhskoi avtonomnoi oblasti Azerbaidzhanskoi SSR, 1918–1925; Dokumenty i materialy. Baku: Azerneshr, 1989.

Kämalä, "Ana Yurdum—Azärbayjan," *Azärbayjan,* no. 12 (1979).

Khagani Shirvani, *Üräk Döyünütüläri.* Baku: Ganjlik, 1979.

————. *Khagani Shirvani; Sechilmish äsärläri.* Baku: Azerneshr, 1978.

Melikov-Zardabi, Hasan. *Äkinji, 1875–1877 (Tam mätni).* Baku, 1979.

Nagornyi karabakh: razum pobedit; Dokumenty i materialy. Baku: Institute of Party History, Marxism-Leninism Institute, 1989.

Naselenie imperii po perepisi 28–go ianvaria 1897 goda po uezdam. St. Petersburg: S. P. Iakovlev, 1897.

Nasreddin Tusi, *Akhlagi Näsiri.* Baku: Elm, 1980. Translation, with annotations and notes, from Persian.

————. *Tansugnameji Elkhani (Javahirname).* Baku: Elm, 1984.

Obzor deiatel'nosti Soveta Narodnykh Komissarov i Vysshego ekonomicheskogo Soveta ZSFSR. Tiflis, 1927.

Otchet TsK AKP(b) VI s"ezdy AKP(b). Baku, 1924.

Perepis' naseleniia gor. Baku, 1903. Baku: Kaspii, 1905.

Perepis' naseleniia gor. Baku, 1913. Baku: Kaspii, 1916.

"Programma narodnogo fronta Azerbaidzhana." English translation in *Caucasus and Central Asian Chronicle* 8, no. 4 (August 1989).

Rabochee dvizhenie v Azerbaidzhane v gody novogo revoliutsionnogo pod"ema (1910–1914 gg.); Dokumenty i materialy. Baku: Academy of Sciences, 1967.

Rabochee dvizhenie v Baku v gody pervoi russkoi revoliutsii; Dokumenty i materialy. Baku: Academy of Sciences, 1962.

Russian Empire, Ministry of Finance, *Ezhegodnik* (Annual, yearbook). St. Petersburg: Ministry of Finance, 1869–1916.

————. *Obzor Vneshnei torgovlii* (annual). St. Petersburg: Ministry of Finance, 1833–1863.

Rustemkhanlï, Sabir. *Ömür kitabï.* Baku: Ganjlik, 1989.

————. "Sagh ol, ana dilim." *Azärbayjan,* no. 6 (1982).

Spiski nasel'ennykh mest' rossiisskoi imperii. Vol. 65, pt. 1. Tiflis: Kavkazskii statisticheskii komitet, 1870.

Spisok uchebnykh zavedenii viedomostva ministerstva narodnogo prosvieshcheniia (krome nachal'nykh) po gorodam i seleniia. St. Petersburg, 1913.

Svod zakonov rossiiskoi imperii, vol. 14, chap. 3. St. Petersburg, 1857.

Tekin, Talat. *A Grammar of Orkhon Turkic.* Indiana University Uralic and Altaic Series. Vol. 69. Bloomington: Indiana University Press, 1968.

Yusuf Hass Khajib, *Kutadgu Bilig.* Translated by Robert Dankoff as *Wisdom of Royal Glory.* Chicago: University of Chicago Press, 1983.

Memoirs, Autobiography

Broido, Eva. *Memoirs of a Revolutionary.* Translated by Vera Broido. London: Oxford University Press, 1967.

Cebesoy, Gen. Ali Fuad. *Moskova Hatırları.* Ankara, 1982.

Dumas, Alexandre. *Adventures in the Caucasus.* New York, 1963.

Kazim Karabekir, *İstiklal harbimiz.* Istanbul, 1960.

Keykurun (Sheyh Zamanli), Naki. *Azerbaycan istiklal mücadelesinin hatıraları.* Istanbul: Azerbaycan Gençlik Derneği, 1964.

Togan, Zeki Velidi. *Hatıralar.* Istanbul, 1969.

Yurtsever, A. Vahap. "Azerbaycan İstiklal savaşından sahneler," *Azerbaycan* (Istanbul). May–June, July–August 1955; May–June, July–August 1956.

Periodicals

The title of the periodical is followed by the issuing body and date of first issue. For those periodicals no longer issued, period of activity is noted rather than time of first issue. AzTk = Azerbaijan Turkish.

AACAR BULLETIN	Association for the Advancement of Central Asian Research, Amherst, Massachusetts; 1988.
Ädäbiyyat vä Injäsänät	(literary weekly) Writers' Union and Ministry of Culture, January 1934; AzTk.
Ädalät	Union of Jurists of Azerbaijan, July 1990; AzTk.
Akhïn	Academy of Sciences branch of the APF, January 1990; AzTk.
Aydïnlïg	Gayghï Society (refugee relief), August 1990; AzTk.
Azadlïk	(weekly) Azerbaijan Popular Front; December 1989; bilingual.
Azärbayjan	(literary monthly) Azerbaijan Writer's Union; 1923; AzTk.
Azärbayjan	(weekly) People's Aid Committee to Karabagh; October 1989; bilingual.
Azerbaijan	(Paris) Émigré, 1920s–30s; AzTk.
Azerbaycan	(Ankara, Turkey) Émigré, 1950s.

Azärbayjan Kommunisti	(monthly journal) CC AzCP; 1920; AzTk.
Azerbaycan yurt bilgisi	(Istanbul) Émigré; 1930s.
Bakï (daily)	Baku Committee AzCP; 1958; AzTk.
Bakinskii Rabochii	CC AzCP, Soviet of Ministers, Supreme Soviet; 1906.
Baku	(daily) Pre-revolutionary; in Russian.
Caucasus and Central Asian Chronicle	(London) Formerly *Central Asian Newsletter* (Oxford); 1981.
Central Asian Survey	(London) 1982.
Dedem Gorgud/ Dedem Korkut	(independent literary-arts weekly) Summer 1991; AzTk.
Dirchelish	Dirchelish (Resurgence) party, spring 1989; AzTk.
Elm	(newspaper) Azerbaijan Academy of Sciences; 1984; bilingual.
FVChP	(special bulletin) Azerbaijan Popoular Front; spring 1990; AzTk.
Feryad	Ministry of Oil and Gas; Ministry of Chemical and Oil Refining Industries, October 1990; AzTk.
Gala	(town of Masally; "independent" literary-arts newspaper) January 1991; AzTk.
Ganjlik/Molodost'	(monthly magazine) CC Azerbaijan Komsomol; 1988; one issue in Russian, one in AzTk.
Garabagh	AzCP oblast' Organization Committee, 1990; AzTk.
Gobustan	(monthly arts journal) Azerbaijan Writers' Union and Ministry of Culture Press; 1969; AzTk.
Ilham	"Ittifagteatr" Creative Production Union, Azerbaijan branch of USSR Theater Union, November 1990; AzTk.
Istiglal	Social Democratic Party of Azerbaijan; spring 1990; bilingual.
Izvestiia	Azerbaijan State University; Russian in 1920s; then bilingual.
Journal of the Institute of Muslim Minority Affairs	Institute of Muslim Minority Affairs (London); 1981.
Kaspii	(prerevolutionary daily) Russian.
Kavkazskii kalendar	(annual prerevolutionary information almanac) Tiflis.
Khäbärlär/Izvestiia	(quarterly) Series in History, Philosophy and Law, Academy of Sciences; probably 1930s; bilingual.
Khäzär	(monthly journal of "translations and literary relations") Azerbaijan Writers' Union; January 1990; AzTk.
Kommunist	(Baku) AzCP; 1919; AzTk.
Kurtuluş	(Berlin) Society for the Salvation (Kurtuluş) of Azerbaijan (émigré); 1934–39(?).

Meydan	Azerbaijan Popular Front, October region (Baku) branch; fall 1989; AzTk.
Mübarizä	Union of Afghanistan Veterans for Azerbaijan Republican Territory Unity; November 1990; AzTk.
Novoe Russkoe Slovo	(New York) Émigré; 1930s.
Odlar Yurdu	Vatan (Azerbaijan Friendship Society; 1960; AzTk (Latin, Cyrillic, and Arabic script editions).
Panorama Azerbaidzhana	(Moscow) Plenipotentiary Representatives of the Azerbaijan Republic; January 1991.
Posledniaia novosti	(Paris) Émigré; 1920–30s.
Respublika	Soviet of Ministers of AzSSR, July 1990; AzTk.
Sähär	(daily) Economic supplement to *Kommunist*; 1989; AzTk.
Shusha	Shusha raikom (regional committee AzCP) and regional soviet of people's deputies; 1932; AzTk.
Tanïdïm	Tanïdïm Charitable Society; April 1991; AzTk.
Tarikh	Supplement to *Elm* by Academy historians; September 1990; AzTk.
Umid	(Moscow) "Independent Azerbaijan Information Center"; spring 1990; bilingual.
Vätän	(Ganje) Ganje section of the Azerbaijan Popular Front; late 1989 or January 1990; AzTk.
Vätän säsi	Azerbaijan Society of Refugees; April 1990; AzTk.
Vestnik Giandzhi	(Ganje) Ganje gorkom (city committee AzCP) and city soviet of people's deputies; 1922.
Yeni Fikir	AzSSR Committee on Publishing and Kitap (Book) Committee); October 1989; AzTk.
Yeni Kavkaziye	(Istanbul) Émigré; 1920s.
Yurtdash	Union for Ties to Co-nationals Living Outside the Union, January 1991; AzTk.

Dissertations

Altstadt, Audrey L. "The Azerbaijani Turkish Community of Baku before World War I." University of Chicago, 1983.

Aslani, Sadulla Shahverdy oglu. "Obrazovanie Iranskoi partii 'Edzhtimaiiun-e Amiiun (Mudzhakhid).'" Baku: Azerbaijan State University, 1975.

Blank, Stephen. "The Unknown Commissariat: The Soviet Commissariat of Nationalities, 1917–1924." University of Chicago, 1979.

Guseinova (Huseinova), Dina Sadyg gyzy. "Razvitie morskogo transporta, formirovanie kadrov rabochikh-moriakov Azerbaidzhana i ikh revoliutsionnye vystupleniia (90-e gody XIX v.—1907 g.)," Baku: Azerbaijan Academy of Sciences, 1975.

Musaev, M. "Razvitie torgovli goroda Baku v period kapitalizma (1860–1917 gg.)." Baku: Academy of Sciences, 1970.

Newpaper Accounts, Op-Ed Articles, Party Position Papers

Abaskulieva, E., and R. Mustafa. "Trevozhnye dni i nochi." *BR* 23 November 1988.

Abbasov, Äläkbär. "Vätän Khidmät Demäkdir." *Azärbaijan*, no. 11 (1986).

———. "Tarikhi hünär." *Az Kom*, no. 1 (1983).

Abdullayev, Bähruz, "Milli Münasibätlärin inkishafïnda aparïjï güvvä." *Az Kom*, no. 3 (1987).

Agamalioglu, S. "Dve nadezhdy na odno i to zhe polozhenie." *BR*, 11 January 1927.

Aghayev, Emil. "Khäzärin taleyi." *Azärbayjan*, no. 10 (1979).

Alekberli. "Azerbaidzhano-tiurkskaia literatura; doklad tov. Alekberli na vsesoiuznom s"ezde pisatelei." *Pr*, 23 August 1934.

Äliyäv, Rähim. "Gyrkh günün düsünjäläri." *Azärb* (n), 2 March 1990.

Äliyeva, Z., F. Süleymanov, A. Hüseynzadä. "Khalg Maarifïnin Väzifäläri." *Az Kom*, no. 1 (1978).

Allahverdiyev, R. "Bashlïja istigamät üzrä." *Az Kom*, no. 9 (1986).

Äqbär, M. "Türqçe telegraf olmaz." *Kom*, 6 August 1931.

An Azerbaijani (pseud.). "Musavat-Ittihad Fä'aliyeti." *Kom*, 17 June 1927.

Azertekin, A. "Bir adamdan alinacak ders." *Azerbaycan* (Ankara), May–June 1956.

Baghirov, Mir Jafar. "Piat' let pobed i dostizhenii." *ZV*, 28 April 1925.

"Baku, Erevan: trevozhnaia osen'." *Kom Pr*, 27 November 1988.

Burbyg, Lt. Col. N. "Na nochnykh ulitsakh Kirovobada," *KZ*, 30 November 1988.

Dashdämirov, Ä. "Ideolozhi ishin bä'zi aktual problemläri." *Az Kom*, no. 4 (1987).

Dash-demir (pseud.?). "Azerbaycan Devlet üniversitesi 1919–1934." *Kurtuluş*, November 1934.

Demidov, N., and Z. Kadymbekov. "Vremia otvetstvennykh deistvii." *Pr*, 5 December 1988.

Dzhapparov, Z. "Protivostoianie, kotoroe mozhet zavesti v tupik reshenie problem." *BR*, 12 January 1990.

———. "Trevozhnyi ianvar' v Lenkorani." *BR*, 17 January 1990.

Efendiyev, Mamed Sadykh. "Za podlinno narodnyi azerbaidzhanskii iazyk." *BR*, 22 July 1937.

Estekov, Almaz. "Politicheskaia otsenka sobytii v Baku." *Turkestan*, no. 1, January–February 1990.

Falichev, Colonel O. "Pravda sil'nee vsego." *KZ*, 22 December 1988.

Gasïmzadä, Gasïm. "Garshïlïglï ädäbi tä'sir problemi." *Azärbayjan*, no. 1 (1980.)

Gändilov, S., and S. Ähmädova. "Partiya häyatïnïn äsas ganunu." *Az Kom*, no. 6 (1986).

Häsänäliyev, N. "Abidälär layejd münasibät." *Az Kom*, no. 4 (1987).

Huseinov, M(irza) D(avud). "Ideia nezavisimosti Azerbaidzhana i partiia mussavat; I. Do fevral'skoi revoliutsii." *ZV*, 28 April 1925.

Ibrahimov, Eldeniz. "Nuzhno trezvo otsenit' situatsiiu." *BR*, 16 January 1990.

Ibrahimov, Mirzä. "Jänubda dirchälish," Azärbayjan, no. 1 (1980).

"Ideolozhi ishimizin bä'zi mäsäläläri haggïnda," *Az Kom*, no. 5 (1968).

"Informatsiia predsedatelia presidiuma verkhovnogo soveta Azerbaidzhanskoi SSR Tatlieva S. B." *BR*, 18 June 1988.

"Iranda antikommunizm ideologiyasïnïn bä'zi jähätläri." *Az Kom*, no. 7 (1965).

"K sobytiiam v Nagornom Karabakhe," *Pr*, 10 May 1989.

Karayev, A. H. "Ne tez unuttunuz biz ki unutmamishig." *Kom*, 11 August 1927.

———. "Musavatcilarin yal da'vasy; Deterding köperkleri bogushurlar." *Kom*, 29 January 1929.

Keller, William. "Nationalists in Azerbaijan Win Big Concessions from Party Chief." *New York Times*, 12 October 1989.

Kuliyev, Mustafa. "Makhinatsii 'nationalistov'." *BR*, 13 July 1927.

———. "M. E. Resulzadenin jeni manevrasi." *Kom*, 31 August; 2, 3 September 1931.

———. "Nasledie prokliatogo proshlogo." *BR*, 25 July 1927.

Lynev, R., and A. Stepanova. "Baku, 26 noiabria." *Izv*, 27 November, 1988.

———. "Razgovor na ploshchadi." *Izv*, 28 November 1988.

———. "Vchera, 29 noiabria, Baku." *Izv*, 20 November 1988.

Malikhov, Giyaz. "Tiurkskii vopros: puti vykhod iz krizisa." *Azärb* (n), 24 March 1990.

Mämmädov, Kh. "Dövlät statistikasï yenidängurma yolunda." *Az Kom*, no. 12 (1986).

"Mechty musavatistov." *BR*, 13 April 1927.

"Milli azadlïg häräkatï vä müasir antikommunizmä garshï mübarizä mäsäläri." *Az Kom*, no. 12 (1971).

Mikhailov, Konstantin. "Trevozhnei dni Apsherona." *Sobesednik*, no. 3 (January 1989).

"Mir zemle Karabakha; Ot konfrontatsii—k bor'be za perestroiku." *Pr*, 15 January 1989.

Musabekov, Gh(azanfar?). "Duşman kara kahinda canlanma." *Kom*, 3 June 1927.

———. "Pod znakom neuklonnogo rosta." *ZV*, 28 April 1925.

"Musavatisty o 'natsional'nom dvizhenii'." *BR*, 23 May 1927.

"Nä veririk, nä alïrïg? Azärbayjan-Ermänistan." *Sähär*, 13 January 1990.

"Natsional'nyi tragediia." *Ümid*, January 1990.

"O russkom iazyke." *PN*, July 1938.

"Obrashchenie armian zhivushchikh v Shushinskom raione." *BR*, 17 June 1988.

"Obrashchenie gruppy predstavitelei Azerbaidzhana v adres s"ezda narodnykh deputatov SSSR; Ne dopuskat' razhiganiia strastei." *BR*, 30 May 1989.

"Obrashchenie predstavitelia TsK KPSS i Prezidiuma Verkhovnogo Soveta SSSR v Nagorno-Karabakhskoi avtonomnoi oblasti." *Kom*, 25 September 1988.

"On vypolnial sluzhebnyi dolg." *Vyshka*, 2 February 1990.

Orakhelashvili, M. "Im slezy—trudiashchimsia radost'." *ZV*, 17 December 1926.

Osmanzadä, Süleyman. "Bir vätän böyüyür." *Azärbayjan*, no. 5 (1982).

"Papag mikrob yuvasïdïr." *Kom*, 19 November 1928.

"Partiinoe stroitel'stvo; Vesti neustannuiu bor'bu s velikoderzhavnym shovinizmom, kak glavnoi opastnostiu i mestnym natsioinalizmom." *BR*, 7 October 1931.

Pir (pseud.). "Pervye lastochki proletarskoi literatury." *BR*, 8 July 1927.

Polonskii, L. "Tri priezda." *BR*, 14 August 1988.

Räfiyev, Kh. "Khalgïn gälbindä." *Az Kom*, no. 5 (1987).

Rähimov, K. N. "Mäktäb islahatï vä respublikada khalg maarifinin ughurlu adïmlarï." *Azärbayjan mäktäbi*, no. 1 (1986).

Romanov, A. and A. Tepliuk. "Baku." *Kom Pr*, 30 November 1990.

———. "Baku, Erevan: trevozhnaia osen'." *Kom Pr*, 27 November 1988.

———. "Men'she emotsii, bol'she mudrosti!" *Kom Pr*, 1 December 1988.

———. "Slukhi i fakty." *Kom Pr*, 29 November 1988.

Rozhnov, Georgii. "Doroga bez kontsa." *Vyshka*, 11 February 1990.

"S.A." (pseud.). "Musavatskie shavki." *BR*, 3 January 1927.

Shatrov, Mikhail. "Prizyvaiu k pazumu i vole." *Izv*, 28 November 1988.

Shiräliyev, M., and M. Mämmädov. "Dilimizin sälisliyinä diggäti artïrag." *Az Kom*, no. 9 (1974).

Siniakob, P., and B. Fomin, "Pochemu pogibli eti liudi?" *Molodezh Azebaidzhana*, 3 February 1990.

Sinitsyn, Vladimir. "Chernaia pamiat'." *Sel'skaia zhizn'*, 21 October 1988.

Sirus (pseud.). "Chaiji Jälal vä Köroghlu." *Azärbayjan*, no. 6 (1987).

"Sluzhit' narodu—schast'e!" *Gänjlik/ Molodost'*, no. 6 (1988).

"Tofik Ismailov: S nadezhdoi smotriu." *Vyshka*, 25 February 1990.

"Topkhana obretaet pervozdannyi vid." *Izv*, 28 November 1988.

"Trevogi pogranichnoi Astary." *KZ*, 1 December 1988.

"Türk-Tatar Äksinkilabchilar," *Kom*, 24 December 1925.

Vahabzadä, Bähtiyar, and Suleiman S. Äliyarov, "Redaksiya pochtundan." *Azärbayjan*, no. 2 (1988).

Vaksberg, Arkadii. "Burnye aplodismenty." *Literaturnaia gazeta*, 21 September 1988.

Väliyäv, Kemal. "Bir daha Dädä Gorgud she'rläri haggïnda." *Azärbayjan*, no. 11 (1981).

Vladykin, Major O. "Aktivisty razdora." *KZ*, 16 December 1988.

Yunusova, Leyla. "Pestraia palitra neformal'nykh dvizhenii v Azerbaidzhane." *NRS*, 19 September 1989.

———. "Mera otvetstvennosti politika." *Istiglal*, no. 4 (April 1990).

"Zaiavlenie chlena pravleniia NFA Etibara Mamedova na press konferentsii v Moskve." *Akhïn*, no. 3 (1990).

Zeynalov, A. "Ijtimai amayin sosialistjasina täshkili," *Az Kom*, no. 1 (1968).

SECONDARY SOURCES

Äfändiyev, P. *Azärbayjan shifani khalg ädäbiyyatï.* Baku: Maarif, 1981.

Ähmädov, Teymur. *Näriman Närimanov.* Baku, 1977.

Akhundov, B. I. *Monopolisticheskii kapital v dorevoliutsionnoi bakinskoi neftianoi promyshlennosti.* Moscow, 1959.

Akhundov, Davud Aghaoglu. *Arkhitektura drevnego i rannesrednevekogo Azerbaidzhana.* Baku: Azerneshr, 1986.

Alexiev, Alex. "Soviet Nationalities in German Wartime Strategy 1941–1945." Santa Monica, Calif.: Rand Corp, R-2772-NA 1982.

———, and S. Enders Wimbush, eds. *Ethnic Minorities in the Red Army; Asset or Liability?* Boulder, Colo., and London: Westview, 1988.

Aliev, I. Ed. *Voprosy istorii Kavkazskoi Albanii.* Baku, 1962.

Aliiarov [Äliyarov], Suleiman S. "Internatsional'nyi sostav i edinstvo proletariata Azerbaidzhana (kanun i period pervoi mirovoi voiny)." *Uchenye Zapiski.* Series on History and Philosophy Azerbaijan State University, no. 6 (1973).

———. "Iz istorii gosudarstvenno-monopolisticheskogo kapitalizma v Rossii: Osoboe soveshchanie no toplivu i neftianye monopolii." *Istoriia SSSR*, no. 6 (1977).

———. "Izmeneniia v sostav rabochikh Baku v gody pervoi mirovoi voiny." *Istoriia SSSR*, no. 2 (1969).

———. *Neftianye monopolii v Azerbaidzhane v period pervoi mirovoi voiny.* Baku, 1974.

———. "Redaksiya pochtundan." *Azärbayjan*, no. 9 (1988).

———. "Trud A. M. Stopani 'Neftepromyshlennyi rabochii i ego biudzhet' kak istochnik." *Uchenye zapiski.* Series on History and Philosophy Azerbaijan State University, no. 7 (1978).

Allahverdiyev, B. *Kitablar haggïnda kitab.* Baku: Gänjlik, 1972.

Altstadt, Audrey L. "Baku City Duma: Arena for Elite Conflict." *CAS 5*, nos. 3/4 (1986).

———. "Critical Essay-Review of D. B. Seidzade's *Iz istorii Azerbaidzhanskoi burzhuazii.*" *Kritika* (publication of the Harvard University History Department), no. 4 (1984).

———. "The Forgotten Factor: The Shi'ite Mullahs of Azerbaijan." In Chantal

Lemercier-Quelquejay, Gilles Veinstein, and S. Enders Wimbush, eds., *Passé Turco-Tatar, Présent Soviétique*. Paris: Editions Peeters, 1986.

―――. "Guseinov, Ali." *Modern Encyclopedia of Russian and Soviet History*. (1982) 13:204–6.

―――. "Muslim Workers and the Labor Movement in Pre-War Baku." In Sabri M. Akural, ed., *Turkic Culture: Continuity and Change*. Indiana University Turkish Studies Series, no. 6. Bloomington: Indiana University Press, 1987.

Arasli̇, H. *Böyük Azärbayjan shairi Füzuli*. Baku, 1958.

Arsharuni, A., and Kh. Gabdullin. *Ocherki panislamizma i pantiurkizma v Rossii*. Moscow: Bezbozhnik, 1931. (Reprinted as no. 18 in the reprint series of the Society for Central Asian Studies, London, 1990).

Ashurbeyli, Sara B. *Gosudarstvo Shirvanshakhov: VI–XVI vv*. Baku: Elm, 1983.

―――. *Ocherki istorii srednevekovogo Baku, VIII—Nachalo XIX vv*. Baku: Academy of Sciences, 1964.

Atkin, Muriel. *Russia and Iran, 1780–1828*. Minneapolis: University of Minnesota Press, 1980.

―――. "The Strange Death of Ebrahim Dhalil Khan of Qarabagh," *Iranian Studies* 12 (1979).

Azärbayjan filologiya mäsäläläri, no. 2, Baku, 1984.

"Azerbaidzhanskii iazyk v sfere vysshego obrazovaniia." *Razvitie natsional'nykh iazykov v sviazi s ikh funktsionirovaniem v sfere vysshego obrazovaniia*. Moscow: Nauka, 1982.

Azerbaijanian Poetry: An Anthology. Ed., Mirza Ibrahimov. Moscow: Progress Publishers, 1969.

Azärbayjani̇n igtisadi tarikhinin aktual problemläri. Baku: Elm, 1978.

Baddeley, J. F. *The Russian Conquest of the Caucasus*. New York, 1969.

Bagirova, R. G. "Razvitie transporta Azerbaidzhana v period postroeniia fundamenta sotsialisticheskoi ekonomiki (1926–1932 gg.)." In *Azärbayjani̇n igtisadi tarikhinin aktual problemläri*. Baku, 1978.

"Bästäkari̇n yüksäk väzifäsi vä amali̇." *Azärbayjan*, no. 11 (1979).

Bennigsen, Alexandre. "The Crisis of Turkic National Epics, 1951–1952; Local Nationalism or Internationalism?" *Canadian Slavonic Papers* 17, nos. 2–3 (1975).

―――, and Chantal Lemercier-Quelquejay. *Islam in the Soviet Union*. Translated by Geoffrey Wheeler. London: Pall Mall, 1967.

―――, and S. Enders Wimbush. *Muslim National Communism in the Soviet Union*. Chicago: University of Chicago Press, 1979.

―――, and S. Enders Wimbush. *Mystics and Commissars: Sufism in the Soviet Union*. London: Hurst, 1985.

―――, and Marie Broxup. *The Islamic Threat to the Soviet State*. New York: St. Martin's, 1983.

Bilinsky, Yaroslav. "The Soviet Education Laws of 1958–59 and Soviet Nationalities Policy." *Soviet Studies* 14, no. 2 (October 1962).

Blank, Stephen. *Stalin and the Narkomnats: Sorcerer as Apprentice.* Forthcoming.

Bok, A. D. "Usloviia byta rabochikh-neftianikov g. Baku." In *Usloviia byta rabochikh v dorevoliutsionnoi Rossii (po dannym biudzhetnykh obsledovanii),* ed. N. K. Drukhin. Moscow: Sotsekon, 1958.

Bor-Ramenskii, E. "Iranskaia revoliutsiia 1905–1911 gg. i bol'shevikov Zakavkaz'ia." *Krasnyi Arkhiv,* no. 5 (1941).

Bournoutian, George. "The Ethnic Composition and Socio-Economic Condition of Eastern Armenia in the First Half of the Nineteenth Century." In Ronald Grigor Suny, ed., *Transcaucasia: Nationalism and Social Change.* Ann Arbor, 1983.

Buniatov, Ziya. *Azerbaidzhan v VII–IX vekov.* Baku: Elm, 1965.

———. *Azärbayjan VII–IX äsrlärdä.* Baku: Elm, 1989.

———. *Gosudarstvo Atabekov Azerbaidzhana.* Baku, 1978.

D.Z.T. (Jeyhun Hajibeyli). *La Première République Musulmane: L'Azerbaidjan.* Paris: Editions Ernest Leroux, 1919 (extracted from *Revue du Monde Musulman,* 1919).

Efendiev, M. M. *Gasan-bek Zardabi.* Moscow: Medgiz, 1961.

"Ekonomika Nagorno-Karabakhskoi avtonomnoi oblasti Azerbaidzhanskoi SSR: Problemy i perspektivy." *Azärbayjan Khalg täsärrüfati/ Narodnoe khoziaistvo Azerbaidzhana,* no. 7 (1988).

Essad Bey (Lev Nissenbaum). *Blood and Oil in the Orient.* Translated by Elsa Schuster. New York: Simon and Schuster, 1937.

Fatullaev, Sh. S. *Gradostroitel'stvo Baku, XIX-nachale XX vekov.* Leningrad: Stroizdat, 1978.

Feshbach, Murray. "Trends in the Soviet Muslim Population: Demographic Aspects." In Yaacov Ro'i, ed., *The USSR and the Muslim World.* London, 1984.

First All-Union Conference of Historian-Marxists (December 1928–January 1929). *Trudy,* Moscow (1929).

Fursenko, A. A. *Neftianye tresty i mirovaia politika 1880–1918 gg.* Moscow-Leningrad, 1965.

Gasanov, I. M. "Iz istorii krest'ianskogo dvizheniia v Azerbaidzhane v gody pervoi russkoi revoliutsii." In *Azerbaijan v gody pervoi russkoi revoliutsii.* Baku: Elm, 1966.

Geibullaev, G. *Toponimiia Azerbaidzhana.* Baku, 1986.

Geiushev (Göyüshev), Z. G. *Filosofskaia mysl' v sovetskom Azerbaidzhane; kratkii ocherk.* Baku: Elm, 1979.

Golden, Peter B. *Khazar Studies.* Budapest: Hungarian Academy of Sciences, 1980.

———. "The Turkic Peoples and Caucasia." In Ronald Grigor Suny, ed., *Transcaucasia: Nationalism and Social Change.* Ann Arbor, 1983.

Guliev, A. N. *Bakinskii proletariat v gody novogo revoliutsionnogo pod'ema.* Baku: Azerneshr, 1963.

Guliyev, Villayät. "Nizamidän Saib Täbriziyä gädär (Ingilis shärgshunasï G. Auslinin (1770–1845) ädäbiyyatïmïz haggïnda gejdläri)." *Azärbayjan,* no. 11 (1979).

Guseinov, Ragim. *Ocherki revoliutsionnogo dvizheniia v Azerbaidzhane.* Baku, 1926.

Gustafson, Thane, and Dawn Mann. "Gorbachev's Next Gamble." *Problems of Communism* 36, no. 4 (July–August 1987).

Hadjibeyli, Jeyhun. *See* D.Z.T. and Khadzhibeili, Dzheikhun.

Hajibäyov, Uzeir. *Ordan Burdan.* Compiled by Mirabbas Aslanov. Baku: Yaziji, 1981.

Hamm, Michael, ed. *The City in Late Imperial Russia.* Bloomington: Indiana University Press, 1986.

Handbook of the Major Soviet Nationalities, ed. Z. Katz, R. Rogers, and F. Harned. New York: Free Press, 1975.

Hegaard, Steven E. "Nationalism in Azerbaijan in the Era of Brezhnev." In George W. Simmonds, ed., *Nationalism in the USSR and Eastern Europe in the Era of Brezhnev and Kosygin.* Detroit, 1976.

Hitchins, Keith. "The Caucasian Albanians and the Arab Caliphate in the Seventh and Eighth Centuries." In *Bedi Kartlisa: revue de kartvélologie.* Vol. 42. Paris, 1984.

———. "Fuzuli." In *Modern Encyclopedia of Russian and Soviet Literatures.* Vol. 8, pp. 75–80.

Howard, Harry N. *The King-Crane Commission.* Beirut, 1963.

Huseinov, Akif. "Näshrimiz vä kechmishimiz." *Azärbayjan,* no. 10 (1982).

Ingram, Edward. *The Beginning of the Great Game in Asia 1828–1834.* Oxford, 1979.

Ismailov, Mahmud A. "Nauchnaia sessiia v Institute istorii i Filosofii Akademii Nauk Azerbaidzhanskoi SSR." *Trudy* (Academy of Sciences, Institute of History) 4 (1955).

———. "Gornaia promyshlennost' i mekhanicheskoe proizvodstvo Azerbaidzhana v period kapitalizma." In *Materialy po ekonomicheskoi istorii Azerbaidzhana.* Baku: Azerneshr, 1970.

Istoricheskaia geografiia Azerbaidzhana. Ed. Ziya Buniatov. Baku: Elm, 1987.

Istoriia Azerbaidzhana/Azärbayjan Tarikhi. 3 vols. Baku: Azerbaijan Academy of Sciences, 1958–63.

Istoriia Azerbaidzhana. Baku, 1979.

Istoriia natsional'no-gosudarstvennogo stroitel'stva v SSSR. Volume 1: *Natsional'no-gosudarstvennogo stroitel'stva v SSSR v perekhodnyi period ot kapitalizma k sotsializmu (1917–1936 gg);* Volume 2: *Natsional'no-gosudarstvennogo stroitel'stva v SSSR v period sotsializma i stroitel'stva kommunizma (1937–1972).* Moscow: Mysl', 1972.

Kadishev, A. B. *Interventsiia i grazhdanskaia voina v Zakavkaz'e.* Moscow: Ministry of Defense, 1960.

Karenin, Anatolii Aleksandrovich. *Sultan Mejid Äfändiyev.* Translated by M. Taghizade. Baku, 1963.

"Kavkaz GPU'a yardim." *Kurtuluş,* no. 1 (November 1934).

Kazemzade, Firuz. *Struggle for the Transcaucasus (1917–1921).* New York: Philosophical Library, 1951.

Kaziev, M. A. *Meshadi Azizbekov (Zhizn' i deiatel'nost')*. Baku, 1976.

———. *Nariman Narimanov (Zhizn' i deiatel'nost')*. Baku, 1970.

Kerimbekov, A. "Razvitie sotsialisticheskogo sorevnovaniia na Azerbaidzhanskoi zheleznoi doroge v gody predvoennykh piatiletok." In *Azärbayjanïn igtisadi tarikhinin aktual problemläri*. Baku: Elm, 1978.

Kerimov, Kh. "Kapitalizmdän sosializmä kechid dövrü münasibätläri sistemindä ämäk haggï." In *Azärbayjanïn igtisadi tarikhinin aktual problemaläri*. Baku: Elm, 1978.

Khadzhibeili, Dzheikhun (Hadjibeyli, Jeyhun). *Antiislamistskaia propaganda i ee metody v Azerbaidzhane*. Munich: Institute for the Study of the USSR, 1957.

Khälilov, Penah. "Häyatïmïz vä näshrimiz." *Azärbayjan*, no. 1 (1982).

Khazar, Mirza. "The *Birlik* Society in the Azerbaijani Democratic Movement." *RL Report*, 23 August 1989.

Kharmandarian, S. V. *Lenin i stanovlenie zakavkazskoi federatsii, 1921–1923*. Erevan: Aiastan, 1969.

Köcherli (Kocharlinskii), Firuddin. *Literatura Azerbaidzhanskikh Tatar*. Tiflis, 1925.

Köcherli, Firuddin(son). *Marksizm-Leninizm vä Azärbayjanda demokratik ijtimai fikir*. Baku, 1976.

Kuznetsova, N. A., and L. M. Kulagina. *Iz istorii sovetskogo vostokovedeniia*. Moscow, 1970.

Lazzerini, Edward J. "Hümmat." In *Modern Ecyclopedia of Russian and Soviet History (MERSH)*. Vol. 14.

Lenin milli siyasätinin yetirmäasi; Nahkjivan MSSR'in 50 illiyi. Baku, 1974.

Libaridian, Gerard J. "Revolution and Liberation in the 1892 and 1907 Programs of the Dashnaktsutun." In Ronald Grigor Suny, ed., *Transcaucasia: Nationalism and Social Change*. Ann Arbor, 1983.

Madatov, Garish Ali. *Azerbaidzhan v Velikoi Otechestvennoi voine*. Baku: Elm, 1975.

———. *Pobeda sovetskoi vlasti v Nakhichevani i obrazovanie Nakhichevanskoi ASSR*. Baku: Academy of Sciences, 1968.

Malanchuk, V. E. *Istoricheskii opyt KPSS po resheniiu natsional'nogo voprosa i razvitiiu natsional'nykh otnoshenii v SSSR*. Moscow: Vyshaia Shkola, 1972.

Mämmädli, Gulam, comp. *Javid - Ömrüboyu; häyatï vä yaradïjlïg salnamäsi; 1882–1941*. Baku: Yaziji, 1982.

———. *Molla Näsreddin*. Baku, 1984.

Materialy po ekonomicheskoi istorii Azerbaidzhana. Baku: Azerneshr, 1970.

McAuley, Alastair. "The Soviet Muslim Population: Trends in Living Standards, 1960–75." In Y. Ro'i, ed., *The USSR and the Muslim World*. London: George Allen and Unwin, 1984.

McKay, John. "Baku Oil and Transcaucasian Pipelines, 1883–1891: A Study in Tsarist Economic Policy." *Slavic Review* 43, no. 4 (Winter 1984).

———. "Entrepreneurship and the Emergence of the Russian Petroleum Industry,

1813–1881." In *Research in Economic History: A Research Annual*, ed. Paul Uselding. Vol 8. Greenwich, Conn.: 1983.

Melikov, Javanshir. "V zalozhnikakh u klana." *Sotsialisticheskaia industriia*, 23 October 1988.

Mil'man, A. Sh. *Azerbaidzhanskaia SSR—Suverennoe gosudarstvo v sostave SSSR*. Baku: Azerneshr, 1971.

————. *Politicheskii stroi Azerbaidzhana x XIX- Nachale XX vekov*. Baku: Azerneshr, 1966.

Minorsky, Vladimir. "Caucasica IV: Sahl ibn Sunbat of Shakki and Arran. The Caucasian Vassals of Marzuban in 344/955." In *The Turks, Iran and the Caucasus in the Middle Ages*. London: Variorum Reprints, 1978 (from *Bulletin of the School of Oriental and African Studies* 15/3, London [1953]).

———— (trans.). *A History of Sharvan and Darbend in the 10th–11th Centuries*. Cambridge, 1958.

Mirähmädov, Äziz. *Azärbayjan Molla Näsreddini*. Baku, 1980.

Mitzakis, John. *A Handbook of the Russian Oil Industry*. London, 1913.

Musaev, M. *XX [Iyirminji] äsrin ävvälärindä Bakï shähärini tijareti (1900–1917)*. Baku: Elm, 1974.

————. *XIX [On dokuzunju] äsrin sonlarïnda Bakï shärhärini tijareti (1883–1900)*. Baku: Elm, 1972.

————. "Milli kapitalïn tekamülü" in *Azärbayjanïn igtisadi tarikhinin aktual problemläri*. Baku: Elm, 1978.

Näbiyäv, Bäkir. "Epik zhanr vä müasir häyat." *Azärbayjan*, no. 7 (1986).

Narimanov, Nariman. "K istorii revoliutsii v okrainakh," *Khäbärlär/ Izvestiia*, Series in History, Philosophy and Law, Azerbaijan Academy of Sciences, no. 4 (1989).

Näsibzadä, Näsib. *Azärbayjan demokratik respublikasi*. Baku, 1989.

————. "Azärbayjan Demokratik Respublikasi: Istiglal Soraghïnda." *Elm*, 12, 19, 26 August and 2, 9 September 1989, and *Odlar Yurdu*, no. 17 (448) (September 1989), Cyrillic script.

Nissman, David B. *The Soviet Union and Iranian Azerbaijan: The Uses of Nationalism for Political Penetration*. Boulder, Colo.: Westview, 1987.

Novruzov, Hajï. "Mäktäb ateistlär yetishdirir," *Azärbayjan mäktäbi*, no. 6 (1987).

Ocherk istorii Azerbaidzhanskoi sovetskoi literatury. Moscow: USSR Academy of Sciences, 1963.

Öke, Mim Kemal. "Prof. Arminius Vambery and Anglo-Ottoman Relations 1889–1907." *Turkish Studies Association Bulletin* 9, no. 2 (1985).

Paksoy, H. B. *Alpamysh; Central Asian Identity under Russian Rule*. Hartford, Conn.: Association for the Advancement of Central Asian Research, 1989.

————. "Central Asia's New Dastans." *CAS* 6, no. 1 (1987).

————. "Elements of Humor in Central Asia: The Example of the Journal *Molla Nasreddin* in Azerbaijan." In *Turkestan als historischer Faktor und politische Idee*, ed. Prof. Dr. Erling von Mende. Köln: Studienverlag, 1988.

———. "Introduction to the *Dastan Dede Korkut*." In *Soviet Anthropology and Archaeology* Vol. 29, no. 1, 1990.

———. "Nationality and Religion: Three Observations from Ömer Seyfettin." *CAS* 3, no. 3 (1984).

Pashaev, Nazar A. *Pobeda kulturnoi revoliutsii v sovetskom Azerbaidzhane*. Moscow: Nauka, 1976.

Pazhitnov, K. A. *Ocherki po istorii bakinskoi neftedobyvaiushchei promyshlennosti*. Moscow, 1940.

Pershke, S., and L. Pershke. *Russkaia neftianaia promyshlennost'; ee razvitie i sovremennoe polozhenie v statisticheskikh dannykh*. Tiflis, 1913.

Pipes, Richard. *Formation of the Soviet Union, 1917–1923*, rev. ed. Cambridge, Mass.: Harvard University Press, 1964.

Pokshishevskii, V. V. *Polozhenie bakinskogo proletariata nakanune revoliutsii (1914–1917 gg)*. Baku, 1927.

Raevskii, A. *Angliiskaia interventsiia i musavatskoe pravitel'stvo*. Baku, 1927.

Rahr, Alexander. "The Composition of the Politburo and the Secretariat of the CC of the CPSU." Radio Liberty Research, *RL* 236/87 (26 June 1987) (Munich).

Rakowska-Harmstone, Teresa, et al. *The Warsaw Pact: A Question of Cohesion*. Phase 2, Volume 3. An Operational Research and Analysis Establishment Extramural Paper of the Canadian Department of National Defense, No. 39. Ottawa, 1986.

Reese, William. "Religious Revival and Nationalism in Caucasian Events." *RL* Report, 5 December 1988.

Rhinelander, L. H. "Viceroy Vorontsov's Administration of the Caucasus." In Ronald Grigor Suny, ed., *Transcaucasia: Nationalism and Social Change*. Ann Arbor, 1983.

Rorlich, Azade-Ayşe, "The 'Äli Bayramov' Club, The Journal *Shärg Gadïnï* and the Socialization of Azeri Women, 1920–1930." *CAS* 5, nos. 3/4 (1986).

———. "Not by History Alone: The Retrieval of the Past among the Tatars and the Azeris." *CAS* 3, no. 2 (1984).

———. *Volga Tatars; Profile in National Resilience*. Studies of Nationalities in the USSR series. Stanford: Hoover Institution Press, 1986.

Rustämov, Izzät. *Häsänbey Zärbadi*. Baku, 1969.

Rustamova, Kh. "Iz istorii natsionalizatsii neftianoi promyshlennosti Azerbaidzhana (1920 g.)." *Uchenye zapiski*, Azerbaijan State University, 1963.

Säfärli, A., and Kh. Yusifov. *Gädim vä orta äsrlär Azärbayjan ädäbiyyati*. Baku: Maarif, 1982.

Salamzade (Sälämzadä), A. V. *Arkhitektura Azerbaidzhana XVI–XIX vv*. Baku, 1964.

———, and K. M. Mämmädzadä. *Arazboyu abidälär*. Baku, 1979.

Samedov, Iu. *Rasprostranenie marksizma v Azerbaidzhane*. 2 vols. Baku: Elm, 1966.

Sef, S. E. *Bor'ba za oktiabr' v Zakavkaz'i*. Tiflis, 1932.

Seidzade, D. B. *Iz istorii Azerbaidzhanskoi burzhuazii.* Baku, 1978.

Seyidov, Yusuf, and Samet Älizadä. *Klassik Azärbayjan shairleri söz haggïnda.* Baku: Gänjlik, 1977.

Sharif, Aziz. "Azärbayjan musigisinin atasï." *Azärbayjan,* no. 12 (1981).

Shaw, Stanford, J., and Ezel Kural Shaw. *The History of the Ottoman Empire and Modern Turkey.* Vol. 2. Cambridge, Eng.: Cambridge University Press, 1977.

Soper, John. "Shakeup in the Uzbek Literary Elite." *CAS* 1, no. 4 (1983).

40 [sorok] let Nakhichevanskoi ASSR. Baku: Azerneshr, 1964.

Steklov, A. P. *Revoliutsionnaia deiatel'nost' bol'shevistskikh organizatsii na kavkaz-'skom fronte, 1914–1917 gg.* Tbilisi: Sabchota Sakartvelo, 1969.

Sumbatzade, A. S. *Azerbaidzhanskaia istoriografiia XIX–XX vekov.* Baku: Elm, 1987.

———. *Kubinskoi vosstanie 1837 g.* Baku: Elm, 1961.

Sumer, Faruk. "Oğuzlara Ait Destani Mahiyetde Eserler." *Dil. Tarih, Coğrafya Fakultesi Dergisi.* Ankara University, 1959.

Suny, Ronald G. *The Baku Commune: Class and Nationality in the Russian Revolution.* Princeton, 1972.

———. "A Journeyman for the Revolution: Stalin and the Labor Movement in Russian Baku, June 1907–May 1908." *Soviet Studies* 3 (1971).

———. "Transcaucasia: Cultural Cohesion and Ethnic Revival in a Multinational Society." In Lubomyr Hajda and Mark Beissinger, eds. *The Nationalities Factor in Soviet Politics and Society.* John M. Olin Critical Issues Series, Russian Research Center, Harvard University. Boulder, Colo.: Westview Press, 1990.

———, ed. *Transcaucasia: Nationalism and Social Change.* University of Michigan Slavic and Eastern European Series. No. 2. Ann Arbor, 1983.

Swietochowski, Tadeusz. *Russian Azerbaijan, 1905–1920; The Shaping of National Identity in a Muslim Community.* Cambridge, Eng., and New York: Cambridge University Press, 1985.

———. "Hümmit Party: Socialism and the National Question in Russian Azerbaijan, 1904–1920." *Cahiers du monde Russe et Sovietique* 19, nos. 1–2 (1978).

Taghiyev, Husein. *Azärbayjanda kitabkhanajïlïg ishi.* Baku, 1964.

Taghiyeva, Sh. A. "Näriman Närimanovun 1905–1911-ji illär Iran ingilabï ilä älagädär fäaliyyäti haggïnda." *Izvestiia,* Series on History, Philosophy and Law, Academy of Sciences of Azerbaijan, no. 3 (1973).

Tairzade (Tahirzadä), N. "Sostav uchachshikhsia bakinskogo real'nogo uchilishche v poslednei chetverti XIX veka." *Izvestiia,* Series on History, Philosophy and Law, Academy of Sciences of Azerbaijan, no. 3 (1981).

———. "Vechernie kursy prosvetitel'nogo obshchestva 'Nijat' (1908–1914)." *Izvestiia,* Series on History, Philosophy and Law, Academy of Sciences of Azerbaijan, no. 1 (1976).

Tillett, Lowell. *The Great Friendship.* Chapel Hill: University of North Carolina, 1969.

Togan, Zeki Velidi. *Bugünkü Türk İli Türkistan ve Yakın Tarihi.* 2d ed. Istanbul, 1981.

Tokarzhevskii, E. A. *Ocherki istorii Sovetskogo Azerbaidzhana v period perekhoda na mirnuiu rabotu po vosstanovleniiu narodnogo khoziaistva (1921–1925 gg.).* Baku, 1956.

Tskitishvili, K. *Zakavkaz'e v partizanskoi voine, 1941–1945 gg.* Tiflis, 1973.

Ullman, Richard H. *Britain and the Russian Civil War.* Vol. 2. Anglo-Soviet Relations series, 1917–1921. Princeton: Princeton University Press, 1968.

Velichko, V. L. *Kavkaz; Russkoe delo i mezhduplemennye voprosy.* St. Petersburg, 1904 (reprinted Baku: Elm, 1990).

Vucinich, Wayne. "Structure of Soviet Orientology." In Vucinich, ed., *Russia and Asia: Essays on the Influence of Russia on the Asian Peoples.* Stanford: Hoover Institution Press, 1972.

Wimbush, S. Enders. "Why Geidar Aliev?" *CAS* 1, no. 4 (1983).

————, ed. *Soviet Nationalities in Strategic Perspective.* London: Croom Helm, 1985.

Wright, Richard E. "On the Origins of Caucasian Village Rugs," *Oriental Rug Review* 10, no. 4 (April/May 1990).

Woods, John. *The Aqquyunlu: Clan, Confederation, and Empire.* Minneapolis: Bibliotheca Islamica, 1976.

Wurm, Stefan. *The Turkic Languages of Central Asia: Problems of Planned Culture Contact.* Central Asian Research Centre in association with St. Anthony's College, Oxford University, 1954.

————. *Turkic Peoples of the USSR; Their Historical Background, Their Languages, and the Development of Soviet Linguistic Policy.* Central Asian Research Centre in association with St. Anthony's College, Oxford University, 1954.

Zemtsov, Ilya. *Partiia ili mafia?* Paris: Les Editeurs Reunis, 1976.

Index

About the Author

AUDREY L. ALTSTADT received her Ph.D. from the University of Chicago and has received postdoctoral fellowships from the Russian Research Center at Harvard University and the George F. Kennan Institute of Advanced Russian Studies. She conducted research in Baku, Azerbaijan, during 1980–81 and 1984–85 and was the first American to gain access to the Azerbaijan State Historical Archives. She is currently a member of the history department at the University of Massachusetts at Amherst.